DEBATING CUBAN EXCEPTIONALISM

DEBATING CUBAN EXCEPTIONALISM

Edited by

Bert Hoffmann
and
Laurence Whitehead

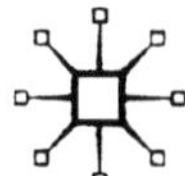

DEBATING CUBAN EXCEPTIONALISM

First published in 2007 by
PALGRAVE MACMILLAN™
175 Fifth Avenue, New York, N.Y. 10010 and
Houndmills, Basingstoke, Hampshire, England RG21 6XS
Companies and representatives throughout the world.

PALGRAVE MACMILLAN is the global academic imprint of the Palgrave Macmillan division of St. Martin's Press, LLC and of Palgrave Macmillan Ltd. Macmillan® is a registered trademark in the United States, United Kingdom and other countries. Palgrave is a registered trademark in the European Union and other countries.

ISBN-13: 978–1–4039–8075–5
ISBN-10: 1–4039–8075–6

Library of Congress Cataloging-in-Publication Data

Debating Cuban exceptionalism / edited by Bert Hoffmann and Laurence Whitehead.
        p. cm.—(Studies of the Americas)
    Includes bibliographical references and index.
    Contents: On Cuban political exceptionalism / Laurence Whitehead—Cuba : from exception to democratization? / Andrew Arato—How exceptional is the Cuban economy? / Emily Morris—The gatekeeper state : limited economic reforms and regime survival in Cuba, 1989–2002 / Javier Corrales—Cuba : consensus in retreat / Haroldo Alfonso Dilla—Cuba's dilemma of simultaneity : the link between the political and national question / Bert Hoffmann—The Cuban-American political machine : reflections on its origins and perpetuation / Alejandro Portes—Rethinking civil society and religion in Cuba / Margaret C. Crahan and Ariel Armony—The knots of memory : culture, reconciliation, and democracy in Cuba / Rafael Rojas.
    ISBN 1–4039–8075–6 (alk. paper)
    1. Cuba—Politics and government—1959–1990. 2. Cuba—Politics and government—1990– 3. Political culture—Cuba. 4. Socialism—Cuba. 5. Cuba—Forecasting. I. Whitehead, Laurence. II. Hoffmann, Bert.

F1788.D33 2007
972.9106′4—dc22   2006049198

A catalogue record for this book is available from the British Library.

Design by Newgen Imaging Systems (P) Ltd., Chennai, India.

First edition: May 2007

10 9 8 7 6 5 4 3 2 1

Printed in the United States of America.

Contents

List of Figures

List of Tables

.

Preface

Claus Offe

The fall of the Berlin Wall on November 9, 1989 and the subsequent definitive demise of state socialism have shaped the configuration of political forces and agendas of domestic politics in many countries, as well as much of international politics since, with just one superpower in place. It must be added to this truism, however, that the demise of state socialism (as defined by state ownership of productive assets, monopolistic political parties, and at best limited guarantees of civil liberties) was an entirely European event: *all* of the European state-socialist countries (for the time being with the exception of Byelorussia), but *only* the countries whose capitals are located on European territory have taken at least the initial steps toward the transition to some form of liberal democratic capitalism, whereas all the non-European socialist states did not experience economic and political regime changes of comparable proportions. These non-European cases include those of China, North Korea, Vietnam—and Cuba.

Cuba is the focus of the present volume. The conference at which first drafts of chapters found here were presented and debated took place in Berlin in October 2003. It was hosted by the New School University in New York, the Ford Foundation and the Humboldt University in Berlin. I had the honor to serve as the host on behalf of the latter institution. Somewhat unusually, the fact was that, while the conference was about Cuba and the challenges ahead that affect Cuba, only some of the conference participants could pass as "Cuba experts." As I am not a "Cuba expert," these introductory remarks will be short. All the participants, however, have studied, lived through, or are involved deeply either scholarly and/or politically in transformations of and transitions from various forms of state socialism. So the conference was, and was intended to be, a learning experience in comparative contemporary state socialism and its aftermath. What participants tried to understand in this comparative perspective is the nature of Cuban socialism, the reasons for the persistence of "the Cuban model" on the island, the internal and external challenges this model is currently exposed to, and the alternative ways these challenges can conceivably be coped with in the complex interaction between elite and nonelite actors, as well as between domestic and international forces.

One thing about Cuba is certain: it is a puzzle, or a particularly hard case to understand and predict in terms of the comparative study of state-socialist systems and their capacity to survive, adjust, or shift toward some kind of post-socialist economic and political regime. If anything, one might have expected that Cuban socialism, given its numerous vulnerabilities (benignly called a *período especial* [special period] by Cuban leaders) after the end of the massive economic support the Soviet Union (USSR) gave Cuba, would share the fate of its great sponsor after 1991. A dozen or so factors, however, immediately come to mind that make the Cuban model and its continued existence a thoroughly exceptional case: its relatively small size as an island republic; its geographic location, just half an hour of flight time away from the territory of the only superpower; its resulting role of "David" facing "Goliath"; its role as a target of both military and economic sanctions and hostilities initiated by that neighbor; the fact that for the first time in its history, beginning in 1992, it was no longer dependent upon or supported by an overseas "sponsoring power," be it Spain, the United States, or the Soviet Union; the fact that Fidel Castro has now been in power continuously for more than 45 years, a longer time than any other leader in the twentieth century, and the equally unparalleled (seemingly somewhat declining) international prestige and charisma of both the man and the "Cuban model" he inaugurated; the fact that a large part of the population has left the country and is spearheading a vehement—if divided—external opposition from Miami and other locations in the United States, and doing so with the generous political support of American authorities and other political forces; the fact that Cuban society is increasingly divided not just between domestic and external segments of the population but also between those who have, in a variety of ways, access to foreign currency and those who do not; the sharp decline in economic output that occurred as a consequence of the breakdown of the Soviet Union; a looming succession crisis that is to be anticipated when Fidel (or his brother, for that matter) is no longer leading the country; the gradual if inconsistent adjustment to the new economic situation through the admission of foreign direct investment, the buildup of a tourism industry, and the adoption of the U.S. dollar as a second currency, as well as the reluctant liberalization of the market for small agricultural and commercial business; the erratic pattern of harsh repression and partial concessions in a general authoritarian context of little respect for human rights, and the ensuing absence of a minimally coherent and robust internal opposition that might become a potential counterelite; the exemplary record in the provision of public health and educational services that is matched by no other country at a comparable stage of economic development; the consistent propensity of the Cuban leadership to "go it alone," and the failure to negotiate alliances and coalitions with external partners (such as the European Union [EU] or some of its member states); and, last but not least, a political culture marked by the values of solidarity, national independence, and a cult of defiance and self-sacrificing heroism.

What is demonstrated and discussed in the individual chapters of this volume is which of these features of the Cuban model (and others) can and must be treated as robust and parametric, and which are amenable to change and can therefore contribute to the generation of solutions that create a way to overcome the country's highly precarious situation.

After the fall of the Berlin Wall, the other historical event of our time is, of course, the attack on Washington and New York on September 11, 2001. As a consequence of these events, both the notion of how democracies can be brought into being, and the evaluation of what democracies are good for, seem to have fundamentally changed. I remember watching a one-hour TV program on Cuba in New York in mid-April 2003 that was sponsored by a major U.S. think tank. This was shortly before the American president was about to declare victory in the U.S. military campaign in Iraq. The sophisticated and knowledgeable speaker dealt with the general situation in Cuba and recent massive human rights violations, particularly the sentencing of 75 Cuban opposition activists to a monstrous number of several years in prison. In conclusion, that expert came close to arguing that, given that global attention is currently fixed on military action in Iraq, it might be a good idea to get rid of the Cuban regime by military means and replace it by an entirely different, democratic regime. While this is far from the official position of the American administration, it seemed to me that the suggestion was nonetheless symptomatic in that the question of regime change was clearly conceived of by the speaker as something that could be orchestrated from "the outside." The meaning of the term "to democratize" has, as it were, recently turned from a reflexive verb ("doing something to oneself"[1]) into a transitive verb ("making someone else the object of one's democratizing action"). In the latter version, the activity of "democratizing an Other" must face the obvious paradox of bestowing democratic self-determination upon some collectivity that is, in the act of "receiving the gift," simultaneously deprived of its alleged democratic self-determination.

Let me try to elaborate briefly on the nature of this change in the "grammar" of democratization. There used to be a time, to give a highly stylized account of the intellectual history of democratization theory, when it was generally believed that democracies emerged in societies where all the structural prerequisites of democracy (such as an educated middle class, economic prosperity, and urbanization, among other requirements) were present in the social structure that taken together constitute a "mature" society that can then both adopt and sustain a democratic regime type, which is thought of as inherently desirable as it guarantees liberty and the safe enjoyment of individual freedom by citizens. In other words, the theory claimed that the evolution of *social structures* generates *citizens* who desire to adopt *democracy* as popular sovereignty for the *intrinsic* value of being liberated from predemocratic forms of rule. All four italicized terms in this equation seem to have changed after the hitherto virtually unknown activities of "state building," "nation building," and "democracy promotion" became catchwords and strategic patterns of international politics. These strategies are being experimented since the start of the new century in the "failed states" of Afghanistan, Iraq, and, on a smaller scale, in Bosnia and Kosovo. Instead of the maturity of appropriate social structures being seen as a "prerequisite" for democratization, democracy is now something that is held to be possible if the right actors are in place and guide their decisions in the right way—and this is possible almost anywhere and at any time, regardless of the level of modernization attained by any given society. External actors, rather than the citizenry of the country to be democratized, are believed to have the capacity to impose democratic regimes. And the motivation for doing so has not primarily to do with the intrinsic value of liberty of the people that are thereby destined to enjoy democracy; rather, it has to do with the interest of the external democratizing agent and with an instrumental calculus that this will enhance the latter's security—following the maxim that democracies are less dangerous than nondemocracies insofar as they are less likely to engage in international or civil wars, or to become bases of nonstate international violence ("terrorism"). There is a further semantic shift that appears to have been triggered by September 11 and the American-led "war on terrorism" that is worth noting here: the widely observable substitution in political discourse of "security" for "peace" as the strategic objective of international politics. (Achieving "security" means depriving the enemy of the *capability* to inflict hostile action upon the agent that consequently made secure, whereas "peace" connotes some form of reconciliation and thus emphasizes the overcoming of hostile *intentions* or the transformation of a former enemy into a nonenemy.)

All these shifts in the international environment need to be taken into consideration when probing into the many economic, political, military, cultural challenges that Cuba and its "model" is currently exposed to, and the available and feasible responses to these challenges. Asking this question implies assuming that Cuba's future will be significantly different from its present, whether for better or worse. Who are the actors and political forces that are going to cope with these challenges, and how and to what extent can we predict, as well as evaluate, probable outcomes? In dealing with these questions, the authors contributing to this volume have refrained, for the most part, from advocating a political program or plan for action, which is beyond the competence of social scientists anyway (and all the more so as most of the contributors are not Cuban citizens). That restraint, however, does not preclude the possibility of testing alternative futures along two obvious—albeit inherently contested—dimensions: are they desirable or not, and do they seem realistic or not? Applying these two distinctions, one might even go on to specify who the actors, or coalitions of actors may be who are likely to pave the way toward a future that is both realistic and desirable, and which actors stand in the way of such favorable outcomes. These actors are, at any rate, numerous in kind and include the population of the island and its various collective actors, the varied coalitions of Cubans abroad, external actors such as the United States, the EU, the United Nations, and its organizations, as well as a number of Latin American countries.

When exploring the realm of the possible, as well as the subset of desirable possibilities, we need to keep in mind the limitations of our prognostic capacities as social scientists. It has been said that history is driven by three kinds of forces: accidents, evolutions, and intentions. We do not know the proportional mix of these forces, and the role played by accidental events at least is unpredictable by definition. The transitions that took place in Central and Eastern Europe in and after 1989 demonstrate that today's realities can well be such that yesterday's even most enlightened prophets had to consider them beyond the realm of the possible.

Such difficulties, however, are no excuse to blur the line between wishful thinking and the more scholarly procedure of thoughtful wishing. Even if history has pleasant surprises in stock, these do not come about by dint of visions and wishes alone. Circumstances that are beyond the control of visionaries must play their role as facilitating contextual conditions that are favorable for and supportive of such visions. In the case of Cuba, the vision was simple enough. At the initiative of Oswaldo Payá, the petition of the Varela Project was started in 2002 and signed by thousands of Cubans who thereby asked the National Assembly to launch a referendum comprising five demands. These demands pertained to the guarantee of universally recognized human rights, an amnesty for all political prisoners, the liberalization of economic activity, the adoption of a fair electoral law, and the actual holding of general elections under that law. For most of us, it is probably easy to agree that demands such as those posed by the Varela Project must be fulfilled if any desirable Cuban future is to materialize, although the means by which— and the order in which—these five demands may be realized is open to political debate. In particular, the question remains whether raising such demands and supporting them from the outside will be self-defeating or whether they may actually strengthen the prospects for a desirable future.

Currently, there is a lot of advice being given to various actors as to what they should do, or refrain from doing, in order to achieve desirable responses to these challenges. It is not the primary purpose of this volume to add to this long list. The purpose and questions are more analytical: What kind of advice is actually being given, what are the intentions of those who proffer such advice, who needs and appreciates it, and which advice makes a realistic assessment of the capacities of the various actors involved to follow through with it? What kind of goals, strategies, and alliances do policy recommendations entail? Such an analytic approach is in line with what scholars are able to do. As scholars, we lack the authority to give political advice or to make political demands—although this is an authority that we fully enjoy as citizens of our respective countries, of course.

The authority of giving advice is often claimed on the basis of analogy: "We have followed a certain strategy and succeeded, and so, if you are in a similar situation, you had better emulate what we did if you want to achieve a similarly positive outcome." This is an example of what I like to call "flowerpot thinking": the same seeds in another pot are assumed to allow the blooming of the same plant that we cultivated in a prior, parallel context. Following this line of thought, three East European citizens who happen to have served once as presidents of Poland, the Czech Republic, and Hungary offered advice in September 2003 that they felt was relevant to actors engaged in the Cuban experience, and therefore called for externally sponsored civil society opposition—the models in mind were Polish *Solidarnosc* and similar East European movements that sprung up in their countries before 1989. The Achilles heel of such advice is, of course, the analogy such advice is based on. What if Cuba is a different kind of plant, and what if the rule of Cuban "exceptionalism" applies?

Needless to say, not all transitions from authoritarian rule, not even transitions from state-socialist authoritarianism, are alike. Flowerpot thinking is a common fallacy when considering the challenges facing Cuba. Such thinking is bound to fail for many reasons, some of which are explored in this volume. To highlight just two: first, the transitions in Central and Eastern Europe took place in a context when nations where trying to escape from the supranational regimes of the Warsaw Pact, the Council for Mutual Economic Assistance (CMEA), and the hegemonic rule of the Soviet Union. They also took place in an international political context when these nations could confidently expect that, once achieved, national liberation would be honored and respected by their Western neighbors, and that they would be invited to join another much more liberal supranational regime that is more respectful of autonomy: the EU (as well as the North Atlantic Treaty Organization, NATO). None of this remotely applies to Cuba. Cubans overwhelmingly anticipate that a transition from authoritarian state socialism will not result in a gain, but rather in a considerable loss of national autonomy and in a demolition of what are held to be its accomplishments.

There is another facet of Cuban exceptionalism that is highly conspicuous, and that is the "David effect," which means that the Cuban Revolution from its inception has received more attention, support, admiration, and global solidarity than any other state-socialist regime ever has, with the possible exception of the Soviet Union in its first decade of existence.

Karl W. Deutsch offered one of the most well-known insights of modern political science: he defined power as the privilege of power holders *not* to learn. It must be said that the Cuban leadership seems to have made quite extensive use of this prerogative at various points in its recent history. One of the less dramatic instances of this is illustrated by the fact that, despite sustained efforts to the contrary, not a single Cuban participated, with a permission granted by the Cuban government, in the academic conference from which this volume originated. Similarly, His Excellency the Cuban Ambassador to Germany failed consistently even to respond to a formal invitation to honor that conference with an opening statement. At the same time, the Cuban impasse or deadlock has become so manifest and undeniable that it underlines the urgency of thinking—including thoughtful wishing—about the political and economic future of the island and its people.

Note

1. In this sense, Laurence Whitehead refers to the "reflexive and self-directing characteristics of democratization." See Laurence Whitehead, *Democratization. Theory and Experience* (Oxford: Oxford University Press, 2002), p. 35.

Acknowledgments

Following the chronology of events that led to this volume, the authors want to thank all those who organized and supported the conference on "Cuba: The Challenges Ahead" at Berlin's Humboldt University in October 2–5, 2003 that gave birth to this endeavor. It was here that, at a lunch time talk with Andrew Arato and Claus Offe, who chaired and hosted the conference, the sparkling waters of the Spree river embarked us on a project that would bring the debate on Cuban exceptionalism to a broader audience. However, the present volume went very much astray since then; almost half of the texts in this volume have been added from other sources. Thanks are due to *Foro Internacional* (Mexico), and the *Latin American Research Review* for granting permission to publish the articles by Alejandro Portes and Javier Corrales, respectively. We thank all those who at some stage were involved in the translation and revision of these texts published, and particularly Alexandra Barahona de Brito who was so helpful in turning our manuscripts into publishable form. Finally, the authors also want to thank Nuffield College of Oxford University and the Institute for Ibero-American Studies of the German Institute for Global and Area Studies in Hamburg for their support of this project.

List of Abbreviations*

AC	Acción Católica (Catholic Action)
ACP	African Caribbean and Pacific
ADR	Acción Democrática Revolucionaria (Revolutionary Democratic Action)
AFSC	American Friends Service Committee
ANC	African National Congress
ANAP	Asociación Nacional de Agricultores Pequeños de Cuba (National Association of Small Farmers)
ANPP	Asamblea Nacional del Poder Popular de la República de Cuba (National Assembly of Popular Power)
APSC	Asamblea para la Promoción de la Sociedad Civil (Assembly to Promote Civil Society)
ASCE	Association for the Study of the Cuban Economy
BP	Buró Político (del Partido Comunista de Cuba)
CANF	Cuban American National Foundation
CARITAS	Catholic Relief Service
CC	Comité Central (del Partido Comunista de Cuba)
CC	Concilio Cubano
CCD	Comité Cubano por la Democracia (Cuban Committee for Democracy)—United States
CCRD	Centro Cristiano de Reflexión y Diálogo (Christian Center for Reflection and Dialogue)
CDR	Comité de la Defensa de la Revolución
CEA	Centro de Estudios sobre América
CFCR	Centro de Formación Cívica y Religiosa (Center for Civic and Religious Formation)
CIA	Central Intelligence Agency
CIS	Commonwealth of Independent States
CMEA/ COMECON	Council for Mutual Economic Assistance
CSB	Central and Southeastern Europe and the Baltic Countries
CTC	Confederación de Trabajadores de Cuba
CUC	Convertible Cuban Peso

* Unless otherwise indicated, all country-specific acronyms refer to Cuba.

CVR	Comisión de Verdad y Reconciliación—Peru (Commission of Truth and Reconciliation)
DR	Directorio Revolucionario
EBRD	European Bank of Reconstruction and Development
ETECSA	Empresa de Telecomunicaciones de Cuba, SA
EIU	Economist Intelligence Unit
EU	European Union
FDI	Foreign Direct Investment
FRG	Federal Republic of Germany
FSLN	Frente Sandinista de Liberación Nacional (Sandinista National Liberation Front)—Nicaragua
FTZ	Free Trade Zone
GAESA	Grupo de Administráción de Empresas
GONGO	Government-organized nongovernmental organization
GDP	Gross Domestic Product
GDR	German Democratic Republic
GM	Grupo Montecristi (Montecristi Group)
IAIHR	Inter-American Institute of Human Rights
ICAIC	Instituto Cubano de Arte e Industria Cinematográficos (Cuban Institute of Cinematographic Art and Industry)
IDB	Inter-American Development Bank
IMF	International Monetary Fund
ILO	International Labor Organization
INS	U.S. Immigration and Naturalization Service
JP	Junta Patriotica—Miami, FL
M-26	Movimiento 26 de Julio
MCL	Movimiento Cristiano de Liberación (Christian Liberation Movement)
MDC	Movimiento Demócrata Cristiano (Christian Democratic Movement)
MRP	Movimiento Revolucionario del Pueblo (Revolutionary Movement of the People)
MRR	Movimiento de Recuperación Revolucionaria (Movement for the Revolutionary Recuperation)
MRTA	Movimiento Revolucionario Tupac Amaru—Peru (Tupac Amaru Revolutionary Movement)
NCO	Noncommissioned officer
NGO	Nongovernmental organization
NED	National Endowment for Democracy—United States
OAS	Organization of American States
ONE	Oficina Nacional de Estadísticas
OUSI	Office of United States Interests
OXFAM	Oxford Committee for Famine Relief
PCC	Partido Comunista de Cuba (Cuban Communist Party)
PDC	Plataforma Democrática Cubana (Cuban Democratic Platform)

PIC	Partido Independiente de Color (Independent Party of Color)
PRI	Partido Revolucionario Institucional—Mexico (Revolutionary Institutional Party)
PSOE	Partido Socialista Obrero de Español (Spanish Socialist Workers Party)
PSP	Partido Socialista Popular (Popular Socialist Party)
SOE	State-owned enterprise
TRC	Truth and Reconciliation Comission—South Africa
UBPC	Unidades Básicas de Producción Cooperativa
UC	Unidad Cubana (Cuban Unity)
UN	United Nations
UNDP	United Nations Development Programme
UNEAC	Unión de Escritores y Artistas de Cuba (Writers and Artists' Union of Cuba)
UNHRC	United Nations Human Rights Commission
UNJC	Unión Nacional de Juristas de Cuba (National Union of Jurists of Cuba)
USSR	Union of Soviet Socialist Republics
WAQI	Radio Mambí—Miami, FL
WB	World Bank
WTO	World Trade Organization
WQBA	La Cubanísima—Miami, FL

Chapter 1

On Cuban Political Exceptionalism

Laurence Whitehead

Introduction

Comparative politics is a curious field of academic endeavor. It is about detecting commonalities between political processes that are in many of the most fundamental respects unique. All political histories are exceptional, but the political history of Cuba is so to an exceptional degree, as is demonstrated here. This chapter seeks to place current discussions about the foreseeable demise of the Castro regime, and alternative post-Castro scenarios, in a broader historical and comparative perspective. The objective is to explore the implications of Cuban political exceptionalism and not to essentialize it. Such an exploration is intended to broaden the repertoire of resources for thinking about possible post-Castro and even postcommunist transition scenarios. It should not be expected to generate any highly predictive conclusions, since an exceptionalist tradition can develop in multiple directions.

The first section reviews the major features of Cuban political history that deviate from what one might call a standard pattern and that therefore support the notion of Cuban exceptionalism. Its main purpose is to remind the reader of this recurring characteristic. However, it is also necessary to make some brief and tentative comments about possible explanations for it.

The second section reflects on the consequences of persistently following a deviant path. If theories of cumulative causation or path dependence have any merit then the way we model future choices and outcomes for post-Castro Cuba ought to take into account the island's deeply entrenched record of political exceptionalism. Standard models of regime transition and democratization that work reasonably well across a broad range of "normal" cases may not offer adequate guidance when extended to truly deviant cases.

The third section turns from the past to the present. Whatever the weight of Cuban history, in the early years of the twenty-first century the island has had and will continue to also contend with overwhelmingly strong international pressures to adjust, conform, or "integrate,"[1] into a system the requirements of which are radically at variance with many aspects of the currently existing and strongly embedded Castro regime. Standard power political and realist approaches to international relations would predict that however deviant Cuban politics may have been in the past, the objective realities are now stacked so heavily against nonconformity with external norms that the past (i.e., the Cuban Revolution) is bound to be more or less comprehensively dismantled or even liquidated. If so, a fairly standard (nonexceptional) outcome can be foreseen, and the only discussion becomes how to manage the intervening process of adjustment or transformation. This seems to be the intellectual framework within which most academic analyses of Cuban politics is located now, and it may soon be vindicated by experience. However, this framework glosses over the evidence of Cuban exceptionalism reviewed in this chapter and disregards its cumulative consequences. Moreover, such analyses have so far failed to predict the course of Cuban politics since the breakup of the Soviet bloc over a decade ago. In an attempt to fill these lacunae the fourth section of the chapter contrasts realist and "constructivist" approaches to the analysis of Cuba's current political impasse.[2]

The fifth section goes on to probe the limits of the "exceptionalist" interpretation, selecting the liberal constitutionalism of Benjamin Constant as an appropriately "universalist" alternative perspective. The chapter concludes with a reminder that Cuba's future possibilities remain highly contested and quite open. It comments on the Varela project, in the light of a theoretical reflection on the scope and limits to what might, on the most generous of interpretations, be classified as a democratic outcome in Cuba.[3] If we are to prepare for unanticipated developments and political surprises we need to keep in mind not only a standard framework of analysis but also alternative possible angles on the dynamics of Cuban politics and interactions between the island and the world.

Cuban Politics: How Exceptional, and Why?[4]

When Napoleon exported his version of politics to the Iberian Peninsula, one eventual result was to deal a deathblow to European colonial rule in the Western Hemisphere. The only exceptions were Cuba and Puerto Rico. When Cuba eventually broke away from Spanish rule and became an independent republic it was again out of step. This was a time when the rest of the Latin American republics were nearing their first centenary celebrations and when imperial rule was expanding, not contracting, in most of Africa and Asia. Again, the course of Cuban politics was desynchronized from broader political trends. Indeed, Cuba was an exception even among the territories detached from Spain as a result of the war of 1898. Puerto Rico and the Philippines were governed as U.S. colonial possessions. Only Cuba secured independent statehood. The nature of Cuban independence was also sui generis. Of all the decolonization of the past century no other independent state was subjected to anything as intrusive as the Platt Amendment, with its externally imposed constitutional provisions (including acknowledging the right of a foreign state to land troops and assume governing powers under specified, externally determined, conditions).[5] Cuba's formally sovereign political system was also subject to external institutionalized supervision every time the U.S. Congress reallocated its sugar import quotas. In the long comparative history of military coups in the twentieth century, there are many cases of generals seizing power and not a few examples when leaders came from the ranks of colonels. But the Cuban Sergeants Revolt of 1933, which led to the 25 years of the Batistato, involved a fracture within the military hierarchy at a lower level than has been known anywhere else (setting aside cases where the hierarchy itself disintegrates and the institution breaks up). Similarly, the frustrated revolution of 1933 was itself an almost unparalleled reaction to the Great Depression (the only more or less comparable experience being that of the Chilean Socialist Republic of the previous year). But then, with the possible exception of the Philippines under Marcos, it is hard to find examples of multiparty democracy as violent and corrupt as that which prevailed in Cuba between 1940 and 1952. What all this indicates is that Cuban political exceptionalism has deep historical roots.

Cuban political exceptionalism was a highly developed characteristic long before Fidel Castro's apparently crackpot decision to attack the Moncada Barracks and then land an expeditionary force of insurgents brought from Mexico in the *Granma*. These unpromising beginnings gave rise to the extraordinary, and again unprecedented,[6] spectacle of a fully equipped military regime allowing itself to be defeated first politically, and then militarily, in the course of a short and not so bloody guerrilla war. By the time Castro had consolidated his hold on the government in Havana and then reassigned his country from the U.S.-led "free world" to the Soviet bloc, the once unthinkable had become daily fare in Cuban politics. However political logic might operate in the rest of the world, a quite different set of possibilities and imperatives applied on this island. This is certainly not to imply that there were no constraints (indeed, the Castro regime soon learnt some harsh lessons about world politics and laws of economics that it had initially believed it could disregard) but rather to underscore that the course of Cuban politics remained deviant from all standard patterns.

Cuba is the only communist-ruled country where the local Communist Party did not play a leading role in the seizure of power; where the Soviet Union was not expecting, let alone directing, the takeover; and where the ruling party was not even formally constituted until over a decade after the revolution. It is the only communist-ruled country where the "class war" was waged principally by means of the wholesale expulsion of the propertied class to a neighboring country ("externalizing" that class but leaving it substantially intact). It is the only constituent part of the Soviet bloc to have remained under the same leadership and system of government in place before the fall of the Berlin Wall. It is the only surviving communist-ruled country (apart from North Korea) where private ownership and the market economy remain essentially suppressed by the authorities. It is the only country in the world to have been directly and continuously ruled by the same individual for over 46 years. It is the only country in the Western Hemisphere denied membership of the Organization of American States (OAS) and the Summit of the

Americas process. It is the only country ever to have succeeded in isolating the United States in a series of international votes (strictly speaking the roll call was the United States, Israel, and the Marshall Islands versus the world, in a succession of votes of over extraterritoriality).

No doubt, one could extend and refine this list of ways in which Cuban politics have been exceptional, but the above suffices for our purposes. The obvious questions that then arise are: Why was Cuba so different from everywhere else for so long? Does it make sense to suppose that after all this exceptionalism Cuba can readily revert to normal patterns of politics any time soon? This chapter is more concerned with the second question, but some consideration of the long-run sources of Cuban exceptionalism is necessary before we can focus on the present and on future prospects.

Although geography is not sufficient to determine destiny, Cuba's geopolitical predicament provides a critical insight into the structural characteristics promoting and sustaining this extraordinary record of political exceptionalism. As the largest island in the Caribbean, and as the seat of one of the great ports and administrative cities of the world, Cuba was the essential naval link between Spain and the rest of her transatlantic empire. It was the most valuable and strategic location south of the U.S. mainland as the North American continent filled up with settlers and as the U.S. South struggled to counteract the supremacy of the Yankee North. When the United States acquired a major navy, the possession (or failing that, the neutralization) of Cuba became a sine qua non condition for Washington to project its sea power to more distant locations. During the Cold War the possession of secure military facilities behind the U.S. security perimeter was such an asset to Moscow that it was worth extraordinary subsidies. Even today, one of the Cuban regime's most valuable bargaining counters remains its location. It can protect the United States from instability and drug trafficking or it can threaten to unleash further waves of mass immigration, and it can attract tourists from less equable climes to counteract the economic sanctions imposed by its most immediate neighbor. These geographical advantages (and the associated burdens of proximity to the United States) provide any Cuban government with an opportunity structure that differs from that available to any other nation in the world. Many of the exceptional developments described earlier in the chapter derive at least partially from this distinctive geopolitical profile.

Another clue to Cuban exceptionalism lies in the machinery of social control available to the island's rulers. Although some attempts have been made to establish more than one center of political activity within the territory, Cuba is not like Hispaniola, which can support both Haiti and the Dominican Republic. It is not like Colombia, with its intermontane basins and its *republiquetas.* Havana has long dominated its hinterland, almost all of which is readily accessible from the coast. There has almost always been one hierarchical authority that exercises social control throughout the entire territory, due to good internal and coastal communications and the natural boundaries of the island's insularity. Ever since the days of slavery and the traumas of the Haitian slave revolt, Cuban rulers have taken care to ensure that order was maintained uniformly throughout their large and fertile island. Political control over entry and exit to the island has given successive rulers remarkable power to shape its demography and to regulate its political identity. Thus, under Spanish rule the mass importation of slaves from Africa, accompanied by a far more selective importation of overseers and administrators from Spain, configured the enduring colonial political order. Once on the island, the black population was trapped. It could neither move elsewhere nor free itself. As a result, slavery persisted into the 1880s. Under the semi-sovereign, Plattist republic a different pattern of immigration and racial hierarchy was promoted by governments beholden to the United States (and especially to the segregationist South). The Batistato restricted immigration and used this power to help structure and control a labor movement that could serve its interests. The revolution oversaw the exit of one-tenth of the population, thereby achieving a massive mostly nonviolent redistribution of assets and life chances. In contrast to other socialist revolutions, Cuba needed no major civil war and no gulag to achieve this transformation, since its insularity and proximity to a welcoming Florida offered an exceptionalist solution—albeit one with it its own exceptionalist political consequences. Its secure island base has also enabled the Castro regime to operate forcefully on the international stage, including the "export" of teachers, soldiers, doctors, and construction workers to friendly states. This exceptionally large-scale and sustained program of international solidarity projects the message of the regime far beyond the range achievable by other nations of a comparable size. Again, the foundation for this is the distinctive solidity of the island's geopolitical base. In consequence, key issues for any post-Castro regime will be the terms on which those who wish to leave the island are to be granted exit permits; the basis on which those who wish to return can regain their citizenship—and perhaps even a restitution of their assets; and whether or not the island's future rulers can maintain or redeploy any of their cohorts of internationalists. This extremely concise review may at least suffice to demonstrate that the island's physical location, integration, and insularity have made its successive demographic policies a fundamental instrument of the Cuban state's regulation and direction of society. To some extent, similar patterns can also be discerned elsewhere, but Cuban history provides an exceptionally forceful and sustained demonstration of the long-term and transformative power of this particular form of social control. In addition, the predominance of the capital city and the sophistication of the resulting administrative structure made any bid for power an all-or-nothing game. This helps to explain how independence could be deferred for so long and why the Platt Amendment did not generate the pluralist equilibrium possibly imagined by its more thoughtful authors. It also helps explain why in 1933 the Cuban armed forces fractured not vertically, but horizontally (with noncommissioned officers [NCOs] pitted against their seniors). It makes the assault on the Moncada barracks more rational than most historians have appreciated, and it helps to explain why when Batista failed to crush a few rebels in the Sierra Maestra the whole edifice of control unraveled so quickly and completely. It tells us why Kennedy's failure at the Bay of Pigs laid the foundations for such a durable and indigestible communist regime in America's "backyard," and it also helps explain the regime's ability to block organized resistance even after the collapse or overthrow of all other Soviet bloc communist regimes.

Putting these two structural characteristics together it may be possible to generate partial explanations for other features of Cuban political exceptionalism. The combination of geopolitical predicament and unified social control helps to explain why the timing of critical developments in Cuban politics was so out of line with the timing of similar processes elsewhere. In turn, this helps to explain a pattern of powerful but frustrated political initiatives (notably the failed war for full independence, the frustrated revolution of 1933, and the failed experiment in competitive party politics in the 1940s), each of which is likely to have helped pave the wave for Castro's revolution, and to erode likely potential sources of resistance to it. The broad pattern seems to be that while internal conditions may have favored comprehensive political reorganization, geopolitical constraints kept blocking standard political outcomes. The interplay between these two logics generated a cycle of successive frustrations, each of which elicited nonstandard projects and responses.

The two structural characteristics briefly summarized above are insufficient to account for all the distinctive features catalogued above. They are both sketched rather than fully delineated. But they serve to confirm two points that are essential for the main argument presented here. Cuban exceptionalism preceded the 1959 revolution. And it would be rash to assume that its structural foundations are about to disappear just because the lifespan of Fidel Castro may soon be drawing to a close.

Exceptionalism, Counterfactuals, and Cumulative Causation

One of the key difficulties of historical explanation is how to specify the counterfactual alternatives to what actually happens. If we are to consider the "paths not taken" and the historical "might-have-beens" that can provide a yardstick for the evaluation of actual historical outcomes we need well-specified counterfactuals. But while we may be able to identify quite clearly what actually happened, there is in principle an unlimited supply of possible alternatives that did *not* take place. One advantage of viewing Cuban political history within the exceptionalist framework is that it can help to bring order to this kind of analysis, because it can highlight certain standard outcomes that were typical elsewhere and thereby focus attention on why Cuba was different and on the consequences that might follow from that difference.

Thus, it is not arbitrary to compare what actually happened with the counterfactual hypothesis that Cuba *might have* attained her independence at the same time as all the other Spanish republics; or that Cuban communism *might have* collapsed when all other Soviet bloc regimes did. Of course this kind of question always leaves much room for debate, but if there is a clear standard pattern then its implications can be laid out with a fair degree of detail and precision, and the main consequences of deviating from it can also be identified with some confidence.

Viewed from this perspective, it becomes clear that each time Cuban politics deviated from the standard or expected pattern one consequence was to increase the likelihood that the following stage would also be nonstandard. If Cuba had become independent at the "normal" time it would not have experienced the Platt Amendment version of semisovereign constitutionalism. If Cuba had not experienced the Platt Amendment regime, its armed forces would almost certainly not have fractured at the NCO level, as they did in 1933. If the Sergeants' Revolt had not taken that form then the 25 years of the Batistato would have been impossible, and some other, perhaps more robust or even more legitimate, form of domination would have been established. Without the Batistato it is hard to see how Castroism could have gathered the same strength or prevailed with so little internal resistance. The extremely distinctive features of the Castro regime no doubt owe much to the personal trajectory and character of its leader, but they are also partially determined by these preceding considerations and by the many repeated national frustrations arising from prior U.S.-Cuban interactions. The essential claim here is not that every link in the historical chain can only be understood in the terms just described, but rather that each link was exceptional in a way that can be specified by comparative analysis and, furthermore, that cumulatively each of these exceptional outcomes added to the probability of further deviations from a standard path, all clearing the way for what eventually become the Castro regime.

If path dependence has any explanatory value in the field of comparative politics, then the lack of conformity between the Cuban and other, more typical, sequences should lead us to expect cumulatively more divergent outcomes. But if this argument holds for the course of Cuban politics over the twentieth century it also carries implications about how much we should expect standard models to predict outcomes in the present and future as well.

One way of tracking these implications is by examining the consequences of being a latecomer. Cuba was a latecomer to independence, which meant that by the time the republic came into existence its creators already had knowledge of how the same process had turned out elsewhere. Not only were they constrained by the different context of independence (after 1900 as opposed to during the 1820s), but they were also guided in their strategic thinking by their understanding of preceding processes. Cuba was also a latecomer to communism. Not only did Cuban communism differ from its predecessors in that it was not an imposition following the advance of the Red Army, but it also took a different form because the lessons of Stalinism were being digested by communists following Khrushchev's secret speech of 1956, and the Cuban leadership was aware of the differences between Russian and Chinese variants of communism. And as the Cuban regime did not collapse at the same time as the Soviet bloc, the leadership in Havana has had time to reflect on how transitions to postcommunism can work, what their consequences may be, and how to prepare for what was an unanticipated shock for its predecessors. So if Cuba eventually democratizes, its transition path may not replicate that of other Latin American countries, among other reasons because it will happen so much later, and this difference in timing will give rise to differences in understanding on the part of the key actors involved.

In summary, for reasons such as those outlined above, the logic of domestic politics suggests Cuban exceptionalism is more likely to reproduce itself (through eccentric path dependency, cumulative causation, and the consequences of timing differences) than to be dissolved. It would probably require some massive external imposition for such political deviance to be eliminated. And even in the occurrence of such an event the prevailing logic would be that of U.S. hegemony, rather than some "end of history" liberal convergence.

Ways Out of the Impasse: Realist versus Constructivist Perspectives

My interpretation is that the political situation in Cuba consists of an impasse between a domestically based commitment not to liquidate the legacy of the revolution and an externally driven imperative to integrate Cuba into an international system that is fundamentally incompatible with the preservation of most of that legacy. The clash between these two forces has dominated the political scene for at least the past decade, and my view is that although there have been some interesting shifts of emphasis and partial attempts at accommodation they have not resolved the underlying problem. Hence my characterization of the present as an impasse, and moreover one that could easily persist into the medium-term future.

Before we can evaluate possible ways out of an impasse it is necessary to specify its nature. Experience suggests that in the short to medium term it is quite likely that the existing balance of forces will remain stable. The Cuban regime may roughly maintain its current course, and the United States may maintain its unilateral sanctions without extending its scope and securing major concessions from Havana.[7] This is what can be described as an impasse. To the extent that the conflict continues but neither side budges, it could be argued that the deadlock suits both sides, in that both may regard it as the lesser of evils when compared to either yielding or acting more aggressively. However, even when such an impasse persists for a long period it does not necessarily follow that the underlying equilibrium is truly stable. In addition to the contingent factors that could destabilize the situation (such as the death of Castro, or the involvement of the Unites States in higher priority conflicts elsewhere) there is a deeper source of tension. And that is that even if both sides reluctantly conclude that the present deadlock is the lesser of evils, they still both adhere to incompatible views of the eventual outcome. Each side still believes that if the cost of extending the conflict is endured for long enough the other side may eventually be forced to back down. Official Washington continues to believe that, in the end, the Cuban regime will have to capitulate and that when it does the Cuban people will disassociate themselves from most or all of what the United States views as the unpalatable doctrines and practices that have emanated from Havana.[8] A still dominant group in the Cuban leadership evidently believes that if Castro regime remains solid in its determination to resist the dictates of Washington, then sooner or later the hostility of the U.S. government will weaken, American pragmatism will come to the fore, and some continuation of the present postrevolutionary political system will be reluctantly accepted.

So long as these two incompatible expectations persist the resulting impasse will remain a *tug-of-war* rather than a stable equilibrium. But in a tug-of-war, no matter how static the apparent balance of forces, each side is in fact expending great energy in an attempt to weaken the other. In this particular instance, it is the Cuban economy and the future well-being of the Cuban people that is most weakened by the persistence of the impasse, although Washington also suffers various inconveniences.

With these considerations in mind we can now attempt to theorize the possible ways out of the impasse. The most influential set of theories belong to what can be summarily labeled a realist perspective. The object of this section is to sketch out the broad realist approach and then to contrast it with an alternative theoretical standpoint that can (again loosely) be labeled constructivist. Admittedly, this dichotomy between realism and constructivism is a simplification. Both positions can be refined and perhaps partially reconciled. But this is not a theoretical chapter, and a simple dichotomous reading provides us with a heuristic devise that illuminates the Cuban experience. If standard "realism" explained the essential features of Cuban politics, then that would refute the thesis of Cuban "exceptionalism." If realism fails, however, then my argument in favor of Cuban exceptionalism can be incorporated into the more general explanatory framework offered by constructivism.

A central argument here is that realism does *not* provide very good guidance as to how Cuba reached its present state. It omits some key explanatory variables that are better illuminated from a constructivist perspective. If this is true of the past and present, then realist approaches may continue to mislead us, when applied to Cuba's prospective future "integration" into the international system. The constructivist alternative generates insights into the course of Cuban politics that are invisible from a realist standpoint, notably the insights derived from cumulative causation and path dependence.

From the realist perspective deviations from a standard path should not become cumulative because realists assume that when a political actor chooses an inappropriate or irrational course, the resulting high costs will lead them to correct the error. Either that, or those who bear the costs of the error acquire an incentive to change their leadership. On this model of political behavior it would not have been rational to attack the Moncada barracks in the first place, since the chance of success seemed so low, and the cost of failure was extreme.[9] Once the Moncada attack had failed, realists would not expect a second adventure to be attempted, and if it were they would not expect it to attract much support. Realism is not a promising framework for the prediction of social revolution in general, and it cannot obviously be applied to explaining the Cuban upheaval of 1959. Nor would realists expect a fragile new revolutionary regime to switch alliances from the United States to the Soviet Union, or to risk a nuclear war over the introduction of missiles behind the U.S. defense perimeter. Realists would not predict a long chain of apparently unrealistic revolutionary policies, each followed by further acts of even greater voluntarism in defiance of what they must regard as the objective logic of the situation. Still less would they predict that such deviant behavior might be accompanied by growing support and eventual success (in part due to the polarized reactions triggered by the deviant behavior). Finally, they would not predict that the resulting regime could last for approximately half a century, and outlive all its early sources of support. In short, conventional realism does not predict the behavior of the Castro regime. Indeed, confronted by the intractable realities of Cuban politics a significant strand of realist analysis has been reduced to the conclusion that Castro must be "mad."

How would a constructivist perspective change this analysis? Take the example of sanctions. From a realist perspective sanctions are simply a cost that any rational actor will try to avoid provided the price of securing relief is not too great. But on several occasions—in the late 1970s, and again in 1996—it is plausible to argue that the Cuban regime faced the possibility that sanctions against it might be lifted, and acted in ways calculated to avert that outcome. If Cuba was not the object of unilateral (internationally illegitimate) sanctions by an overbearing enemy, then the discursive consequences would be serious. Externally, it could lose its "David" status and become just another relatively needy and somewhat unsuccessful Caribbean nation. Domestically too in the absence of a clear, visible, and constantly renewed indication of external aggression, the regime would have to change its explanation for the shortages and frustrations of daily life on the island. From a constructivist perspective these "soft" or presentational aspects of the sanctions issue could weigh more heavily with Cuban policy makers than the hard material consequences of the punishment. Put in more realist language, a certain type of political strategy—characteristic of actors in a position of material weakness but organizational autonomy—may be to convert objective loss and material sacrifice into political advantage. But once conventional realism is relaxed to allow costs and benefits to be redefined according to incommensurable and subjective criteria it loses the parsimony that provides its major theoretical justification. This less "realistic" version of realism (the shift from an instrumental to a symbolic calculation of advantage) is not just a practice of the present Cuban government, of course. It may offer some chance of success— or at least vindicate—the structurally weaker side in any conflict: it may be the loser's last resort. So, for example, it is also relevant to the Palestinian intifada or to the boycotts of segregated facilities in the American South in the 1960s. It applies to hunger strikers, Buddhist self-immolators, and Kamikaze pilots.

All these variants of political action involve courting suffering (defying the logic of conventional realism), to turn the tables on the strong or to generate solidarity among the weak, or—failing that—at least to transmit a message of defiance.

The example of sanctions helps demonstrate how a constructivist perspective might provide an explanation for political events that would be unintelligible or irrational from a strictly realist viewpoint. It could help to explain not just the attack on the Moncada barracks but also the priority that Cuba has attached to outmaneuvering the U.S. delegation at the United Nations Commission on Human Rights (UNHRC). What palpable benefit does Havana derive from all the efforts it expends to secure such a diplomatic victory? A constructivist approach offers clues to what would otherwise seem an inexplicable pattern of behavior.[10]

But here we need to add another important point. Constructivism does not just attempt to explain the wasteful and quirky behavior of eccentric and minor political actors. It aims to illuminate political interactions more broadly. So we need to consider whether the behavior of Cuba's external partners and adversaries also requires analysis from within this perspective, rather than being explicable in purely realist terms. For example, can Washington's long-standing and internationally unpopular stance toward the Castro regime be accounted for in terms of a realist cost-benefit analysis, or is it also driven by other considerations?[11] More generally, has the long-term exceptionalism of Cuban politics induced a wide array of international actors to base their relations with successive rulers of the island more on symbolic considerations than on the realpolitik that is generally assumed to prevail in international affairs?

A major argument of this chapter is that the constructivist perspective deserves consideration when interpreting the island's relations with all three categories of partners: backers, sympathizers, and opponents. It can be applied to pre-1958 Cuba as well as to the postrevolutionary period, and it may continue to influence Cuban affairs even after a prospective post-Castro regime transition.

This argument can be developed by considering each category of partners in turn. First, there are *the backers*. Over the long run Cuba has been the protégé of three successive major external controllers and protectors: Spain until 1898, the United States until 1959, and the Union of Soviet Socialist Republics (USSR) until 1992. Thus, mostly for geopolitical reasons, the island has almost always found itself in an asymmetric and exclusivist relationship with a single great power. Only after the dissolution of the Soviet Union in 1992 have the rulers of Cuba conducted their affairs without the exceptional support and constraints arising from such an intense and privileged dependence (and there are signs that Chávez's Venezuela and even China may now be being enlisted as partial surrogates in this role). Until then, these tight reciprocal relations were charged with symbolism and characterized by feelings of love and hate. They were far removed from the rational pursuit of self-interest between autonomous unitary actors, as postulated by the realist

school. This may seem a banal observation in the case of Spain, since Cuba
was after all a colonial possession at the time. However, even then, the
emotional and symbolic dimensions of the relationship were unusual, since
Cuba was the *loyal* colony that remained after most of the empire had broken
away. Moreover, Cuba was an exceptionally wealthy and glorious possession,
with a magnificent capital city and an unusually prosperous and modern
economy. The Cuban élite had to be wooed by Spain, for if they had chosen
annexation by the United States there was little their European rulers could
have done to stop them. Consequently, Spain invested a huge amount of
political and psychological capital in nurturing its special relationship with
Cuba. When the island was eventually lost, this was *el desastre* (the disaster),
a shattering diminution of Spain's role in the world and of Spanish national
self-esteem. Cubans understood the intimacy and passion of this relationship, and it colored their attitude toward themselves and toward the rest of
the world. This, at least, would be the line of argument that constructivists
could deploy to differentiate themselves from the realists.

Then, for 60 years, Cuba experienced a peculiarly lopsided and ambivalent
relationship with the world's newly emerging dominant power, the United
States.[12] The Platt Amendment was the formal expression of this curious
desencuentro. From a constructivist perspective we need to identify the interpretative structure behind that odd constitutional format. Why did Washington
grant Cuba its independence, why did it retain *arrières pensées* (second
thoughts) about this generosity, and why was it so flabbergasted when anti-
Americanism proved to have such virulent popular appeal? Perhaps the key
point is that the United States expected to combine the advantages of semi-
colonial control over an absolutely strategic neighbor with the good conscience
of demonstrating that it was not just another imperialist power, that it would
establish and guarantee the autonomous rights to which a modern nation was
entitled, and that the Cuban people would themselves endorse America's self-
definition as a benign neighbor. From a constructivist standpoint, then, the
most unforgivable aspect of the Cuban Revolution might not be the loss of
property or even the military setback (although these were certainly painful
enough, at least during the 1960s) The most enduring offence might rather be
the discourse of the Cuban Revolution, its systematic denigration the U.S.
government and its tireless verbal assaults on North American self-esteem. From
this standpoint it makes sense that whereas Washington can now forge partner-
ships with Russia and China, and can lift sanctions against Vietnam, something
more is demanded of the Cubans. On this view, Washington's underlying goal
is not be so much that the Cuban state acknowledge its objective weakness, but
rather that the Cuban people repudiate the comprehensive indictment of
American state policy that official Havana has reiterated so relentlessly since
1959. If there is a symbolic and emotional component in United States
attitudes toward the Castro regime, the psychological relationship is again
reciprocal. Cuban leaders are fascinated by the United States, and they study
American policies with obsessive attention. This could be understood simply
as a logical response to geopolitical realities, but a full profile of Cuban

perceptions of the United States would demonstrate its emotional and identitarian content, which goes beyond mere instrumental rationality. (The same is even more the case for Puerto Rico). Cubans pride themselves on their ability to understand and perhaps even to manipulate U.S. reactions, albeit according to a logic that may be more expressive than utilitarian. Their discourse and strategy rests on a belief that Cuba's importance, its value to the world, arises from its valor in articulating general truths that others are too opportunist to express outright. Here at any rate is how a constructivist position might be differentiated from that of a traditional realist.

Cuba's third privileged relationship, with the USSR, can also be analyzed within a similar framework. Castro's enthusiasm for a socialist internal transformation and a pro-Soviet realignment of the Third World was an ideological victory more inspiring than anything that the post-Stalinist bureaucrats in the Kremlin could hope to conjure up from their own resources. The Cuban Revolution offered the USSR external validation for Moscow's otherwise not very plausible claims about the superiority of its political system and the necessary course of world history. The Cubans knew far more about the United States than other peoples of the world, and had benefited more than most from U.S. investment and political influence. If *these* people asserted (for their own reasons, rather than in deference to Soviet compulsion) that the world's most advanced capitalist nation was hypocritical and exploitative, this provided Moscow with an ideological vindication of exceptional value. The Cuban gesture came at precisely the moment when Moscow most needed it (when the breach with China had led to the withdrawal of all Soviet aid from Beijing). Moreover it was backed by an expressive willingness to assume risks and absorb costs in order to prove Cuba's new allegiance was irreversible. Even the unidealistic bureaucrats of the Kremlin found it impossible to resist the ardor of Cuba's courtship (although some of them had occasion to rue Khrushchev's impulsiveness, and what they called his "hare-brained" schemes, after it was too late to reestablish distance between Havana and Moscow). The "love-hate" dimension of this relationship became particularly evident after Gorbachev's rise to power in Moscow, which was matched by what Cuba described, in undisguised criticism of the Soviet model, the "rectification of errors and negative tendencies." But, in truth, the ambivalence was there all along, as can be seen from the eccentric history of the ruling party itself (the first purge of a pro-Soviet "microfaction" took place in the early 1960s).

Finally, after 1992, Cuba found itself for the first time bereft of any major external protector. The Chinese Communists, the Spanish Socialists, the Mexican Institutional Revolutionary Party (Partido Revolucionario Institucional [PRI]) and the Canadian Liberals have all flirted with the idea of partially filling this vacuum, only to recoil (for reasons to be considered below under the heading of "sympathizers"). The Venezuela of President Chávez has only recently stepped up to this vacancy, and its resources and staying power remain to be tested. The intense and privileged relationships to which the Cubans have for so long been accustomed are beyond the range of any of these external political actors, most of whom lack either the material resources or the psychological dispositions to take on such a demanding "mistress." Therefore, from a constructivist viewpoint, we need to enquire about the symbolic and emotional significance for Cuba of attempting to "go it alone." From a constructivist perspective, this can be approached indirectly by examining how Cuba handles its remaining relationships with sympathizers and opponents.

The dominant relationship with *sympathizers* is to castigate them for faint-heartedness, and to pressurize them to emulate the Cuban level of valor and self-sacrifice. In due course this polarizes potential supporters between the "unconditionals" and the disillusioned ("traitors" in Castroist terms). A succession of leftist intellectuals, from Jean Paul Sartre to Jorge Castañeda, has experienced this unpleasant fate at the hands of the Cuban Revolution. But it is important to note that a similar polarization occurs in Miami, and it seems that this Cuban political style has a long historical pedigree. Thus, many of those who had sympathized with Cuba's long war of independence against Spain found they were caught in just such a vice. In extremes, Machado and Batista also squeezed allies and sympathizers into the boxes of "unconditionals" and "untrustworthies." This suggests that ideas of compromise and coalition building, of meeting the other party halfway, may not be deeply rooted in the Cuban political tradition. Fidel's attempt to upstage all the other 50 national leaders at the March 2002 Monterrey Summit on the financing of development is only one of his most recent in a characteristically extended sequence of displays of intransigence. Cuba's conflict with the European Union (EU) over the jailing of 75 dissidents in 2003 followed a similar pattern. The absence of an external protector has not as yet diminished the current Cuban regime's proclivity for such performances. Indeed it may even be hypothesized that the psychological need for this kind of expressive politics is all the greater in times of isolation and weakness. Whether this style of political action would disappear as Cuba "reintegrates" into the international system is an open question, but the historical record raises some doubts.

Then there is the relationship with outright *opponents.* Arguably, Cuban exceptionalism and intransigence would eventually be eroded by the interplay of external pluralist pressures if Havana faced no unifying and overbearing opponent to reenergize the struggle for self-affirmation. But although Cuba no longer has a privileged protector it still has a galvanizing external antagonist. At least that is how the authorities in Havana still construct their understanding of the world, and that worldview helps them screen out a more sordid calculus of the costs and benefits of each choice.

The foregoing constructivist analysis has already offered some suggestions why Washington can still be counted on to play its appointed aggressor role. U.S. national pride and self-understanding requires the Cuban people to apologize and retract, not just to cut a pragmatic deal. In addition, the intransigeance of Havana is mirrored by the intransigeance of Miami (with each feeding off the other) which in turn constrains Washington's room for maneuver. But let us make the mental experiment, and imagine that despite these strong forces some future U.S. government *did* try unilaterally to step back from this unproductive confrontation. The experience of the Carter administration, and the treatment regularly meted out to potential sympathizers who were not unconditional both suggest that Havana would not make it easy to negotiate a *détente*. From a constructivist perspective we could anticipate that even in its current condition of objective weakness the Cuban authorities might prefer the comfort of their exceptionalism to the internally divisive and disorienting consequences of a compromise *salida* (exit). Each concession might therefore be followed by a stepped-up demand. In practice, it is difficult to envisage a pragmatic end to this discursive clash. Neither side can easily cool the rhetoric, for the discourse is an essential part of the political reality. It is what binds both political communities together. That, at least, is where a constructivist analysis might differ from a conventional bargaining strength perspective on Cuba's future course.

"Liberal Constitutionalism" or
"Cuban Exceptionalism"?

This section tests the plausibility of the "exceptionalist" thesis from a different standpoint. The previous section drew on international relations theory, and examined the history of Cuba's geopolitical experience during the twentieth century. It exposed the limits of realism and highlighted the relevance of a constructivist perspective that would account for the island's repeated deviations from expected patterns, at least up until the present day. But looking to the future, and drawing on what has been learnt about the comparative politics of democratization, we might nevertheless conclude that the conditions for such deviancy are now coming to an end. In many other countries (including a wide range of former communist regimes) we have witnessed convergence on a remarkably standard pattern of democratic transition. Liberal constitutionalism has become the dominant form of political organization throughout the Western Hemisphere, and international pressures to conform to that model have grown evermore relentless over the past decade. This section therefore reflects on liberal constitutional universalism and how it might apply to contemporary Cuba. Without attempting a predictive conclusion, it also explores the continuing plausibility of "exceptionalist" arguments that might nullify tendencies toward a liberal convergence.

At this point some possible misconceptions about the meaning of "exceptionalism" may need to be addressed. No one is claiming that Cuban exceptionalism is so exceptional that it cannot be compared with other countries or that its future is predetermined by its past. Instead, the "exceptionalist" claim would be that Cuba does not "fit" with most standard social science templates or models; it does not provide a simple moral lesson to the rest of the world—be it a lesson of virtue to be admired and imitated by all others as Castro would have it, or as lesson in what is evil, as the Bush administration would have it. The island's distinctive political history and characteristics mean that one should be very cautious in drawing inferences from Cuba's trajectory—either about how the rest of the world can be organized, or about where the people of Cuba are bound to go next (either as a matter of necessity or of morality). The more we focus on what is unusual about the island's political experience, the less likely it is that we can derive simple lessons that will be easily transferable or applicable elsewhere. And the more we direct attention to its complexities and eccentricities the less certain we can be about what constitutes either the most probable or the most desirable way forward for the Cuban people. Their past does not prescribe their future, because standard models that may work elsewhere need to be adapted considerably to fit their circumstances and understanding, and also because the paralysis arising from their geopolitical deadlock and their polarized ideological debate precludes the Cuban people from undertaking the free enquiry and broad, open deliberation needed to decide who they really want to be, and where—given their special constraints—they would like to go next. It is in these respects that one could argue legitimately theories of Cuban political exceptionalism.

But however strong the arguments in favor of Cuban "exceptionalism" they can never entirely neutralize social forces that have proved to be binding elsewhere. Cuba may be an island, but it is very much part of the wider world, as its people certainly know, and as its political leaders have always recognized. All claims about exceptionalism can therefore be no more than relative. They concern questions of timing, balance, and interpretation. The version of exceptionalism promoted by the Castro regime is as follows: "We may be small and isolated, but it is the rest of the world that is wrong. That is why we owe it to others (as well as to our own people), to maintain our deviant standpoint despite the heavy costs we have to bear. And that is also why our sympathizers owe it to us to create the conditions for us to continue to do this." Whatever else one thinks about this position, it clearly involves making universalistic claims. So whether one is a defender or a critic of the Cuban Revolution, arguments about Cuban exceptionalism have to be weighed against claims that situate Cuba within some global framework of interpretation.

In this section of the chapter the framework selected for consideration is that provided by doctrines of constitutional liberalism. This is because it has historical roots in Cuba,[13] and because it provides one influential source of guidance about how Cuba might eventually evolve once the inflexibility of the Castro regime begins to relax. The question for consideration here is whether the "exceptionalist" interpretation advanced earlier in this chapter is sufficient to preclude the normal functioning of constitutional liberalism on the island within the foreseeable future, or how it might distort it. A more familiar way of posing the same questions would be to enquire not whether "Cuban exceptionalism" may impede a standard constitutional democracy, but more specifically whether the legacy of either "Castroism" or "the Cuban Revolution" may produce this effect. It is tough to disentangle the relationship between the two levels of analysis since the latter is so much the most visible and indeed exaggerated manifestation of the former. The advantage of trying to pose the question in terms of exceptionalism rather than Castroism is that it may offer some escape from the rigid ideological stereotypes (for and against) that so dominate the public debate and that therefore obstruct efforts to situate Cuba in a comparative perspective. But after 46 years of absolute power exercised from a single viewpoint it becomes very difficult to distinguish which political legacies are attributable to the Cuban Revolution and which derive from further back.

The comparative evidence from other contemporary democratizations is only a very rough guide to the constraining effects of such legacies given Cuba's highly distinctive trajectory, and is fairly inconclusive in any case. The deaths of Franco and Salazar were followed fairly soon by the installation of surprisingly conventional constitutional democracies—albeit with a "revolutionary" interregnum in the case of Portugal. Indeed, in these cases there was little overt evidence of the previous political regimes survived, although the outcome was more mixed in Latin American comparators such as the Dominican Republic and Paraguay. But in any case these were all deeply antirevolutionary regimes. The diverse postcommunist successor states of the USSR and Yugoslavia also present a varied picture, with much stronger political legacies persisting in some countries than in others. Afghanistan and Iraq, both traumatized by decades of war and extremes of domestic brutality, were thought by many Western observers to be *tabulae rasa* on which new constitutional democratic edifices could easily be constructed, although experience so far suggests that these superstructures rest on very weak foundations, and the past may easily return to obstruct the future. Arguably, we should expect to find Cuba among the cases where prior legacies are most constraining, both because of the frustrated nationalism described above, and because the revolution may have penetrated more deeply into the national consciousness than elsewhere. This is hard to verify, but we do know that the revolutionary leader has ruled far longer, and has persisted with more vigor than most in attempting to project his legacy into his country's future.

The Post-Napoleonic Precedent:
Benjamin Constant

Standard theories of democratic transition tend to generalize from a wide variety of relatively short-term contemporary instances of "regime change." They lack much historical depth, and try to homogenize processes that are in reality long-term, complex, and partially open-ended.[14] But if Cuban politics has followed a distinctive trajectory for over a century of sovereign national existence, and if there are grounds to expect Cuba's historical legacy to exert a particularly strong constraining influence on future developments, then the most useful way to bring comparative political insights to bear on this case may be to extend the time frame and range of examples taken to be relevant. This section adopts that strategy, reviewing the case of France after the downfall of Emperor Napoleon in 1815.

The French Revolution of 1789, like that of Cuba in 1959, awakened idealistic hopes of political liberation and mass participation, but in due course gave rise to an extremely personalist political regime. When Napoleon's tenure of power was finally brought to an end by external defeat coupled with internal exhaustion and dissension, liberals such as Benjamin Constant were faced with a dilemma that could also prove relevant to a post-Castro Cuba.

Constant's central preoccupation was with the political legacy of the French Revolution and what he regarded as the Napoleonic usurpation of its emancipatory potential. He tried to identify the despotic features of the regime that he believed were sure to perish, and to separate those from what he considered to be the enduring features of modern liberty, which could not be eradicated and had to be recognized and protected by the successor regime. Of course, the Cuban case is separated from his concerns both by two centuries and the Atlantic Ocean, but Constant pitched his arguments in a universal form, and so his analysis provides us with a fairly appropriate yardstick for comparing the universalizing logic of constitutional liberalism with this chapter's claims about the "exceptionalism" of Cuba's historical trajectory.

Constant built his case around two propositions that jointly explained why both the ideals of the French Revolution were worthy of respect and also why, in practice, they had proved so flawed and untenable. From this he derived a set of political principles that he held to apply to all representative governments in the modern world. They can be summed up by the phrase liberal constitutionalism (meaning the protection of individual rights, including those to private property, division of powers, judicial independence, press freedom, an elected assembly, and civil control over the military, among others). The two key propositions were, first, that the liberty of the Ancients differed from the foundations of liberty in the modern world in that the former was collective and the latter individual; and second, that a revolution made in the name of freedom was a noble enterprise but that if it promoted the Ancient instead of the modern idea of liberty it would become oppressive and thus doomed to fail. His solution was not to reject the revolutionary enterprise, but to advocate that it be refounded according to modern principles of individual freedom.

Analysts of contemporary Cuba can find striking passages in the work of Constant that may seem to foreshadow key aspects of the island's political trajectory after 1958. Critics of the Castro regime can hardly fail to recognize it in such passages as this: "It is somewhat remarkable that uniformity should never have encountered greater favor than in a revolution made in the name of the rights and the liberty of men. The spirit of the system was first entranced by symmetry. The love of power soon discovered what immense advantages symmetry could procure for it. . . . Today admiration for uniformity, a genuine admiration in some narrow minds, if affected by many servile ones, is received as a religious dogma, by a crowd of assiduous echoers of any favored opinion."[15]

But friends of the Cuban Revolution can also find some passages in Constant that reflect their views:

> The aim of our reformers was noble and generous. Who among us did not feel
> his heart beat with hope at the outset of the course which they seemed to open

up? And shame, even today, on whoever does not feel the need to declare that acknowledging a few errors committed by our first guides does not mean blighting their memory or disowning the opinions which the friends of mankind have professed throughout the ages. . . . Especially when we lived under vicious governments, which, without being strong, were repressive in their effects; absurd in their principles; wretched in action; governments which had as their strength arbitrary power; for their purpose the belittling of mankind; and which some individuals still dare to praise to us today.[16]

Instead of rallying to either camp in the ideological dispute over the justification of the French Revolution, Constant invoked historical necessity as the authority for his conclusion that only liberal constitutionalism could resolve the postrevolutionary impasse. He was clear that Napoleon's personal system of rule could not be institutionalized, because it ran counter to what he viewed as the individualistic foundations of modern liberty. He therefore anticipated the opportunism and defections that accompanied the waning power of the supreme ruler. The move from a personal despotism to a more stable and institutional regime based on individual liberty would require consulting with the freely expressed opinions of the ordinary citizens of France. He knew that unconditional defenders of Napoleonic rule would not favor such freedom, nor would the émigrés, hungry for a restoration of the ancien regime. But neither of these power contenders could supplant the will of the French people, who needed the freedom to deliberate on their own preferences for the future: "[I]f authority will only remain silent, the individuals will speak up, the clash of ideas will generate enlightenment, and it will soon be impossible to mistake the general feeling. You have here an infallible as well as easy means, freedom of the press; that freedom to which we must always return; that freedom which is as necessary to governments as it is to the people; that freedom, the violation of which, in this respect, is a crime against the state."[17]

Given his declared intention to provide a prescription to all modern representative governments, his writings may be invoked to support a liberal internationalist universalism (antiexceptionalism). On this view, Cuban political exceptionalism must be a time-limited deviation, and liberal universalism applies to this Caribbean island as much as elsewhere. It is indeed possible that something close to his prescription of liberal constitutionalism will prove the most widely acceptable formula for stabilizing a post-Castro transition to democracy, and for reintegrating Cuba into the regional community of American states. That is not only what a wide range of external authorities and advisers are urging, it is also what the 11,000 Cuban signatories to the Varela Project called for in the spring of 2002. Constant's analysis helps clarify the logic of this position.

Nevertheless, both the political trajectory of France after the fall of Napoleon and the checkered history of Constant's own efforts to promote stable constitutionalism in that country caution against accepting his analysis as a conclusive refutation of Cuban exceptionalism. Certainly, liberal constitutionalism followed an erratic path in the two centuries after Constant wrote these words, even in France. Neither Bonapartists nor Legitimists could be relied on to operate within Constant's proposed constitutional framework after 1815, and the effects of revolution and counterrevolution on French popular opinion were to produce not a consensus on liberal restraints but a clash of rival ideological projects that destabilized French politics for at least another half century, if not more permanently. (Not for nothing is the current regime in France known as the Fifth Republic). So despite Constant, the post-Napoleonic precedent suggests that a post-Castro Cuba could continue resisting the "end of history" logic of liberal constitutional convergence for generations to come. Cuban exceptionalism is not necessarily about to be eclipsed by inevitable regime change to a monotone consolidated democracy. In fact, applying Constant's terminology we would have to enquire whether twenty-first century Cuba even now belongs to what he called "the modern world." For him, the modern spirit of individualism was founded on commerce,[18] as well as on certain expectations of freedom of choice, and independence of action beyond the scope of collective constraint. He contrasted this to the system of "liberty" in antiquity, which "consisted in exercising collectively, but directly, several parts of the complete sovereignty. . . . But if this was what the ancients called liberty, they admitted as compatible with this collective freedom the complete subjection of the individual to the authority of the community . . . all private actions were submitted to severe surveillance. . . ."[19]

Postrevolutionary Cuba seems closer to Constant's Sparta than to the characteristics he attributed to the modern world.[20] Neither in the realm of commerce and private ownership, nor in the domain of individual rights of opinion and expression does the situation on the island correspond to what this founder of liberal constitutionalism took to be the inherent features of modern liberty.[21] So here too, within the framework of this universalizing theory, Cuba's claims to "exceptionalism," or that it deviates from a presumably universal standard of social organization, once again require attention.

Constant also analyzed the demise of what he called "the most complete despotism that has ever existed,"[22] referring to the 14 years of Napoleon's personal supremacy. In Cuba, the equivalent period already exceeds 46 years, quite long enough to obliterate the moral inheritance of previous generations (a loss that Constant described as a "treasure," and considered "an incalculable evil for a people").[23] As it turned out, even the 14 years of Napoleonic rule produced such an impact on French collective consciousness that half a century later attempts were still being made to recreate it. The legacy of Castroism is hardly likely to be more easily eliminated. As a final argument in defense of the exceptionalism thesis, the Cuban Revolution has long been encircled and besieged by much more powerful forces from without, whereas the Napoleonic Empire collapsed mostly from inner contradictions after expanding and dominating its weaker neighbors. The claims of national unity against overbearing adversity have reinforced Cuba's political resilience and disposition to defy external prescriptions. This source of exceptionalism in Cuba may not yet be exhausted either.

Tentative Conclusions about an
Uncertain Transition

In Cuba as elsewhere the past remains an imperfect guide to the future. So even though Cuban political exceptionalism has a remarkable pedigree, it cannot necessarily be extrapolated indefinitely into the twenty-first century. Similarly, although constructivism may help to explain some features of Cuban political dynamics that are inexplicable from a narrowly realist perspective, the understanding that it generates is not highly predictive. Nor is it helpful to overstress the dichotomy between realism and constructivism. After all, all the episodes described above have real as well as symbolic consequences. Those old enough to remember the Missile Crisis can hardly dismiss the emotions it aroused as being purely subjective, and the division of so many Cuban families is a real wound to both sides, not a mere verbal disagreement. In any case, the criticism of "realism" is a largely artificial academic construct. A sounder version of realism would take discursive and symbolic considerations into account wherever it could be shown that they were more than mere window dressing. Constructivism and exceptionalism are compatible with this more interpretative version of realism. Similar considerations apply to Constant's liberal universalism. For heuristic purposes it was useful to contrast it with the "exceptionalism" argument laid out here. But again, the dichotomy should not be overstressed. In practice, throughout his political career Constant struggled with the awkward fact that French political realities proved stubbornly resistant to his universalizing liberalism. At one point he even compromised himself as an adviser to Napoleon (after the return from Elba) and later had to face the Legitimist reaction. Although there was a space for the development of political liberalism in the wake of the French Revolution, it was only one doctrine in competition with other serious rivals. Similarly, Cuban exceptionalism and even the legacy of the Cuban Revolution include certain precedents that potentially can be developed in a liberal constitutional direction, even though the main thrust of these political traditions is clearly illiberal. It should not be forgotten that there was a long-running tradition of liberal constitutionalism prior to the 1959 revolution (indeed Castro's "History Will Absolve Me" speech was an appeal to the 1940 constitution). Even now, although the Varela Project is currently blocked, both Castro and his moderate opponents have, in fact, united on the underlying principle that it is for the citizens of Cuba to determine the form of their government using the institutional devises provided by the 1976 constitution. What can be declared "irrevocable" by a referendum can also at some later date be revoked according to the same procedure.

Elsewhere, in a much more general and theoretical discussion of democracy and democratization, I have referred to both postrevolutionary Cuba and Iran as "hard cases" that test the limits of our standard terminology on such questions.[24] It may well be the case that these revolutions have both exhausted their followers, and can no longer rely on the spontaneous support of national majorities, just as Constant argued about post-Napoleonic France. However, given the less than universal confirmation of Constant's faith in commerce and individual liberally in the modern world, there is a wider range of possibilities that requires consideration. For one current of opinion dominant in Washington and Miami, the democratization of Cuba involves subordination to the will of the U.S. Congress, as laid down in the Helms-Burton Act, which specifies who will be disbarred and what international obligations will take priority over Cuban laws. We may label this a return to the "Plattist" conception of semisovereign democracy known to the Cuba people between 1902 and 1933. Another alternative with a clear historical foundation and some significant support (notably in Spain and Mexico) would resuscitate the broad framework of the 1940 constitution and classify that as Cuba's best basis for redemocratization. This would most closely correspond to standard social science ideas on the subject, and would go furthest toward minimizing the extent of future political exceptionalism in Cuba, but it may be the case that the material and subjective conditions for it may have been destroyed by the past half century of division and ideological conflict. A third logical possibility would be that many of the social and institutional transformations of the revolutionary period might have to be accepted as the basis for a future and more democratic Cuban polity. The socialist constitution of 1976 enshrines the monopoly of a single party, and this has now been ratified in a façade-style referendum. It would clearly require extensive modification before it could begin to provide the basis for a regime founded on the freely expressed will of the Cuban people. Nevertheless, this too remains a possible starting point for Cuban democratization. The eventual trajectory of post-Castro political evolution could, in principle, be shaped by any one of these three competing projects, or perhaps by some synthesis of all three.

What the Cuban people will choose is far from self-evident at this stage, not least because the timing and circumstances of their choice are still so unclear, but also because of lack of consensus about which "Cuban people" should have the right to determine the outcome. In these conditions we can reach no more than highly tentative conclusions about what remains an extremely uncertain transition. Far from assuming that Cuba is necessarily destined eventually to fall into line with "standard" social science assumptions concerning a stable liberal democratic end point, the spectrums of future possible regimes still seems wide open. Experience elsewhere indicates that radically different political settlements can be found sheltering under the capacious international standard of recognized democracies. (Some are even trying to persuade us that contemporary Afghanistan and Iraq merit this designation; few hesitate to accord it to regimes as controversial and diverse as those now established in, say, Guatemala or Israel). Thus, even though a post-Castro Cuban regime may have no choice but to seek external recognition as a democracy, this could prove a lose constraint. And it would still be compatible with the continuation of strong elements of national "exceptionalism."

The assumption underlying this analysis is that if Cuba is to democratize the ultimate basis will have to be an unconstrained choice by the Cuban people. If they genuinely and freely chose to persist in their political exceptionalism, my theoretical argument is that that would have to count as a democratic choice. This thought experiment widens the scope of democratic constitutionalism well beyond current conventional thinking, and can perhaps be accused of providing a veneer of democratic legitimacy to a regime that would not, either in its origins or its inner convictions, respect the popular will. However, this theoretical standpoint on democracy and democratization carries at least three implications that are powerful protections against authoritarian misuse. First, if the people's choice is to be truly free, the election campaign must allow voters full access to the arguments of both sides, and they must be convinced that they choose without fear of retaliation. Second, even if they were freely to choose the 1976 constitution they must retain the right subsequently to change their minds. And third, freedom of debate must include free exchange of ideas internationally as well as internally. Over time, this would mean either that Cubans would manage to convince the rest of the Americas of the legitimacy of their decision to be different, or international opinion would tend to convert Cuban opinion to the superiority of a more standard variant of constitutional democracy. ("Over time" may not mean quickly, at least if one considers how long it took to reconcile French republicanism with the other European variants of democracy).

This thought experiment can now be compared with the Castro regime's actual political practice, as illustrated by its reaction to the Varela Project. In response to the 11,000 signatures petitioning for free elections and other reforms, Castro authorized a popular plebiscite in favor of amending the 1976 constitution to make socialism "irrevocable." Out of a total population of 11.2 million, 8,198,237 signatures were collected, and in early July 2002 the National Assembly carried the amendment by 559 votes in favor, with 19 not present and none against. The organizers of the Varela Project had offered the Cuban Communist Party (Partido Comunista de Cuba [PCC]) the opportunity to demonstrate its respect for the freely expressed opinions of the people, and this was its reply. The experiment was judged too risky, and instead the ruling party put on an orchestrated display of unity, thus vindicating the classic liberal thesis that there can be no pluralism in a state-dominated economy. For the standpoint of this chapter, this was yet another assertion of Cuban voluntarism and exceptionalism. Even in China and Iran, such a performance would now be viewed with embarrassment. It requires a suspension of disbelief that cannot indefinitely conceal the realities of Castro's mortality, and of the regime's untenable isolation. Those who signed and voted as they did are all too aware that nothing has been permanently resolved, but they obeyed the logic of "double morality" in a besieged political system.

This, then, is the starting point from which any eventual regime transition may have to depart. Under such conditions it is not possible to estimate which currents of opinion will turn out to have most support, or what new synthesis of collective aspirations can be constructed, once a genuine opening gets underway (as eventually it surely will). Much will depend upon precise timing and circumstances, which can only be speculated upon. Thus Cuba's prospective transition is subject to great uncertainties and—like its politics more generally—could well prove nonstandard. What can be anticipated is that it will not be straightforward to establish public confidence in the exercise of freedom of opinion and expression.

Yet any genuinely democratic outcome in Cuba requires the development of a civic dialogue in which alternative viewpoints can be formulated and exchanged without fear of sanction. Under such conditions we can also anticipate confrontations between long-frozen and antagonistic positions on fundamental issues. Constant's questions about France would surely reappear: what should be dismantled and what can be preserved from the entire legacy of the revolution, and indeed of the first century of the Cuban Republic? Since the United States will not annex Cuba, but will almost inevitably exercise immense influence over any transitional regime, what balance can be established between the desire for national autonomy and reliance on external guidance? On the domestic side, what constitutional system can combine the diffusion of responsibility and the acknowledgment of diversity with the generation of consent and the effective management of public policies?

These are the most sweeping and foundational of issues for any democratic system, and the consequence of Cuba's long record of political exceptionalism is that the basic groundwork for a civic dialogue on such issues has yet to be laid. But in the absence of civic dialogue, and of a collective agreement on how to address such foundational issues, any attempt at regime transition will be profoundly unsettling. In short, not only the timing but also the structure and content of a post-Castro transition remain outstandingly uncertain. Such conditions provide fertile ground for the perpetuation of Cuba's secular tradition of political exceptionalism.

Both in practical terms, and also in terms of democratic theory, Cuba is a "hard case." This chapter has argued that its political exceptionalism is deeply rooted and may not end any time soon. It has also probed into challenge that Cuba has posed, and may continue to pose, to two currently influential types of "universalism"—realism in international relations, and liberal constitutionalism in comparative politics. The jury is still out on how these theoretical and practical challenges are likely to be resolved.

Notes

1. Using the language of the title of the conference at which a first version of this chapter was presented.
2. For the international relations debate between realists and constructivists see Walter Carlsnaes, Thomas Risse, and Beth A. Simmons (eds.), *A Handbook of International Relations* (New York: Sage, 2001), chapters 3–5.
3. Initiated in 2002, Varela involved a petition to the National Assembly signed by over 10,000 Cubans, calling for a referendum on provisions to liberalize the economy, to ensure respect for human rights and amnesty political prisoners, and to hold general elections under a new and fairer electoral law.

4. A chapter of this type contains many historical assertions that are not developed in detail and have therefore not been sourced. My interpretations are solely my own responsibility but draw on the three relevant chapters of the *Cambridge History of Latin America* and their accompanying bibliographies, as follows: Leslie A. Bethell (ed.), *Cuba: A Short History* (Cambridge: Cambridge University Press, 1993), particularly the chapters by Luis E. Aguilar ("Cuba, c. 1860–c. 1930," pp. 21–56); Louis A. Pérez Jr. ("Cuba, c. 1930–c. 1959," pp. 57–94); and Jorge I. Domínguez ("Cuba since 1959," pp. 95–148).

5. Perhaps the closest analogy was with Britain's occupation of Egypt between 1882 and the outright declaration of a Protectorate in 1914. This comparison seems to have occurred to U.S. Secretary of State Elihu Root, although the contrasts are also evident.

6. Somoza in 1979 is the closest analogy, one that was very influenced by the Cuban precedent.

7. Recent events associated with the Varela Project—former President Carter's live broadcast on Cuban television, President Bush's reaffirmation of Washington's sanctions policy, followed by President Castro's sponsorship of the signature campaign to make the revolution "irrevocable"—all fit within this pattern.

8. In mid-2005, Secretary of State Condoleezza Rice appointed Caleb MacCarry as her Cuban "transition coordinator," confirming the official U.S. commitment to this postulated endgame.

9. A cost-benefit analysis of this type cannot accommodate the actions of a suicide bomber or make sense of a phrase such as *¡Patria o Muerte, Venceremos!* (Homeland or Death, We Will Prevail!) Despite the evident political potency of such a political style, under conventional realism it becomes irrational, perhaps even inexplicable.

10. For the purposes of this chapter constructivism is a broad perspective rather than a precise technique. It is a style of political explanation that regards rhetoric and discourse as potentially motivating and constraining and that views extended sequences of interactions among political actors (who either may be collective or individual depending upon the political process in question) as driven partly by emotion and psychology, not purely by rational calculation of interest. More generally, many political beliefs and justifications for action are held to be "social constructed" rather than derived directly from objective determinants. Some critics object to constructivism on the grounds that its explanatory conclusions are typically indeterminate (not predictive). But many political processes are *ex-ante* (beforehand) open-ended through social persuasion and construction. In principle, there is no reason why attending to discursive and psychological factors must reduce the precision of an explanatory account.

11. For a recent survey article that emphasizes the irrational elements in the U.S. stance toward revolutionary Cuba see Louis A. Pérez Jr., "Fear and Loathing of Fidel Castro: Sources of US Policy toward Cuba," *Journal of Latin American Studies*, 34 (2), May 2002: 227–254.

12. For a recent survey of a century of U.S. policy toward Cuba, focusing on the supposed objective of democracy promotion, see Lars Schoultz, "Blessings of Liberty: The United States and the Promotion of Democracy in Cuba," *Journal of Latin American Studies*, 34 (2), May 2002: 397–425.

13. Traditional socialism offered one possible global framework within which to place the Cuban experience, but in current conditions that does not seem the most fruitful way to test the limits of the exceptionalism argument.

14. This argument is more fully developed in my *Democratization: Theory and Experience* (New York: Oxford University Press, 2002) and also in my "Freezing the Flow," *Taiwan Journal of Democracy*, 1 (1), 2005: 1–20.

15. Biancamaría Fontana (ed.), *Constant: Political Writings* (Cambridge: Cambridge University Press, 1988), pp. 73–74.

16. Ibid., p. 317.

17. Ibid., p. 150.

18. "Commerce makes the interference of arbitrary power in our existence more vexatious than it was in the past, and this because, our speculations being more diversified, arbitrary power must multiply itself to reach them; but at the same time commerce makes it easier to evade the influence of arbitrary power because it changes the very nature of property, and thereby makes it virtually impossible to seize." Ibid., p. 140. Neither Cuba nor Russia nor China conformed to this model in the twentieth century, nor indeed did Nazi Germany.

19. Ibid., p. 311.

20. The point of this observation is not to gloss over the fundamental differences separating ancient Sparta from contemporary Cuba but only to suggest that even in a world two centuries more "modern" than the one known to Benjamin Constant, we continue to encounter an unexpectedly wide variety of political experiments and trajectories.

21. Constant's contrast between the ancients and the moderns is now considered much overdrawn, and it would be equally exaggerated to equate Cuba with his description of the ancients. After all, on the issue of religious toleration, so critical for Constant, contemporary Cuba is now more liberal.

22. Benjamin Constant, *Écrits Politiques* (Paris: Gallimard, 1997), p. 753 (my translation).

23. Ibid., p. 74.

24. Laurence Whitehead, *Democratization: Theory and Experience* (Oxford: Oxford University Press, 2002), p. 23.

Chapter 2

Cuba: From Exception to Democratization?

Andrew Arato

I am not an expert on Cuba: although I have learned many things about Latin America from my students, I have not had the good fortune to learn about Cuba to the same extent. So, even the familiar notion of Cuban exceptionalism that Laurence Whitehead so eloquently describes in this book was new in a sense. From a familiarity with international history I knew, of course, that Cuba was not part of the wave of anticolonial, republican revolutions that swept through Spanish America during the first quarter of the nineteenth century, and I knew that the island was the last major Spanish colony in the Western Hemisphere until the Spanish-American War. And from U.S. history, I was also familiar with Cuba's special status, as symbolized by the Platt Amendment that was forcibly incorporated into the country's first republican constitution and was bolstered by repeated direct and indirect U.S. interventions in Cuban internal affairs. Finally as a student of comparative democratic transitions in communist Eastern Europe, I was very much aware that Cuba belonged neither to the set of democratizing countries of the 1980s or early 1990s. What I had not realized until reading Laurence Whitehead's contribution to this volume is that these three separate and exceptional circumstances may very well be interrelated. I had always thought and hoped that Cuba might simply become a belated member of either sequence of transitions, or of both, and that it would simply take longer to begin and end that process in Cuban than in Latin America's other most protracted case—that of Mexico. My view was that because the Cuban dictatorship, like the Mexican, was the product of an indigenous social revolution, this fact and the regime's attendant special legitimacy resources might lead regime forces to initiate a protracted transition carefully controlled "from above."[1] Whatever the normative desirability of such a path as compared with others (such a lengthy process usually makes it more vulnerable to uncertainty and reversal), this seemed to be the most likely kind of transition in Cuba.

I have since been forced to consider a second hypothesis, which is that Cuba cannot possibly join the Latin American or Eastern European transition series because its exceptionalism has postponed the process for too long and because the international context has changed since those earlier transition processes and is especially crucial in the case of Cuba. More specifically, the democratic transitions in the 1970s and early 1990s were domestically driven. The role of external and international factors was important, but it was restricted to "soft" interventionism in the form of human rights campaigns, public political support for domestic actors, influence exercised by nongovernmental organizations, cultural exchanges and financial incentives, the promise of admission to international bodies, and, less frequently, sanctions. These actions influenced domestic developments, facilitating the emergence, organization, and institutionalized learning experiences for domestic actors. But in all these cases external input stopped well short of military intervention, not least because the Cold War balance survived even though the Soviet Empire had already begun to crumble. All this created the international context in which the Central and East European transitions took place, and even those of South Africa and other countries on that continent. The Soviet Union was strong enough to fend off military interventions in its sphere of influence, but it was too weak to police it effectively and resist initiatives and movements that relied on peaceful grassroots mobilization. Also, either it was unable to interfere or was no longer interested in interfering with the African countries (the African National Congress [ANC] had to look elsewhere for support, with dramatic consequences for both the timing and the quality of the South African transition).

The vocabulary of these earlier processes—the emphasis on human rights, international civil society and the public sphere—is still with us, but it now operates in a very different context, for two reasons in particular. First, there are now states, dictatorial regimes, and regions that resist the logic of democratization of previous decades. Competing ideologies such as Islamic fundamentalism offer the hope of positive change for many living under decrepit, secular regimes, but these ideologies do not espouse democracy, open civil societies, and public debate. Second, with the Cold War bipolar world gone, there is a new willingness and capacity of multilateral organizations and states—particularly of a unilateral United States—to intervene militarily in contexts that were once "off limits" for balance-of-power considerations. One manifestation of this was the "new" or humanitarian interventionism of the 1990s that gave external actors the "right" to intervene in the face of impending or ongoing systematic and gross violations of fundamental rights. The idea that such interventions might be carried out to promote democracy was not part of that thinking, however. The intervention in Iraq was perhaps the first (or second, if the more justified and legal war in Afghanistan is taken into account) of what may become a new, second series of transitions, in which the central feature of international involvement in domestic political change is the existence of a lone superpower whose international power is not curbed by other forces.

When speculating about the "Cuban transition," the question arises whether the country will belong to any previous series, if any. As shown by the case of the Ukraine, the impact of the current international context is not insignificant when a country undergoes a transition that fits in with the earlier varieties. The open political interference of foreign states contrasts with the interventions of the 1990s, which were "softer" and largely nonstate. In the case of Cuba, since the United States is the most important foreign state actor, one must consider seriously that Cuba may belong to the second series. The United States may not attack Cuba—the superpower is much too preoccupied elsewhere and its international bonafides are in tatters—but there are many other possible opportunities for hard intervention, not just of the Iraqi kind. Hard intervention may come in response to an internal breakdown or civil war. It may occur as a result of the deployment of state resources that are short of military means but can powerfully shape a transition process and diminish its autonomous logic.

The possibility of hard or quasi-hard intervention (not inconceivable at the time of writing) means that external interference is probably already a factor in internal politics. While it would be absurd to attribute hard-line policies of the Cuban regime to a threat from the United States, it is certainly the case that Cuban elites and Cuban society are aware of the new role of the United States in the world. So the hardening of the regime may be a sign that Cuba is already behaving as a member of the second series, in which the external factor is predominant. This may be why it preemptively crushes seeds of dissent (as the Iranian authorities have done) on the grounds that domestic opponents are preparing the ground for an Iraqi-style external intervention. However, one can argue the opposite as well: the failure of U.S. engagement in Iraq, and the fact that Washington is busy elsewhere, may have the opposite effect, although it is unclear whether it is the weakness or the aggressiveness of the United States that the Cuban population perceives when listening to local or Miami-based media outlets, both of which affirm the power of the United States, albeit for opposite reasons.

Is Cuba likely to join the first series of democratic transitions, and, if so, under what conditions? It is to be hoped that its exceptionalism proves less exceptional after all and that Cuba will be simply a belated member of the Latin American and Eastern European democratic transitions of the last decades of the twentieth century. The question then arises to what extent the possibility of external intervention has already influenced and may affect the timing and nature of a transition in Cuba. My first fallible hypothesis is that Cuban exceptionalism—a function of a particular history and a unique geostrategic circumstance—has already affected the "when" (timing) and will influence the "how" (path) of its transition, but it will not lead to a reconsolidation of a dictatorship that has exposed the country to such severe economic and social crisis. This hypothesis can be justified on three grounds. First, as in other Soviet-type economies, it is not possible to reform Cuba's resource-constrained and shortage-plagued economy,[2] particularly because the almost limitless external supply of resources has dried up. Second, a replacement (as opposed to mere supplementation) of a Soviet by a capitalist economy cannot be politically stabilized as it has been in China, given Cuba's very different cultural political context and the absence of comparably vast, domestic, and private agricultural resources. Third, Cuba is again exposed to external attempts to change the regime, and no one should entirely exclude the possibility of U.S. military intervention if the Cuban regime maintains its current course—either with or without domestic or external Cuban backing. The first two points indicate why a reconstructed dictatorship is unlikely, and the third point indicates that muddling through is not a long-term option. So my second hypothesis is that it is still possible for Cuba to become the last of the Latin American and one of the last communist transitions to democracy. The question, then, is when and how.

Lacking prophetic qualities and knowing that social science is not very good at prediction, I cannot answer the "when" question. However, if the above hypothesis is correct, the transition would have to be initiated at least in the first decade of the twenty-first century otherwise there is little justification for including Cuba in a set that includes the Argentina (early 1980s), Brazil (mid 1970s–mid-1980s), Chile (early to late 1980s), and Mexico (mid-1970s to late 1990s). It must be admitted that even if the Cuban transition occurs within this time frame, this offers no definitive proof of the validity of my hypothesis. If the still viable dictatorship were to be overthrown from the outside as a part of a new post-Iraq wave of externally imposed transitions,[3] for example, Cuba would belong neither to Latin American nor to the Central and East European set of transitions, all of which were *primarily* domestically initiated and conducted processes of change.[4] It is doubtful that externally imposed regime change will lead to a consolidated democracy in most circumstances.[5] However, this is unfortunately insufficient to deter current power holders in Washington from engaging in such attempts.[6] So, the most serious rival alternative to my hypothesis is not the indefinite survival of the current regime but a grave external or internal crisis leading to U.S. intervention, a possibility that fits the Cuban exceptionalism argument. And in that case, Cuba would belong to the new series of regime change that includes Afghanistan and Iraq. The likelihood of one or another of these two hypotheses being correct depends on the actions of key current and future actors inside and outside Cuba and the current regime.[7]

Obviously, domestically managed transitions to democracy may be steered from above, below, or by both simultaneously when there is negotiation and compromise. Against the mainstream of transition literature,[8] however, (and the Mexican case bears this out), liberalization (*abertura* or *glasnost*) can "succeed" when it takes the form of repeatedly reiterated and partial electoral reforms.[9] For middle-aged or even older reform initiators all that matters is that they remain in power sufficiently long and that they and their supporters successfully implant legal structures that will preserve not only their civil and political rights but also the rights of their clients and dependents.

Two other transition paths are possible. First, when the regime lacks legitimacy and/or expectations of long-term stability are absent or rapidly declining, a regime (or its reformist elements) may realize that controlled self-transformation is the only way to avoid complete breakdown in the future. If they recognize this, then they will seek out allies and engage in negotiations to ensure a compromise settlement. Initially, regime actors will offer relatively few concessions but if the opposition is and remains united experience indicates that full agreement around new constitutional and democratic principles is possible and even likely (the cases of Spain, Hungary, and South Africa are examples in this regard). Only military governments can impose the conditions of exit from power (as in Chile, although it was not until the very end that the transition was actually negotiated) or force the democratic opposition to accept undemocratic concessions (as in Brazil). State parties generally accept personal and political legal guarantees to transform themselves into parties that can contest competitive elections.[10] However, if regime actors are unavailable (or overly weak) to undertake such efforts, then the outcome may be internal collapse or regime overthrow resulting from revolutionary mass action and a counterelite assault (as in Romania) or from nonviolent popular pressure (as in Argentina, the German Democratic Republic, and Czechoslovakia).

From a normative point of view, negotiated transitions are much preferable to incremental regime-led reformism or to insurrection followed by collapse. There is now solid evidence to prove that negotiated transitions tend to produce the best democratic constitutional outcomes and tend to offer the best hopes for post-transition consolidation. Incremental regime-led reform can sustain a dictatorship for unexpectedly long periods, and it makes it difficult to institute a coherent structure for democratic politics that is strong enough to resist authoritarian reversion. Moreover, revolutions and insurrectionary coups usually tempt actors to impose new "totalizing" solutions that may result in a new kind of dictatorship. Having said this, dictatorships are likely to prefer a top-down reformist option, and there are always radical oppositionists who feel that anything short of a full revolutionary rupture constitutes a betrayal of the "cause." So the best chance for a negotiated transition occurs when top-down reform is *no longer* possible and when a revolutionary solution is *not yet* feasible. That moment will come for Cuba, but it will not last forever and has to be taken advantage of at the right time.

As noted above, like Mexico, Cuba could be an ideal candidate for top-down reformist change But this is where exceptionalism comes in. The initiation of a reform process generally requires ruling elite reformists to be willing to and able to win the argument within the regime. But in Cuba much depends on the personal choices of a leader who has never been predisposed to reformism, and, furthermore, the regime can portray all external pressure and all opposition and factionalism as a treasonable attempt to weaken the unity of a small country facing a very powerful external enemy. Moreover, the remaining legitimacy resources of the regime are linked to Cuba's exceptional status: the regime is widely seen as the defender of the country's national sovereignty against American imperial aspirations, an idea amply supported both by both the history of U.S.-Cuban relations and aggressive economic sanctions, as symbolized by the Helms-Burton legislation. In other words, the

United States is both an advocate of Cuban democratization *and* a threat to Cuban sovereignty and independence; so democratization can be represented by the regime as a form of capitulation to foreign pressure and as incompatible with the defense of national independence, and advocates of reform misrepresented as supporters of external intervention and as enemies of Cuban national sovereignty.

If it is true that any successful reform from above requires that people have some hope of long-term economic stability, then it may follow that this kind of process could have been initiated when the Soviet empire began to collapse in the early 1990s. This is no longer feasible given the radical nature of Cuban economic decline. In other words, there is little chance that a liberalizing regime will be able to avoid the social conflicts that would inevitably be unleashed. If this is true, then the thesis of an inevitably unsuccessful liberalization holds. Indeed, it can be assumed that all members of the elite are conscious of this problem and therefore resist even initiating liberalization.[11] According to mainstream transitions literature this also means that a negotiated transition would be impossible, as it is posited that democratization presupposes liberalization (independent actors capable of negotiating with the regime cannot emerge unless civil society has been built up, and this cannot happen without liberalization or decompression).[12]

There are several reasons to question this logic, however. The incredible success of the Varela Project in conditions of severe repression indicates that significant political actors can emerge relatively quickly in Cuba. Further, while the older generation of Miami Cubans has long sidelined a peaceful and negotiated compromise solution, the younger generation of post-Mariel exiles seems to be fundamentally different. There is now important external support for nonviolent democratic initiatives. The international learning process about the virtues of negotiated transitions that began in Spain and that continued in Central Europe, Latin America, and South Africa has apparently had an important influence on Cuban intellectual communities both in and outside the island. So if the leadership fears a crisis, collapse, or even external intervention in the medium term and if it were then to accept a negotiated settlement, it would certainly find partners to embark on a genuinely historical compromise.

There are three types of hard-liners that would oppose any such solution: members of the regime, the exile community, and of the U.S. administration. These groups are each others' best allies, at least in the short term. But the long-term plans of these groups vary. The hard-line exiles and their American political backers hope for revolutionary change, preferably domestically driven but if needs be through timely external intervention. Despite the blow that the U.S. intervention in Iraq may have dealt to this vision, there remains significant international support for a limited interpretation of state sovereignty (sovereignty is conditional upon popular sovereignty and respect for human rights). This latter view can be used to justify the Cuba's external "liberation." What is missing is an immediate pretext for military intervention.

But this may change, particularly if reform from above or a negotiated settlement become impossible.

Contrary to what regime hard-liners say, the best protection of sovereignty may not be a dictatorship but a democracy supported by other Latin American democracies. Democracy is unthinkable without sovereignty, since a country without significant autonomy shifts decision-making power from the people and their representatives to external actors and institutions. In the current international context, the reverse may also be true to some extent. Legitimately or not, dictatorships will be more exposed to external intervention than democracies, the integrity of which can be defended by arguments of national *and* popular sovereignty. Without underestimating the possibility of foreign intervention and influence in divided and conflict-ridden democracies (look at Chile in the 1970s and Chávez's Venezuela), the response to the danger of intervention cannot be dictatorship or even a populist and highly conflictive democracy; it must be a democratic regime that is capable of transforming former and potential enemies to opponents that share a common loyalty to a democratic constitution.

There are several preconditions that must be met if this outcome is to win the day and eliminate the possibility of a violent internal or external overthrow of the regime. First, Cuban democrats at home and abroad must transform their discourse. This is already happening. There is more talk of compromise, negotiation, and reconciliation than of violent overthrow. This trend should be supported. The right atmosphere for negotiated settlement is not created by radical anticommunist talk of totalitarianism, but rather by dialogue about a past that all sides can learn from. Second, all reform attempts by the regime, even timid and seemingly insignificant, should be welcomed. Insufficient as they may be, their importance lies in their being undertaken in the first place. They may very well provide opportunities for a negotiated settlement. Equally, however, it is very important that sections of the opposition should not accept meaningless acts of reform as being serious, and it must be made clear that the details have to be negotiated and that one-sided impositions are not acceptable. Whatever the situation ten or more years ago, Cuba no longer has the time for a protracted and messy process of top-down reform. Third, it will have to be made clear that a growing part of the exile community and opposition forces at home do not support continued sanctions or interference in Cuban affairs through the Helms-Burton Act. At the same time, however, the U.S. government should not be pressed to abandon all forms of pressure. A good starting point would be to reverse recent, harsher discriminatory rules about family members and other U.S. citizens visiting Cuba. There is much support for this within the exile community, and it is surprising that the Democratic Party did not campaign vigorously on the issue in Florida during the last U.S. election.

Future candidates of both the major U.S. parties should be urged to adopt a new policy for Cuba. Contrary to the dominant stereotype, there is support for such a change within the Cuban exile community. As U.S. government attitudes may change only very slowly (or fail to materialize), however, there should be strong encouragement for a much more active policy toward Cuba by the European Union (EU) and Latin America. It is important to persuade Cuban elites that there are important counterweights to a United States that may exploit any conflicts during a process of democratization to attack the island's sovereignty. Finally, it is necessary to unite all important Cuban groups at home and in exile in support of a minimum program for a negotiated transition and a historical compromise. It should be made clear that only the groups accepting such a program will be able to participate in any future negotiated settlement.

On a more speculative note, what could happen after a genuine and negotiated transition begins? It may seem premature to ask this question, but this debate can help to promote positive attitudes and risk taking on the part of regime elites. Following Hannah Arendt, it may be worth distinguishing between the liberation and constitution-making phases of a transition or a revolution. External interference and intervention are not just a problem for liberation (a phase that ends with the production of a minimum set of rules to initiate an open political process) but also for institution and constitution building. As we have seen in Iraq, it is possible for an external power to try to dominate at least the most important part of this second phase.[13] It is even possible for an indigenous and autonomous process of liberation to be taken over by an outside power at the stage of institutional transformation, as in the case of the old German Democratic Republic (GDR). Although there is no "other Cuba" to absorb Cuba, the United States and the exile community could very well intervene with financial, expert, and human support and dramatically influence the process of institutional transformation. In other words, an indigenous and autonomous process can easily be overtaken by forces that are very difficult to control once they are set in motion. So it is important to design anticipatory plans and forms of organization. This is a matter for the exile community first and foremost. No democratic process can keep it from political participation in Cuba. As long as it is seen as closely linked with U.S. foreign policy, however, nationalist forces in Cuba to which the regime can and will appeal to will see that community as an external agent ready to hijack any transition process. This means that many who might otherwise support a transition prefer not to do so. The only answer to this problem is to implement confidence-building measures that involve a gradual disengagement from U.S. policy and politics, and a search for new allies elsewhere in the world. There are many candidates in Europe, starting with Spain, and also in Latin America (such as Mexico and the Southern Cone countries). The formation of an explicitly political group with a new profile and a developed transitional program would make a difference, as long as its distance from U.S. interests is crystal clear. I cannot say whether a political organization of this kind can exist abroad in the current context, but it would certainly be an asset and its platform should be clear about its commitment to reconciliation, a peaceful and negotiated transition, and the preservation of national independence.

In conclusion, it can be said that a negotiated settlement is the best way to ensure a relatively rapid transition to democracy and democratization in Cuba. Reform from above is no longer very likely, and it would not, in any case, lead to a democratic outcome for a long time. Revolutionary rupture and its likely companion, civil war, would expose Cuba to (or be the result of) U.S. intervention. Even if successful, intervention would inaugurate an era of retaliation against and suppression of beneficiaries of the old regime, real or supposed. And as history teaches us, from Paris to Baghdad, this is not a suitable way to go about democratic consolidation. Cuban democrats and their friends should therefore do all that is possible to facilitate the kind of negotiated transition that turns former enemies into political opponents.

Notes

1. Andrew Arato, "Interpreting 1989," chapter 1, in *Civil Society, Constitution and Legitimacy* (Lanham, MD: Rowman and Littlefield, 2000), pp. 1–42.
2. Janos Kornai, "The Reproduction of Shortage," in Janos Kornai (ed.), *Contradictions and Dilemmas: Studies on the Socialist Economy and Society* (Harvard, MA: MIT Press, 1986), pp. 6–32.
3. This is a possible neoconservative interpretation of President George W. Bush's November 6, 2003 speech to the National Endowment for Democracy (NED).
4. I acknowledge Laurence Whitehead's caveat in this regard. All transitions have their internal and external aspects. However, the relative weight of these factors differs immensely from the 1980s and 1990s, and in the case of Iraq, a case of external imposition of democracy.
5. See Andrew Arato, "The Occupation of Iraq and the Difficult Transition from Dictatorship," *Constellations*, 10 (3), September 2003: 408–424.
6. What lessons will be learned from Iraq? U.S. officials may merely conclude that such interventions should be confined to less complex societies and be closer to home. The domestic reasons for external adventurism that I think are inherent to constitutionally weak but presidentially strong systems (particularly in times of crisis) are unlikely to disappear.
7. Of course, if the Cuban regime were externally overthrown at the start or in the middle of a process of liberalization or democratization, the veracity of my initial hypothesis could never be tested. I consider such a possibility unlikely but unfortunately not impossible.
8. See Adam Przeworski, *Democracy and the Market: Political and Economic Reforms in Eastern Europe and Latin America* (Cambridge: Cambridge University Press, 1991).
9. Andrew Arato, "The Round Tables, Democratic Institutions and the Problem of Justice," in András Bozoki (ed.), *The Round Table of 1989. The Genesis of Hungarian Democracy: Analysis and Documents* (Budapest: Central European University Press, 2002).
10. Ibid.
11. It is also possible that the dominant elements of a new regime constellation delude themselves like so many of their predecessors, as Przeworski vividly describes in *Democracy and the Market*. In that case, inevitably unsuccessful attempts to liberalize and control the consequences of liberalization would

indicate that the window for a negotiated settlement is open, although it will not remain so forever.

12. See also Alfred Stepan (ed.), *Democratizing Brazil: Problems of Transition and Consolidation* (Oxford: Oxford University Press, 1989), particularly the introduction. See also Przeworski, *Democracy and the Market*.

13. Andrew Arato, "Interim Imposition," *Ethics and International Affairs*, 18 (3), Winter 2004: 25–51.

Chapter 3

How Exceptional Is the Cuban Economy?

Emily Morris

Introduction

There were good reasons why in 1990 Cuba's economy was expected to collapse along with the Soviet economic bloc. Economic dependency on Council for Mutual Economic Assistance (COMECON) trade and finance was extreme: in 1989, the Cuban economy was an open one, with an imports-gross domestic product (GDP) ratio of 35 percent, and the COMECON trade bloc accounted for around 80 percent of all trade. The bloc also provided the external financing to cover a large current account deficit, amounting to more than 10 percent of GDP.[1] Of total exports, sugar accounted for 80 percent, and the COMECON preferential sugar price was around three times the world market price, a benefit worth around 12 percent of GDP. The extent of Cuban dependence on COMECON thus meant that when the trading bloc collapsed around one quarter of GDP was immediately wiped off Cuba's national income, even before the effects of economic dislocation were added, as import capacity fell by 70 percent between 1990 and 1993 (see figure 3.1).

In addition to suffering this sharp external shock, unlike other transition economics Cuba could not draw on official multilateral capital flows when the crisis struck.[2] It also had no preferential trade agreements with other partners (of the sort enjoyed by Central American and Caribbean countries exporting to the United States, or by African Caribbean and Pacific [ACP] countries exporting to the European Union [EU]) and was barred from trade with its natural trade partner, the United States. Moreover, restrictions on external economic relations were further compounded by the Torricelli Law in 1992 and Helms-Burton Act in 1996.

Real GDP measures during such a period of collapse and structural change need to be treated with some caution, but the official Cuban real GDP data shows a decline of 35 percent in 1989–1993, and on the basis of the available information this estimate seems reasonable. This makes Cuba one of the worst hit among the transition economies.[3] Lacking access to external support to lift

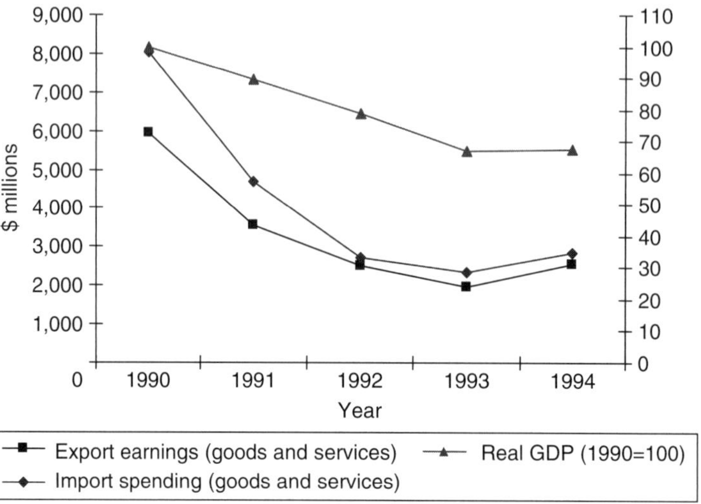

Figure 3.1   Import Capacity and GDP Collapse (1990–1994)

Sources: Banco Central de Cuba, annual reports, 1994–2004 (Havana: BCC); *Oficina Nacional de Estadísticas, Anuario estadístico de Cuba,* annual reports, 1994–2005 (Havana: ONE). Figures are EIU estimates.

it out of its difficulties, it seemed that Cuba would be forced to accept a disadvantageous transition to a market economy, like most of its fellow former COMECON members. It was seen as only a matter of time before the Cuban exception was liquidated, and the country would follow the rest of Latin America in a painful capitulation. But despite the Cuban government's refusal to follow the transition path, the Cuban economy survived, and from the mid-1990s it began to grow. In fact, its overall performance in terms of GDP recovery has been broadly in line with the average for the other "transition economies."[4] In 1990–2000, it was even slightly above the transition economy average although its relative performance has weakened since 2000.

Cuba's recovery defied expectations. It had appeared self-evident that the collapse of COMECON would necessitate liberalizing reforms to enable Cuba to adapt to the new external conditions. The surprisingly good relative economic performance, despite Cuba's rejection of an economic "transition" therefore requires explanation. An assessment of the strengths and weaknesses of the "Cuban model" provides some clues as to whether it is a viable exception.

Explaining Cuba's Economic Performance

The Benefits of Liberalization

One explanation for Cuba's favorable performance relative to expectations is that, despite the government's insistence on following its own path and rejecting prescriptions for liberalizing reforms, some significant economic reforms were introduced. In this sense, the economy's survival and growth would not be exceptional but merely the predicted outcome of reform. Most obviously, opening to international markets has played an important part in rebuilding Cuba's import capacity since 1990. With an exceptionally hard budget constraint in terms of foreign exchange, it was imperative for Cuba to find alternative sources of external earnings quickly. This was done: by 2003, foreign currency earnings (excluding capital inflows) had been restored to their 1990 level, and since then they have risen further (see figure 3.2 and appendix 1 of this chapter). Although total import capacity has still not been restored to its precrisis level, on current trends this can be achieved within the next few years, and important liberalizing reforms have been introduced to that end. Decision making in enterprises linked to external trade has been decentralized so that newly constituted semiautonomous state-owned corporations are able to negotiate directly with overseas suppliers, investors, and customers. A stream of joint ventures and other agreements with foreign businesses has not only helped to transform Cuba's productive structure but also has profoundly changed its economic system and business culture. For the first time there was competition (albeit limited) among state enterprises, and some of the ministries that had previously been part of the central planning apparatus had their role reduced to oversight of some semiautonomous enterprises, and strategic planning.

Two sectors have led the Cuban external adjustment: tourism and nickel. The expansion of tourism has been achieved as a result of the opening to foreign capital and to management and marketing agreements. Gross earnings

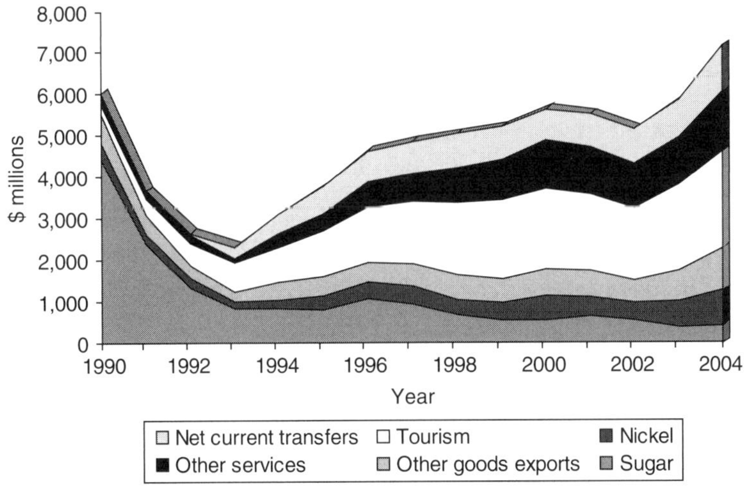

Figure 3.2 Cuba: Current Account Inflows

Sources: Banco Central de Cuba, annual economic reports, 1994–2004 (Havana: BCC); *Oficina Nacional de Estadísticas, Anuario estadístico de Cuba,* annual reports, 1994–2005 (Havana: ONE). Figures are EIU estimates.

from tourism rose significantly from under $250 million in 1990 to over $2.5 billion in 2005. The recovery and expansion of the nickel industry has also been achieved through new links with foreign businesses, with joint venture agreements with Canadian partners playing the main part. The latter have provided a major injection of capital investment, and the new vertical links for nickel processing needed to replace previous arrangements with Soviet partners. As a result of these, nickel output, which fell from 47,000 tons in 1989 to 27,000 in 1994, recovered to around 75,000 tons in 2005. Export earnings from nickel, which had dropped from around $500 million in 1989 to $200 million in 1994, have since recovered to over $1 billion (according to Economist Intelligence Unit estimates for 2005), helped by favorable prices.

Although tourism and nickel account for more than half of the recovery of import capacity, there has also been a significant contribution from expansion of exports of other goods and services. These exports have also been facilitated by restructuring and liberalizing measures. The export of goods other than sugar and nickel has been backed by foreign direct investment (FDI) and production and marketing agreements with foreign partners. These include agreements for the financing of tobacco and citrus production, and international marketing, with the most significant agreements concerning rum and cigars. The pharmaceuticals sector has also started to make a significant contribution to foreign exchange earnings. At the start of the 1990s, heavy state investment in this sector seemed to be producing disappointing results, but the limited available information suggests that by 2005 both exports of manufactured medicines and profits from production licenses had started to make a significant contribution to earnings.[5] Again, the breakthrough has been the result of the industry's opening to foreign business and adaptation to conditions in overseas markets. "Other services" include not only air passenger transport associated with the growth of tourism but also exports of cultural services, licenses, and patents. Expansion of these has been facilitated by reforms that have given relative autonomy to Cuban enterprises and fostered entrepreneurial activity. Since 2004, earnings in the other services category have been given a boost by payments for the services of thousands of doctors and other professionals working in Venezuela under a bilateral agreement (see below), but even before this extra stimulus, services exports were on a strong upward path.

A strong increase in net current transfers has also played an important part in the recovery of import capacity. Data on the composition of these inflows is sparse and unreliable, but an increase in the remittances component will have been encouraged by the legalization of the holding of hard currency in 1993, while transfers associated with the informal tourism sector will have grown broadly in line with the expansion of tourism.[6]

Restructuring of the external sector has not only involved export industries but also other industries connected with international trade and payments. These include importers and infrastructure activities associated with trade.

The new types of semiautonomous state-owned corporations have appeared in telecoms, the power industry, oil and gas, the financial system, and among trading companies. The foreign sources of capital and exposure to international business practices have brought much needed modernization and increases in output and efficiency in these areas. In telecoms, a joint venture established in 1994 has resulted in new investments to increase the number of fixed telephone lines by 70 percent, digitize most of the telephone network, and build a national fiber-optic network.[7] In the power industry, new investment may not have been sufficient to solve the problem of power cuts, but it has nonetheless played a crucial role in preventing the collapse of electricity generation. In the oil and gas sector, progress has been greater, with output up from 0.7 million tons of oil in 1990 to 3.7 million tons in 2005, producing an import saving of more than $1 billion. Moreover, industry observers have commented favorably on the high technical and environmental standards of the new oil and gas investments (which are concentrated close to the important tourist resort at Varadero). In finance, like tourism, the industry has been modernized and restructured to create a set of new, semiautonomous competing banks. New financial instruments have been introduced to facilitate external trade, and banks have made major investments in new technology.

Cuban policy makers have described the reforms to the external economy as an "adjustment" to the new external conditions, rather than a "transition" or "liberalization." Whatever term is used, the measures adopted achieved a rapid integration of Cuba's external sector with the global market economy. Many Cuban enterprises, and whole industries, have restructured in order to adjust from producing quotas under the COMECON arrangements to the need to compete at world market prices. The result has been a dramatic change in the productive structure of the Cuban economy, with a level of labor productivity in the new sectors far higher than that of the rest of the economy.

Within the domestic economy, liberalizing reforms have been much more limited. The most significant of these have been the opening of free agricultural markets, the legalization of new categories of self-employment, and permissions for small private restaurants and bed and breakfasts. These openings have been eagerly welcomed by both buyers and sellers, providing employment and improving the supply of food and personal services, despite the restrictions and regulations imposed on them. Despite their limitations, they have been credited with relieving the social and political tensions created by economic hardship and restrictions. And although prices remain fixed by the planning system, there have been adjustments to individual prices of some goods to influence consumption and reduce subsidies—including adjustments to the price of imported fuels to encourage energy conservation and the introduction of user charges for some nonessential public services. In this sense, the role of the price mechanism has expanded, helping to improve the efficiency of the allocation of some scarce resources.

Costs and Benefits of the Persistence
of a Command Economy

While the limited degree of liberalization provides some of the explanation for Cuba's ability to make the economic adjustment after 1990, it cannot be the full explanation, as performance has been so much stronger than it would have been if the degree of reform—which has been so much less extensive than in other transition economies—were the main determinant of performance. In other words, the survival of much of the central planning system in Cuba does not appear to have inhibited growth as much as expected. To understand this, it is useful to explore the strengths as well as weaknesses of the Cuban planning system in responding to crisis and recovery.

Costs

According to the various systems of scoring the degree of transition developed by the World Bank (WB) and the European Bank of Reconstruction and Development (EBRD), Cuba is very low in the reform ranking.[8] The state retains ownership of almost all productive capital and—with the exception only of small farmers and a small number of tightly constrained legally self-employed—it still forbids private enterprise by Cubans. Aside from the agricultural and handicraft markets introduced in 1994, domestic prices are still set by the planning authorities, as are the official exchange rate and all wages in the formal sector, even for joint ventures. The existence of two exchange rates distorts decision making in both the formal and informal sectors. Inputs for production, including labor, are still largely allocated by the planning system, despite the claim that material balances have been replaced by the use of profit and loss accounting. The allocation of finance is still mainly controlled by the central planning authorities despite the development of the new financial system that increases the role of the Central Bank, using interest rates as one means of rationing credit.

The hindrance to economic performance arising from continued state control has been explored at length not only by commentators outside Cuba but also by economists within the country, who use a different vocabulary and more measured criticism.[9] Evidence of poor performance includes the very low level of domestic investment and FDI, low productivity, and lack of entrepreneurship. Whenever economic growth has faltered (as in 1997–1998 and again in 2001–2003) the slowdown has been cited as proof that the Cuban model is unsustainable, even if it may have succeeded in creating some limited recovery. Evidence of weaker relative growth performance since 2000 supports the view that Cuba's recovery has been running out of steam and needs further reform.

Even where liberalization has been greatest, in the sectors linked to the recovery of the external accounts, the limits imposed by the Cuban state on the opening to foreign business have inhibited performance. Cuba has attracted a low level of foreign direct investment compared with other countries in transition.[10] With weak domestic savings, the overall national rate of investment has remained very low, hindering recovery.[11] Potential foreign investors have been turned away, and foreign businesses with existing licenses to operate in Cuba have been refused renewal of licenses or had them abruptly withdrawn. Rigid planning priorities and lack of restructuring have inhibited export diversification, leaving continued high dependence on a small number of traditional products: nickel, cigars, sugar, fish, and citrus.

Job creation in the new export-oriented industries has been inhibited by tight regulation of the terms for foreign investors. The Cuban authorities, by setting relatively high dollar wage costs for joint ventures with foreign partners, have blocked many potential employment-creating activities.[12] This is particularly true for the development of new manufacturing industries and explains the failure of Cuba's experiment with free trade zones (FTZs).[13] Instead of allowing the creation of these jobs, the state has preferred to maintain high levels of disguised unemployment by subsidizing loss-making production or by paying the wages of workers who are either working at extremely low levels of productivity or laid off on a portion of their pay.[14]

Within the rest of the economy, where there has been less liberalization, the results have been much worse than in the privileged sectors prioritized to restore foreign exchange earnings. Real output data published by the National Statistics Office (Oficina Nacional de Estadísticas [ONE]) shows that the only sectors that had recovered their 1990 level of output by 2003 (the latest year for which full data are available at the time of writing were services, minerals, and electricity, gas, and water—reflecting the recovery of tourism, nickel, and power, all resulting from the external opening.[15] In contrast, the overall level of manufacturing output was still 16 percent lower than in 1989, agriculture 40 percent lower, and construction 55 percent lower. Within the manufacturing sector, the only major product categories that had recovered were cigars and spirits, both linked to exports. Output of nearly every other manufactured product in 2003 was still between 30 percent and 70 percent lower than it had been in 1989, and average labor productivity remained well below its 1990 level.

Cuba's flourishing informal economy reflects the failure of the official economy. The rapid growth of the informal economy in the early 1990s can be directly attributed to the failure to liberalize prices during the economic contraction.[16] As national income declined, official prices and nominal wages were held constant. The inevitable result was shortages, leading to an increase in black market prices (including the black market price of hard currency). Just as inevitably, black market traders and informal producers stepped in to fill the unmet demand. Since then, instead of liberalizing prices and allowing free markets to correct the conditions that create Cuba's "second economy,"[17] the government has rigidly kept most prices fixed and has sought to repress informal economic activity.

The openings to free markets that were made within the domestic economy were undertaken with reluctance. The agricultural markets were introduced in response to a crisis in the late summer of 1994, and the official justification given for the openings to self-employment and private restaurants and lodgings have stressed their status as responses to the economic difficulties and not the start of something more profound. These small openings to private enterprise have not yet been abolished, but the authorities have imposed ever tighter regulations since the late 1990s, limiting their scope. More than a decade after the economic crisis, the shortages and broad divergences between official and black market prices persist and the informal economy has continued to thrive. The continued severe imbalances within the Cuban economy—with the existence of two exchange rates, fixed prices, very low real wages for Cubans within the peso economy, and prohibition of legal private sector activity spawning a vast informal sector—are impeding economic recovery, indicating that liberalization might bring improvements. The perverse incentives arising from the gaps between official and unofficial price sets, and the debilitating separation of the external from the domestic economy, not only undermine the performance of the formal economy but also create severe social strains. By prohibiting the development of new small enterprises, the government has reduced the supply of goods and services that would improve living conditions, hampered the growth of productive employment, and held back the overall level of economic activity.

Despite the much vaunted enterprise restructuring under the *perfeccionamiento empresarial* (business improvement) program, much of the inefficient and bureaucratic management of state enterprises remains intact. Enterprises have been required to produce profit and loss accounts, but this has not brought the anticipated increase in enterprise autonomy because prices are still fixed, and inputs and outputs still largely dictated by the planning authorities. Anecdotal reports suggest that changes to the system of planning have resulted in confusion and conflicting targets. The improvement in food supply resulting from the legalization of free agricultural markets in 1994 has been severely constrained by the limitations placed on the distribution of supplies of agricultural inputs, and by quotas for production for the state distribution system at fixed prices that limit the possibilities for producing for the free markets and the minimal scope for developing systems of distribution. Similarly, the reorganization of agriculture anticipated when state farms were converted into Basic Units for Cooperative Production (Unidades Básicas de Producción Cooperativa [UBPC]) failed to materialize. The new cooperatives were still tied to quotas and state prices, and as a result most have continued to report losses, making them dependent on the authorities for subsidies, thus negating what little autonomy they had gained.

The performance of the main traditional export industry, sugar, which has remained under state control, has been cited as a clear example of the failure of the Cuban model. With the loss of the COMECON subsidy, the industry was doomed. Low investment over many years and heavy dependence on imported inputs rendered the industry uneconomic at world market prices. Lacking the foreign exchange to pay for inputs of fuel, fertilizers, pesticides, or spare parts, the industry has collapsed, with the harvest plummeting from over 8 million tons to around 2 million tons. However, the level of employment in the industry was maintained throughout the 1990s. Policy toward the sector appeared frozen: the government neither made any effort to provide the investment needed to increase productivity and make the sector economic nor allowed it to contract. Instead, each year the harvest was a disappointment, and in the assessments that followed, the underperformance was blamed on the weather and inadequate organization, as well as the lack of inputs or spare parts. As a result, for years the Cuban economy has been weighed down by the burden of the subsidy for the ill-fated industry. And even when a restructuring plan was finally announced in 2002, the workers were allowed to continue to draw wages; as a result, burden of the subsidy to the sugar industry has remained.[18]

In the second half of the 1990s the pace of reform slowed, and since 2000 the trend toward liberalization appears to have been reversed. This reform retrenchment coincided with a slowdown in Cuba's growth rates in 2001–2003, leaving Cuba lagging in performance relative to other transition economies. The domestic economy's continued stagnation has been widely interpreted as evidence that the Cuban model cannot be sustained, so that the Cuban exception will eventually finally capitulate.

Benefits

In spite of the drawbacks of conservatism the economy has done much better than expected, suggesting that there might have been some positive effects of conservatism to offset the negative ones that predictably provide the focus for so much of the Cuban transition literature. The benefits from natural resource endowments—beaches for tourism and large nickel reserves—are not sufficient to explain why the Cuban economy was able to make its recovery in the absence of external support. Studies of transition in other formerly centrally planned economies provide some clues. They have observed that under some conditions economic liberalization can produce negative effects. Where institutions and regulations were too weak to ensure efficient outcomes, transition has created markets that work badly, hampering growth and development. Rent-seeking behavior has distorted policy formation, and state capacity has been weakened. There are also cases in which the transition economy's state sold its assets at disadvantageous terms. Poorly functioning markets have resulted in inefficient outcomes, and have imposed enormous social costs, reflected in health and social indicators. In the case of Cuba, it can be argued that in some respects resistance to transition blueprints has enabled the economy to avoid some of the pitfalls experienced elsewhere as well as shielding the most disadvantaged from the worst effects of economic crisis and transformation.

Cuba's most obvious advantage was institutional stability. Throughout the crisis of transition recession, the state retained the capacity to govern, avoiding the disruption caused by the collapse of administrative structures, skills, and revenue-collecting capacity experienced in countries undergoing full simultaneous political and economic transition. In Cuba, total government revenue has remained between 50 and 60 percent of GDP, allowing the state to provide a minimum (although reduced) standard of health, education, and welfare services, maintain employment through job creation initiatives and subsidies to loss-making industries, and sustain its own capacity for administration and law enforcement. This contrasts with the loss of state capacity elsewhere, where damage to regulating and tax-collecting capacity has impeded the efficient functioning of liberalized markets, human capital has been lost, and health and social security systems has suffered more severely.[19]

Connected to this strength, in terms of economic performance, has been Cuba's success in stabilizing the economy. In response to the collapse in the value of the peso in 1990–1994, the Cuban government introduced a major package of selective adjustments to the system of prices and subsidies. Some prices on nonessential goods were raised, user charges were introduced on some public services, government administration was streamlined, and enterprise subsidies were cut. As a result, the overall fiscal imbalance was rectified, and the value of the Cuban peso (Ps) rose from a low of Ps 120-$1 before the 1994 stabilization package to around Ps 25-$1 within a year.[20]

In the sectors linked to the external recovery, restrictions on the scope of liberalization have also produced some benefits. For example, Cuba's refusal to allow wholesale privatization, while it has undoubtedly limited the gains from higher capital inflows and competition, has prevented the sale of major national assets on disadvantageous terms. The Cuban state has used its monopoly ownership and control of national resources to compensate for the bargaining disadvantage arising from its lack of access to hard currency, very limited international business experience, and the fact that the economy was closed off from the United States, the country that would otherwise have provided Cuba's main natural market source of financing and pool of potential investors. Instead of opening up a market for the sale of state assets to foreign buyers, the Cuban state has negotiated individually with potential foreign investors. In each case, it has sought to maximize the benefit to the Cuban economy. Its objectives have been explicitly stated: to gain access to capital, technology/know-how, or markets. This precluded investors that were purely seeking to gain access to the Cuban market or purchase assets in the hope of capital gains. Agreements with foreign partners for joint ventures have specified investment commitments, as well as technology transfer, management restructuring, and marketing contributions.[21] Although a large number of foreign investors were frustrated, some of those who did manage to gain a foothold in Cuba through negotiation with the authorities have prospered while making a significant contribution to Cuba's restructuring and recovery. In fact, with its relatively low level of foreign direct investment and very small national investment-GDP ratio, Cuba's real GDP growth-investment ratio—an indicator of overall "investment efficiency"—is exceptionally high.

Another benefit of limiting the scope of market relations with foreign investors is that the government has been able to control its development strategy. In tourism, it has been able to manage the branding of Cuba in the market. Tourist operators hoping to market casinos have been blocked, sex tourism has been discouraged[22], and hotel developments have been restricted to protect Cuba's heritage and environment from negative externalities. This insistence on adherence to guidelines informed by strategic planning is not unique to planned economies. Although they inevitably draw criticism from frustrated investors, planning restrictions can bring benefits in terms of development objectives, and in the case of Cuba it can be argued that in some respects they have done so.[23]

Even on employment creation, it is not clear whether Cuba's policies have necessarily been completely detrimental compared with the outcomes that might have been expected from more rapid liberalization. It is arguable that the imposition of high labor costs for foreign investors was economically rational from the perspective of the Cuban state-owned economy with its large welfare system. The average full economic cost of Cuban labor is far higher than the nominal peso wage, because of the cost of nonwage entitlements (including health, education, social security, and subsidized consumption of basic goods and utilities) provided by the state. As a result, the government would, in effect, have been subsidizing the foreign investor if it had dropped the labor cost below its economic cost. The true cost of labor may not be as high as the hard currency amounts demanded from foreign partners, but by keeping labor costs high the Cuban state has encouraged the development of high value-added activities. It has also been able to use the labor payments to cross-subsidize the low peso payments to employees of the Cuban state and its enterprises.

Similarly, in the sugar sector, the special characteristics of the economy during the 1990s suggest that policy may not have been as irrational as it appeared. The true economic cost of keeping laborers in the sugar industry was not as large as the sugar subsidy. In the context of its acute scarcity in the early 1990s, foreign exchange had a high economic value (as reflected in the black market exchange rate), so it was economically beneficial to continue with any activity that yielded a positive hard currency balance, even if it were tiny compared to the peso costs. Moreover, with the state committed to providing social security and all the associated benefits, the extra cost to the state of paying the wages and running costs for sugar production was less than it appeared. And finally, with no alternative employment or other activities to offer in the sugar-growing areas, closure of the mills would have led people to migrate to other parts of the country in search of work, compounding the problems of overcrowding and burden on overstretched infrastructure in the towns, particularly Havana. Therefore, in the context of an extreme shortage of foreign exchange, high social security costs, and a lack of alternative employment, a case can be made for propping up the sugar industry with such a huge subsidy, and delaying rationalization until the economy improved and new employment opportunities were starting to open up.

The greatest policy rigidities, and the greatest degree of stagnation, have been within the domestic economy, and it is here that the need for further liberalization appears most urgent. However, it is not only ideological rigidity that gives rise to hesitation on the part of the Cuban authorities. The price distortions and controls on private enterprise that create the black markets and prevent economic adjustment are embedded in the Cuban system for delivering its commitment to universal access to basic goods and full employment, through the subsidized ration system and bloated public sector. The lack of liberalization within the domestic economy is therefore closely tied to Cuba's overperformance compared with other transition economies in terms of maintaining employment and providing a guaranteed minimum level of nutrition, health, and education to the whole population—not to mention the contribution to political stability played by the lack of abrupt rationalization of employment. In this sense, Cuban policy has traded economic efficiency and growth for a commitment to meet basic needs and desire to minimize social upheaval.

In the proposals for transition drawn up by proponents of full liberalization, large amounts of foreign assistance are envisaged to ensure the maintenance of the social safety net and public services during the transition. In the absence of such support, Cuban policy makers have had to find a different way to manage change while providing social protection. They have argued that the adjustment of the exchange rate is central to this process. Rather than unleash huge inflation and dislocation by liberalizing the economy under current conditions, the aim should be to gradually restore the real value of the Cuban peso as the economy recovers, in order to close the gap between official and market prices, wages and exchange rates. Although the discourse of political leaders presents exchange rate appreciation as simply a means of restoring more equitable relative incomes, some economists in Cuba have described currency adjustment in terms of creating preconditions for increasing the role of markets within the domestic economy. Without a unified exchange rate, relative prices are chaotic and distorted, and free markets are unable to function efficiently. Progress has been slower than hoped, despite the fiscal discipline and gradual economic improvement. The unofficial value of the Cuban peso appreciated only slightly in 1995–2001, from Ps 25-$1 to Ps 19-$1 (prompted by a decline in tourism in 2001), and then slipped back again to Ps 25–26-$1, where it remained until early 2005. The undervaluation of the Cuban peso continues to create serious distortions, encourage illegality, and hamper the integration of the domestic and external economies. Nonetheless, there are arguably merits to the preference for gradual adjustment rather than a sudden shock, in the context of Cuba's lack of external support and the high priority given to welfare and social stability.

Recent Policy Shifts

The Cuban economy has been kept afloat, defying expectations, thanks to the introduction of reforms necessary to restore external earnings. The cost of relative policy conservatism was clearly offset by some of its benefits in the first decade post-COMECON. Rapid growth and high levels of productivity have been achieved in some sectors, health indicators have been relatively good, and human capital has been preserved. However, by the early 2000s the recovery was losing steam. Persistent imbalances within the domestic economy suggested that Cuba's model was not a sustainable one that could ensure economic development. The longer the imbalances persisted, the greater the net welfare loss of failing to address the problems by reforming the system. Further economic reforms seemed to be needed to bring dynamism to the domestic economy, but public statements by Cuban government figures continue to insist that transition is not an option. However, at the time of writing, a series of measures have been adopted that suggest a departure in economic strategy, although the direction may not be clear.

The strand of the new policy that has caused most concern involves recentralization of decision making. Enterprise managers have been deprived of some of their decision-making powers concerning the management of hard currency; the budding private enterprise sector has been squeezed tightly, with licenses for self-employment or small businesses being revoked; and the state auditing and tax-collecting systems have been expanded and strengthened. These measures, introduced amidst speeches condemning "economic crime," indiscipline, and waste, have been interpreted as a reversal of the decentralizing and liberalizing reforms of the 1990s. Politically, they have been presented as such, with officials stressing the need to end the illicit gains of those working in the thriving external sector and fighting a rearguard action against corruption and the misappropriation of funds. At the same time, the economy has been de-dollarized, with the withdrawal of the U.S. dollar from circulation and its replacement with the Cuban convertible peso (CUC), and the role of the Central Bank has increased in the management and allocation of foreign currency. At first, the withdrawal of the U.S. dollar from domestic circulation in late 2004 was interpreted as no more than an attempt by the authorities to round up the hard currency held by the population and encourage remittance and tourist income in currencies other than the U.S. dollar. However, the announcement in early 2005 that the convertible peso was to be revalued against the U.S. dollar marked an important new departure. For the first time, the Cuban currency was unpegged from the value of the U.S. dollar. This had been made possible by the regulations introduced to separate enterprise accounts in U.S. dollars and convertible pesos, suggesting that the move had been carefully planned.

This move was coupled with the first modest revaluation of the unofficial value of the Cuban peso from Ps 26-CUC 1 to Ps 22-CUC 1.[24] Although most peso earners have little disposable income to convert into convertible peso to make purchases at the hard currency retail outlets, the revaluation brought some improvement in their purchasing power. The revaluation was followed by a series of announcements of increases in pay and pensions. Again, the increases are modest relative to the increases needed to restore the real purchasing power of peso incomes to their precrisis levels, but they mark a first step in this direction. It is a necessary step toward expanding consumer demand to strengthen the market for domestically produced consumer goods and services.

The exchange rate reforms and increases in nominal peso incomes have begun to reduce some of the price distortions in the domestic economy.

The real value of Cuban peso incomes have been slightly increased, while the purchasing power of hard currencies have been reduced, thus curtailing the degree of privilege enjoyed by employees of joint enterprises and trading companies and those in receipt of remittances or informal dollar earnings. Taken together with the shift toward recentralization of economic management, they herald a new phase in Cuba's recovery, in which auditing has been strengthened and the Central Bank's role as regulator of financial flows has been enhanced while both household spending and public investment are set to increase markedly.

The increase in consumer spending and public investment has been made possible by the change in Cuba's external conditions that began in 2004. The Cuban Revolution's always-politicized external economic relations have been profoundly altered by the arrival of its two new saviors: an alternative political partner and economic benefactor, in the form of Venezuela's Hugo Chávez, and a new source of commercial credit, in the form of communist China. The reform of the system for handling foreign currency can be viewed as an adaptation to the need to handle large new flows of external finance, and increases in peso incomes and public investment can be seen as a response to the new resources available to the government thanks to benefits of new trade with Venezuela. Chinese investment plans in Cuba involve spending amounting to something in the region of 7 percent of Cuba's import spending, and the size of proposed new lines of credit would increase import capacity by the same amount again. The sale of the services of thousands of doctors and other professionals to Venezuela appears to have made an enormous contribution to the government's resources. There are no official figures for the earnings from this, but unofficial Cuban estimates suggest that the deal brings a new income stream of as much as $750 million, raising import capacity by about another 10 percent and the government's hard currency resources by a much larger percentage. Agreements with Venezuela also provide a buffer against movements in world oil prices, and the promise of large amounts of new investment in the energy infrastructure.

Both the centralization of control of foreign currency and expansion of public sector wages and investment appear to reinforce a statist, centrally directed model of economic management, but, as with earlier reforms, appearances may not reflect the full picture. An enhanced role for the Central Bank as regulator of the financial system could mark a shift away from the old planning system based on material balances toward one in which the allocation of finance is based more on market forces. The increase in real consumer spending could be the start of a move away from consumption dominated by state provision of basic needs toward an economy that responds to consumer preferences. Such a shift would create new reform challenges for the Cuban system of economic management.

Current indications are that trade and financial links with China and Venezuela are set to expand quickly in the coming years, while other new sources of foreign currency earnings are also beginning to emerge. The diversification of markets has been the result of U.S. sanctions that block the free development of Cuban-U.S. economic relations, and, in the long run, this could be beneficial for export diversification. Current high prices for both nickel and oil have compounded the mutual benefits from existing commodity-based trade with both China and Venezuela, and have enhanced the potential for oil exploration and development in Cuban territorial waters in the Mexican Gulf.[25] Cuba's investments in human development and scientific research have also opened up other potential areas for growth. There have been reports of discussions about the export and licensed production of Cuban biotechnology products in agreements with China and India for example, which would add hundreds of millions of dollars to Cuba's import capacity, and become the first signs of export activity in the information technology sector. All this suggests that the Cuban external adjustment will continue.

Conclusions: Does Cuba Provide an Alternative Model?

Cuba's strategy for coping with the collapse of the Soviet bloc has been unique. Not only did Cuba not undergo the standard post-Soviet transition to market via collapse and privatization, but it also resisted the more gradualist, or social democratic, variant of managed transition.[26] And despite the continuing, even tightening U.S. embargo and relative isolation from other economies, the Cuban economy—while still very weak and distorted—has performed surprisingly well. However, the characterization of Cuba as a "transition laggard" is an oversimplification. In fact there has been more extensive liberalization than either Cuban policy makers or their detractors like to admit. This liberalization has played an important part in the economic recovery since the mid-1990s.

It has been argued, on good evidence, that economic performance would have been better if the Cuban authorities had been less resistant to transition, but it has been less commonly appreciated that the Cuban model has spared the economy from some of the pitfalls of rapid liberalization. In these respects, Cuban policy can be seen as a relatively successful response to its specific conditions and priorities.

While this chapter has drawn attention to some of the positive outcomes of the Cuban model, it has also highlighted the persistence of severe economic weaknesses, and described the imperative for further changes in the way the economic system operates. The dual economy, with a stagnant domestic sector and the dynamic and efficient externally linked sector, has created severe economic difficulties as well as social and political tensions. To integrate the two halves, further reforms, including liberalization of the domestic economy, will be needed. Recent changes in economic management have been widely interpreted as a reversal of existing reforms that will compound the existing difficulties. However, the Cuban model is one of creative adaptation to circumstances, and there is no reason to expect this to change. The recent shifts in policy should be seen as the latest responses to a change in circumstances, and understood as part of a strategy that includes the expansion of the role of financial markets and consumer preferences, as well as strengthening regulation and clamping down on private enterprise.

Since 1990, even while the political rhetoric has continued to emphasize rejection of the prescriptions of liberalization, sufficient liberalizing reforms have been introduced to ensure the survival of a socialist alternative in the heart of the Americas. The exceptionalism of the Cuban Revolution rests as much on its propensity to respond to change as on its insistence on pursuing a separate path. Its resistance of the prescriptions of transition, widely predicted to bring its downfall, has proved to have some benefits, although it also leaves the economy burdened by severe and persistent weaknesses. It still remains an open question whether the Cuban model, based on an insistence on following a separate path, will eventually prove capable of survival, or whether in the end it is forced to capitulate by embarking on the economic transition long thought to have been inevitable.

Appendix 1 Sources of Foreign Exchange for Imports ($ million)

Year	1990	1991	1992	1993	1994	1995	1996	1997	1998	1999	2000	2001	2002	2003	2004	2005
Sugar	4,338	2,288	1,240	758	760	714	976	853	599	463	453	550	448	289	324	154
Nickel	398	240	241	160	201	331	423	416	345	410	599	465	432	620	860	1,053
Other goods exports	679	452	298	218	421	462	467	554	596	584	626	646	522	746	1,008	1,170
Tourism	243	402	550	720	850	1,100	1,333	1,515	1,759	1,901	1,948	1,840	1,769	2,052	2,329	2,686
Other services	283	182	192	112	310	428	596	636	833	954	1,166	1,114	1,067	1,148	1,351	1,654
Net current transfers	−13	18	43	263	470	646	744	792	813	799	740	813	820	915	1,100	878
Net factor services inflows	−456	−334	−248	−264	−423	−525	−493	−483	−449	−514	−622	−502	−600	−650	−800	−687
Capital account inflows minus increase in reserves	2,545	1,454	421	372	260	518	167	437	392	462	859	653	296	155	−146	233
Total imports	8,017	4,702	2,737	2,339	2,849	3,675	4,213	4,720	4,889	5,057	5,768	5,579	4,754	5,274	6,026	7,141

Sources: Banco Central de Cuba, Annual Economic Report 1994–2004 BCC, Havana, *Oficina Nacional de Estadisticas, Anuario Estadistico de Cuba*; annual, 1994–2005 ONE, Havana 1994–1995. Figures are EIU estimates.

Appendix 2 Transition Recession

	Consecutive years of output decline	Cumulative output decline (%)	Real GDP, 2000 (1990 = 100)	Real GDP, 2005 (1990 = 100)[b]
Central and Southeastern Europe and the Baltics[a]	3.8	22.6	106.5	
Albania	3	33	110	145
Bulgaria	4	16	81	103
Croatia	4	36	87	107
Czech Republic	3	12	99	116
Estonia	5	35	85	119
Hungary	4	15	109	130
Latvia	6	51	61	87
Lithuania	5	44	67	95
Poland	2	6	112	130
Romania	3	21	144	192
Slovak Republic	4	23	82	103
Slovenia	3	14	105	124
Commonwealth of Independent States[a]	6.5	50.5	62.7	
Armenia	4	63	67	112
Azerbaijan	6	60	55	98
Belarus	6	35	88	n.a.
Georgia	5	78	29	58
Kazakhstan	6	41	90	146
Kyrgyz Republic	6	50	66	85
Moldova	7	63	35	48
Russian Federation	7	40	64	86
Tajikistan	7	50	48	n.a.
Turkmenistan	8	48	76	n.a.
Ukraine	10	59	43	64
Uzbekistan	6	18	95	117
Cuba[c]	3	35	87	102
Output decline during the Great Depression, 1930–1934				
France	3	11		
Germany	3	16		
United Kingdom	2	6		
United States of America	4	27		

Notes:

[a] Simple average, except for the index of 1990 GDP, which shows population-weighted averages.

[b] Using EIU estimates for real GDP growth, 2001–2005.

[c] Using EIU data, based on Cuban official GDP growth series.

Sources: World Bank, *Transition—The First Ten Years: Analysis and Lessons for Eastern Europe and the Former Soviet Union*, Washington, DC, November 2001, p. 5; Economist Intelligence Unit, Country Data.

Appendix 3 Real GDP by Sector

Year	Gross Domestic Product (1997 prices)[a]													
	1990	1991	1992	1993	1994	1995	1996	1997	1998	1999	2000	2001	2002	2003
GDP total[b]	30, 507	27,245	24,090	20,506	20,653	21,159	22,819	23,439	23,476	24,956	26,482	27,268	27,686	28,502
Agriculture	2,909	2,211	1,983	1,532	1,457	1,516	1,781	1,823	1,566	1,748	1,907	1,924	1,876	1,921
Industry	8,984	7,774	6,165	5,262	5,599	6,043	6,642	6,996	6,552	7,018	7,560	7,429	7,462	7,465
Mining	178	159	205	187	190	296	345	354	313	321	427	412	464	472
Construction	4,201	3,023	1,682	1,074	1,069	1,148	1,500	1,545	1,504	1,616	1,752	1,658	1,619	1,690
Electricity, gas, and water supply	483	453	402	356	372	408	423	452	469	507	572	578	592	611
Manufacturing	5,292	4,790	3,999	3,540	3,810	4,055	4,375	4,645	4,267	4,574	4,810	4,781	4,788	4,693
Services	18,112	16,894	15,815	13,606	13,410	13,322	14,056	14,284	15,020	15,857	16,670	17,579	18,010	18,739

Notes:
[a] The published official sources provide the series for 1997 prices only from 1996 on. Previous years are estimates based on growth rates given in the previous series that were based on 1981 prices.
[b] Components do not add to the total. A small residual includes import duties from 1996 and, before 1996, the adjustment due to rebasing.

Source: Oficina Nacional de Estadística, *Anuario Estadistico de Cuba*.

Notes

1. This is an Economist Intelligence Unit (EIU) estimate, based on official data for the trade deficit in 1989 ($2.73 billion), and an estimate of the dollar value of GDP.

2. U.S. sanctions barred lending to Cuba from the relevant regional multilateral institution, the Inter-American Development Bank (IDB), as well as from the International Monetary Fund (IMF) and the World Bank (WB). Cuba has received only very small amounts of official financing, mainly from UN agencies. Ritter describes the external financial support available to other countries as the means of "jump-starting" the economies. See Archibald R. M. Ritter (ed.), *The Cuban Economy* (Pittsburgh, PA: University of Pittsburgh Press, 2004), p. 10.

3. In the absence of reliable data for many of the transition economies in the early 1990s, an approximation of the "transition recession" given by the World Bank (1992) is provided in appendix 2 of this chapter. It puts the average cumulative output decline of Eastern European countries (not Commonwealth of Independent States [CIS] countries) following the collapse of COMECON at 22.6 percent, with the average number of consecutive years of decline at 3.8 percent. The CIS countries fared worse, with an average decline of 50.5 percent and average number of consecutive years of decline at 6.5 percent.

4. The World Bank (World Bank, *Transition: The First Ten Years. Analysis and Lessons for Eastern Europe and the Former Soviet Union* [Washington DC: World Bank, 2002], p. 5) and the *Economist Intelligence Unit* estimates (shown in appendix 2) demonstrate that Cuba's overall performance was slightly above the average between 1990 and 2000. Cuba performed better over the first decade than the average for the CIS states but more poorly than the average for Central and Southeastern Europe and the Baltic (CSB) countries. Of the four countries that suffered similar declines to Cuba's in the transition recession (Albania, Belarus, Croatia, and Estonia), the average degree of recovery of real GDP by 2000 was very close to that of Cuba: their average level of GDP in 2000 was 93 percent of the 1990 level, compared with Cuba's 87 percent. However, Cuba's relative performance is below average in 2000–2005 but still well above the worst performers.

5. Press reports in 2005 suggest that annual earnings from the biotechnology sector have reached than $300 million and are rising rapidly. It is unclear whether this figure is for merchandise exports only or includes income from licences.

6. There has been some confusion in discussions about these flows, with the total for net current transfers sometimes being mistaken for the total for remittances alone.

7. However, telephone density remains extremely low. According to UN Development Programme (UNDP) data, UNDP Web site, http://hdr.org/hdr2006/statistics/indicators/120.html. In 2004 there were still only 68 lines per 1,000 inhabitants, under half the average for the Latin American and Caribbean region.

8. The European Bank for Reconstruction and Development (EBRD) *Transition Reports* (London: EBRD, 1988) provides scoring systems for transition. For example, the 1998 report used eight criteria: large-scale privatization, small-scale privatization, governance and enterprise restructuring, price liberalization, trade and foreign exchange system, competition policy, banking reform and interest rate liberalization, and securities markets and nonbank financial institutions. Whichever scoring system is used, Cuba's overall score is among the lowest.

9. These include an extensive "Cuban transition" research program based in the United States, with support from the U.S. government. In this literature (including an annual volume of papers presented at the Association for the Study of the Cuban Economy's (ASCE) conference, called *Cuba in Transition* [Maryland: ASCE, 2004]), the many failings of Cuban economic management have been extensively examined, and the overall framework for a hypothetical transition, as well as transition plans for individual sectors, are being worked out.

10. The strong correlation between the degree of transition and FDI inflows is noted by the EBRD (*Transition Reports*, p. 81) and the World Bank (*Transition*, p. 7) reports that FDI inflows in the 1990s averaged just 0.9 percent of GDP in the 1992–1995 period in other transition economies, but in 1996–1999 it accelerated to an average of around 3 percent of GDP; in Cuba net FDI inflows were at a similar level in 1992–1995, at 0.9 percent of GDP, but it failed to accelerate in line with other transition economies in 1996–1999, remaining at only 1 percent of GDP during this period.

11. Ritter notes that domestic savings were only 2.3 percent of GDP in 1993 and gross national investment was only 5.2 percent of GDP in 1994. He reckons that levels of net investment for much of the 1990s were probably negative, with the capital stock deteriorating more rapidly than it could be replaced. Certainly roads, railways, public buildings, housing, and water services deteriorated over this period. Ritter (ed.), *The Cuban Economy*, p. 6.

12. Although exact details are not published, the range appears to average around \$400–\$600 per month. These are the amounts paid by the enterprise for Cuban workers; the workers are then paid their salaries in pesos. At the unofficial but legal *Cadeca* exchange rate (which is available only within Cuba and applies only to personal transactions), the U.S. dollar has been valued at 20–26 pesos for the past decade. This would seem to imply that the workers receive less than one-twentieth of the amount paid to the state. However, this is not the full picture for two reasons. First, Cuban workers' entitlements to goods and services at heavily subsidized prices means that the purchasing power of peso incomes is much higher than their value at the *Cadeca* exchange rate. Second, foreign businesses provide additional benefits in kind besides frequently making extra, unofficial payments "under the table."

13. The idea of creating export-oriented manufacturing in the FTZs was also doomed to failure because of Cuba's lack of access to the U.S. market.

14. Official unemployment figures, even during the worst of the crisis, were very low. Workers laid off are not officially unemployed as they remain on the payroll of their employer, receiving a proportion of their salary. New entrants to the labor market are also excluded, as they do not qualify as part of the working population. The official rate of unemployment has been announced each year since 1994, when it was given as 6.5 percent of the working population. It peaked at 7.9 percent in 1995, and then it fell each year to only 1.9 percent by 2004. The true rate of underemployment, or proportion of people of working population either laid off in jobs that could be described as disguised unemployment (because productivity is so low, although they remain employed in order to keep the unemployment rate down) or waiting to find their first job, has been unofficially estimated to be as high as 50 percent.

15. Real GDP data is in appendix 2.

16. A huge nominal fiscal deficit in 1990–1993 led to the collapse of the Cuban peso's market value.

17. "Second economy" described and explained in Jorge F. Pérez-López, *Cuba's Second Economy* (New Brunswick, NJ: Transaction Books, 1995).

18. The plan included the transfer of around half of the agricultural land under sugar for other uses and closure of around half of the mills, with the state undertaking to maintain the salaries of the workforce during retraining and redeployment. Around half a million people were directly employed in the industry before the restructuring, implying that some 2 million, or 18 percent of the population, were dependent on it. The harvest fell from 3.6 million tons in the 2002–2003 crop year (compared with more than 8 million tons in 1989–1990) to only 1.3 million tons in 2004–2005.

19. Education, health, and welfare services undoubtedly suffered, but mortality rates and educational performance indicators suggest that universal provision was maintained. A comparison between the trends in the UNDP *Human Development Report* (UNDP, *Transition 1999: The Human Cost of Transition* [New York: UNDP, 1999]) highlights the Cuban exception in this respect, with a very much smaller deterioration in health indicators despite the decline in total resources available.

20. According to official statistics (from the Banco Central de Cuba (Cuban Central Bank, BCC) and the Oficina Nacional de Estadísticas or National Statistics Office [ONE]), the fiscal deficit was cut from 34.5 percent of GDP in 1994 to 7.4 percent in 1994 and only 2.4 percent by 1996; since then it has averaged less than 3 percent of GDP.

21. The terms of agreements varied, but full privatization has never yet been ceded. The preferred arrangement stipulates that the foreign partner, instead of simply paying for a share of the enterprise, provides an investment commitment in return for its share. In the case of the first "100 percent privatization" of a power utility on the Isle of Youth, the foreign partner was not purchasing the enterprise but leasing it for a fixed period. The biggest straightforward transfer of ownership was in the case of the enterprise responsible for international marketing of Cuban cigars, in which the buyer paid up front for a 50 percent stake in the enterprise in return for a share of future sales.

22. The control of sex tourism has strengthened after initial apparent laxity. In the early 1990s, when the value of the Cuban peso dived to Ps 120-$1 and unemployment and underemployment swelled, the incentives for prostitution were such that it was impossible to repress. Policy has evolved since then, with gradually increasing success, based on an integrated, multiagency approach with the emphasis moving away from police work to attention to the marketing of tourism as well as education, social welfare, and employment creation.

23. The main issues in terms of public benefit and economic efficiency are not whether such guidelines exist but whether they have a clear rationale and are implemented fairly and efficiently. The Cuban authorities have sought to clearly set out the legal framework for contracts with foreign partners, although it appears that the idiosyncrasies of the Cuban system have had some deterrent effect and complicated disputes settlement. The lack of transparency in the Cuban policy-making process has also deterred investors, and unexplained changes in policy have added to both frustrations and operating risk. Nonetheless, it is possible to argue that there have been some developmental benefits.

24. The unofficial exchange rate is that used for personal transactions, and available at the *Cadecas* exchange houses; the official rate, used for accounting purposes, is still Ps 1-CUC 1.
25. The U.S. geological survey has estimated that Cuban territorial waters in the Mexican Gulf, which are just starting to be explored, could yield up to 5 billion barrels of oil.
26. Such as the path envisaged by its advisers from the Spanish Socialist Party (Partido Socialista Obrero de Español [PSOE]).

Chapter 4

The Gatekeeper State: Limited Economic Reforms and Regime Survival in Cuba, 1989–2002

Javier Corrales

Introduction

In the 1990s the Cuban regime displayed two unexpected characteristics. One was survival. The other was the implementation of uneven economic reforms, meaning that some sectors of the economy were revamped, while others remained untouched. This chapter connects these two outcomes by arguing that uneven economic reforms explain regime survival. Uneven economic reforms served to strengthen the power of the state vis-à-vis society, and within the state, the power of hard-liners. This new type of state, which I call the gatekeeper state, dominates society through a new mechanism—it fragments the economy into different sectors of varying degrees of profitability and then determines which citizens have access to each respective sector. While some authoritarian regimes stay alive by providing widespread economic growth, the Cuban regime in the 1990s has survived by restricting access to capitalist rewards. This has permitted the incumbents to navigate through societal pressures and postpone regime transition.

The continuity of the Cuban political regime in the 1990s has amazed most Cubanologists of every persuasion.[1] Despite the demise of dictatorships in Latin America and most of the Soviet bloc, Cuba's regime has remained unabashedly authoritarian. This continuity in politics contrasts with the discontinuities in economics. Between 1993 and 1996, Cuba opened new sectors to foreign direct investment (FDI), liberalized farm markets, legalized the possession of U.S. dollars and new forms of self-employment, and reduced the fiscal deficit by cutting spending.

Compared to economic reforms elsewhere in Latin America, Cuba's reforms were timid. Cuba fell short of privatizing any state-owned enterprises (SOEs), liberalizing financial markets, and permitting full-scale profit making, as most aggressive reformers in Latin America did in the 1990s.[2] Cuba also fell short in comparison to communist China and Vietnam in the 1990s, which allowed the rise of a private business sector.[3] However, compared to the

Cuban Revolution's own past, Cuba's economic reforms were profound. The few sectors that were targeted for reform actually underwent unprecedented change. Economically, therefore, the Cuban regime displayed a combination of both significant reform in some areas, and reform avoidance in many others.

Many scholars in the mid-1990s believed that economic reforms were a preamble of things to come in politics: economic opening would yield political opening. To their surprise, this did not happen, and this chapter attempts to explain why. Specifically, I argue that the uneven nature of economic reforms contributed to regime survival. First, the uneven economic reforms served to mislead—in fact, completely fool—those actors who in the early 1990s were pressuring for deep economic and political opening. The reforms allowed the state to give the impression that the regime was moving toward the market—the type of signal that was necessary to placate the pressures coming from reform advocates—when in fact, the government never intended to follow that path. Instead, the government intended to side with the hard-liners.

The other reason is that uneven economic reforms magnified the power of the state by enhancing its capacity to dispense inducements and constraints. It is normally believed that economic openings hurt incumbent politicians (at least in the short term), and may even undermine authoritarian states in general. This is because market reforms agitate society by creating losers and winners, both of whom put pressure on the state. To survive these societal pressures, states must build new coalitions with new actors,[4] show some reform accomplishment such as restored growth,[5] and move on to "second-stage reforms" by making state institutions less corrupt and more transparent.[6]

In Cuba, these societal pressures never became that strong, and thus the state did not have to bother much with any of the above policies. The reforms were carried out in a manner that enlarged the leverage of the state over society, rather than diminishing it. Advocates of market reforms argue that an open economy unleashes economic forces and agents that can act as checks on state power.[7] Yet, when reformers enact circumscribed rather than full-fledged market reforms the power of the state may not decline. In Cuba, limited reforms actually enhanced the power of the state by converting it into the gatekeeper of a new and highly valuable commodity: the small and profitable externally connected sector. As a gatekeeper, the state has increased the payoff of cooperating with it: the state rewards (or elicits) societal loyalty by dispensing access to this sector. In many ways, the Cuban state has transformed the way it interacts with society: while the number of winners is decreasing, the reward that actors obtain for endorsing the state is becoming more valuable. This has lessened the prospects of regime change.

The Resilience of (One-Party) Authoritarian Regimes

Incumbents in authoritarian regimes stand a better chance of surviving internal and external shocks than in democracies.[8] Bruce Bueno de Mesquita et al. argue that this phenomenon can be explained by the differences in size of the winning coalition, defined as the members of the population whose support is essential for the survival of the government.[9] Incumbents in democracies require, by definition, large winning coalitions, at least large enough to beat their rivals in electoral contests. Incumbents in authoritarian regimes, by definition, do not require large winning coalitions to stay in office. They are sustained by a small segment of the population.

To stay in office, incumbents in both democracies and authoritarian regimes must do the same: please or reward their winning coalition with "things of value." Precisely because winning coalitions in authoritarian regimes are smaller, it is easier and less costly for the incumbents to please them. So, in the context of a huge crisis, the incumbents in authoritarian regimes will still find enough "pork" to please the small winning coalition. In a one-party dominant authoritarian regime, the incumbents enjoy even "greater political resources": they can use bureaucratic privileges for recruiting a minimal number of subordinates.[10] If the winning coalition was larger, as in the case of a democracy, it would be harder to find sufficient things of value for the entire coalition. In principle, therefore, it is easier for authoritarian regimes to maintain the loyalty of the core group during economic crisis than it is for democracies. With fewer favors, they can achieve far greater loyalty among the reduced number of actors that support them.

Cuba qualifies as a small winning coalition regime. The pillar of the regime includes three selective groups: the party (with a membership in 1997 of 780,000 in a country of 11.4 million), the military (with 50,000 troops in 1999), and the security apparatus, whose size is unknown.[11] As long as enough things of value can be provided to these actors—which is not too costly because this is not a large group—their loyalty can be preserved even during harsh times.

Pressure for Reform and the Dilemma of
Market Reforms for Authoritarian Regimes

In their model about the survivability of authoritarian regimes, Bueno de Mesquita et al. fail to consider the possibility of internal splits within the winning coalition.[12] Other theorists have shown that deep economic crises create divisions among incumbent forces, whether democratic or authoritarian, regarding how to respond to the economic crisis. The split occurs between soft-liners (in favor of economic reform) and hard-liners (who are reform-adverse).[13] In authoritarian regimes, the split can occur along yet another dimension: namely, what to do politically? Some will favor political opening while others prefer hardening.[14] Although the incidence of splits is less frequent in single-party authoritarian regimes as opposed to military or personalistic regimes,[15] these splits have nonetheless occurred in one-party states such as Mexico, Korea, and Taiwan, leading to regime change.[16]

Pressure for economic reform also comes from external actors. The literature on economic reform stresses that during economic crises, incumbents are desperate to obtain external allies. Cuba's potential new external allies (mostly in Europe and Latin America) pressed for economic reform. Some of them (such as Spain and Mexico) were deep reformers themselves and pushed Cuba to become one as well.[17] With its capital stock depreciated, and unable to make new investments, Cuba simply could not ignore the demands of investors.[18]

Finally, pressure also comes from society at large. Economic hardship causes citizens to demand economic relief. In 1989, the collapse of the Soviet bloc plunged Cuba into a severe depression. The gross domestic product (GDP) plummeted from 20.8 million pesos in 1989 to 16.7 million pesos in 1993.[19] This was one of the worst depressions in the history of Latin America. Food consumption levels, to mention one indicator of personal hardship, plummeted from 3,109 calories a day in 1989 to 2,357 calories by 1996, a dramatic 24 percent drop in just a few years.[20] The regime had reasons to fear urban riots, and offering relief to society was imperative.

Yet the regime also had justifiable reasons to fear alienating the hard-liners, the largest group within the winning coalition.[21] Reforms could make hard-liners feel politically abandoned. The danger was that they would see their views ignored by Castro, feel the costs of reforms more profoundly than other sectors,[22] and witness the possible increase in power of political rivals given that economic reforms give rise to new, possibly wealthier, societal actors.[23]

The Cuban state thus faced a dilemma starting in 1989. Reforms were necessary to please some members of the winning coalition and incorporate new members. Yet, reforms risked alienating the largest sector of the winning coalition, the hard-liners. Castro had to make a decision—either side with the *duros* (hard-liners) or the soft-liners. The rest of this chapter argues that after making some concessions to soft-liners in 1993–1995, Castro ultimately sided with the *duros*.

A Small Opening to Soft-Liners in 1993–1995

In mid-1993, after four years of consecutive annual GDP contraction, the Cuban government finally felt cornered.[24] Pressures to liberalize were ubiquitous. Less than two years prior to 1993, at the 1991 Fourth Party Congress, the politburo discussed major reforms, but cavalierly shelved them.[25] By 1993, the economy still showed no signs of improving and pressures continued to mount. To what extent did the leadership accommodate these pressures? I answer this question by looking first at cabinet changes and then at adopted policies.

It is not easy to gauge the political divisions within the top echelon of the Cuban government, a regime that is well known for its hermetic politics and an obsession with portraying an image of unity. Yet, there is one way, however imperfect, to discern internal divisions: examining the number of changes in the cabinet and the entry of new faces. Figure 4.1 shows the number of cabinet changes in Cuba from 1979 to 2002.[26] Several points stand out. First, large cabinet reshufflings are not correlated with economic performance.

If so, regression analysis of cabinet changes as the dependent variable and economic growth rates as the explanatory variable would yield a negative coefficient. Instead the coefficient is positive (0.1193) and statistically insignificant (t-statistic 0.481034).

Second, large cabinet reshufflings in Cuba are instead associated with (1) changes in economic policy direction and (2) purging campaigns. Figure 4.1 shows 3 major cabinet reshufflings: in 1993–1995 (20 changes in 3 years, or an average change of 20 percent of the cabinet per year), in 1985–1986 (16 changes in 2 years, or an average change of 23.5 percent of the cabinet per year), and in 1989 (6 changes in 1 year, or a change of 17.6 percent of the cabinet). Two of these episodes coincide fully with deep policy changes: specifically, the 1993–1995 changes coincide with the period of deepest market reforms; while the 1985–1986 changes came right after the period of market reform reversals (Rectification). The 1989 change is not related to economic policy changes but to a political witch hunt, that is, the Ochoa affair of 1989—the largest purging of the military and the cabinet since the 1960s. Undoubtedly, the Cuban cabinet underwent a significant change in 1993–1995, both in terms of reshuffling and, more significantly, entry of new faces. Sixteen new individuals entered the cabinet during this period, perhaps the largest inflow in decades. I will call this the 1993–1995 cohort. This cohort came close to matching the number of the old guards in the cabinet—those who entered prior to 1993 (some dating to the 1970s), henceforth the pre-1993 cohort (see table 4.1).

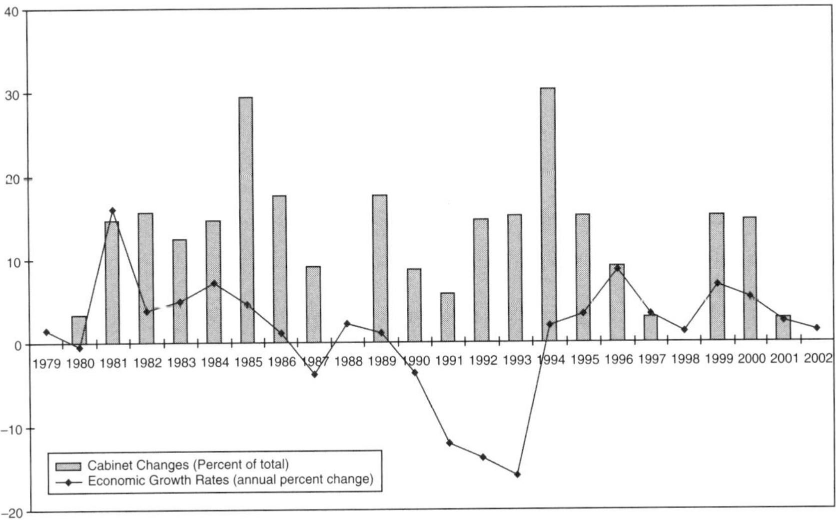

Figure 4.1 Economic Performance and Cabinet Changes in Cuba (1979–2002)

Sources: Economic growth rates from 1980 to 1990, GSP Rate (%), Carmelo Mesa-Lago et al., *Market, Socialist, and Mixed Economies: Comparative Policy and Performance, Chile, Cuba and Costa Rica* (Baltimore, MD: Johns Hopkins University Press, 2000); from 1991 to 2002, gross domestic product, CEPAL, *Balance preliminar de las economías de América Latina y el Caribe; anexo estadístico* (Santiago de Chile: CEPAL, 1992–2003); cabinet changes, *Europa World Year Book* (London: Europa Publications Limited, 1979–2003).

Table 4.1   Old Guards and Newcomers in Cuba's Cabinets (1996–2002)

Cohort/Career background	Total incoming members 1993–1995 cohort	Cabinet composition	
		Early 1996 cohort	Early 2002 cohort
Total pre-1993 cohort		23	17
Total 1993–1995 cohort	**16**	**15**	**9**
Technocrat	5	4	3
Military	2	2	0
High-ranking political official	5	5	2
Former vice minister	4	4	4
Total cabinet in early 1996		38	
Total 1996–2002 cohort			10
Technocrat			1
Military			2
High-ranking political official			4
Former vice minister			3
Total cabinet in early 2002			36

Source: Europa World Year Book. Various Years. London: Europa Publications Limited.

It is clear that during the peak of economic reform (1993–1995), Castro did not hand over the cabinet entirely to newcomers. Early in 1996 the cabinet still remained under the control of the pre-1993 cohort, with 23 of 38 seats (see table 4.1). Nevertheless, the space provided to newcomers was not minuscule—15 seats, including crucial positions such as foreign relations and economy and planning.

Is it possible to assume that the balance between the pre-1993 and 1993–1995 cohorts represents an estimate of the balance between the *duros* and reformers? Answering this requires conducting interviews and examining the policy positions of each cabinet member, which is impossible to do in Cuba. One must rely instead on less direct methods of inference.

For the pre-1993 cohort, it is easy to infer that most members in office in early 1993 were *duros.* The reason is that most of them were survivors of the Ochoa affair of mid-1989 and, further, implemented the Rectification. The Ochoa affair was the most virulent crackdown against reformers—or *gorbachevistas*—that is, sympathizers of Gorbachev's model of simultaneously opening the economy (perestroika) and politics (glasnost).[27] The government executed four high-ranking military officers, sentenced almost two dozen government officials to prison (including two former ministers), and fired or demoted many more. The fact that the pre-1993 cohort stayed in the cabinet throughout Rectification suggests that they must have felt quite comfortable with hard-line economic policies or, at the very least, were "closeted" reformers.[28]

For the 1993–1995 cohort, on the other hand, such inferences are more complicated. On the one hand, a theoretical reason exists to expect this group to be more in favor of reform: the policy orientation of hired ministers often reflects the policy direction of the period of recruitment, and 1993–1995 is the period of greatest market opening.[29] Yet, to suggest that the 1993–1995 cohort was entirely composed of reformers is a stretch. Castro might have recruited conservatives to oversee the newcomers.[30]

What is nonetheless feasible is to examine the profile of hired ministers and make some observations about the hiring preferences of the national executive. In filling cabinet posts during economic crises, governments juggle two objectives—maximizing technocratic competence and political loyalty.[31] Governments need to recruit technically competent individuals capable of confronting the economic challenges and implementing complex policy changes, but they also need individuals who are committed to the political survival of the government.

To satisfy this dual requirement of technocratic competence and loyalty, two combinations have been impossible in Cuba. One is the combination of a candidate scoring high on both technocratic expertise and loyalty. This is an impossible fantasy since finding such a person is improbable . The other impossible combination is a candidate who is neither technocratic nor loyal. No government would hire such a candidate. The only possible choices are the following:

Technocrats. These are highly trained individuals with experience in international, business, financial, or nonpolitically oriented circles. Most Latin American reforming governments in the late 1980s and early 1990s recruited cabinet members from this pool. This option was also available in Cuba, given the rise of semi-independent researchers who had studied in or traveled to reform-oriented countries such as the Soviet Union, China, Western Europe, and Latin America in the late 1980s.[32] For the Executive, the advantage of recruiting technocrats was injecting technical competence, more international respect, and new ideas into the cabinet; the risk was incorporating individuals of unproven loyalty to the Cuban Revolution.

Vice ministers. Another way to inject technical expertise is to appoint individuals who occupy second-rank positions in ministries (such as vice ministers). Because vice ministers are often in charge of the operational functions of ministries, they acquire technical expertise. The advantage of recruiting this group is more proven loyalty than group one, but at the cost of fresh ideas since vice ministers often represent policy continuity rather than new thinking.

Military officials. Instead of relying on civilian technocrats or vice ministers, whose loyalties are untested, the government could recruit from the military, whose loyalty (especially after the Ochoa affair) was assured. The military is often a close proxy of technocrats, given its experience running large-scale operations, traveling abroad, and acting as a laboratory of policy innovation.[33] Recruiting from this group would allow the government to incorporate technical competence without sacrificing as much loyalty as would be the case with technocrats.

High-ranking political officials. These are individuals who had a distinguished career in the revolutionary struggles of the 1950s and 1960s; held some high level office at a national level political organ (e.g., member of the Political Bureau [Buró Político, BP] of the Cuban Communist Party [Partido Comunista de Cuba, PCC], the National Assembly [Asamblea Nacional del Poder Popular de la República de Cuba, ANPP], or the labor confederation, the Confederation of Cuban Workers [Confederación de Trabajadores de Cuba, CTC]); or had a close relationship with the president (like the special adviser to Fidel Castro). Recruiting from this group allows the government to maximize loyalty at the expense of technocratic competence.

What choices did Fidel Castro make in 1993–1995? A review of the background of the 16 members of the 1993–1995 cohort shows that Castro opted to balance risk (see table 4.1).[34] On the one hand, he chose technical expertise (five technocrats).[35] On the other hand, he balanced this choice by also appointing from the three other pools (four vice ministers,[36] two military officers,[37] and five high-ranking officials).[38] Each of these groups allowed Castro to incorporate higher degrees of loyalty.

The 1993–1995 cohort thus incorporated a new breed—albeit a small one. Only a small group within this cohort represented a true break from the past—the five technocrats. They were not the independent, neoliberal, internationally connected "technopols" typical of Latin American ministries of the early 1990s. However, they represented new blood that was less tied to the political status quo. Together with the few closeted reformers who might have existed in the pre-1993 cohort, one could speak of the emergence of a less orthodox group. This was not a faction, defined as a group of likeminded minorities helping each other politically to advance their ideas against majorities. Factions have not existed in the Cuban cabinet since the 1960s. But it is enough evidence of diversity to suggest that the cabinet was more pluralistic in early 1996 than in early 1993. However, it is also evident that the newcomers were not majoritarian—neither within their cohort nor within the cabinet. They had to share political spaces with the old-timers and *duros*.

The limited pluralism of 1996 was short-lived. Ultimately, Castro sided with the *duros*. I reach this conclusion based on the following reasons: A government that is siding with hard-liners tends, first, to reform cautiously (rather than sweepingly), creating "power reserves" for the hard-liners, defined as domains of policy that remain under control of the hard-liners and, second, to discontinue the reforms as soon as the economy recovers. Cuba's post-1993 economic reforms confirm both hypotheses.

Power Reserves for Hard-Liners: Opening and Restricting in 1993–1995

The pattern of economic liberalization that Cuba started in 1993 conforms to the power reserve hypothesis. In broad strokes, there are two ways to introduce economic reforms. One is to pursue all-out reform (shock therapy). The other is to introduce the least amount of reform possible (gradual reform). In the late 1980s and early 1990s, most Latin American administrations in deep economic crises chose the first strategy. Cuba in 1993 chose the latter. The government liberalized selectively, and in every liberalized sector, it introduced substantial restrictions.

In agriculture, for instance, the state permitted transforming state farms into cooperatives—the Basic Units of Cooperative Production (Unidades Básicas de Producción Cooperativa [UBPC]) in September 1993, and the emergence of farmers' markets in October 1994. But, UBPCs were denied autonomy. The state determines production plans, sets the price of products, and monopolizes the distribution of goods and inputs such as fertilizers, fuels, pesticides, and equipment.[39] The state also approves which farmers can form or join a cooperative.

In the external sector, the state allowed up to 100 percent foreign ownership of local businesses in September 1995. However, of the 368 entities with foreign capital in 2000,[40] only 1 is believed to be 100 percent foreign-owned. The rest are joint ventures with the state, suggesting that the state is forcing its way into these businesses. In hiring workers, joint ventures must hire from a list of candidates provided by the state. Joint ventures are required to pay all wages to the state (in dollars) rather than directly to workers, and the state then pays the workers in undervalued pesos, thereby realizing a huge profit. This violates the International Labour Organization (ILO) convention banning the confiscation of wages and the interference of labor's right to choose employment.[41]

In exchange rate policy, the government depenalized dollar holding, derogating Article 140 of the Penal Code in July 1993. And yet, to capture these dollars, the government opened approximately 275 shops where dollar holders can buy goods and pay a sales tax of 140 percent on most products.[42] The state holds a monopoly over all dollar-transacted retail trade, estimated at 73.6 percent of GDP.[43]

In microeconomics, the state allowed self-employment with Decree 141 of September 1993. But from the start, the self-employed were banned from hiring labor and operating in many sectors, essentially killing the possibility of expansion. *Paladares* (private restaurants) are required to do most wholesale business with the state: inputs (including many foods) have to be acquired from state stores, where prices are 20 to 40 percent higher.[44] Already in

January 1994, the Cuban government began to crack down on the self-employed with the order to close hundreds of *paladares*.[45] Fines can be as high as 1,000 pesos for each chair over the limit.[46] In 1995, a draft law to allow Cubans to own and operate private businesses, which was strongly endorsed by the Spanish government, was shelved.

In telecommunications, the government created a special Ministry of Computing and Communications (Decree Law 204), to promote the "massive use of services and products related to information technology, communications, and computing."[47] Yet, electronic mail access is only permitted in the workplace; users typically share a single account; Internet cafes or connections in public libraries are restricted; and no Internet service providers exist. Only nongovernmental organizations (NGOs) that are neutral or loyal to the regime are allowed access.[48] Resolution 383/2001 prohibits the sale of computers, printing equipment, photocopiers, or any other means of mass printing to any Cuban association or citizen without a permit granted by the Ministry of Foreign Trade. Cuba thus has one of the lowest levels of Internet connectivity in the Americas.[49]

Finally, in the area of human and capital flows, the state liberalized remittances (including allowing Cubans to open checking accounts in dollars) and facilitated trips by Cuban exiles. Remittances benefited 60 percent of the population by 2000.[50] However, Cuba has the highest restrictions on and transfer cost for remittances among 11 Central American and Caribbean countries.[51] The average transference cost in Cuba was $28 for every $250 sent, whereas in Ecuador, which receives a comparable amount of remittances, the transfer cost was $19.50 in 2001. Remittances can be cashed in government-owned or joint venture channels only. Remittances are taxed through an over appreciated exchange rate of one to one, through value-added taxes on final sales, or through taxes on interest earned by bank deposits.[52] In the area of migration, Cuba is one of the few countries in the world requiring exit visas—eligible to politically safe citizens for a fee of approximately $300.

In short, the restrictions in each of Cuba's presumably "most liberalized" sectors are weighty. Cruz and Seleny label them "segmented marketization."[53] I propose instead stealth statism. Behind the pretense of market reforms, the Cuban government ended up magnifying the power of the state to decide who can benefit from market activities and by how much. The point of this opening-and-restricting style of economic reform was twofold. First, it served as a fooling devise. The government managed to create the illusion in 1993–1995 that Cuba was indeed committed to market-oriented change. This was necessary to alleviate the mounting pressure for change at home and abroad. Political economists agree that economic policy can often be used by governments to issue signals. Governments can announce audacious policies ("overshooting") for no reason other than to compel skeptics to take the government seriously, as many Latin American presidents did in the early 1990s. Reform demanders were skeptical of Castro's intentions. Castro needed to change those expectations. Hence, it was necessary to take bold steps or at least appear to be doing so. In reality, behind every reform, there was a provision expanding the restrictive capacity of the state.

The second objective was to reward the *duros* within the government.[54] The restrictions reassured the *duros* that the reforms would not go too far. More crucially, it gave the *duros* a privileged new role: gatekeepers to the new economy. They became the principal beneficiaries of the economic gains of the reforms and the sole arbiters of access to these gains.

Once Out of the Woods . . .

Another indicator that the Executive favored the *duros* was the sluggish pace of reform after recovery. A true reform-minded administration, in which reforming technocrats have the upper hand, tries to broaden and deepen the reforms after recovery. Technocrats argue that the reforms are working and, thus, push for more. In contrast, an Executive committed to pleasing the hard-liners does the opposite, decelerating and maybe even discontinuing the reforms.

This is what happened in Cuba. Between 1995 and 2000, the Cuban economy recovered, as GDP per capita increased at an average annual rate of 3.4 percent. While not enough to offset the decline of the early 1990s (in 2001, Cuba's GDP was still 20 percent below the 1989 level), the recovery did soften political pressures on the government. The government responded by slowing down and reversing reforms and has not since considered seriously pursuing the other reform projects such as legalizing private property, liberalizing the labor market, and privatizing SOEs.[55] The policy reversal began in January 1996, precisely when Cuba was enjoying its best economic performance in some time. One of the hard-liners in the Central Committee (Comité Central [CC]) declared that the party cadre "must form an ideological trench . . . from which the Marxist ideology . . . can be defended and from which diversionist ideology can be countered."[56] In March 1996, Raúl Castro delivered his famous antireform speech to the BP, in which he lambasted the reforms and the reformers within and outside the party.[57] The government then launched attacks against the intellectual community and political dissidents.[58] By 2000, the pace of approved foreign joint ventures slowed down considerably with the increase in *trabas*, or bureaucratic obstacles, for new approvals.[59] Vice President Carlos Lage also criticized the foreign trade zones, and the government began to privilege SOEs over foreign corporations in the granting of contracts and shifted attention to apparent distractions (such as vague processes of reforming SOEs or *perfeccionamiento empresarial*),[60] and more disturbingly, increasing restrictions on self-employment.

We now know that the reforming administrations' proclivity for losing interest in reform in Latin America is not uncommon. Weyland borrows from prospect theory to explain this phenomenon, arguing that actors become risk takers if they find themselves in the "domain of losses," and risk-averse, in the "domain of gains."[61] This theory predicts that state leaders will initiate risky reforms if they face an intense economic crisis (the "domain of losses") but will avoid risky reforms once the economic crisis ends (as when they enter the "domain of gains"). In Cuba, the slowdown of reforms coincided with the country's economic recovery between 1995 and 2000.

Yet, the slowdown of reform was more complicated than simply losing an appetite for risk. In fact, the government's propensity toward risk did not disappear at all, evidenced by its decision to punish reform winners (with penalties on the self-employed, heavy taxation of *paladares*, increased restrictions on FDI, and open criticisms of major trading partners, such as Mexico and Spain). Few reformers in Latin America and Eastern Europe have had an open policy of penalizing reform winners, even after losing interest in reforms. If anything, the tendency has been to overprotect the winners, in part because turning against winners is politically risky.[62] In Cuba, however, the state has had no qualms about this, and the only winners who it has sought to protect are the *duros.*

The Victory of the Old Guard: The 2002 Cabinet

Little question remains that by the late 1990s the reform advocates had been politically weakened, not just in terms of the extent to which their policies were being watered down, rejected, or reversed, but also in terms of their presence in the cabinet. A look at retirements after 1996 shows the victory of the old guard. By early 2002, six of the 15 members of the 1993–1995 cohort in office in 1996 had exited the cabinet, a retirement rate of 40 percent. In contrast, eight of the 23 members of the pre-1993 cohort in office in 1996 had exited by 2002, a retirement rate of 34.8 percent. This is still an over count, since three of the pre-1993 cohort died in office, two of whom were replaced by old guards, thus the net retirement rate of the pre-1993 cohort drops to a low 15 percent. The net retirement rate (which excludes those who exited due to deaths and includes replacements by old-timers) is 3 of 20.

One would expect the retirement rate of the old guard—for reasons of age alone—to be significantly higher than the rate for other groups. In fact, the opposite occurred in Cuba. The pre-1993 cohort dominated the 2002 cabinet, holding seventeen positions, including three of the four vice presidencies (the 1993–1995 cohort held nine positions, and the 1996–2002 cohort held ten positions).

Furthermore, the 1996–2002 cohort shows a departure in the hiring preference that prevailed in 1993–1995, away from nonestablishment individuals (table 4.1). Only one technocrat was recruited, so that by 2002 there were only four technocrats left in the cabinet. Most cabinet members were political loyalists and establishment figures: seventeen from the pre-1993 cohort plus six high-ranking political officials, one military officer, and seven former vice ministers.

In sum, by the early 2000s, the Cuban regime returned to the homogeneous conservatism of the early 1990s, both in terms of policy and leadership. This is probably one reason why the return of economic hardship in 2001–2003 did not produce calls for market reforms within the government or that the political crackdown of 2003 did not produce cabinet resignations. The survival of old-timers and nonreformers in the Cuban cabinet is simply remarkable, as remarkable as the survival of the regime itself.

The New Gatekeeper State

The economic reforms of 1993–1995 transformed Cuba into a state capitalist economy. Latin America's political economists should recognize this term. State capitalism is the term used to describe many Latin American economies prior to the 1980s, in which the state achieved dominance by maintaining a mixed economy which it heavily dominated. Indeed, it was customary to speak of the "triple alliance" between the state, multinationals, and domestic capitalists that promoted, yet also distorted, development.[63] Cuba comes closer to this model today than at any other point since the early twentieth century with one important modification: there are no private domestic capitalists (and, by extension, middle sectors). Capitalism in Cuba consists of a double alliance between a nondemocratic state and multinationals.

That this alliance has magnified the power of the Cuban state becomes evident when one examines how the reforms have fragmented the economy. As many point out, the Cuban economy is fragmented into at least three sectors, in increasing order of profitability: the old statist sector, the informal sector, and the new joint state-external sector. The old statist sector is stagnant if not contracting (as is the case with the sugar industry). The informal sector is large, but as is typical of sectors where property rights are not specified, its growth is unlikely to yield widespread prosperity.[64] Finally, the joint state-external sector is truly thriving (particularly the tourism, nickel, and citrus production sectors).

The state is profiting from this fragmented economy in two ways. First, there is an economic gain as the statist economy is living off of the profits of the state-external sector.[65] The second gain is political and more important. The state has emerged as the gatekeeper of the thriving state-external sector. The state alone gets to decide which Cuban citizens can enter this sector, and access is reserved for core members of the winning coalition—the ruling party, the military, and collaborators. For instance, party leaders help decide who gets to participate in the nonstate sector (mixed enterprises, cooperatives, self-employed, among others), which in 2000 absorbed 22.5 percent of total workers, up from 8.2 percent in 1981.[66] The party is even more directly involved in staffing the external-state sector, the most lucrative of all.[67] Tourism alone supports 100,000 jobs in Cuba.[68] Only friends of the PCC get recommended for jobs in tourism and joint ventures. The state keeps all Cubans away from tourist facilities but rewards politically well-behaved Cubans with packages in these resorts. It does the same with communication services. For instance, the Cuban telephone company (Empresa de Telecomunicaciones de Cuba, SA [ETECSA]), a joint venture between the state and an Italian firm, has reiterated that only friends of the PCC and volunteers in Committees for the Defense of the Revolution

(Comités de la Defensa de la Revolución [CDR]) will receive access to telephone and Internet services.[69]

The other beneficiary of the reforms is the military, which manages tourist properties, participates in many joint ventures, and controls key cabinet positions connected to the external sector such as telecommunications. The Armed Forces Ministry, under the direction of Fidel Castro's brother Raúl, runs the Enterprises Administration Group (Grupo de Administráción de Empresas [GAESA]), a huge business conglomerate. GAESA is presided over by military officials close to Raúl: General Julio Casas (president) and Mayor Luis Alberto Rodriguez (general director), who is Raúl Castro's son-in-law. GAESA holds some of Cuba's most lucrative businesses such as Gaviota (which operates more than 30 hotels); Tecnotex, SA (which handles import needs of firms in the holding); Aerogaviota (a small tourist aviation company); Almest (which builds hotels for international tourism); Almacenes Universal (which controls several free trade zones); and Antex (which provides technical and engineering assistance abroad).[70]

Citizens who do not want to accept the low wages of state jobs and do not qualify for jobs in the external sector join the informal sector.[71] However, citizens cannot fully escape the power of the gatekeeper state even there. The government retains a monopoly over banks, exchange houses, and retail stores so that a percentage of every financial transaction in the informal economy ends up in the hands of the state.

Most important, the government holds citizens participating in the informal/illegal market hostage by acting as a selective enforcer. Most informal market activities are illegal. But as with prostitution, the state often allows those informal activities while reserving the right to enforce the law at any given moment and catching lawbreakers by surprise—what Aguirre calls the combination of "openness and rigidity" in a system of formal and informal controls.[72] Citizens operating in informal markets can never dismiss the possibility of a crackdown and, thus, live in constant anxiety. The state uses its own resources to bribe authorities, including members of the CDRs, to look the other way. Either way, it dominates citizens by tolerating informal activities on the one hand, while simultaneously cracking down on them unpredictably.

Two Models of Self-Perpetuation: China and Cuba

Comparing Cuba with China in the 1990s illustrates two different ways in which authoritarian regimes seek self-perpetuation. All authoritarian regimes rely on force to stay in power.[73] This much is obvious. But beyond this, as argued above, authoritarian regimes must also offer other things of value to their winning coalitions. One model is to deliver spectacular economic growth, sometimes achieved by giving free rein to market forces, betting that the market will generate new economic winners. High economic growth allows authoritarian states to sustain themselves by enlarging the size of the winning coalition with two new types of supporters: market winners (citizens who gain economically from the reforms) and admirers (citizens who marvel at the regime's economic performance). As long as the state succeeds in co-opting many of the new winners, generating admirers, and protecting enough losers, it has a good chance of surviving.

An alternative model is to be complacent about weak economic growth altogether, or rather to keep economic growth circumscribed to small pockets of the economy. Here, the survival strategy of the state hinges not on expanding the size of the winning coalition but on keeping it small in relation to the limited economic gains available—economic scarcity is less perceptible when there are fewer mouths to feed. The trick is to always persuade the remaining members of the winning coalition that siding with the regime is economically more profitable (for them, though not necessarily for the country) than breaking with it. Under this model, introducing small-dose, restricted-access capitalism is rational. Not many actors win, but those who do are rewarded and become obsequious to, or tolerant of, the regime. Authoritarian regimes either provide economic growth (and offer hope that the winning coalition expands) or limit growth and keep the winning coalition small and thus satisfied with the little that is available.

China in the 1990s exemplifies the first model. In its effort to deliver spectacular economic growth, the Chinese state became the largest promoter of private sector wealth in the history of socialist countries. Private investment as a share of GDP increased from an insignificant 3.7 percent in 1980 to 17 percent in 1999, higher than Chile and one of the highest in the world (see table 4.2). By 2000, private firms generated 50 percent of China's GDP.[74] Although the Chinese government continues to impose limits on the private sector, it nonetheless continues to make room for the domestic private sector.[75] For example, in 1999 the Chinese congress amended its constitution to recognize the private sector, and in 2000, it enacted a law of sole proprietorship that protects the interests of investors and creditors.[76] In 2001, Chinese President Jiang Zemin called for the ruling party to accept nontraditional classes, including private businessmen,[77] and China joined the World Trade Organization (WTO), requiring that China improve property rights and ease restrictions on investment.[78] Simultaneously, the Chinese government continued to subsidize the inefficient state sector as a way to protect labor from market competition. The Chinese state is still prepared to repress those economic winners who express dissent.[79] But its main strategy of self-perpetuation consists of generating an even larger number of new winners, converting some of them into new allies and hoping that even the losers remain appreciative of state protection.

Cuba in the 1990s exemplifies the second model. Table 4.2 shows the effects of Cuba's policy of discouraging the private sector.[80] In 2000, private resource flows (the sum of FDI and remittances) that entered Cuba accounted for only 4.2 percent of GDP, one of the lowest in the world (equivalent to Malawi). If one excludes remittances, private resource flows decline to an insignificant 1.5 percent of GDP.[81] With these low levels of resources, economic growth will always be somewhat anemic, and pockets of wealth in the island will be limited. The gatekeeper state's only option is to keep the winning coalition as small as possible.

Table 4.2   Foreign Investment and Soldiers

Year	Private investment as % of GDP			Soldiers per 1,000 inhabitants		
	1980	1990	2000	1989	1999	Change
Postmilitary regimes						
Argentina	19.2	9.4	15.4	3	2	−0.33
Chile	11.2	18.4	16.4	7.4	5.9	−0.20
Post-anticapitalist regimes						
Nicaragua	n.a.[c]	11.2	19	18.7	2.5	−0.87
China	3.7	8.3	17.0[a]	3.5	1.9	−0.46
Vietnam	n.a.	n.a.	8.8[b]	19.2	6.2	−0.68
Cuba	n.a.	n.a.	4.2	28.5	4.5	−0.84

Notes

[a] 1999.

[b] Estimate.

[c] n.a. = not available.

Sources. For private investment in Argentina, Chile, Nicaragua and China see Stephen Everhart and Mariusz A. Sumlinski, "Trends in Private Investment in Developing Countries: Statistics for 1970–2000 and the Impact on Private Investment of Corruption and the Quality of Public Investment," IFC Discussion Paper No. 44 (Washington, DC: World Bank, 2001). For Vietnam, see Liesbert Steer, "The Private Sector in Vietnam," obtained from the International Finance Corporation (IFC), Washington, DC (mimeo), 2001, p. 25. For Cuba, see Ministerio de Hacienda, *Anuario Estadístico de Cuba* (Havana, Cuba: Ministerio de Hacienda, Dirección General de Estadística, 2001). Soldiers per 1,000 inhabitants taken from U.S. Arms Control and Disarmament Agency, *World Military Expenditures and Arms Transfers* (Washington, DC: U.S. Arms Control and Disarmament Agency, 1989), and *World Military Expenditures and Arms Transfers* (Washington, DC: U.S. Arms Control and Disarmament Agency, 2000).

Both models of self-perpetuation carry risks. The risk of the Chinese strategy is that there is no guarantee that the new economic winners will be loyal to, or feel awed by, the regime. Economic winners can turn antiauthoritarian (as happened in South Korea and Taiwan) and sometimes even anti-incumbent (as happened in Chile in the 1980s and in Mexico and Peru in the 1990s). The risk of the Cuban strategy is twofold. The first is the difficulty and trickiness of determining the right size of the winning coalition. Second, the policy of repressing independent means of earning a living, which is necessary for the state to act as the gatekeeper of profitable sectors, will upset many citizens.

Because of these risks, neither regime can be said to be in a stable equilibrium. However, the Cuban state seems to be managing these risks fairly well.[82] This becomes clear by looking at the requirements of the gatekeeper state and how the Cuban state has met them. I have argued that the gatekeeper state must meet three requirements to survive. First, it must capture most of the gains from capitalism. Second, it must keep the size of the winning coalition small enough. Third, it must retain a monopoly over the transfer of gains to the members of its winning coalition. The section on power reserves showed how effectively the Cuban state has met the first requirement. In what follows, I show how the Cuban state is meeting the other two requirements just as well.

Evidence on behalf of the second requirement is clearest at the level of the military. Table 4.2 shows that in comparison with two former nationalist military regimes in Latin America (Chile and Argentina) and three former anticapitalist regimes (China, Vietnam, and Nicaragua), the Cuban military has experienced a profound shrinkage in soldiers—a huge 84 percent drop. Many may attribute this to the decline in activism of Cuba's foreign policy. It is also a rational strategy to reduce the size of the winning coalition. In Latin America's new democracies, as well as in China and Vietnam, the state has reduced the size of the old winners (the military) and has welcomed new winners (market-based investors). In Cuba, however, the state has reduced the size of the old winners to a far greater degree without making room for new winners outside the traditional ancillary institutions of the state.

At the party level, evidence of shrinkage is more complicated. On the one hand, party membership seems to have increased by 232,457 between 1992 and 1996.[83] If true, this means that membership increased from 5.7 percent to approximately 7.1 percent of the population. This is impressive, but in itself is not evidence of an expansion of the winning coalition. An increase in party membership is relatively cheap for the state because it does not burden the state with significant additional costs, in contrast to membership in the military, which expands the payroll and adds pension and other costs.

Rather than party membership per se, the key indicator of the size of the winning coalition is the size of the party's leadership—the group that runs the gatekeeper state. Here, the evidence of shrinkage is irrefutable. In the early 1990s, Castro reorganized the CC of the PCC, eliminating many positions and introducing stricter criteria for the selection of leaders, which "facilitated rooting out reformers or contrarians."[84] Prior to the 1991 Fourth Party Congress, the number of CC departments was reduced from 19 to 9, and the staff was cut by 50 percent.[85] In 1997, the CC was purged from 225 to 150 members.[86]

Evidence also exists that the Cuban regime has become more intolerant of independent means of earning a living (the third requirement listed earlier). Government-imposed restrictions on the formal independent sector (self-employment) are well known.[87] In the early 2000s, the clampdown was extended to informal sectors, with two prominent targets: street vendors (*vendedores ambulantes*) and taxi-bike operators (*bicitaxis*).

The clampdown of taxi-bikes illustrates the political logic of the gatekeeper state. Taxi-bikes are Cuban rickshaws. They emerged following the government's decision to sell Chinese-made bikes at affordable prices to help the population cope with the transportation crisis of the early 1990s. Using old car parts and homemade canopies, many Cubans converted their bikes into tricycles for two passengers. Initially, taxi-bikes served residential areas. However, they have become a tourist attraction for many willing tourists who take them despite their slow speeds. From February 2001, the Cuban government has launched an attack against taxi-bike operators, frequently harassing and fining them. In February–March 2003, this campaign intensified in Havana, leading to the arrest of the director of the union of taxi-bikes.

The repression of the taxi-bike market shows not only the logic but also the precariousness of the Cuban model. The gatekeeper state is never free from stress. The first stress point is at the gate itself. Consider the options available to repressed taxi-bike operators. One option is to try to enter the tourist taxi sector, where the operator can earn an impressive $467 per month, significantly beating the average wage in the public sector of $6 per month.[88] If that fails, the taxi-bike operator could qualify for the more accessible job of tourist policeman, where he can earn $31 a month. But to get either job, the repressed taxi-bike operator must befriend, maybe even bribe, authorities at the party or CDRs. This illustrates, paradoxically, why repressing the taxi driver might not generate political subversion against the state and might but, on the contrary, generate citizen compliance with, and bribes to, the state. In either case, state officials win, earning either compliance or bribes. Because of the pressure to join profitable sectors, state officials know that the viability of the regime depends on maintaining the sturdiness of the gate and the selectivity of those who can go through it.

The second pressure point is the repression itself. The repression of self-employment opportunities has not received as much international condemnation as the repression of human rights activists, such as the arrest and quick sentencing of 78 dissidents and the execution of three hijacker-defectors in April 2003. It is nonetheless one of the most intrusive ways in which the Cuban state routinely controls citizens. Because markets become irrepressible once they achieve a certain size, the gatekeeper state must always act preemptively, disbanding them before they prosper. If the Cuban state continues to act preemptively against such markets, it may be successful in prolonging its life.

These two features of the gatekeeper state—preemptive repression and monopoly over access to capitalist rewards—help to account for the paradoxical nature of Cuban politics in the 1990s. They explain why membership in the PCC has risen in the very same country in which dissent, defections, and alienation are also rising.[89]

Conclusion: Limited Economic Reforms and Regime Transition

This chapter challenges several notions in the literature on Cuba as well as on market reforms and regime transition. Some authors suggest that Cuba's new political economy offers respite from the suffocating statism of the 1980s and that PCC control over society has somewhat softened. This chapter argues instead that the Cuban state and its ancillary organs, such as the party remain quite controlling.

The state has invented a new "racket" (to borrow from Tilly)[90] that works as follows: the state creates small market pockets—the few sectors open to FDI are transacted in dollars—in an island of economic poverty and stagnation. The state becomes the sole gatekeeper of such pockets, exclusively deciding who gains access to them. This new state is powerful in a different way than was the case under the pre-1993 command-economy model. Previously, only one economy existed—the state sector—and all nondissidents were guaranteed access to it. Because it was the "only pie" to be distributed among many, the value of each piece was significantly discounted. In the new economic model, however, the state distributes pieces from three different pies. The most valuable pie, the state-external economy, is distributed among the smallest portion of the population, namely, the winning coalition. The state is in a position to offer a more valuable reward to loyalists than before. It can also offer a more onerous punishment to dissidents in the form of exclusion from the most desirable pie. The predominant incentive for citizens is therefore to "leave the state peso economy."[91] One exit is Miami; another is to befriend or bribe a government official. This explains why Cubans today display a high incidence of both exit and opportunistic loyalty.

Another feature of the literature on Cuba is that there is some optimism that the economic reforms of the 1990s generated a constituency inside the government favorable to further liberalization. The argument is based on the idea that the "in" groups, after witnessing the benefits of the market, are now prepared to extend them. Instead, I argue that signs point in the opposite direction. The pressure for reform within the government might have been significant earlier, perhaps peaking in 1993–1995, but it has since subsided. Technocrats at the cabinet level have been displaced, and actors who are running and profiting from the gatekeeper state are not necessarily interested in expanding economic liberties. Instead, they have adopted the preference of ordinary cartel members, clamoring for more state protection against competitors and higher barriers to their arenas of wealth.

One can now begin to understand the two puzzles outlined in the introduction. The combination of risk taking and risk aversion in economic reform is explained by the split in preferences within and outside the winning coalition in the early 1990s. The survival of the regime is explained by the state's acquired capacity to distribute inducements and constraints by fragmenting the economy into different pieces of different value and monopolizing access to the most valuable piece.

A central conclusion of this chapter is that it makes no sense to think of Cuba as a market economy, just as it makes no sense to see it as a socialist economy. Cuba's new economic model is not a market-oriented model because there is no freedom of association, no property rights for citizens, and no price freedom—all indispensable for capitalism. It is not socialist either because the state is now the guarantor, in fact, the generator, of enormous inequalities: the state determines who has access to the thriving state-external sector; everyone else is either a loser or a mere survivor. The state is thus directly responsible for the rise of inequality in Cuba.[92]

That said, it is clear that Cuba did introduce a small dose of capitalism, and it is worth asking what impact has this has on the prospects for democratization. Market economies are usually considered a necessary though not sufficient precondition for democratic development.[93] However, while market openings can yield democratic gains, they can also be politically corrosive, allowing democratic gains to coexist with democratic setbacks. Market reforms may create a leaner and thus "meaner" state that either establishes a tyranny of technocratic, efficiency, and austerity values and practices[94] or overwhelms institutions of accountability.[95] Alternatively, market reforms may weaken civil society by aggrandizing the privileges of the already well-off and lessening the power of marginalized groups.[96]

In Cuba, the way in which market reforms have eroded democracy is different. First, Cuba's reforms were far more restrained, meaning that more room for the "meaner" state prevails in decisions about the allocation of resources, and thus, fewer spaces exist for autonomous societal groups to flourish. Second, despite their limited nature, reforms in Cuba generated serious societal inequalities, which are more politicized because they are determined by the state more than by market forces. Finally, reforms have virtually precluded the rise of institutions of accountability. In Latin America, market reforms may have undermined institutions of democratic accountability, but seldom did they cancel them out altogether. In Cuba, these institutions of accountability were nonexistent prior to the reforms, and their possible rise was thwarted because reforms in the 1990s empowered exclusively the one group that opposed them the most—the *duros*.

The Cuban case thus illustrates the complicated relationship between market reforms and democratization. The relationship is not linear. Instead, it resembles an inverted J-curve. During the early stages of reform, when a communist state launches market openings (as was the case in Cuba in 1993–1996), one can envision a moment of political liberalization in which democratization is possible: the move from a command-economy to a more mixed one creates more political opportunities for political change. But if economic reforms are aborted, the consequence is the rise of a gatekeeper state. The regime does not return to the same levels of totalitarian restrictions that existed at the outset, but it decidedly moves in a nondemocratic direction.

Authoritarian regimes face two options for survival. They either produce high levels of economic gains, which allow them to expand the size of the winning coalition, or they restrict economic gains, in which case, they must restrict the size of the winning coalition. Both options require restrictions on dissent. But in the latter, the state must be far more vigilant of civil society,[97] always ensuring the selectivity of the gate.

Introducing capitalism in small doses is like applying a small amount of bleach. If the bleach is applied in a concentrated form to one item of clothing, regardless of how small a portion, it will leave a stain. If the bleach is too diluted in water, there is no bleaching effect. In Cuba, capitalism has been introduced in small doses and unevenly—concentrated in some sectors; diluted in others. In the external-state sector, capitalism has been applied in concentrated form, transforming the beneficiaries into stained monopolists. Elsewhere in Cuban society, small-dose capitalism has been diluted with so much statism that it has had little effect in yielding a wealth-holding, entrepreneurial, middle-sector society. Insofar as the emergence of middle-sector status boosts the bargaining leverage of society vis-à-vis an authoritarian state, one must conclude that at least this form of democratic pressure is weak in Cuba.

It is no wonder that Fidel Castro reiterates, as vociferously as he does, that he will not give up socialism in Cuba. He is reaffirming a commitment to a system of state governance that, however unequal and unwieldy, is quite efficient in generating loyalty and rewards within a small winning coalition. It is also easy to understand why Fidel Castro is not alone among Cubans in displaying a preference for keeping things as they are. Few Cubans gain from it, but those who count politically for the regime gain a lot.

Notes

1. See, e.g., Darren Hawkins, "Democratization Theory and Non-Transitions: Insights from Cuba," *Comparative Politics*, 33 (4), July 2001: 441–461; Jaime Suchlicki, "Castro's Cuba: Continuity Instead of Change," in Susan Kaufman Purcell and David Rothkopf (eds.), *Cuba: The Contours of Change* (Boulder, CO: Lynne Rienner, 2000), pp. 57–79; Benigno Aguirre, "The Stability of Cuba's Political System," in Eloise Linger and John Coleman (eds.), *Cuban Transitions at the Millennium* (Largo, MD: International Development Options, 2000), pp. 273–278; Haroldo Alfonso Dilla, "Cuba: La reforma económica, la reestructuración social y la política," *Estudios Latinoamericanos: Nueva Época*, 4 (7), January–June 1997: 165–178; Carollee Bengelsdorf, *The Problem of Democracy in Cuba. Between Vision and Reality* (New York: Oxford University Press, 1994); Archibald R. M. Ritter, "Cuba's Economic Strategy and Alternative Futures," in Jorge F. Pérez-López (ed.), *Cuba at a Crossroads: Politics and Economics after the Fourth Party Congress* (Gainesville, FL: University Press of Florida, 1994), pp. 67–93; and Jorge I. Domínguez, "The Secrets of Castro's Staying Power," *Foreign Affairs*, 72 (2), Spring 1993: 97–107.
2. By 1999, the accumulated privatization revenues of the top 9 privatizing countries in Latin America amounted to 9.1 percent of GDP, among the highest in the world (based on Eduardo Lora, *Index of Economic Reforms in Latin America*, mimeo, Inter-American Development Bank, Washington, DC, 2001). Average private investment in Latin America increased from 13.6 to 16.5 percent of GDP between 1989 and 1998 (based on Stephen S. Everhart and Mariusz A. Sumlinski, "Trends in Private Investment in Developing Countries, 1970–2000," International Finance Corporation Discussion Paper 44, International Finance Corporation, Washington, DC, September 2001).
3. Claes Brundenius and John Weeks (eds.), *Globalization and Third World Socialism: Cuba and Vietnam* (New York: Palgrave Macmillan, 2001).
4. See Edward Gibson, "The Populist Road to Market Reform: Policy and Electoral Coalition in Mexico and Argentina," *World Politics*, 49 (3), April 1997: 339–370.
5. Karen L. Remmer, "Elections and Economics in Contemporary Latin America," in Carol Wise and Riordan Roett (eds.), *Post-Stabilization Politics in Latin America* (Washington, DC: Brookings Institution Press, 2003), pp. 31–55; Kurt Weyland, *The Politics of Market Reform in Fragile Democracies: Argentina, Brazil, Peru, and Venezuela* (Princeton, NJ: Princeton University Press, 2002); and Stephen Haggard and Robert Kaufman, *The Political Economy of Democratic Transitions* (Princeton, NJ: Princeton University Press, 1995).

6. Manuel Pastor Jr. and Carol Wise, "The Politics of Second Generation Reforms," *Journal of Democracy*, 10 (3), July 1999: 34–48.

7. See Milton Friedman (with Rose D. Friedman), *Capitalism and Freedom* (Chicago, IL: University of Chicago Press, 1962); Francis Fukuyama, "The End of History," *The National Interest*, 16, Summer 1989: 3–18; and John Williamson, "What Should the World Bank Think about the Washington Consensus," *World Bank Research Observer*, 15 (2), August 2000: 251–270.

8. Adam Przeworski et al., *Democracy and Development: Political Institutions and Well-Being in the World, 1950–1990* (New York: Cambridge University Press, 2000), p. 109.

9. Bruce Bueno de Mesquita et al., "Political Institutions, Political Survival, and Policy Success," in Bruce Bueno de Mesquita and Hilton L. Root (eds.), *Governing for Prosperity* (New Haven, CT: Yale University Press, 2000), pp. 59–84; and Barbara Geddes, "What Do We Know about Democratization after Twenty Years?" *Annual Review of Political Science*, 2, 1999: 115–144.

10. Haggard and Kaufman, *The Political Economy of Democratic Transitions*, p. 13.

11. Suchlicki, "Castro's Cuba."

12. De Mesquita et al., "Political Institutions, Political Survival, and Policy Success."

13. Adam Przeworski et al., *Democracy and the Market: Political and Economic Reforms in Eastern Europe and Latin America* (New York: Cambridge University Press, 1991); Haggard and Kaufman, *The Political Economy of Democratic Transitions;* and Javier Corrales, *Presidents without Parties: The Politics of Economic Reform in Argentina and Venezuela in the 1990s* (University Park, PA: Pennsylvania State University Press, 2002).

14. Guillermo O'Donnell and Philippe C. Schmitter, *Transitions from Authoritarian Rule: Tentative Conclusions about Uncertain Democracies* (Baltimore, MD: Johns Hopkins University Press, 1986).

15. See Geddes, "What Do We Know about Democratization after Twenty Years?"; and Haggard and Kaufman, *The Political Economy of Democratic Transitions*, pp. 11–13.

16. Dorothy J. Solinger, "Ending One-Party Dominance: Korea, Taiwan, Mexico," *Journal of Democracy*, 12 (1), January 2001: 30–42.

17. Julio Carranza Valdés, Luis Gutiérrez Urdaneta, and Pedro Monreal González, *Cuba: Restructuring the Economy: A Continuing Debate* (London: Institute of Latin American Studies of the University of London, 1996).

18. Andrew Zimbalist, "Whither the Cuban Economy?" in Purcell and Rothkopf (eds.), *Cuba*, pp. 13–29.

19. Comisión Económica para América Latina y el Caribe (CEPAL), *La economía cubana: Reformas estructurales y desempeño en los noventa* (Santiago: CEPAL, 2001).

20. *Cubanalysis*, n.d.

21. William M. LeoGrande, "The Cuban Communist Party and Electoral Politics: Adaptation, Succession, and Transition," *Cuban Transition Project, Institute for Cuban and Cuban-American Studies Mimeo* (Coral Gables, FL: University of Miami, 2002); and Wayne S. Smith, "Cuba's Long Reform," *Foreign Affairs*, 75 (2), March–April 1996: 99–112.

22. Marifeli Pérez-Stable, "Caught in a Contradiction: Cuban Socialism between Mobilization and Normalization," *Comparative Politics*, 32 (1), October 1999: 63–82.

23. Yi Feng et al., "Political Institutions, Economic Growth, and Democratic Evolution: The Pacific Asian Scenario," in de Mesquita and Root (eds.), *Governing for Prosperity*, p. 204

24. See Carmelo Mesa-Lago et al., *Market, Socialist, and Mixed Economies: Comparative Policy and Performance, Chile, Cuba and Costa Rica* (Baltimore, MD: Johns Hopkins University Press, 2000).

25. Although scholars initially argued that in 1991 the government began to liberalize economically, in retrospect, the decisions were rather hesitant. Other than the relegalization of family-based service work, nothing was done to ease the strictest restrictions of the "Rectification" period. Rectification was the name that the government gave its mid-1986 decision to close the economic openings of the 1970s such as farmers' markets and self-employment. In the words of Eusebio Mujal-León and Joshua Busby, Rectification was a return to totalitarianism after a period of "softer post-totalitarianism," making Cuba one of the least liberalized economies in the communist world. See Eusebio Mujal-León and Joshua W. Busby, "Much Ado about Something? Regime Change in Cuba," *Problems of Post-Communism*, 48 (6), November–December 2001: 6–18. See also Consuelo Cruz and Anna Seleny, "Reform and Counter-Reform: The Path to Market in Hungary and Cuba," *Comparative Politics*, 34 (2), January 2002: 211–231; "Learned, Healthy . . . and Skinny," *Cubanalysis*, 13, mimeo, n.d.; Carmelo Mesa-Lago, "Un ajiaco cubano-alemán sobre la tercera reforma agraria de Cuba," *Encuentro* (Madrid), 18, Fall 2000: 254–258; Susan Eva Eckstein, *Back from the Future: Cuba under Castro* (Princeton, NJ: Princeton University Press, 1994); Mesa-Lago et al., *Market, Socialist, and Mixed Economies;* Bengelsdorf, *The Problem of Democracy in Cuba;* Andrew Zimbalist, "Reforming Cuba's Economic System from Within," in Pérez-López (ed.), *Cuba at a Crossroads*, pp. 220–237. Even though officials recognized that Rectification proved to be ruinous (see, e.g., Marta Beatriz Roque Cabello and Manuel Sánchez Herrero, "Background: Cuba's Economic Reforms: An Overview," in Jorge F. Pérez-López and Matías F. Travieso-Díaz (eds.), *Perspectives on Cuban Economic Reforms* (Phoenix, AZ: Arizona State University Center for Latin American Studies 30, 1998, pp. 9–17)), this antimarket stand was reaffirmed in 1991. See Jorge I. Domínguez, "The Political Impact on Cuba of the Reform and Collapse of Communist Regimes," in Carmelo Mesa-Lago (ed.), *Cuba after the Cold War* (Pittsburgh, PA: University of Pittsburgh Dominguez, 1993), pp. 99–132; LeoGrande, "The Cuban Communist Party and Electoral Politics"; Pérez-López (ed.), *Cuba at a Crossroads;* and *Miami Herald*, September 28, 1992, p. 12A. The few economic changes approved were nothing more than policies already in place during Rectification: more austerity and price hikes; more foreign investment; and more joint ventures, mostly in tourism, which had been allowed since 1982. See Mesa-Lago et al., *Market, Socialist, and Mixed Economies*, p. 299; Mauricio Font, "Crisis and Reform in Cuba," in Miguel Ángel Centeno and Mauricio Font (eds.), *Towards a New Cuba?: Legacies of a Revolution* (Boulder, CO: Lynne Rienner, 1997), pp. 109–133; and Eckstein, *Back from the Future*, pp. 60–87. To weather the crisis, the only economic right that Cubans in Havana received was the freedom to raise their own pigs and grow their own home vegetable gardens ("victory gardens"). See Eckstein, *Back from the Future*, pp. 109–12.

26. All data on cabinet changes were drawn from *Europa World Year Book* (London: Europa Publications Limited, 1979–2003).

27. The government accused General Arnaldo Ochoa of leading a "macrofaction" involved in drug trafficking and other economic crimes. There is disagreement about whether Ochoa himself favored domestic reforms, but it is agreed that he challenged Castro's military policies in Angola. Ochoa was probably executed more for his potential as a coup plotter than for anything else. Yet, the government used the Ochoa excuse to purge the cabinet of *gorbachevistas*. See Josep M. Colomer, "Los militares 'duros' y la transición en Cuba," *Encuentro de la Cultura Cubana*, 26–27, Fall–Winter 2002–2003: 148–167; Frank O. Mora, "From Fidelismo to Raulismo: Civilian Control of the Military in Cuba," *Problems of Post-Communism*, 46 (2), March–April 1999: 25–38; Eckstein, *Back from the Future*; Juan M. del Águila, "The Party, the Fourth Congress, and the Process of Counter Reform," in Pérez-López (ed.), *Cuba at a Crossroads*, pp. 19–40; and Julia Preston, "The Trial that Shook Cuba," *New York Review*, December 7, 1989, pp. 24–31.

28. The last known official suspected of supporting some degree of glasnost for Cuba was Carlos Aldana, a high-ranking member of the Political Bureau of the Comunist Party (not a minister), but he too was expelled in September 1992 presumably for his proreform views. See Esther Vera and Josep M. Colomer, "El Nacional-Catolicismo de Fidel Castro," *Claves de Razón Práctica*, 81, 1998: 14–19; Jorge I. Dominguez, "The Political Impact on Cuba of the Reform and Collapse of Communist Regimes"; Howard W. French, "Castro Steers a Suffering Nation for Confrontation," *New York Times*, October 12, 1992, p. A3. For a skeptical view on Aldana's reform proclivities, see Juan M. del Águila, "The Party, the Fourth Congress, and the Process of Counter Reform."

29. Jorge L. Domínguez (ed.), *Technopols: Freeing Politics and Markets in Latin America in the 1990s* (University Park, PA: Pennsylvania State University Press, 1997).

30. One hypothesis is that these cabinet changes constituted a mere technical downgrading, an effort to replace competent people with younger, easier to manipulate "yes-men." See the declarations by Cuban defector Alcibiades Hidalgo, former adviser to Raúl Castro in *El Nuevo Herald*, July 28 and 30, 2002.

31. See Barbara Geddes, *Politician's Dilemma: Building State Capacity in Latin America* (Berkeley, CA: University of California Press, 1994).

32. Domingo Amuchastegui, "Las FAR: Del poder absoluto al control de las reformas," *Encuentro de la Cultura Cubana*, 26–27, 2002–2003: 133–147.

33. Juan Carlos Espinosa, "Vanguard of the State: The Cuban Armed Forces in Transition," *Problems of Post-Communism*, 48 (6), November/December 2001: 19.

34. Classified ministers according to their professional position prior to being appointed, based on data provided by the international press and Granma, the official organ of the Cuban Communist Party. There was no background information for the pre-1993 cohort.

35. Juan M. Junco del Pino, Osvaldo Martínez, Jose Luis Rodríguez, Francisco Soberón, and Carlos Dotres.

36. Barbara Castillo, Ibrahim Ferradaz, Jose Manuel Millares, and Jesús Pérez.

37. Silvano Colas Sánchez and Orlando Rodriguez Romay.

38. Alfredo Jordan, Wilfredo Lopez, Roberto Robaina, Nelson Torres, and Salvador Valdéz.

39. Mesa-Lago, "Un ajiaco," p. 256.
40. CEPAL, *La economía cubana*.
41. Matías F. Travieso-Díaz and Charles P. Trumbull, "Foreign Investment in Cuba: Prospects and Perils," mimeo, 2002.
42. Archibald R. M. Ritter and Nicholas Rowe, "Cuba: From 'Dollarization' to 'Euroization' or Peso Reconsolidation?" *Latin American Politics and Society*, 44 (2), Summer 2002: 99–124; and Zimbalist, "Whither the Cuban Economy?" p. 18.
43. Ritter and Rowe, "Cuba: From 'Dollarization' to 'Euroization' or Peso Reconsolidation?" p. 107.
44. *Miami Herald*, March 27, 1997.
45. *Miami Herald*, January 29, 1994.
46. *Miami Herald*, March 27, 1997.
47. See http://www.cubagob.cu. Accessed September 2003 (and again January 8, 2007).
48. Taylor C. Boas, "The Dictator's Dilemma: The Internet and U.S. Policy toward Cuba," *Washington Quarterly*, 23 (3), 2000: 62–63.
49. Javier Corrales, "Lessons from Latin America," in Leslie Simon, Javier Corrales, and Don Wolfenson (eds.), *Democracy and the Internet* (Washington, DC: Woodrow Wilson Center Press, 2002), pp. 30–66.
50. Mesa-Lago et al., *Market, Socialist, and Mixed Economies*, pp. 7–8.
51. Manuel Orozco, "Globalization and Migration: The Impact of Family Remittances in Latin America," *Latin American Politics and Society*, 44 (2), Summer 2002: 41–65.
52. Lorena Barberia, "Remittances to Cuba: An Evaluation of Cuban and U.S. Government Policy Measures," Working Paper 15, September 2002, at http://web.mit.edu/cis/www/ migration/pubs/rrwp/15_remittances.pdf. Accessed September 2003 (and again January 8, 2007).
53. Cruz and Seleny, "Reform and Counter-Reform."
54. Manuel Pastor Jr., "After the Deluge? Cuba's Potential as a Market Economy," in Purcell and Rothkopf (eds.), *Cuba*, pp. 31–55.
55. See Jorge F. Pérez-López, "Waiting for Godot: Cuba's Stalled Reforms and the Continuing Economic Crisis," *Problems of Post Communism*, 48 (6), November/December 2001: 43–55.
56. *Miami Herald*, January 16, 1996.
57. See also Pérez-López, "Waiting for Godot," p. 51.
58. *Miami Herald*, May 2, 1996.
59. Travieso-Díaz and Trumbull, "Foreign Investment in Cuba"; *Economist*, July 4, 2002.
60. The goal of *perfeccionamiento empresarial* is to make SOEs less reliant on direct subsidies and more sensitive to price signals by making them more autonomous. See *Economist Intelligence Unit*, February 2001. Over 1,100 of 3,000 SOEs were targeted for reform; as of 2001, only 88 SOEs had completed the process.
61. Weyland, *The Politics of Market Reform in Fragile Democracies*.
62. Joel Hellman, "Winners Take All," *World Politics*, 50 (2), January 1998: 203–234; and Hector Schamis, "Distributional Coalitions and the Politics of Economic Reform in Latin America," *World Politics*, 51 (2), January 1999: 236–268.

63. Peter Evans, *Dependent Development: The Alliance of Multinational, State and Local Capital in Brazil* (Princeton, NJ: Princeton University Press, 1979).

64. Mancur Olson, *Power and Prosperity: Outgrowing Communist and Capitalist Dictatorships* (New York: Basic Books, 2000), pp. 173–199.

65. Ana Julia Jatar-Hausmann, *The Cuban Way* (West Hartford, CT: Kumarian Press, 1999); and Purcell and Rothkopf, *Cuba.*

66. *Economist Intelligence Unit,* November 2001.

67. See the declaration by Marcos Portal, Minister of Basic Industry, Associated Press, September 6, 1995.

68. Miguel Alejandro Figueras, "Cuba's Tourism Sector," Seminar at Smith College, Northampton, MA, September 10, 2001.

69. Directorio Democrático Cubano, *Informe parcial de violaciones a los derechos humanos en Cuba, Febrero 2001–Febrero 2002,* at http://www.procubalibre. org.ar. Accessed September 2003 (and again January 8, 2007).

70. Victor Afanasiev, "Fuerzas armadas y política revolucionaria: El caso de Cuba de 1959 a los años 90," in Lilian Bobea (ed.), *Soldados y ciudadanos en el Caribe* (Santo Domingo: FLACSO, 2002), pp. 207–254; and G. Fernández and M. A. Menéndez, "The Economic Power of the Castro Brothers," *Diario 16,* June 24, 2001, at http://www.cubacenter.org/media. Accessed September 2003 (and again January 8, 2007) and at http://www.autentico.org/oa09602.php. Accessed January 8, 2007. See also Espinosa, "Vanguard of the State."

71. The difference in income across different types of economies is immense. The ratio between the average wage in the traditional and other economies can be up to 70 times, compared to a ratio of only 5 to 1 between highest- and lowest-paid workers at the end of the 1980s. See Rikke Fabienke, "Labor Markets and Income Distribution during Crisis and Reform," in Brundenius and Weeks (eds.), *Globalization and Third World Socialism,* p. 125.

72. Benigno Aguirre, "Social Control in Cuba," *Latin American Politics and Society,* 44 (2), Summer 2002: 67–98.

73. Przeworski et al., *Democracy and Development,* p. 271.

74. Asian Development Bank, *Country Economic Review: People's Republic of China,* mimeo, Asian Development Bank, August 2002; and Asian Development Bank, *Asian Development Outlook* (Oxford: Oxford University Press, 2003).

75. Yasheng Huang, *Selling China: Foreign Direct Investment during the Reform Era* (New York: Cambridge University Press, 2003).

76. Ibid.

77. STRATFOR, "Calls for Widening Base Portend Struggle for Future of Chinese Communist Party," July 5, 2001, at http://www.stratfor.org. Accessed September 2003 (and again January 8, 2007).

78. Asian Development Bank, *Country Economic Review.*

79. In June 2003, for instance, the state penalized the Dawu Group, one of China's largest private companies, by confiscating assets, freezing its bank accounts, and arresting its wealthy founder Sun Dawu for publicly opposing Beijing's policies. STRATFOR, "China's Rich Try to Rival Communist Party's Power?" June 6, 2003, at http://www.stratfor.org. Accessed September 2003 (and again January 8, 2007).

80. Scholars debate the reasons for unimpressive and declining levels of FDI in Cuba, some blaming it on the U.S. embargo. See, e.g., Paolo Spadoni, "The

Impact of the Helms-Burton Legislation on Foreign Investment in Cuba," paper presented at the XI Annual Conference of the Association for the Study of the Cuban Economy, Coral Gables, FL, August 2–4, 2001. For others on the internal embargo or the restrictions on doing business in Cuba, see, e.g., Gary M. Shiffman, "Castro's Choices: The Economics of Economic Sanctions," paper presented at the XII Annual Conference of the Association for the Study of the Cuban Economy, Coral Gables, FL, August 1–3, 2002; and Travieso-Díaz and Trumbull, "Foreign Investment in Cuba"; Maria C. Werlau, "Foreign Investment in Cuba: The Limits of Commercial Engagement," *World Affairs*, 160 (2), Fall 1997: 51–69.

81. This figure is small in comparison to China. FDI in China amounted to 4.1 percent of GDP in 2000. See Organisation for Economic Cooperation and Development, *China in the World Economy: The Domestic Policy Challenges* (Paris: OECD Synthesis Report, 2002).

82. For an assessment of how the Chinese regime is handling its risks, see An Chen, "Capitalist Development, Entrepreneurial Class and Democratization in China," *Political Science Quarterly*, 117 (3), Fall 2002: 401–422; and Mary E. Gallagher, "Reform and Openness: Why China's Economic Reforms Have Delayed Democracy," *World Politics*, 54 (3), April 2002: 338–372.

83. See http://www.pcc.cu/construc.htm. Accessed September 2003 (and again January 8, 2007).

84. del Águila, "The Party, the Fourth Congress, and the Process of Counter Reform," p. 29.

85. LeoGrande, "The Cuban Communist Party and Electoral Politics."

86. Inter Press Service, October 13, 1997.

87. See Jatar-Hausmann, *The Cuban Way;* Ted Henken, "Condemned to Informality: Cuba's Experiments with Self-Employment During the Special Period (The Case of the Bed and Breakfasts)," in Lisandro Pérez, *Cuban Studies* 33 (Pittsburgh, PA: University of Pittsburgh Press, 2002); and Ted Henken, " 'Vale Todo' (Anything Goes): Cuba's Paladares," paper presented at the XII Annual Meeting of the Association for the Study of the Cuban Economy, Coral Gables, FL, August 1–3, 2002.

88. These figures were taken from Mesa-Lago et al., *Market, Socialist, and Mixed Economies*, p. 3.

89. Damián Fernández, *Cuba and the Politics of Passion* (Austin, TX: University of Texas Press, 2000).

90. Charles Tilly, "War-Making and State-Making as Organized Crime," in Peter B. Evans, Dietrich Rueschemeyer, and Theda Skocpol (eds.), *Bringing the State Back In* (New York: Cambridge University Press, 1985), pp. 169–191.

91. Ritter and Rowe, "Cuba: From 'Dollarization' to 'Euroization' or Peso Reconsolidation?" p. 109.

92. Some estimates contend that the Gini coefficient, an indicator of income inequality that ranges from 0 to 1, skyrocketed from 0.22 in 1986 to 0.55 in 1995, similar to pre-1959 levels. Fabienke, "Labor Markets and Income Distribution during Crisis and Reform," pp. 102–129; and Carmelo Mesa-Lago, "Testing the Assumptions Concerning the Effects of German Pension Reform Based on Latin American and Eastern European Outcomes," *European Journal of Social Security*, 4, 2002: 285–330.

93. Friedman (with Friedman), *Capitalism and Freedom*.

94. See Miguel Ángel Centeno and Patricio Silva (eds.), *The Politics of Expertise in Latin America* (New York: St. Martin's, 1998).

95. An example is Guillermo O'Donnell, "Delegative Democracy," *Journal of Democracy*, 5 (1), January 1994: 55–69.

96. Philip Oxhorn and Graciela Ducatenzeiler, "The Problematic Relationship between Economic and Political Liberalization: Some Theoretical Considerations," in Philip Oxhorn and Pamela K. Starr (eds.), *Markets and Democracy in Latin America: Conflict or Convergence?* (Boulder, CO: Lynne Rienner, 1999), pp. 13–41.

97. Haroldo Alfonso Dilla and Philip Oxhorn, "The Virtues and Misfortunes of Civil Society in Cuba," *Latin American Perspectives*, 124 (4), July 2002: 11–30.

Chapter 5

Cuba: Consensus in Retreat

Haroldo Alfonso Dilla

Introduction

Even at its most decadent, the Cuban Revolution continues to captivate global attention. The revolution turned the page on the radical anticapitalist projects that once won the minds and hearts of millions of people and in the name of Marxism and socialism, achieved the social justice, national independence, and economic development that peripheral capitalism failed to produce. But the revolution failed to construct a viable alternative to the capitalist order and has become an isolated dissident within the global capitalist system. Moreover, it has failed politically: Marxism plays the role of ideological legitimization, but endogenous authoritarian forms have prevailed.

So the kind of transition that can be discussed in the case of Cuba is not fundamentally one toward democracy but rather toward some form of peripheral capitalism. This process is already underway and is perfectly compatible with many of the authoritarian habits of the Cuban political regime. The global capitalist system requires that Cuba establish clear rules for market competition and an adequate context for the "probability calculus" that Weber deemed vital for functioning mercantilism to flourish. The United States is a key player in all this, and its geopolitical ambitions demand that any new system in Cuba should entail an organic alignment with Washington, and the kind of government that can prevent undesirable situations such as uncontrolled surges in immigration flows, or operative freedom for drug traffickers.

This chapter focuses on the Cuban transition debate, notably the details of a possible transition to a liberal regime, the potential actors involved, and the pacts they may establish. Institutionalizing a liberal system of rules may result in democracy and a positive climate for political and civil liberties, but such a regime would function imperfectly and be far from ideal. More importantly, it will likely reverse many of the Cuban Revolution's social victories and eliminate "inconvenient" arenas for participation that exist in Cuba today. And democracy would remain a variable dependent on the demands of capitalist accumulation.

All of this may sound obvious, but it is important to understand the systemic, constitutive factors of the Cuban social revolutionary pact and Cuban public consensus and the extent to which will shape initial conditions of a transition. As Terry Karl and Philippe Schmitter say, it is necessary to observe "structural contingencies" in processes of political change.[1] Thus, to recognize the actors at stake, their capacity for action, and the complexity of the goals they may pursue, it is necessary to understand the underlying social context.

There is no agreement regarding the state of political consensus on the island. The exiled intellectual community tends to describe a disenchanted, cynical, and fearful populace that still swears loyalty to the system and upholds the supposed "immutability" of the regime. However, while the effects of regime repression have clearly had a very powerful dissuasive impact on potential opposition and protest, repression cannot explain the fact that Cubans participate on a massive scale in the cacophonous marches and countermarches organized by the Cuban government and in Cuba's singular electoral processes, despite a process of growing impoverishment. These descriptions are therefore an example of wishful thinking rather than accurate descriptions of reality. Equally deceptive are the analyses proffered by Cuba's official intellectuals, who posit a situation of monolithic unified support for Fatherland, Revolution, and Socialism. Understanding the reality is crucial: Cuba's future path will depend on the how the revolutionary social contract and social consensus evolve and interact—in some ways, these two variables and their interrelationship can be said to define the political history of the country of the past four decades.

From Founding Pact to Subsidized Consensus

The Cuban Revolution was based on a founding social pact between the revolutionary political class and popular sectors that was founded upon a project of social justice, national autonomy, development, and democracy. But it was an asymmetrical pact forged under conditions that were particularly favorable to the ruling class. Cuban society suffered a radical transformation with the elimination of its bourgeoisie and a significant part of its middle classes as domestic political actors. The homogeneity that emerged as a result of this elimination allowed the state to define "the people" in a very restricted way: they were the classes and social sectors that had least benefited from the capitalist system. The people once played a central role in various struggles for social, political, and national rights, but they were limited by low standards of education and a clientilistic political tradition. Thus, popular organizations such as the labor unions and agricultural associations were used to support the institutions of the revolution, and they gradually became merely the famed "transmission belts" of Leninist party politics.

The aggressive counterrevolutionary stance of the United States and Cuban émigré groups were essential catalysts: the growing radicalism of social and political transformation policies—especially notable in 1960–1968— was legitimated by the argument that it was necessary to defend national sovereignty, a central feature of the revolutionary project and in popular cultural politics.

Like any other foundational project, Cuba fused radically different categories—nation, revolution, the people, socialism—and subsumed individual differences in an idealized vision of the collective. More importantly, it was a project based on a pre-Athenian notion of politics that merged power with authority, legislator with community, and law with morality. Although this project had the virtue of revealing the "moral fragility of positive law"— an intrinsic problem of liberal democracy—it also had the effect of turning all acts of dissidence into direct attacks on the community that were therefore deserving of punishment and ostracism.[2] So political democracy was restricted to local participation and freedom, and rights were restricted to the new administrators, whose monopoly over the definition of the "collective desideratum" gave them the unique power to excommunicate anyone who failed to comply with their vision.

From its unchallenged heights, the revolutionary political class was able to adapt the revolutionary agenda and to turn democracy into a variable contingent upon the achievement of other objectives. The term democracy disappeared from political discourse for more than five years, and when it made a comeback in the early 1970s it was limited to ensure the preservation of the new bureaucratic configuration of power.

Cuba's entrance into the Soviet bloc gave the country subsidized access to a more flexible market with lower interest rates and less than competitive technology. As proved by the events of the 1990s, this was no long-term blessing, but it did constitute a viable medium-term option. It provided national security guarantees, and it gave the regime a surprising level of autonomy from the social body as the economic production model ceased to depend on internal factors of productivity, investor efficiency and savings. Soviet subsidies accentuated the asymmetry of the revolutionary alliance. It produced a complex social structure and form of social mobility that contradicted the initial ideals of the revolution. But from the vantage point of 1975–1985 this may have been the best of all possible worlds for the by then less revolutionary, older, and more bureaucratic Cuban leaders.

Three basic factors permitted a rearticulation of the social alliance and the notion of consensus in the "Soviet" era. First, the state's continued monopoly on the distribution economic resources concentrated decision-making powers in the hands of a small group of individuals who also had the power to determine how supplies would be distributed, including the supply of information. The role of the market and of currency was drastically limited. Central planning left little room for entrepreneurial decision making and was organized in a way that blocked effective horizontal exchanges.

Second, the political system gained control of, and allowed mobility for, the actors capable of articulating the system: the party, its social organizations, and its media outlets, as well as the masses. The latter lacked even an elementary level of autonomy, but specific sectoral social interests were represented, including through municipal levels arenas of participation. Despite its highly centralized nature, the Cuban state preserved various channels to evaluate social needs, design policy, and receive feedback within a relatively wide resource margin.

Third, the state retained an equally monopolistic capacity to produce and transmit a credible and legitimizing ideology. It created a teleological paradigm that merged what are usually three separate realms: what is real, what is ideal, and what is practical. It was able to produce a coherent doctrine or ideology that reconciled upward mobility and enrichment with global insertion in an apparently ever-expanding "socialist camp." And given its points of contact with the national political culture, including the nationalist ethos of political actors, this was an effective doctrinal instrument.

The foundations of this world began to crumble toward the end of the 1980s, and collapsed when the Soviet bloc disintegrated and Cuba lost the external support that had subsidized its "utopian" experiment for 25 years. This history is well recorded and for the purposes of this chapter, it must suffice to say that after various antimarket experiments, the Cuban government was finally forced to implement an economic reform program that despite its incoherencies and partial reversals, definitely initiated Cuba's gradual reinsertion into the global capitalist economy. This process and its associated social dynamics is the key to understanding contemporary Cuban society. The incendiary rhetoric and apocalyptic speeches and the myriad street demonstrations of the past decade are merely the most visible manifestation of "collateral damage" produced by this historical shift.

Systemic Inconsistencies and the Penury of Consensus

Contrary to the dire predictions of right-wing Cuban exiles, and despite severe economic crisis and social impoverishment, the Cuban regime has not collapsed. Castro's "final hour"[3] has yet to come. This is a historical achievement that has thwarted the long-awaited (and frankly shameful) counterrevolutionary vengeance sought by émigrés. Nonetheless, it is equally the case that the Cuban government has been forced to face far greater and more complex difficulties than before and must implement measures that will cause further structural imbalances and threaten the political consensus. The Cuban political class is increasingly caught in a contradictory situation: it must respond effectively to the demands of accumulation and sustain a commitment to social revolution, but it must also maintain the pillars to reproduce its political power and agenda.

Initially, the regime responded by seeking to open up spaces for debate, allowing social mobilization around new issues, and by instituting economic reforms. This promising phase came to an abrupt end in 1996. Since then, politics has been driven by short-term objectives, exacerbated nationalism, and characterized by accentuated authoritarianism as well as the self-serving actions of individuals within the regime. Pluralism and diversity within the revolutionary camp, condemned by the Cuban Communist Party (Partido

Comunista de Cuba [PCC]) in 1990, were notions buried by "surreal longings for unanimity."

As noted above, the social revolutionary pact consisted of the political class providing the population with significant social benefits in exchange for a seamless political loyalty. After the mid-1980s, this arrangement began to show signs of exhaustion as Cuban society became increasingly complex, postrevolution class divisions became more accentuated, and the economic model went into decline. The "rectifications" on the eve of the raucous decade of the 1990s constituted an attempt to respond to this downward slide.

The crisis of the 1990s severely limited the state's resource and security-allocating capacities (a pivotal element of the pact) and allowed new actors to play a role in these and other more delicate functions (including ideological and cultural production). Churches, nongovernmental organizations (NGOs), intellectual groups, and various different associations began to criticize the regime. Although they had very limited opportunities to do so, they were able to disseminate their message as the disoriented political class was undergoing recomposition. None of these groups had the deep impact that Cuba's back and front door entrance to the market produced.

The adoption of a market-based logic undermined the egalitarian social pact; more importantly, systematic market insertion created new mechanisms for economic resource allocation and for social mobility, which were beyond the immediate reach of the centralized state. The market—restricted to some dynamic sectors and conforming to the demands of foreign investors—is also an efficient producer of a new kind of ideology. Indeed, the winners in the reform process—the new technocratic-entrepreneurial elite mainly originating from the political class itself—are the most efficient producers of ideology in contemporary Cuba. They show impoverished Cubans that involvement in the marketplace is the best path to individual prosperity. They do this simply by shopping in the scant malls found in the heart of the Cuban capital.

Cuban academics have taken note of this phenomenon from various angles. Nova, Everleny, and Añé emphasize the growing inequality resulting from the economic reform measures and the emergence of an increasing impoverished sector, which is "contained" by what are diminishing social policies and subsidies.[4] Other sociological studies have assessed the ideological and cultural effects of growing inequality and social segregation.[5] It is notable that some recent analyses, though analytically substantial, still conclude that Cuba can establish a superior socialism. Espina, for example, concludes with some semantic ingenuity that these changes represent a "possible alternative socialism"; in a more traditional vein, Hernández says that such developments represent the "reordering [of a] transitional socialism"; Suárez simply says that the result is "a prettier and better socialism." These analysts, whose works are mandatory points of reference in domestic social thought, illustrate just how ideology is produced and socialist rhetoric is transformed in Cuba.

Clearly, political consensus within the Cuban system has eroded under the pressure of growing impoverishment, because of the refusal of the government to initiate a renovated, democratic, socialist project based on democratic principles and because of the persistence of a fundamentalist political discourse that better educated Cuban cannot but disbelieve. The issue is how, and to what degree, the consensus has eroded. In order to answer this question, there are two sources that can be consulted: election results and the few surveys available to date.

Election results constitute the safest quantifiable political indicators, because the ballot is secret and there are no significant reports of fraud or of manipulated results. Under the new electoral law, Cubans have been able to elect National Assembly representatives every five years since 1993. Ballots offer a choice of one candidate for each seat who is nominated by electoral commissions made up of official social organizations. Citizens can vote for all, some, or none of the candidates. If voters choose to vote for "none of the above" the ballot is either annulled or considered a blank vote. The government typically engages in intense preelectoral propaganda campaigns that emphasize the importance of voting for all the nominated candidates, encouraging what is called a "unified vote." According to official rhetoric, this is the only way to vote for the nation, the revolution, and socialism.

There have been three electoral contests since the new law—in 1993, 1998, and 2003—and the proportionality of results was very similar in all cases: between 85 and 90 percent of potential voters followed government instructions and voted for all the candidates. The remaining 10 to 15 percent submitted blank votes, annulled their ballots, or failed to issue a "unified" vote. In the 2003 elections, there were almost 1 million "disobedient" voters. While this is certainly a minority (8 million voted loyally), it is still a significant minority. But not all minority voters are oppositionists, although the extremely polarized atmosphere in which elections have been held does suggest that the minority is highly dissatisfied. These results might indicate that there is a division between a critical minority and a still loyal majority. But this does not account for the fact that the loyal voting bloc may not be homogenous in its support for the regime: they may not, to use the terms of the government, be voting for "the nation, the revolution, and socialism." Interestingly, almost immediately after the 1998 elections the Office of United States Interests (OUSI) announced that it would grant visas for permanent residence in the United States and 732,000 people applied. So a significant number of "loyal" voters obviously wanted to emigrate to the haven of capitalism par excellence, the historical enemy of the Cuban nation for the past 40 years.

In 1994, the year in which the crisis peaked and the *balseros* (boat-people) exodus took place, Cubans were asked in a Gallup survey whether they identified themselves politically as "revolutionaries," "communists," "socialists" or "oppositionists": 48 percent said they were revolutionaries, 11 percent communists, a similar number called themselves socialists, and 23 percent considered themselves oppositionists.[6] So only a small minority had antiregime sentiments, although it is unclear what meaning Cubans attach to the terms revolutionary, socialist, and communist. There is little ideological difference between the latter two labels, and both are committed to the system. However, the majority preference for revolutionary, introduces some doubt, particularly as respondents could always have chosen the more militant socialist and communist labels. By selecting the revolutionary label, individuals might be saying that they recognize social and patriotic victories, and that they do not consider it an option to disown these virtues and become counterrevolutionaries. However, it should be remembered that over the past 150 years, the historical tendency in Cuba has been to identify political virtue with being a revolutionary.[7]

Milán's conclusions are comparable to the Gallup poll results.[8] His survey covered a limited but highly representative sample of 137 homes, distributed among various neighborhoods in the capital. The most notable finding emerging from the interrelated series of indirect questions posed was that 20 percent of interviewees had no hope that in the absence of system restructuring the current regime would bring about any marked improvement in their lives, while 26 percent believed that improvements were only possible under the current political framework. The remaining 47 percent felt that individual effort, rather than reliance on the political regime, was the key to solving existing problems. If one compares these findings with the Gallup poll and elections results, it is possible to conclude that Cuban society is becoming polarized: on the one hand there is a minority divided into pro- and antisystem groups, and on the other, there is a majority that focuses on the achievement of individual goals at the margins of the political system. However, this majority is not for that removed from politics, and its values are not entirely alien to the discourse of the regime, not least because official rhetoric focuses on national political cultural "hard issues" such as patriotism, solidarity, and social equality. It is this majority that passively—and occasionally actively—contributes to the stability of the system, although it has also participated in disruptive activities at critical moments. It is worth noting that future political stability and consensus will depend crucially on this group.

The fact that the PCC governs with the active support of only a minority of the population does not mean that its position is weak. Its power is assured as long as the antisystem minority does not continue to grow. There are points of weakness: support for the Communist Party is primarily based on sectors that are in decline—older, less educated people who are more willing to accept charismatic leadership—and on "opportunists" (the technocratic-entrepreneurial elite and their allies), for whom the protection of the state is a way to ensure the accumulation of wealth. Balancing this out, however, there is the fact that the "antisystem" sector is disorganized, weakened by the urge to migrate to the United States and by the repressive and anathematizing impact of the regime. The historical inability of the opposition to act as a coherent force is an important explanatory factor, one that reverses the causality of the usual explanation of its lack of effectiveness: on this view, while government repression affects the opposition's efficacy (as when its ranks are infiltrated by government agents who act as provocateurs), it is perhaps more relevant that the government is able to repress because the opposition is incoherent and inefficient. In sum, the Cuban state represses opposition groups because the internal costs of repression are lower than the cost of toleration. The international notoriety of certain opposition figures has not translated into national prominence, and this is primarily because of their chronic inability to offer Cuban society any alternative to the cultural politics and values constructed over the last four decades.

The Costly Rationality of the Short Term

After more than a decade since the disappearance of the Soviet bloc, and following an acute economic crisis, the Cuban government has found solutions to some problems and failed to resolve others.[9] Its successes have allowed it to sustain the revolutionary system by preserving its base of support, avoiding extreme poverty, and maintaining reasonable social services. The government has also successfully countered the obsessive hostility of the United States. No less significant for maintaining the consensus has been the regime's capacity to recompose the political class, particularly after the PCC Fifth Congress. However, the government has failed to guarantee sustained economic growth and to return to pre-1989 levels of social economic development. What is more, the government has failed to find ways to ensure the democratic inclusion of diverse social groups, including even the organic sectors that are critical for the survival of the system itself. So, despite high-flowing rhetoric and frequent references to the "march of history" short-term policies have prevailed over strategic, long-term decision making and the sustainability of the meager results achieved is dubious. The main policies of the regime have been outlined as follows: first, the preservation of the foundational revolutionary project through the maintenance of social programs and subsidized consumption quotas; second, the administration of market economy gains through a strong state regulatory presence, including the control and/or co-optation of emerging technocratic-entrepreneurial sectors; third, the fragmentation of traditional as well as emerging economic, political and social actors, and the selective concession of civil and political rights; fourth, low cost repression of disruptive intellectual or social action against the status quo, be it political, intellectual, or through social action, without making distinctions in the politico-ideological spheres; fifth, the maintenance of the traditional consensus-building discourse, notably the nationalist rhetoric that portrays Cuba as the last bastion of dignity in a world beset by troubles such as the war in Iraq or the increased professionalization of the Olympic Games; and finally, the renovation of the political class though the promotion of young cadres within the military or technocratic class, who are distinguished as steadfastly loyal members of the regime's highest authorities.

If the political system is to remain functional, a series of systemic governmental problems must be resolved that cannot be addressed by these six strategies alone. But paradoxically, the solutions to these problems could also have the effect of eroding dramatically the bases of the system they are meant to preserve.

The first challenge is the economy. If it does not grow substantially, then the deficit of accumulated consumption could prove explosive, making it impossible to sustain present social expenditures and exacerbating inequalities in a context of increasingly complex demands and diminishing resources. Even though the adversarial international context (marked by the North American embargo) is problematic, the regime could in theory resort to auxiliary social measures that could have a positive effect on production, services, and employment. Among them are the decentralization of the larger state enterprises in the context of the *perfeccionamiento empresarial* (business improvement) campaign, the legalization of small and medium businesses, and policies to increase the autonomy of the rural cooperative system. But the government has been very reluctant to take these steps. Instead, it has resorted to ideological arguments against procapitalist measures without taking into account that such policies may offer gains in terms of increased worker participation and co-ownership, and more effective cooperatives, all of which would reinforce the presently contracting "spaces" of socialism, and which would in fact be more socialist than current state policy. The reluctance of the Cuban government to move in this direction is not a result of an anticapitalist bias but rather of a corporatist instinct of self-preservation that resists any steps that might generate an autonomous social dynamic and unify what are currently fragmented markets—the latter being an indispensable condition for the successful monitoring of the emerging technocratic-entrepreneurial sector. Consequently, the Cuban leadership has reached a complicated crossroad: the only way to create the conditions for a more productive economy will be to diminish its own power.

The second challenge is the international context. U.S. aggression toward Cuba is a result of its Monroeist tendencies and the need to cater to a domestic political actor. The United States does not want to negotiate with Cuba; it wants an act of submission. The Cuban government, in turn, has used this successfully to consolidate internal support. After four decades of training in the art of confrontation, it is difficult to think of Cuban politics as a separate sphere and conceive of a consensus that does not depend on the maintenance of a real or imagined perception of external threat. However, while the White House is presently in the hands of an irrationally unilateral and ultrarightist sector, the embargo continues to march toward extinction. Again, the Cuban regime, governing a society that has always prioritized its "clients," has demonstrated an ongoing ability to deal with its neighbors by courting economic interests. The key question here is to what extent normalization or a substantial easing of tensions with the United States might weaken the nationalist political discourse (the most solid and credible regime "argument," and the factor that has done the most to prevent a contraction of its broad passive support base).

The third challenge relates to political leadership. The crisis has acutely accentuated personalization and centralization around the figure of Fidel Castro. He has been vital for the preservation of popular support and of the unity of the political class. Fidel Castro has maintained his trademark ability to domesticate dissident tendencies within the postrevolutionary elite and control the recruitment of new cadres while simultaneously convincing most Cubans that the current crisis is still preferable to a market-based future. However, such extreme centralization will create an insoluble problem once the Cuban president disappears either completely or partially from the political scene, particularly as the system lacks internal, coherent negotiation mechanisms. There are two possible results: either the group of active *fidelistas*—individuals whose political affiliation is strongly marked by loyalty to the president—will be fragmented, or the unity of the political class as a whole, apparently viscerally dependent on the control exerted over it by a supreme leader, will break down.

Does this mean that the Cuban political system and the supposedly and proudly "immutable" regime are now highly vulnerable? It certainly does not mean that a transition will occur in an institutional vacuum (the long-held fantasy of the equally "immutable" historical exile leaders and their descendants). Cuba has *almost* all the political actors necessary to negotiate *almost* any kind of political and economic settlement, and the PCC will undoubtedly form the nucleus of whatever new political class emerges. The emphasis on "almost" is important for a sad reason: the future is not bright for a left-wing political alternative based on social equality, environmentally sustainable development, a state responsible for the rights of citizens, and on a democracy that differs from the elitist models that are currently viewed as the necessary "lesser evil." Because of the crisis and impoverishment, and because of the political action of the government, the popular sectors are in an unprecedented state of paralysis, and incipient socialist reform proposals have practically ceased to exist. Almost a decade after the abrupt counterrevolutionary conflicts of 1995–1996, and as never before in the history of the revolution, politics and society continue to lean toward the right. If an alternative socialist transition is to occur, it will be necessary to engage in a critique of revolutionary history and to rescue the idea of socialism from the hands of the class of leaders that hijacked it. And the innumerable social and cultural successes of the past four decades will also have to be vindicated as genuine historical victories. It will be difficult to do this in the midst of the kind of mob catharsis that a transition will likely bring about. But as is said in Tolkein's *Lord of the Rings*, it is important for eras to change, but it is equally important to remember the past.[10]

Notes

1. Terry Lynn Karl and Philippe C. Schmitter, "Dilemas de la democratización en América Latina," *Foro Internacional*, 3, January–March 1991: 27–43.
2. Juan R. Capella, *Fruta prohibida* (Madrid: Editorial Trotta, 1997).
3. Andrés Oppenheimer, *Castro's Final Hour. The Secret Story Behind the Coming Downfall of Communist Cuba* (New York: Simon and Schuster, 1992).
4. See Lia Añé, "La reforma económica y la economía familiar en Cuba," in Mauricio de la Miranda (ed.), *Reforma económica y cambio social en América Latina y el Caribe* (Cali, Colombia: TM Editores, 2000), pp. 126–145; Omar Everleny, "Ciudad de la Habana: Desempeño económico y situación social,"

La Economía Cubana en el 2000, CEEC, Havana, April 2001, pp. 36–45; and Armando Nova, "La nueva relación de producción en la agricultura," *Revista Cuba: Investigaciones Económicas*, January–March 1998: 65–82.

5. See Rafael Hernández, "Sin urna de cristal: Reordenamiento y transición socialista en Cuba," in W. Lozano (ed.), *Cambio político en el Caribe* (Caracas: Nueva Sociedad, 1998), pp. 23–36; Mayra Espina, "Transición y dinámica de los procesos socio-estructurales," in Manuel Monereo, Migual Riera, and Juan Valdés (eds.), *Cuba: Construyendo futuro* (Madrid: Editorial El Viejo Topo, 2000), pp. 9–54; María I. Domínguez, "Generaciones y mentalidades: Existe una conciencia generacional entre los jóvenes cubanos," in Monereo, Riera, and Valdés (eds.), *Cuba: Construyendo futuro*, pp. 55–75; Luis Suárez, *El siglo XXI: Posibilidades y desafíos para la Revolución Cubana* (Havana: Editorial de Ciencias Sociales, 2000).

6. *Cuba Update*, 1995.

7. A study directed by the author of this chapter in four municipalities between 1988 and 1990 found that interviewees felt that being a revolutionary was a necessary and nonnegotiable condition for anyone pursuing political office. However, the label revolutionary is not political but ethical and related to the support of values such as solidarity, love of work, dedication, and loyalty to the community. See Haroldo Alfonso Dilla et al. (eds.), *Participación y desarrollo en los municipios cubanos* (Havana: Centro de Estudios sobre América, 1993).

8. Guillermo Milán, *Los procesos anómicos en la sociedad cubana* (Havana: Instituto de Filosofía, 1998).

9. Haroldo Alfonso Dilla, "Cuba: Los escenarios cambiantes de la gobernabilidad," in Haroldo Alfonso Dilla (ed.), *Los recursos de la gobernabilidad en la Cuenca del Caribe* (Caracas: Nueva Sociedad, 2002).

10. J. R. R. Tolkein, *The Lord of the Rings* (London: Allen and Unwin, 1954).

Chapter 6

Cuba's Dilemma of Simultaneity: The Link between the Political and the National Question

Bert Hoffmann

Introduction

Political science scholars are usually fascinated by great political changes. But in Cuba, what has been spectacular after 1989 is precisely the continuity of the political system in spite of truly dramatic changes in the international context and a profound national economic and social crisis. Against expectations, Cuba's brand of state socialism proved to be immune to the wave of regime change that led to the demise of Communist Party rule in all the Eastern European countries within a brief period of time. From a comparative perspective, therefore, what needs to be explained is Cuba's "nontransition." Claus Offe refers to the "dilemma of simultaneity" in his study of the transformation process in Eastern Europe: in contrast to Southern Europe and Latin America, political regime change toward pluralist, civilian democracy did not call into question the fundaments of the economic system, and, in the former socialist states, political and economic change had to be accomplished simultaneously.[1]

As argued in this chapter, Cuba poses the question of the relationship between economic and political change in an exceptional way. While the political regime has resisted change despite fundamentally changed international conditions since 1989, the reproduction of political authority has not been possible by ensuring economic immobility or maintaining the status quo. Rather, the condition for the political nontransition has been substantial economic change directed by the regime in such a way that political stability has not been severely challenged, even though some of the postulates of classic Cuban socialism have been eroded. After a dramatic crisis in the early 1990s, limited reform measures permitted a modest recovery that converted the regime into the "gatekeeper state," described by Javier Corrales in this volume, and gave it an extraordinary degree of political leverage based on a monopolistic control over access to the dynamic dollarized sectors of the economy and restricted domestic market mechanisms to limited, largely informal, and legally insecure activities.[2]

Claus Offe noted that the "dilemma of simultaneity" in the former socialist states usually included a third "territorial issue . . . the determination of the borders for a state and a population, and the consolidation of these borders within the framework of a European order of states."[3] What Offe calls the "territorial issue" can be conceived more broadly as the national issue or question, centered around issues such as levels of state sovereignty, the role of emigration and emigrant communities, the identity of the nation-state, and the role and uses of nationalism in the political arena. In the Latin American transitions these factors played a minor role. By contrast, in Eastern Europe and the former Soviet Union national question factors were crucially important (e.g., the quest for independence in the Baltic states, the secession of the Central Asian republics, the breakup of Czechoslovakia and the much more violent fragmentation of Yugoslavia, and the very particular case of regime change in the German Democratic Republic [GDR] and its unification with Western Germany).

In Cuba, while political and economic transformation were marked by asynchrony, the political and the national questions are in fact largely intertwined—albeit in accordance with a very different political constellation than was the case in Eastern Europe. It is this simultaneity of the national and the political question and its implications that largely explains the stunning continuity of Cuba's political regime. In sharp contrast to the Eastern European experiences, in Cuba national independence in the face of an over-whelming hegemonic power is the trump card not of the opposition but of the socialist government.

Most of the transitions literature fails to account for the case of Cuba. The four-volume work by O'Donnell, Schmitter, and Whitehead, *Transitions from Authoritarian Rule*, is typical in this regard: it mentions socialist Cuba in passing, but excludes it from the scope of analysis.[4] This is not surprising, since there was no transition in Cuba in the sense of a shift to a Western dem-ocratic kind of political system. But the question of why this did not happen is the reverse of the question of why it happened elsewhere, and exceptions to established patterns or deviant cases can be especially interesting for com-parative purposes. Somewhat surprisingly, "transitology" largely continued to turn a blind eye on Cuba when some of its most leading proponents set out on "travels to the East"[5] after 1989, to explain the upheavals in socialist states by applying the analytical instruments acquired in Latin America.[6] Characteristically, Linz and Stepan, who analyzed transitions and the consoli-dation of democracy in Southern Europe, Latin America, and postcommunist Europe, only once mention Cuba—and prerevolutionary Cuba under Batista at that.[7] There are numerous post-1989 publications on Cuba that use the word transition in their titles, but this should not mislead us: many such works were shaped by the expectation of impending regime change, and the word transition was not used so much as an analytical category for real events but rather as a cipher for hoped-for future developments.[8]

Cuba also was rather marginal in studies about the transformation of the former socialist countries of Eastern Europe although there was scope for comparative work in the economic sphere at least. Economic transformation in Eastern Europe must be understood as part of a process of integration into the world market; equally, although there was no rupture of the political system Cuba was also forced to transform its economy after 1989 to adjust it for insertion into a thoroughly changed world economy. The highlights of this adaptation were the legalization of the U.S. dollar in 1993, the opening up to foreign capital, and the tolerated extension of a huge informal or "black market" economy. So political "transition" and economic "transformation" do not run as parallel as many suppose: intentionally and consciously or not, the Cuban system has undergone considerable economic change but has also avoided a political transition to a pluralist democracy.

Transition studies in the 1980s largely emphasized the decisive importance of domestic factors for democratization. However, the exceptional status of Cuba shows just how immense is the weight of external factors and how the nature of a country's insertion into international politics shapes the domestic arena. In fact, the Cuban case makes it painfully clear how difficult it is to draw a clear distinction between external and domestic factors: if Cuba policy in the United States is a prototypical example of an "intermestic issue,"[9] this is all the more so for Cuba, for which relations with the United States, Europe, or the rest of the world are framed as part of the dichotomous confrontation shaping domestic politics ("with Fidel or with the Yankees").

Getting the Context Right: The Dual Identity of Cuban Socialism

When analyzing Cuba comparatively, the transformation of the former socialist countries of Eastern Europe after 1989 is as much a point of reference as the survival of the socialist states in Asia—China and Vietnam. But Cuba is not neighbored by Poland and Lithuania, nor by China and Vietnam: it is 55 miles west of Haiti, 125 miles east of Mexico, and 90 miles south of the Unites States, and these are much more than mere geographic indications. Indeed, socialist Cuba can only be adequately understood if its dual identity as a socialist country *and* a Latin American country is accounted for.

Broadly speaking, until 1989, revolutionary Cuba was simultaneously a part of the developing Third World and the socialist Second World. The escalating confrontation with the United States led to an alliance with the Soviet Union, which after the proclamation of the "socialist character of the Cuban Revolution" in 1961, translated into an alignment of the island's domestic political structures with the Soviet model, particularly with the so-called process of institutionalization in the 1970s. This alignment culminated in the adoption of the 1976 constitution, the fifth article of which defined the Communist Party (Partido Comunista de Cuba [PCC]) as the Marxist-Leninist vanguard of the working class and the leading force in state and society, as elsewhere between East Berlin and Vladivostok.[10]

But the formal adoption of Soviet-style political structures always coexisted with a strong Latin American identity. Although Cuba became part of the socialist Second World after 1959, it never left the developing Third World. Whereas in Eastern Europe, "returning to Europe" became such a forceful metaphor for hopes of economic well-being and political stability, for the people living between Pinar del Río and Guantánamo, as for the people in the rest of Latin America and the Caribbean, there is no "past Europe" to turn to but only a past of dependent capitalism with high levels of social exclusion, mediated sovereignty, and unfulfilled democratic promises.[11]

The Cuban Revolution's Latin American identity embodies the national aspiration to independence. So the conflict with the United States was not an East-West but rather a North-South conflict. Behind the formal socialist institutions stand the military structures that grew out of the guerrilla war— the foundation of Cuban revolutionary politics. The unquestioned and all-powerful Fidel is not cast from the same mold as Lenin or Stalin, or Tito and Ceaucescu, but is part of the Latin American tradition of caudillo authority and the Cuban tradition of the military leaders of the country's wars of independence and their *mando único* (single leadership). Even today, despite the baroque list of titles acquired under the state-socialist nomenclature (first secretary of the Central Committee [Comité Central, CC] of the PCC, president of the Council of Ministers and of the Council of State), Fidel Castro is first and foremost the *comandante en jefe* (commander-in-chief) of the Cuban Revolution, independently of whether the Cuban Constitution recognizes such a title.

In his memorable essay on *The History, Structure and Ideology of Cuba's Communist Party*, Hans Magnus Enzensberger described the ambivalent relationship of Fidel Castro with the Communist Party, summarizing it thus in 1969: there is "only one thing [that the Communist Party] is not under any circumstance: the core of political power." Noting the ever-present tension between Castro's personalist rule and an imitative bureaucratic socialism, Enzensberger added, "With great pertinacity Fidel escapes the avant-garde that he conjured up. It will never catch up with him. He wants it and he does not want it. The dilemma of Fidel is also that of the PCC, an institution that has now been in the process of being built and destroyed for many years."[12]

Since Enzensberger wrote his famous essay, the "process of institutionalization" equipped the Communist Party with formal committees, congresses, and elective offices. But still, almost 30 years later, Rafael Rojas echoes the analysis of Enzensberger when he writes, "It is blatantly clear that the Cuban Communist Party is not a Gramscian or even Leninist institution. . . . The power of Fidel Castro is not divided or delegated via institutions but rather via persons."[13] In fact, since the onset of crisis in the early 1990s there has been an impressive process of political deinstitutionalization: Communist Party congresses are not held when they are due, elections are constantly rescheduled, regular plenary sessions of the party are skipped, and party statutes are changed without explanation.[14] Moreover, parallel political structures coexist: the Office for the Battle of Ideas, which had become a parallel superministry of sorts that sidestepped the formal competences of existing ministries or state institutions by 2005, is only the most recent but not by any means an isolated case.

This erosion of "socialist legality" has been read as a sign of crisis; however, in many ways it signals a return to pre-Soviet, preinstitutionalization process modes of political organization, which survived as an essential part of Cuban political culture beneath the official surface. What often seems to be a redundant or counterproductive conflict of competences actually serves to maintain Fidel Castro's *mando único* through a very sui generis version of "the separation of powers." The famous (or infamous) slogan *socialismo o muerte* (socialism or death) which so powerfully underscores what has been called the "Numantian"[15] nature of Castro's style of government is not a Marxian, Leninist, or socialist import but is deeply rooted in the Cuban (and indeed Latin American) political tradition. It constitutes a socialist *aggiornamento* (bringing up to date) of Cuba's nineteenth-century national anthem, the concluding line of which proclaims: *¡Morir por la patria es vivir!* (To die for the homeland is to live!).

Cuba's "National Question": The Long Shadow of the United States

Cuba's foremost Latin American quality resides in its relations with the United States and the latter's implications for the national question. While "virtually every one of the East European transitions amounted to national liberation," in Cuba the reverse holds: it is the political nontransition that emerges as the protective cover of national independence.[16] However massive Cuba's dependence on the Soviet Union may have been, the alliance with Moscow was always less of a neocolonial subordination than a means to resist the insolence of the "real" hegemonic power to the North. When Cuba lost its overseas allies after 1989, the regime did not have to invent a new source of legitimization; rather, it brought nationalist resistance back with a vengeance. Article 5 of the 1976 constitution was changed, not to modify the "guiding role" of the PCC but to alter its ultimate mission: rather than being the "vanguard of the working class" of yore, it was to be the "vanguard of the Cuban nation."[17] Until the Cuban Revolution, and from the liberation from Spanish rule, U.S.-Cuban relations were marked by a long tradition of hegemonic ambitions. Cuba became an independent nation in 1902 only after accepting the Platt Amendment, by which the Cuban constitution granted the United States a right to intervene in the affairs of the island. In this context of "mediated sovereignty,"[18] U.S. ambitions to "export democracy" are an indigestible platter indeed. By placing the Cuban Republic under a neocolonial tutelage far removed from "true independence," and by maintaining a highly exclusionary social system that delegitimized the liberal democratic project (to such an extent that Fidel Castro encountered little popular resistance when he did away with what he later called the "pseudo-republic" and *"pluriporquería"* ("pluri-swinery," a play on *pluripartidismo*, or multipartyism). This history still weighs heavily today, not least because Washington's "promotion of democracy" has gone hand in hand with a return to an aggressive unilateral foreign policy and concepts of "benevolent imperialism" are witnessing a remarkable revival.

Exit, Voice, and Cuban-U.S. Relations

Cuban-U.S. relations can not be analyzed as an intergovernmental affair alone. A second strand to which Cuba's political and national questions are linked result from the high level of migration of people from the island to the United States. After the 1959 and in contrast to the state-socialist regimes of Eastern Europe, Cuba kept the door wide open for the emigration of discontent as a political "safety valve."[19] The contrast could not be sharper. As the GDR politburo decided to build the Berlin Wall to stem the "loss of blood" through sustained migration to the West, the Cuban government allowed no less than 230,000 Cubans, mostly from the upper and middle class, to leave the island safely by plane or boat in the period between 1959 and 1962. The emigration of hundreds of thousands of Cubans constituted the great escape valve to avoid social conflict resulting from the radical transformation of the island's economy and society. Nearly 1 million Cubans—starting with the exodus of the old elites, and later with the departure of those dissatisfied from all social backgrounds—emigrated to the United States, most settling in and around Miami. Thus, Cuba became an ideal example of Hirschman's famous "exit" and "voice" model.[20] With his dualist structure of two contrasting reactions (of consumers, members of organizations, or citizens) to a decline in the provision of services or goods, Hirschman postulates an essentially "hydraulic relation" or "seesaw pattern" between the two: the more available the exit option, the less likely that voice is heard.[21] This effect can result from spontaneous or uncoordinated migration decisions "from below," but for Hirschman Cuba after 1959 was a prime example of a state that deliberately used emigration as a "top-down" mechanism of control: "At times, the voice-weakening effect of exit is consciously utilized by the authorities: permitting, favoring, or even ordering the exit of enemies or dissidents has long been one—comparatively civilized—means for autocratic rulers to rid themselves of their critics, a practice revived on a large scale by Castro's Cuba."[22] In other words, at the individual level emigration responds to the political question of whether there is discontent with the present government and living conditions on the island on the playing field of the national question, when people opt to physically leave the Cuban nation-state and go into exile and, over time, become "Cuban-Americans." The first wave of emigration occurred in the years immediately after the triumphant revolution, and a second wave between 1965 and 1973 brought a further 330,000 Cubans to the United States, again mostly from formerly well-off social sectors, who left with an airlift established between Cuba and the United States (notably it was the latter and not Cuba that put an end to this arrangement in 1973). See figure 6.1.

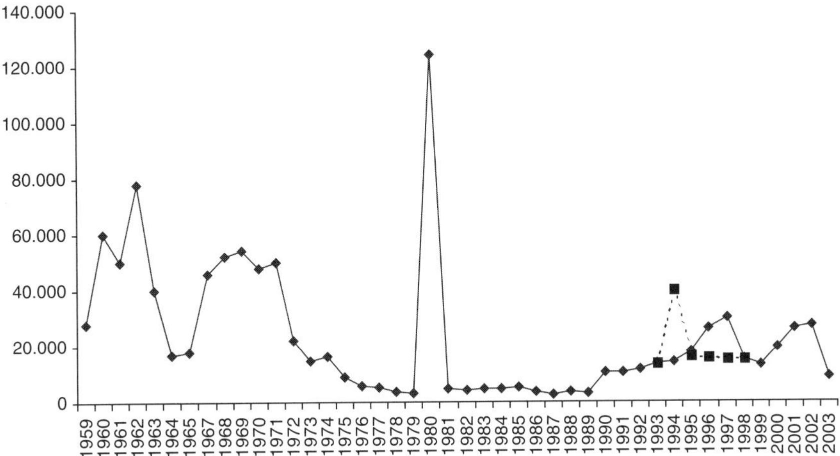

Figure 6.1   Cuban Emigration to the United States (1959–2000)

Note: The *dotted line* (1993–1998) indicates the author's estimates to adjust emigration data to the actual 1994 peak. The data of U.S. immigration statistics refer to legalization in the United States. However, thousands of Cuban immigrants were temporarily interned at the U.S. Guantánamo base during the 1994 *balsero* crisis, formally entering the United States in subsequent years.

Sources: For 1959–1989 see Lisandro Pérez, "De Nueva York a Miami: El desarrollo demográfico de las comunidades cubanas en Estados Unidos," *Encuentro de la Cultura Cubana*, (15), 1999: 20; for 1990–2003 see U.S. Department of Homeland Security, *Yearbook of Immigration Statistics 2003* (Washington, DC: Government Printing Office, 2004), pp. 12–15, also at http://uscis.gov/graphics/shared/aboutus/statistics/2003Yearbook.pdf.

While the number of emigrants fell sharply after 1973, latent emigration pressure accumulated up to 1980 and came to a head with the so-called Mariel exodus. Faced with domestic crisis—more than 15,000 Cuban asylum seekers stormed the grounds of the Peruvian embassy in Havana—the Cuban government resorted again to the exit option, this time without waiting to negotiate a migration accord with the U.S. government. It unilaterally opened the port of Mariel for mass emigration by boat, calling on emigrants in South Florida to evacuate their relatives. Miami Cubans responded to this appeal in great numbers, effectively cooperating with the Cuban government and against the will of the U.S. government. The result was the third wave of emigration: more than 120,000 Cubans left the island in just 5 months.

The fourth wave is associated with the profound post-1989 economic and social crisis. As the number of clandestine boat-people (the *balseros*) steadily rose in the early 1990s, the Cuban government opened the floodgates again, producing the so-called *balseros* crisis of 1994. Again, this wave of emigration was read by politicians and academics alike as an example of the Cuban safety valve at work, with exit undermining voice.[23] A closer analysis of the crisis years since 1989, however, suggests that Hirschman's theory should be modified in two important ways: (1) the focus should be less on the numbers and more on modalities of exit, with the Cuban state politically capitalizing on its gatekeeper role regarding emigration; and (2) it is necessary to address the increasingly transnational character of both voice and exit, which counters the assumed seesaw mechanism at work between the two.

The Castro government has certainly favored exit, but it has equally expended a lot of energy maintaining firm state control over gates to emigration and its modalities. Most importantly, it has insisted on the so-called *salida definitiva* (definitive exit) as a condition for departure, so that emigration is very much a once and for all decision, which is accompanied by the confiscation of property and the need for those who wish to return to acquire a *permiso de entrada* (entry permit) from the Cuban authorities.[24] In addition, emigration involves costly bureaucratic procedures, and sometimes social marginalization or chicanery, once the desire to leave is formally stated, and there are restrictions on those eligible for emigration, particularly children, certain professional groups such as medical doctors, army officials, and anyone holding public or party offices.[25]

Since the state's capacity to enforce these conditions rests on its monopolistic control over access to means of international transportation, an ever-increasing number of boat-people leaving the island clandestinely challenged this position in the early 1990s.[26] In his chapter in this book, Corrales (chapter 4) argues that regime survival was largely possible in the 1990s because of Cuba becoming a gatekeeper state: while dollarization did indeed undermine the traditional concept of a socialist economy, the state eventually strengthened its power over society by preserving its monopoly on access to the emerging dollarized sectors and their far superior income possibilities. Things were not so different with emigration: facing enormous emigration pressure and a sharp increase in illegal departures, the state reasserted its gatekeeper capacity to avoid losing authority over emigration.

But the availability and form of exit are not just domestic decisions. U.S. restrictions on immigration are probably the biggest obstacle for Cubans to overcome if they want to leave the island for what is the country's top destination. Washington's post-1959 "open arms" policy ended with the 1980 Mariel crisis and gave way to a highly ambivalent attitude. At the onset of crisis in the 1990s, there was a bilateral migration accord (signed in 1984 by the Reagan administration), which granted "up to 20,000" U.S. immigration visas to Cubans annually. Actual emigration figures remained very much below this mark, however. In the early 1990s, legally issued immigration visas to Cubans averaged less than 1,000 annually (although the so-called Cuban Adjustment Ac of 1966 was still in place, by which all Cuban nationals who reached the United States—whether legally or not—almost automatically obtained lawful permanent residence.[27]

As a consequence, of the 47,500 Cubans entering the United States between 1990 and 1993, only 11 percent did so with a legitimate immigration visa (see figure 6.2).[28] Almost twice that number, 20 percent, was admitted with a refugee visa issued under a broad interpretation of the category of former political prisoners and their families. Another 17 percent entered

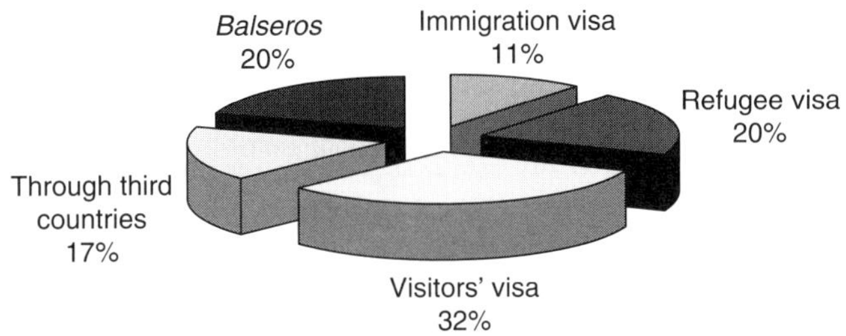

Figure 6.2   Cuban Immigration to the USA (1990–1993) by Form of Arrival

Source: Ernesto Rodríguez Chàvez, *Emigración cubana actual* (Havana: Editorial de Ciencias Sociales, 1993), p. 93.

through third countries under the legal protection of the Exodus Program, jointly organized by the Cuban exiles' most potent lobby organization—the Cuban American National Foundation (CANF)—and the U.S. Immigration and Naturalization Service (INS).

More than half of Cuban immigrants, however, came without the required legal documents. About 32 percent entered with visitors' visas, which they overstayed. Finally, a steadily increasing number—20 percent for the whole period—were *balseros*, the emblematic form of Cuban emigration in the first half of the 1990s. Leaving the island illegally, *balseros* set out to reach U.S. shores on makeshift rafts. They risked their lives in the 90-mile crossing, but once they landed or were intercepted at sea by the U.S. Coast Guard, they, like those overstaying visitor visas, enjoyed full protection of the Cuban Adjustment Act, leading to their ex-postlegalization as immigrants.

The *balseros* symbolized how desperate living conditions had become in Cuba in the media worldwide. However, for the Cuban government the crucial problem was not the negative international image but the fear that kind of illegal emigration would lead to a loss of authority. Stepping up Cuban border guard patrols to intercept *balseros* proved futile. Although the number of interceptions rose significantly, so did the total number of attempts to get into the United States, from 2,000 in 1990 to 15,000 in only the first 7 months of 1994, according to official Cuban data (see table 6.1). As proportions remained stable at roughly three intercepted *balseros* for every one successful arrival on U.S. shores, the dimension of the problem increased.

In fact, uncontrolled exit sparked the most massive articulation of oppositional voice in Cuba during the 1990s: the riots on August 5, 1994, in which hundreds of mostly young Cubans gathered on the *malecón*, Havana's broad coastline avenue, chanting antigovernment slogans and breaking the windows of dollar shops and tourist hotels. This outbreak of voice was dispersed within a few hours without bloodshed, and Fidel Castro appeared on the evening news firmly at the helm of the government countermobilization. It was after this resounding reaffirmation of the state's capacity to subdue voice that the government made an apparently daring move: it declared that borders would be open for a mass exodus of *balseros* in plain daylight and with

Table 6.1 U.S. Immigration Visas for Cubans and Number of Cuban Balseros, Intercepted and Successful (1990–1994)

Year	U.S. Immigration Visas issued to Cubans	*Balseros* intercepted by Cuban border guard	*Balseros* that reached the United States
1990	1,098	1,593	467
1991	1,376	6,596	1,997
1992	910	7,073	2,511
1993	964	11,564	4,208
1994	544	10,975[a]	4,092[a]
Total	4,892	37,801[b]	13,275[b]

Notes: These data do not take into account those who died trying. The author personally saw a dead *balsero* washed ashore in 1994, and there is no reason to doubt that numerous others shared a similar fate. However, there are no formal data available, and estimates not only differ widely but are also subject to misinterpretation as a result of political bias. An example is Holly Ackerman, who writes that "both Cuban and U.S. estimates point to a death rate as high as 75 percent." However, this is highly speculative; her essential reference is to a speech by Fidel Castro in which he provided the data exactly as presented in table 6.1; in this, however, the approximate 75 percent that did not make it to the United States refers not to deaths but to rates of interception and repatriation.

[a] Refers only to the period between January and July 1994.

[b] Refers to the period between January 1990 and July 1994.

Sources: Holly Ackerman, "The *Balsero* Phenomenon, 1991–1994," *Cuban Studies*, 26, 1996: 173; Félix Masud-Piloto, *From Welcomed Exiles to Illegal Immigrants: Cuban Migrants to the U.S., 1959–1995* (Lanham, MD: Rowman and Littlefield, 1996), p. 135. For the balseros a speech by Fidel Castro, see *Granma Internacional*, September 7, 1994, p. 6.

publicly displayed state tolerance. The *balseros* crisis certainly revealed the depth of the country's social crisis, but it was not perceived as a sign of loss of state authority and it also failed to ignite public protest. The state opened the gates, but it did so in a way that ascertained, rather than eroded, its gatekeeper role.

If as Hirschman suggests the *balseros'* exodus served as an escape valve, it also served another, more important, goal: regaining control over emigration by forcing Washington to negotiate. The arrival of hundreds of Cuban boat-people daily had an immediate political impact in the United States. There was widespread public outrage against the Castro government, but the U.S. government also came under pressure to stop this mass inflow of Cubans. The growing unease (to put it mildly) at the prospect of receiving a seemingly endless flow of Cubans led the U.S. Coast Guard to take intercepted *balseros* to the U.S. naval base of Guantánamo Bay instead of Florida, where they were accommodated in refugee camps and became stranded in a legal limbo.[29] Around this time, secret negotiations began and in September 1994, a new U.S.-Cuba migration accord was reached, marking a turning point in two regards. First, the U.S. government accepted the commitment to issue a minimum of 20,000 immigration visas per year instead of the previous "up to 20,000." Second, it announced that boat-people picked up at sea would no longer be granted entry to the United States.[30] The ink on the accord had not yet dried, when the Castro government declared the borders closed to all undocumented emigrants.

For the Cuban government the *balseros* crisis was a risky but in the end highly successful gamble. It obtained a major change in U.S. policy from what seemed like a poor bargaining position prior to the crisis. Turning the U.S. ceiling into the floor of annual immigration visas fits in with the safety-valve theory, but the migration accord was also crucial in restoring the gatekeeper state. It greatly decreased the likelihood of successfully emigrating the *balsero* way, resulting in a massive decline in the number of Cubans illegally leaving the island.

The migration accords left a loophole for special U.S. treatment of Cuban emigrants, since only those apprehended at sea are returned to the island, while those who manage to land ashore continue to benefit from the Cuban Adjustment Act. This so-called wet-foot, dry-foot policy has led to an increase in costly speedboat emigration arranged by professional smugglers, which greatly increase the chances of making it to U.S. territory. The Cuban government has repeatedly attacked these dry-foot loopholes by staging mass demonstrations against the Ley Asesina (the Murderous Law), as it refers to the Cuban Adjustment Act, for inciting illegal emigration. However, between 1997 and 2004 the number of maritime Cuban migrants apprehended by U.S. authorities on land ranged from 400 to 2,400 annually, numbers that pale compared to the *balsero* migration of the early 1990s.[31] With the persistent economic and social crisis, the Cuban emigration potential remains high; in 1998 no less than half a million Cubans formally applied for U.S. immigration visas.[32] Nevertheless, ten years after the *balseros* crisis uncontrolled exit has become much less of a problem, and the Cuban gatekeeper state has prevailed.

Cuba Transnational? Exit as Internationalization of Voice

Emigration holds yet another key to the survival of the Cuban regime that the safety-valve theory cannot adequately account for. Hirschman views the act of emigration as an effective renunciation of voice.[33] But emigration can have a boomerang effect for two reasons. First, there is the classic idea of exile and reentry. Second, and more importantly, however, exit can lead to the externalization of voice. After leaving their country, people who are now not repressed or fearful, can raise their voice all the louder beyond the reach of their state. The Cuban émigré community after 1959 is a prime example of this. While there were attempts to "reenter" island politics via military means, as in the failed Bay of Pigs invasion, the most sustained political activity of that community has been to raise its voice against the Castro government and to exert influence on the U.S. Cuba policy.

Silvia Pedraza wonders whether "those who exited became [the] voice" of Cuban society and whether the émigrés and their highly vocal organizations can adopt the role of the nonexistent independent civil society on the island. Her answer is skeptical since all organizations formed by the exile community "can only be effective to the extent that they are in touch with those inside of Cuba, a condition difficult to fulfill given the Cuban government's capacity to forestall such contacts."[34] Although this is a just observation, she misses a crucial point: the issue is not primarily about substituting for domestic civil society but about the internationalization of voice. The dominant exile organizations have developed a mastery in lobbying Washington, in interacting with and exerting influence on the U.S. government, thus making U.S. Cuba policy a prime example of what has come to be called an intermestic affair (international and domestic considerations are inseparably interwoven).[35] So emigrant voice may in fact have little effect when directed at Cuba, but it has a great deal of weight when articulated via Washington and galvanized by U.S. legislation and U.S. policy toward the island. Although exile organizations celebrate their continued leverage over U.S. Cuba policy, this also is a boon to the Cuban regime. It serves as ever-renewed evidence of the key nationalist thesis of the government in Havana: that all conflict is part of the polarized confrontation between Cuba and the United States, to which there are no in-between alternatives.

A prominent example is the Helms-Burton Act, which was lobbied for intensely by the CANF and passed by U.S. Congress in 1996. This law not only includes an extraterritorial extension of U. S. sanctions but also prescribes in detail the conditions for a democratic transition on the island.[36] Predictably, Cuba's National Assembly passed a strict new law threatening high penalties for dissidents that same year, the Reaffirmation of Cuban Dignity and Sovereignty Act, in reaction to the Helms-Burton Act.[37] Thus, exit not only reduces oppositional voice, but it also produces an internationalization of voice, which the Cuban government then exploits to delegitimize dissenting domestic voice.[38]

As it struggles for economic survival after the demise of its socialist allies in 1989–1991, the Cuban government has found an unexpected ally: emigrants, whose remittances to their relatives on the island became a backbone of economic recovery. The legalization of the U.S. dollar, announced by Fidel Castro in the summer of 1993, was designed precisely to foster family remittances that the government could easily siphon off through rapidly opened dollar stores.[39] Since then, remittances to Cuba have risen to an estimated $1,100 million,[40] far surpassing the combined revenues of the island's traditional export products, sugar, and tobacco; they are second only to the gross revenues of tourism as the country's principal source of foreign currency.[41]

If this challenges traditional notions of the material base for a socialist state, it also questions two basic assumptions of Hirschman's exit category. The first is that exit represents an economic loss for organizations and states, just as it leads to reduced income for a firm. The second is that while voice "can be graduated, all the way from faint grumbling to violent protest," exit is a clear-cut dichotomous category: "One either exits or one does not."[42] Both these arguments lose power with the emergence of transnational networks, through which emigrants keep far-reaching social and economic ties with their countries of origin.[43] Since the 1980s, remittances from emigrants to their relatives at home have increased so greatly that they play a central economic role in a wide array of nations. For Latin America, remittances amounted to no less than $32 billion in 2002, a higher figure than all international aid and development cooperation for the region and at par with the total amount of foreign direct investment.[44]

Given the dimensions, many governments see emigration not only as a stability gain (reducing stress in a tense labor market situation, particularly in the case of low-skilled workers) but moreover as a way to generate hard-currency income through future remittances. Using the Poirine model of remittances as "informal intra-family loan arrangements,"[45] Cuban economist Pedro Monreal concludes that the "export" of emigrants and the "import" of their remittances effectively became a key element in Cuba's world market integration of the 1990s: "Even if for some this may be a troublesome idea: The remittances phenomenon can be seen as an expression of the fact that a significant part of the Cuban economy's 'modern' sector is, de facto, located outside of its national boundaries."[46]

While remittances are the most salient aspect of the new transnational migration networks, as Eckstein points out they have many more implications for both sides, including the transformation of norms, culture, identity, and social and cultural capital.[47]

Little of this has found its way into the general debate on exit and voice. In a recent appraisal of Hirschman's concept and its applications, Dowding et al., although critical, fully endorse the dichotomy of the exit category: "Exit is a fairly crude, binary response . . . operationally, exit is a dichotomous, voice a continuous variable."[48] When applied to migration in today's globalized world, this understanding seems hardly adequate. The particularity of the Cuban case is that remittances not only cross national boundaries but also a profound political and ideological abyss. It is precisely those who opt for exit and who are loyal to their relatives on the island who have generated a source of income that has been decisive for the survival of the regime.[49]

In the run-up to the U.S. 2004 presidential election this paradox led exiled hard-line leaders to lobby for increased restrictions on remittances, in order to tighten economic pressure on the Castro government. This generated severe frictions within the Cuban-American community. While the earliest cohorts of post-1959 emigrants, who maintain few personal ties to the island, backed this measure, it was widely rejected by more recent arrivals. Bush adopted the antiremittances measures with limited risk of electoral losses, since the share of those registered to vote is much smaller among recent immigrants than among the older cohorts. The Cuban government took the tightening of U.S. policy as a welcome pretext to undo one of the economic reform steps it had taken in the mid-1990s, banning the circulation of the U.S. dollar on the island.[50]

Binding the Political with the National Question:
The Case of the Helms-Burton Act

As a result of long-standing hegemonic tradition and interests of U.S. policy, and the political impact of the Cuban émigré community, Cuban U.S. policy effectively stands in the way of any democratization in Cuba. It is worth turning to the Helms-Burton law at this point, as it is closely bound up with the "national question."[51] The law explicitly puts the property claims of the Cuban exiles at the center of U.S. Cuba policy. Most Cubans who emigrated to the United States after 1959 took up U.S. citizenship, and the Helms-Burton Act protects their claims as "the property of U.S. citizens."[52] From a legal perspective, applying U.S. citizenship to Cuban exiles retroactively to the time of the property confiscations flies in the face of international law and prior U.S. jurisprudence. More than 30 years ago the U.S. Foreign Claims Settlement Commission had pronounced that the "principle of international law that eligibility for compensation requires American nationality at the time of loss is so widely understood and universally accepted that citation of authority is hardly necessary."[53] The point here, however, is that these provisions reinterpret the internal Cuban conflict ex post facto as an international conflict in which the revolutionary Cuban state stands not in opposition to Cuban citizens but rather against U.S. citizens and thus the U.S. government. And this internationalized construction shifts the political arena (in which decisions about future political transformations in Cuba are made) away from the island.

U.S. policy could hardly be more supportive of the Cuban government in the latter's attempt to recast all internal struggle as part of a dichotomous us-them conflict. To the extent that this continues, it provides the Cuban leadership with a reliable "ideological" framework within which it can continue to prevent deviant political opinions from gaining space in the national public discourse.

Helms-Burton stipulates a long and detailed catalog of conditions for a democratic transition in Cuba, including the dissolution of the state security apparatus (Section 205a3), the announcement of "free and fair" elections for a new government (Section 205a4), permission for privately owned media and telecommunication companies to operate (Section 205b2A), and the adoption of appropriate steps to return to nationalized property or provide "equitable" compensation to U.S. citizens (Section 205b2D). Washington's requirements extend to the personal: "[A] transition government in Cuba is a government that . . . does not include either Fidel Castro or Raúl Castro" (Section 205a7). From the point of view of Cuban officials no matter how reform-oriented, this catalog as defined by U.S. law describes less a transition government than a situation of complete capitulation. The Helms-Burton Act stipulates still further conditions and requirements for a U.S.-recognized fully fledged "democratically elected government." By unilaterally outlining the future shape of Cuban politics, the latter statement explicitly goes beyond the end of the Castro era, recalling the days of the notorious Platt Amendment, which anchored the right of the United States to intervene in the Cuban constitution in 1909 and became the symbol for the quasi-colonial status of the newly born republic. This is unpalatable even for Cubans who are resolute Castro opponents. Alfredo Durán, a former participant in the Bay of Pigs invasion and currently one of the leaders of moderate exile forces, opposed the bill in a U.S. Senate hearing, saying, "Under Helms-Burton, Cuba would pass from the dictatorship of Fidel Castro to the tutelage of the U.S. Congress. . . . All the requirements in the law establish criteria for democracy in Cuba which only the Cuban people can have the right to determine."[54]

Conclusions

The Cuban government is adamant that Cuba has its own kind of democracy, which simply differs from the Western capitalist model. Anyone who has been to Cuba in recent years, however, can safely conclude that the question of democracy, whatever the variant, has not been fully answered, not even by the Cuban government's last word on the matter—a referendum that led to an outrageous 99.7 percent of popular support for an "untouchable" socialist order. But democratization in Cuba is not just a matter for its people but also for outsiders, particularly the U.S. neocolonial prescription, which is tied up with various interests in the United States and within the emigrant community. In such a context, democratization appears tantamount to unconditional surrender, a prospect that raises serious fears not just for the Cuban elite today but more generally and further into the future.

It may be that U.S. policy is less about promoting a transition government and more about seeking regime breakdown, a change that is not promoted from above but rather results from a collapse of the current system, preferably through a resignation of the Castro government in the wake of social unrest. Where such mobilization "from below" occurred in Eastern Europe, dissatisfaction with the status quo was complemented by hopes for a better future as a result of three interrelated factors: the promise of improved standards of living with the establishment of a market economy, accession to Europe and to societies associated with material improvement (the most prominent example being the unification of the GDR with the Federal Republic of Germany [FRG] and its abandonment of We are the people for We are one People), and a return to a "radiant past" through which a national better self could emerge.[55] In the case of Cuba, all the above are linked to the Cuban emigrant community in the United States and thus to the United States itself. As regards the market economy, the material success story of U.S.-Cubans apparently offers both manifest proof of the promise of a liberal capitalist economy and of the specific capacity of Cubans to operate within such a system. As regards association, Cuban exiles represent a living argument for the advantages of the highest possible attachment with the United States (integration). As regards a radiant past, nobody better embodies the nostalgically idealized prerevolutionary "Golden 1950s" than the exile community.

But to the extent that these promises of a better future are associated with exiled Cubans and the United States, they raise various fearful specters, both for the island elite and the general population. More specifically, there is the threat of the return of the social conflict of the Cuban Revolution, much of which was exported through emigration. It is a situation that raises fears about property claims and of material or moral retaliation for participation in or collaboration with the ancien régime and its attendant ramifications (loss of position, job and functions, outside competition that devalues personal qualifications, resources, and biographies). Further, there is the problem of what are currently sharply polarized positions. When the alternative is either expressed in terms of Down with Fidel!, or alternatively in terms of *Patria o Muerte!*, it is difficult to imagine a peaceful civil process in place of a highly violent confrontation. So, to the extent that promises of a better future are linked to the United States and the exiles, they become politically blocked. These promises appear viable only individually in the form of emigration to the United States but seem unimaginable as a collective Cuban process. The high-wire act of a progressive position on Cuba must be based on continually rejecting the hegemonic ambitions of the United States and advocating a policy that separates the political from the national question. It creates at least an opportunity for dignified reform that should be driven from within (the kind of reform that interested forces on the island could undertake if they were to become sufficiently strong) and rejects the argument that external imposition is a good reason for the Cuban government to brand any quest for democratization as antinational. The 99.7 percent of the referendum should not be the last word of the people on the matter.

Notes

1. Claus Offe, "Capitalism by Democratic Design?" *Social Research*, 58 (4), 1991: 872.
2. Jorge I. Domínguez, Omar Everleny Pérez Villanueva, and Lorena Barberia, *The Cuban Economy at the Start of the Twenty-First Century* (Cambridge, MA: Harvard University Press, 2004); Archibald R. M. Ritter (ed.), *The Cuban Economy* (Pittsburgh, PA: University of Pittsburgh Press, 2004); and Dietmar Dirmoser and Jaime Estay, *Economía y reforma económica en Cuba* (Caracas: Nueva Sociedad, 1997).
3. Offe, "Capitalism by Democratic Design?" pp. 872–873.
4. Guillermo O'Donnell, "Introduction to the Latin American Cases," in Guillermo O'Donnell, Philippe Schmitter, and Laurence Whitehead (eds.), *Transitions from Authoritarian Rule*, 4 vols. Vol. II, *Latin America* (Baltimore, MD: Johns Hopkins University Press, 1986), pp. 9–10.
5. Philippe C. Schmitter and Terry Lynn Karl, "The Conceptual Travels of Transitologists and Consolidationists: How Far to the East Should They Attempt to Go?" *Slavic Review*, 53, Spring 1994: 173–185.
6. Terry Lynn Karl and Philippe C. Schmitter, "Modes of Transition in Latin America, Southern and Eastern Europe," *International Social Science Journal*, 43, May 1991: 269–284; and Guillermo O'Donnell, "The State, Democratization and Some Conceptual Problems: A Latin American View with Glances at Some Post-Communist-Countries," in William C. Smith, Carlos H. Acuña, and Eduardo A. Gamarra (eds.), *Latin American Political Economy in the Age of Neo Liberal Reform: Theoretical and Comparative Perspectives for the 1990s* (New Brunswick: Transaction Books, 1994), pp. 117–125.
7. Juan J. Linz and Alfred Stepan, *Problems of Democratic Transition and Consolidation: Southern Europe, South America, and Post-Communist Europe* (Baltimore, MD: Johns Hopkins University Press, 1996), p. 357. Worthy of

mention is the attempt to place socialist Cuba in the context of international transition research with the Seminar Cuba a la luz de otras transiciones (Cuba in the Light of Other Transitions) conducted by the Instituto de Estudios Cubanos (Institute of Cuban Studies) together with the journal *Encuentro de la Cultura Cubana* in the summer of 1997 in Madrid.

8. In 1990, the Cuban-American Association for the Study of the Cuban Economy published the proceedings of its first annual meeting under the title Cuba in Transition (understood as "the transition of Cuba to a free-market democracy"). Since then, the association has published its proceedings annually under the same title, although developments in Cuba certainly have not measured up to expectations (cf. http://lanic.utexas.edu/la/cb/cuba/asce/). The term free-market democracy used above explicitly conflates of a capitalist economic system with a democratic political regime understood as a "Western" liberal multiparty system. Although this probably represents the dominant current in the literature on Cuba, alternative approaches to discussing democratization processes, such as that by Bengelsdorf, should be noted. See Carollee Bengelsdorf, *The Problem of Democracy in Cuba: Between Vision and Reality* (Oxford: Oxford University Press, 1994). On the island, an intensive academic debate on the scope for more pluralist forms of participation within the socialist system took place in the mid-1990s. Central to this debate were Rafael Hernández, "La sociedad civil y sus alredores," *La Gaceta de Cuba* (Unión Nacional de Escritores y Artistas de Cuba), 1, 1994: 28–31; Hugo Azcuy, "Cuba: ¿Reforma Constitucional o Nueva Constitución?" *Cuadernos de Nuestra América*, 19 (La Habana: Centro de Estudios sobre América, 1994); Hugo Azcuy, "Estado y sociedad civil en Cuba," *Temas* (Havana), October–December 1995: 105–110; and the volumes edited by Alfonso Haoldo Dilla, *La democracia en Cuba y el diferndo con los Estados Unidos* (Havana: CEA, 1995) and *La participacíon en Cuba y los retos del futuro* (Havana: Ediciones CEA, 1996). For a review of that debate see Bert Hoffmann, "Cuba: La reforma desde adentro que no fue," *Encuentro de la Cultura Cubana* (Madrid), 10, 1998: 71–84.

9. Bert Hoffmann, "El cambio imposible: Cuba como 'asunto interméstico' en la política de EE. UU: Consecuencias y perspectivas," in Klaus Bodemer et al. (eds.), *El Triángulo Atlántico. América Latina, Europa y los Estados Unidos en el sistema internacional cambiante* (Sankt Augustin: Konrad-Adenauer-Stiftung/ Arbeitsgemeinschaft Deutsche Lateinamerika-Forschung, 2002), pp. 352–362.

10. Article 5 states, "El Partido Comunista de Cuba, vanguardia organizada marxista-lcninista dc la clase obrera, es la fuerza dirigente de la sociedad y del Estado, que organiza y orienta los esfuerzos comunes hacia los altos fines de la construcción del socialismo y el avance hacia la sociedad comunista." ("The Communist Party of Cuba, the organized Marxist-Leninist vanguard of the working class, is the leading force of society and State, which organizes and orients common efforts toward the high goals of the construction of socialism and progress toward the Communist society.") See República de Cuba, *Constitución de la República de Cuba* (as approved in 1976), at http://pdba.georgetown.edu/Constitutions/Cuba/cuba1976.html. Accessed September 27, 2006.

11. See Marifeli Pérez-Stable, *The Cuban Revolution: Origins, Course and Legacy* (New York: Oxford University Press, 1993).

12. Hans Magnus Enzensberger, "Bildnis einer Partei: Vorgeschichte, Struktur und Ideologie der PCC," *Kursbuch*, October 18, 1969: 215.

13. Rafael Rojas, "Políticas invisibles," in *Encuentro de la Cultura Cubana* 6/7, *Cuba a la luz de otras transiciones* (Madrid), 1997: 24–35.

14. Jorge I. Domínguez, "Comienza una transición hacia el autoritarismo en Cuba?" in *Encuentro de la Cultura Cubana* 6/7, *Cuba a la luz de otras transiciones* (Madrid), 1997: 12.

15. This refers to the city of Numantia, which in 133 BC, after fiercely resisting the forces of the Roman Empire for 20 years, finally fell, with the surviving defenders choosing suicide rather than surrender.

16. Valerie Bunce, "Comparing East and South," *Journal of Democracy*, 6 (3), July 1995: 91.

17. *Constitución de la República de Cuba*, at http://pdba.georgetown.edu/Constitutions/Cuba/cuba1976.html. Accessed September 27, 2006; and *Constitución de la República de Cuba* (including the 1992 reform) at http://www.cuba.cu/gobierno/consti.htm. Accessed September 27, 2006.

18. Pérez-Stable, *The Cuban Revolution*, p. 41.

19. See, e.g., Jorge I. Domínguez, *Cuba: Order and Revolution* (Cambridge, MA: Harvard University Press, 1978); Jorge I. Domínguez, *To Make a World Safe for Revolution: Cuba's Foreign Policy* (Cambridge, MA: Harvard University Press 1989); and Jorge I. Domínguez, "Cuba in a New World," in Abraham F. Lowenthal and Gregory F. Treverton (eds.), *Latin America in a New World* (Boulder, CO: Westview Press, 1994), pp. 203–216.

20. Albert O. Hirschman, *Exit, Voice, and Loyalty: Responses to Decline in Firms, Organizations, and States* (Cambridge, MA: Harvard University Press, 1970).

21. Ibid. Hirschman also introduces a third category, loyalty, which delays exit as well as voice. This third category never received the prominence of exit and voice, and for Hirschman himself it played a secondary role in his later works. See Albert O. Hirschman, "Exit and Voice: An Expanding Sphere of Influence," in Albert O. Hirschman (ed.), *Rival Views of Market Society* (New York: Viking, 1986), pp. 77–101; and Albert O. Hirschman, "Exit, Voice, and the Fate of the German Democratic Republic: An Essay in Conceptual History," *World Politics*, 45 (2), 1993: 173–202 (first published in 1992 as "Abwanderung, Widerspruch und das Schicksal der Deutschen Demokratischen Republik," *Leviathan*, 20 [3], 1992: 330–358). See also Albert O. Hirschman, "Exit, Voice, and the State," in Albert O. Hirschman (ed.), *Essays in Trespassing. Economics to Politics and Beyond* (Cambridge: Cambridge University Press, 1981), pp. 246–265.

22. Hirschman, "Exit and Voice," p. 91. See also by Hirschman, "Exit, Voice, and Loyalty: Further Reflections and a Survey of Recent Contributions," in Hirschman (ed.), *Essays in Trespassing*, pp. 227–228. Among the scholars who have explicitly applied the exit and voice model to the Cuban case and are particularly worthy of note are Josep M. Colomer, "Exit, Voice, and Hostility in Cuba," *International Migration Review*, 34 (2), 2000: 423–442, who uses the concept in a game-theoretic model focusing on the interaction between Cuba and the U.S. government, and Silvia Pedraza, "Democratization and Migration: Cuba's Exodus and the Development of Civil Society—Hindrance or Help?" in Association for the Study of the Cuban Economy (ASCE) (ed.), *Cuba in Transition*, 12, 2002: 247–261, at http://lanic.utexas.edu/project/asce/pdfs/volume12/pedraza.pdf. Accessed September 27, 2006.

23. See, e.g., Ted Henken, "*Balseros, Boteros*, and *El Bombo*: Cuban Immigration to the United States since the 1994 Rafter Crisis And the Persistence of

Special Treatment," paper prepared for the Symposium The Balseros Ten Years Later: No Longer Adrift? Cuban Research Institute, Florida International University, Florida, July 16–17, 2004, pp. 6 and 30.

24. Juan Antonio Blanco, "Sin patria pero, ¿con amo?" *Encuentro en la Red*, May 17, 2004 at http://www.cubaencuentro.com/sociedad/20040517/2acf0b32e45f4b8b8f85a5b44d3f64 20/1.html. Accessed May 18, 2004.

25. Ibid.

26. This was true even in the case of the Mariel boat-lift: although the yachts of Florida-based Cubans served as the means of transportation, the Cuban government had full control over the point of embarkation (Mariel Port) and was thus in a position to put an end to the exodus at any given time.

27. U.S. Congress, *Cuban Adjustment Act* (Public Law 89–732, November 2, 1966, as amended), at http://www.state.gov/www/regions/wha/cuba/publiclaw_89-732.html. Accessed September 27, 2006.

28. For this and what follows see Ernesto Rodríguez Chávez, *Emigración cubana actual* (Havana: Editorial de Ciencias Sociales, 1993), p. 93, who draws on official data from Cuban and U.S. sources.

29. Carmelo Mesa-Lago, "Cuba's Raft Exodus of 1994: Causes, Settlement, Effects, and Future," North-South Center Agenda Paper 12, Miami, FL, 1995.

30. The September 1994 document refers to the transfer of *balseros* picked up at sea to "safe havens" outside the United States (the U.S. Guantánamo base) but the follow-up agreement of May 2, 1995 changed this, and they were sent back to Cuba (with a Cuban government commitment to abstain from any reprisals). The refugees transferred to the U.S. Guantánamo base during 1994 *balsero* crisis were gradually admitted to the United States later as part of the 20,000 quota for yearly legal Cuban migration.

31. Henken, *"Balseros, Boteros,* and *El Bombo,"* p. 15.

32. Ibid., p. 13. More recent data are unavailable as there has been no new visa lottery held since.

33. Hirschman, *Exit, Voice, and Loyalty*, p. 30.

34. Pedraza, "Democratization and Migration," p. 254.

35. Hoffmann, "El cambio imposible," p. 352.

36. Bert Hoffmann, "¿Helms-Burton a perpetuidad? Repercusiones y perspectivas para Cuba, EEUU y Europa," *Nueva Sociedad*, 151 (Caracas), 1997: 57–72.

37. Asamblea Nacional, *Asamblea Nacional: Ley de reafirmación de la dignidad y soberanía cubana* (Havana), December 24, 1996, at http://www.cubavsbloqueo.cu/Default.aspx?tabid 247. Accessed September 27, 2006.

38. Comparison to the GDR is difficult in this aspect. Though considerable in numbers, GDR emigrants never constituted a specific community in the West nor did they settle in any particular region. Except for a number of writers and artists, they hardly raised their voice publicly as ex-GDR citizens.

39. Author's interview with Minister of Economic Affairs José Luis Rodríguez, Havana, in *Die Tageszeitung* (Berlin), November 11, 1993. As long as Western currencies were prohibited, remittances had to be exchanged at the official rate of $1 1 peso, which rendered remittances extremely costly.

40. MIF, *Sending Money Home: An International Comparison of Remittance Markets* (Washington, DC: Inter-American Development Bank, 1993), at http://www.iadb.org/exr/prensa/images/RoundTablesFEB2003.pdf. Accessed September 27, 2006.

41. In the first year after the legalization of the U.S. dollar, the 1994 balance of payments showed an entry of $574.8 million under the heading current transfers, expressly described as "mainly due to income from donations and remittances." Banco Nacional de Cuba (ed.), *Economic Report 1994*, Havana, August 1995, p. 20. For a discussion of different estimates and their methodology, see Pedro Monreal González, "Las remesas familiares en la economía cubana," *Encuentro de la Cultura Cubana* (Madrid), 14 Fall 1999: 50.

42. Hirschman, *Exit, Voice, and Loyalty*, pp. 15 and 16.

43. See, e.g., Alejandro Portes, Luis Eduardo Guarnizo, and Patricia Landolt, "Transnational Communities," *Ethnic and Racial Studies* (special issue), 22 (2), 1999: 316–339; Ludger Pries, *Migration and Transnational Social Spaces* (Aldershot: Ashgate, 1999); and Douglas S. Massey et al., *Worlds in Motion: Understanding International Migration at the End of the Millennium* (New York: Greenwood Press, 1998).

44. MIF, *Sending Money Home*, 11.

45. Bernard Poirine, "A Theory of Remittances as an Implicit Family Loan Arrangement," *World Development*, 25 (4), 1997: 589–611.

46. Monreal González, "Las remesas familiares en la economía cubana," p. 49.

47. Susan Eva Eckstein, "Transnational Networks and Norms, Remittances, and the Transformation of Cuba," in Domínguez, Everleny Pérez Villanueva, and Barberia (eds.), *The Cuban Economy at the Start of the Twenty-First Century*, pp. 319–351.

48. Keith Dowding et al., "Exit, Voice and Loyalty: Analytic and Empirical Developments," *European Journal of Political Research*, 37 (4), 2000: 471.

49. Again, comparison to the GDR is problematic. Transnational social ties between East Germany and West Germany were not created by emigration; rather, the division of Germany cut through existing social ties. Contacts between West Germany and East Germany were not dominated by emigrants from the GDR but rather by family links existing prior to the creation of the GDR. Since Western currencies were forbidden, monetary remittances made little sense; remittances in kind during visits and in the form of packages were common, but they did not play a major role in the GDR's national economy.

50. Fidel Castro, *Mensaje del Comandante en Jefe Fidel Castro Ruíz, leído en la Mesa redonda informativa sobre las nuevas agresiones económicas del gobierno norteamericano y la respuesta cubana, efectuada el 25 de octubre de 2004* (Havana), at http://www.cuba.cu/gobierno/discursos/2004/esp/f251004e.html.

51. Passed by the U.S. Congress in 1996 and named after its initiators, Republican Senator Jesse Helms and Democratic Representative Dan Burton (but officially known as the Cuban Liberty and Democratic Solidarity [Libertad] Act of 1996). See full text at http://www.ustreas.gov/offices/enforcement/ofac/legal/statutes/ libertad.pdf. Accessed January 7, 2007. See also IRELA, *Documentación del seminario El refuerzo del embargo de EEUU contra Cuba: Implicaciones para el comercio y las inversiones*, Conference held at Sitges, Spain, 8–10 July, IRELA, Madrid, 1996; Hoffmann, "¿Helms-Burton a perpetuidad?" p. 1.

52. IRELA, *Documentación del seminario El refuerzo del embargo de EEUU contra Cuba*.

53. Robert Muse, "Legal and Practical Implications of Title III of the Helms-Burton Law," IRELA, *Documentación del seminario El refuerzo del embargo de EEUU contra Cuba*, p. 6.

54. Alfredo Durán, "Testimony to the U.S. Senate of June 14, 1995," *Cuban Affairs/Asuntos Cubanos*, 2 (1–2), Spring–Summer 1995: 3.
55. Michael Burawoy and János Lucás, *The Radiant Past: Ideology and Reality in Hungary's Road to Capitalism* (Chicago, IL: University of Chicago Press, 1992).

Chapter 7

The Cuban-American Political Machine: Reflections on Its Origins and Perpetuation

Alejandro Portes

Introduction

"In order to appraise Miami's present-day development, it is convenient to look at that city in 1959. To simplify, Miami was then a typical southern city, with an important sector of retirees and veterans, whose only interest was the exploitation of tourism during Miami's warm winter months. The growth achieved by Miami has no precedent in the history of the United States. It occurred during what has been called The Great Cuban Miracle. So I believe that those who left the Island after 1959 and those who have arrived more recently with the same faith and hope must feel proud not only of what they achieved for themselves but also what they have accomplished for the entire community."[1] These remarks, written almost 20 years ago by one of the most prominent members of the Miami Cuban establishment, were part of the response of Cuban exiles in that city to attempts by the native Anglo population and its leaders to deal with newcomers and, as it were, 'show them their place' in America's ethnic hierarchy. During the Mariel exodus of 1980, the *Miami Herald*, arguably the principal institution of the old Anglo establishment, led a vigorous campaign to remove the new arrivals from the city. After the end of the exodus, a rapid grassroots mobilization led to an overwhelming vote against the public use of Spanish. "We did not come to Miami to live in a banana republic," proclaimed one of the organizers of the anti-Spanish referendum.[2]

Origins and Paradoxes of Cuban-American Political Power

The Cuban response was extraordinary for its swiftness and scope. Denounced as an increasingly undesirable foreign element, the exiles did not respond with the usual complaints of racism and discrimination; instead they laid claim to the city. Before them, Miami had been an insignificant southern tourist town. The commercial and financial emporium that had suddenly emerged at the tip of Florida was entirely their creation, part of "The Great Cuban Miracle." These were the years in which the Cuban American National Foundation (CANF) was created in 1981 under the leadership of Jorge Más Canosa. They were also the years in which detailed plans were laid out for the achievement of local political power. "The anti-bilingual referendum was a slap in our face," said a Cuban-American local government official in 1981. "People began to feel more Cuban than anyone." Political organization at that time was embryonic, and plans for redress were relatively modest: "[T]o elect a Cuban mayor of the city and perhaps one or two state legislators."[3] By the mid-1980s, these goals had been amply fulfilled: the mayors of Miami, Hialeah, West Miami, and several smaller municipalities were Cuban-born, and there were 10 Cuban-Americans in the state legislature. The momentum toward political hegemony just kept growing. By the early 1990s, Miami Cubans sent two of their own, Lincoln Díaz-Balart and Ileana Ros-Lehtinen to Washington, DC, Republican Party congressional representatives. They were repeatedly reelected throughout the decade without credible opposition.

A study by a liberal think tank, the Center for Public Integrity in Washington, DC, ruefully concluded that the CANF was the most effective ethnic-lobbying organization in Washington, surpassing even the pro-Israeli lobby, which it had originally imitated. The report noted the conservative lobby's "potent, sometimes fearsome" role in shaping U.S. Cuba policy and criticized Más Canosa's access to Washington power brokers as "inordinate" noting that "most foundation heads don't meet with presidents and secretaries of state in every administration."[4]

What had happened? The local Miami Anglo establishment, accustomed as it was to dealing with impoverished racial minorities, had thought that it could deal easily with the seemingly penniless exiles. The ethnic hierarchy of a self-respecting southern city would be promptly restored. They never knew what hit them. For the Cubans were not just another ethnic minority but the displaced elites of their former country, possessors of considerable resources of education, organizational skills, and entrepreneurship. Between 1960 and 1980, thousands of small, medium, and even large firms were created by the former exiles. While their political goals centered on the prompt overthrow of the communist regime in the island, their economic energies focused on recuperating their positions of privilege. *Solidarios* and resourceful, they supported each other with subsidized credit and information and patronized each other as customers. For two decades, the Cuban enclave economy of Miami never ceased to grow.

Policies designed to reassert the hegemony of the dominant group in any community inevitably trigger reactive mobilizations by the excluded. For the most part, these mobilizations are ineffective because of lack of resources. Events in Miami moved along a very different path, however. When the former exiles turned their attention from the political situation in Cuba to that in their adopted country, they brought to the confrontation serious wealth and organizational knowledge. Their mobilization rapidly put the old Miami political establishment on the defensive and then routed it. Consequences of the Cubans' political victory have lasted to our day.

In many ways and with varying undertones of celebration or lament, this story has been told before.[5] Less explored have been the reasons for the perpetuation of the new order that emerged in South Florida in the early and mid-1980s. The Cuban-American elites not only achieved political control of their city but also proceeded to consolidate it during the next two decades eliminating, sometimes with an iron hand, all traces of opposition. This situation gave rise to three paradoxes.

First, immigrants, especially those who are economically successful and have been in the host country for many years, tend to integrate into society's mainstream. Despite their success and their four decades in the United States, Cubans remain apart, having created a distinct political economy in South Florida. This is the *assimilation paradox*.

Second, collective attitudes change, especially when subject to strong external influences. The political outlook of the Miami Cuban establishment is widely regarded as extreme and as out-of-touch with post–Cold War realties. The strident ways in which that outlook has been put forth on repeated occasions made it unpopular, not only in Latin America but in the United States as well. Public opinion surveys consistently place Cubans as one of the least liked groups by the rest of the U.S. population. This is the *intransigence paradox*.

Third, Cuban-American leaders are well aware that by pursuing their militant agenda, they provide the Cuban government with an invaluable symbolic resource. Experts on the island nation have repeatedly argued that the main claim of legitimacy left to Castro's government and one of the major reasons for its continuing existence lies in its credible claim of embodying nationalist opposition against U.S. aggression. Thus, the more Cuban Americans promote U.S. policies hostile to Cuba, the more they contribute to buttress a regime grounded on the defense of national sovereignty.[6] This is the *legitimacy paradox*. In the remainder of this chapter, I explore the reasons for these paradoxical outcomes and the social and institutional mechanisms that have supported their continuation over an extended period.

Why Do They Do It? The Rationale for Political Extremism

For many years, the standard explanation for the anomalous situation in South Florida was the radical character of the Cuban Revolution and the wounds that it inflicted on its many victims. Tens of thousands of people lost their properties without compensations; thousands were imprisoned under harsh conditions; and hundreds more lost their lives before firing squads. The victims and their families could not but harbor a relentless hostility toward the Cuban communist regime and an unquenchable thirst to see it pay for its deeds. This is also the usual explanation advanced by the exiles themselves for actions that the outside world sees as political lunacy. A Cuban-American businessman explained the militant protests orchestrated against the presence in Miami of Cuban artists in this fashion:

> When so many persons have been affected by communism, when so many had to abandon the land where they were born, when people could not visit the cemeteries where their loved ones rest, we do have to protest this kind of thing. Why not? Why do they have to impose on us such a painful thing? A person who has not suffered, who has not had relatives killed, can say coolly that there must be freedom of expression. We know better. It is too hard that they come here, to our center, to tell us these things.[7]

There is little doubt that the experiences of loss in the home country have been a powerful motivating force but, by themselves, they represent an insufficient explanation for the tenacity and resilience of Cuban exile ideology. The traumatic events so vividly described by our informant are, for most Cuban-Americans, a distant memory. A growing number of the people who actually experienced them have now died. Their denunciations are now ritualistically repeated by younger Cuban-Americans who never lived in Cuba and never suffered these traumas. Currently, more than half of the Cuban population of Miami is composed of refugees who came after 1979 and their offspring. Contrary to the exiles of the 1960s, these newer arrivals grew up and were educated under the Revolution, they did not have any properties confiscated, and in most cases, they came for economic reasons and not because of militant opposition to the regime.[8] The perpetuation of the discourse and practice of intransigence is better explained by the confluence of two other forces: first, the consolidation of unanticipated economic and political interests; second the cumulative consequences of past events on cultural practice.

Emergent Interests

The successful mobilizations against local Anglo hegemony had a significant consequence, namely the gradual devolution of political power within the U.S. electoral system to the former exiles. Cuban-American entrepreneurs made the economic contributions that enabled newly minted politicians to win local elections, mainly by mobilizing the Cuban-American vote. It was relatively easy to persuade the mass of Cubans concentrated in Miami to gain U.S. citizenship and register to vote. First, the option of returning to Cuba was blocked, leading to citizenship acquisition as part of the process of long-term settlement.[9] Second, this was already a politically mobilized population; the only requirement was to alter somewhat the direction of this mobilization—from protesting against Castro in the streets to voting in local elections.

With this block of voters solidly behind them, Cuban-Americans could successfully challenge the incumbents, first for municipal office, then for the state legislature, and finally for the U.S. Congress. Once they had been elected, Cuban-American politicians rapidly discovered two important facts. First, there were the considerable gains in status and influence accruing to them by virtue of their office. Second, there were the debts that they had to pay to the businessmen who had contributed to their successful campaigns. Thereafter, Cuban firms in South Florida started to flourish, going from servicing a purely ethnic market to becoming purveyors of goods and services to the mainstream population and to the state. Cuban-American firms laid cable for the local telephone companies, paved Dade County's roads, and built many of the new housing developments.

It helped that the city and county officials who handed out the contracts and the building inspectors who supervised the housing developments were fellow exiles or employees under the control of elected Cuban-American officials. Church and Tower, the company founded by Jorge Más Canosa, became one of the most important Dade County contractors. The Latin Builders Association, grouping all Cuban developers in the county, emerged as one of the most powerful local political lobbies. In time, the contours of what Logan and Molotch call an "urban growth machine" emerged in South Florida, in this instance with a strong Latin undertone.[10]

The basic dynamics of this machine are easy to understand: Cuban-American entrepreneurs contributed to the campaigns of Cuban-American politicians who, once in office, reciprocated the favor. The CANF became the core of this exchange network, ensuring its smooth operation and the strategic targeting of the Cubans' political contributions. In time, not only Cuban-American politicians but mainstream U.S. political figures, such as senators Jesse Helms of North Carolina and Robert Torricelli of New Jersey, became beneficiaries of the former exiles' largesse.

Cubans in Miami discovered that they were doing well by "doing good." Their mobilization against local Anglo attempts to reduce them to the status of another ethnic minority had succeeded beyond all expectations, putting them in control of the levers of local power. That situation, in turn, catapulted politicians and entrepreneurs alike into positions of prominence until the former exiles became the power structure in Miami. The unique growth machine that they created was not, however, without its failings. Many exiles, now in office, seemingly believed that they had been elected in Cuba, not in the United States, and that they could behave accordingly. In time, they found themselves behind bars or were forced to resign.

The popular mayor of Hialeah, Raúl Martínez, was indicted repeatedly by federal authorities, a fact that did not prevent his subsequent reelection. The flamboyant Sergio Pereira was forced to resign in disgrace as Dade County manager. So did Xavier Juárez, a Harvard-trained lawyer and presumed exemplar of a "new" generation of Cuban politicians, after his election as Miami mayor in 1997 proved fraudulent. Even the respected César Odio, for many years the city administrator, lost his job and went to jail on charges of malfeasance. There were so many rigged elections, so much influence peddling and plain stealing of public funds that the Federal Bureau of Investigation had to appoint a special task force for South Florida. At some point, the near bankrupt city of Miami was placed under the direct control of the State of Florida. Federal District Attorney Janet Reno had her hands full in the late 1980s teaching the upstart émigré politicians that Miami was still in the United States and was no banana republic.[11]

By fits and starts, the scandals subsided during the 1990s. The change was due, at least in part, to the learning curve among Cuban political figures hit by so many fines, loss of office, and jail terms. But despite all the setbacks, the political machine created by the former exiles never lost its grip and never ceased to consolidate its position. At the core of this resilience was the remarkable solidity of its electoral base. Cuban-American voters continued to line up at the polls in high numbers and to vote monolithically for their own, sometimes disregarding the candidate's past offenses and jail terms.

That asset insured a near monopoly of elected offices in areas where Cubans constitute a plurality. The behavior of the mass of Cuban voters did not reflect mere ethnic solidarity; instead, it was a direct consequence of an ideology of anticommunism and implacable opposition to the Castro government. In a real sense, a vote cast in Miami was not a vote for a coethnic candidate, but a vote against Castro.[12] Electoral platforms, even for such modest offices as the local school board, had to be carefully tailored to fit this outlook. Conversely, any candidate, Cuban or not, who dared to express some doubts about the righteousness of this position signed his own political death warrant, at least in the Cuban precincts. "He is soft on communism," the old ladies would say on their way to the voting booth, and that fact alone would decide their choice.

This frame of mind explains why Cuban-American politicians have been repeatedly elected without opposition. In particular, the two U.S. representatives, Ileana Ros-Lehtinen and Lincoln Díaz-Balart, have not been sent to Washington in defense of mundane local interests but as ambassadors of a national mission. They are, in the minds of Little Havana voters, the voices of the oppressed Cuban nation and the instruments for its redemption. To the extent that Ros-Lehtinen and Díaz-Balart continue to don the mantle of implacable enemies of Fidel Castro, their reelection has been assured.

More than personal experiences of victimization, it is this concatenation of events that explains the resilience of the Cuban-American machine. The beneficiaries, politicians, and entrepreneurs alike have developed strong vested interests in the continuation of their positions of privilege. To do so, however, they need to keep the electorate in a state of permanent mobilization against the regime in the island. It is this sacred mission—"to free our country from communism"—that translates into votes in Miami. The votes translate, in turn, into powerful offices in Tallahassee and Washington, DC, and into profitable contracts for local entrepreneurs.

The underpinnings of this machine also explain the peculiar situation of entrapment in which some of its members find themselves. Cuban-American politicians who begin to doubt the wisdom of the ideology of intransigence or who become aware of how negatively it bears on the public image of their community must keep silent, because to weaken the fervor of the masses is also to jeopardize their own positions. For the same reason, anyone voicing doubts about the reigning ideology or finding some merit in the policies of the Cuban regime is cast aside and barred entry into the charmed inner circle of the machine.

Cumulative Causation

Many processes in social life build upon themselves. In such instances, present events are determined by similar events in the past that spiral up or down in a cumulative sequence. Examples include individual unemployment, where long spells without a job significantly increase the chances of remaining without one in the future. Market rallies and stampedes are collective examples, where the behavior of certain actors triggers a mass response.[13] One of the key characteristics of cumulative causation is that it progressively eliminates other options, funneling future actions along a narrower path than was possible at the start. Thus, once a person has been convicted of a crime and labeled a social deviant, it becomes difficult for him to return to normal life because the actions of others in his immediate environment tend to reinforce the original label and, hence, exclude him from a range of opportunities. Similarly, a government that becomes known as unreliable in handling its finances will find the doors of international lenders closed, further aggravating its economic situation and leading, in turn, to a new round of unorthodox measures. Vicious circles is the name given in popular parlance to such processes.[14]

Along with the consolidation of political and economic interests requiring continuous popular mobilization, the perpetuation of the Cuban-American machine is also due to a cumulative causation process. It was not inevitable that the cognitive framework that came to dominate the exile community would be right-wing extremism. Other, more moderate ideologies competed for favor in the early years of this community. Reasons for their demise have been examined in detail elsewhere.[15] The key point is that, once the ideology of intransigence became dominant, it fed on itself closing down other options and narrowing with the passage of time.

This narrowing of options has two main manifestations. The first is cognitive, leading to an outlook on the world that is lacking in nuance. Second-generation politicians, born and bred in Miami and who have never been to Cuba, repeat without hesitation the same fervent "anticommunist mantras" and the same calls to arms learned from their elders. They do this, in part, because of political expediency, but there is also an element of genuine conviction. The ideology of intransigence has deprived them of any alternative lens through which to interpret the Cuban revolutionary process or understand the actions of its leaders. The second consequence is more tangible. Built around this ideology, there developed over time a behavioral repertoire that became habitual and necessary. To be part of the community, to be a true "Miami Cuban," having been born on the island and to leave because of political persecution is not enough. It is also necessary to engage in a series of expected behaviors, ranging from supporting right-wing candidates to opposing publicly and loudly anyone voicing sympathies for the Cuban regime. This frame of mind also explains why many aged exiles who are able and would dearly love, under other circumstances, to visit the island refrain from doing so: "My social class doesn't travel to Cuba. Jorge Más Canosa is a saint. We won't break ranks," an elderly exile told Susan Eckstein in the course of her study of the Cuban community.[16]

The same study reports the case of Josefina, an old Cuban woman living in New Jersey who actually went back. She decided to do so because of an 81-year-old sister whom, she feared, she would never see again. Her husband did not accompany her. "I won't visit, I won't return," explained the elderly gentleman. Josefina met her sister, made a peace of sorts with a niece who remained a committed revolutionary, and declared upon return: "It was like Beirut. A country filled with misery and destruction." When her trip drew to a close, Josefina knew "that this was goodbye. I vowed never to return again while Fidel is in power."[17] Eckstein and her collaborator Lorena Barberia found the "Beirut theme" repeated again and again by older exiles who had dared to break the injunction against travel. That their views of "a country filled with destruction" are conditioned by their own community's ideology is made clear by the fact that younger Cuban-Americans living outside of Miami and who have visited the island never dwell on this theme. Indeed, many report quite a different impression:

> I was blown away on my first visit. I grew up thinking that Cuba was like Eastern Europe—gray and fearful. But I found it gorgeous. People have a hard time, but they also have a sense of life. . . . I cried every night because it was the first time I felt at home. Here were Cubans talking with their hands! And I knew their accent![18]

The inertial force of a cumulative causation process helps explain why not only Cuban-American leaders who benefit directly from the Miami political machine but even the mass of exiles who derive little material gain from it continue to uphold the same outlook and to behave accordingly. Theirs is a world in black-and-white, apart from which there is no alternative. After four decades, this self-reinforcing outlook is next to impossible to overcome.

How Do They Do It? The Mechanics
of Continuing Hegemony

Here, I tackle a different question. It is not the same to explain why a social process comes about than to account for its actual inner workings. A process may be beneficial or desirable to certain people, without their wishes being translated into reality. Similarly, once the process is in place, it may be carried along by its own inertial force, but that force may weaken if not reenergized periodically. From an earlier study of the rise of the Cuban enclave economy in Miami, I want to rescue a central notion, namely that it constitutes a moral community.[19] The term moral is not used in its everyday meaning, but to denote the fact that transactions among community members, even the most instrumental, are imbued with the overarching ideology. Adhering to this ideology defines the limits of this community (who is a true Cuban exile, and, therefore, who can claim the protection, social status, and economic opportunities that the community can provide, for example). To understand how this moral community is perpetuated, two general concepts are useful: social capital as a mechanism for social control and ritual as a mechanism for reaffirmation.

The Downside of Social Capital

Social capital, a concept introduced by the French sociologist Pierre Bourdieu and popularized by the American sociologist James S. Coleman, is defined as the ability to access resources by virtue of membership in social networks or larger social structures.[20] Resources can be of any kind—including credit, information, votes, or labor. The central idea is that social capital provides individuals with a privileged means to obtain resources that bypass the market and its rules. It is a privilege granted on the basis of membership. Those who have it gain access to jobs, special rate loans, stock market tips, and voluntary help from friends or neighbors. Nonmembers must purchase these services at market prices or do without.

From the point of view of the recipient, resources mediated by social capital have the character of a "gift." Hence, reasons why recipients would want to participate in these transactions are unproblematic. More difficult to understand is the motivation of donors who appear to be giving away something for nothing. The theoretical literature on this concept identifies several mechanisms that make such transactions possible. For the present analysis, two are relevant. Reciprocity expectations lead members of a community to do favors for each other, in the belief that such favors will be repaid in the future.[21] The key factor that distinguishes these transactions from market exchanges is that the form of repayment is left unspecified. What donors create in these transactions is a diffuse sense of obligation on which they can base future claims. Bounded solidarity is a source of social capital that prompts individuals to help others because of common membership in a given collectivity. Bonds can be of any kind—nationality, class, ethnicity, or family. Regardless of their source, such bonds give rise to a "we-feeling" among those so linked, leading them to prefer each other, even in the absence of reciprocity expectations.[22]

One of the most notable characteristics of the Cuban enclave of Miami, particularly in its early stages, was its internal solidarity, born out of common experiences of forced departure and loss and cemented subsequently by opposition to the regime in the island. The simultaneous growth of Cuban-American economic and political power created a mass of resources and opportunities available to friends and allies. Fellow Cubans stood first in line as recipients of this largesse but only on condition that they adhered strictly to the ideological outlook of the enclave. Cuban-Americans bought from each other, supported each other's firms through concessionary credit and preferences, employed coethnics, and voted monolithically for Cuban candidates. Members of the community—from wealthy entrepreneurs to workers—stood to gain from its reciprocity networks and bounded solidarity.[23]

As elsewhere, these sources of social capital have both their positive consequences and their downside. They create opportunities for individuals, but simultaneously impose social controls over them. Put differently, social capital provides rewards for conformity and disincentives for deviance. The stronger the bonds, the more difficult it is to challenge the dictates of the collectivity. The Cuban enclave constitutes a moral community because of the strength of its social capital and, hence, the unique combination of rewards and punishments with which it holds its members in line.

In the early meetings leading to the creation of the Cuban Committee for Democracy, an organization of centrist Cuban-Americans opposed to the Cuban government *and* to the ideology of the machine, several prominent Miami professionals and entrepreneurs participated enthusiastically, but they eventually dropped out. Their reasons were invariably the same: fear for their jobs and pressure from families afraid of the consequences or opposed to their joining a "communist" organization.[24] These Cubans had effectively traded suppression of their rights to free expression under communism for a similar suppression under capitalism, Miami style. The existence and operation of social capital within the Cuban enclave is thus an important factor explaining the resilience of its political machine: year after year there have been rewards, material and symbolic, for those who toe the line and significant disincentives for those who dare to express a different opinion.

Rituals

Like political leaders the world over intent on hanging onto positions of privilege, the heads of the Miami machine know that its continuation also requires periodic rituals. Rituals fulfill the dual purpose of keeping the crucial mass of supporters involved and reenergizing the collective ideology, adapting it to new circumstances. In Miami, there are two types of rituals: regular and circumstantial. Cuban holidays like Independence Day, or the birthday of Jose Marti are celebrated in Miami as in the island. To these are added days that are part of the history of the exile community, such as the Bay of Pigs landing on April 17, 1961. Such occasions are used by Cuban-American leaders to recommit to their ideological principles, attack the government in Cuba, and request continuing support in the struggle to bring it down. Editorials are read over the enclave's numerous radio stations, led by WAQI (Radio Mambí) and WQBA (La Cubanísima). Listeners are encouraged to participate, which many do vying with each other in their exalted declarations of anticommunist and patriotic fervor. A number of sites in Miami have been imbued with a quasi-sacred meaning in the collective imagination and are, hence, suitable for the celebration of these periodic rituals. The most important of these is the Eternal Flame honoring exile soldiers fallen during the Bay of Pigs invasion. It is located at the heart of the enclave, in the intersection of Calle Ocho (SW 8th Street) and the Cuban Memorial Boulevard (SW 13th Avenue).

A second such site is Freedom Tower, a replica of the Giralda tower of Seville, located in downtown Miami. It served for many years as headquarters of the Federal Cuban Refugee Center that processed hundreds of thousands of new arrivals from the island. It has been recently purchased by the Más Canosa family that announced plans to turn it into a memorial and museum of Cuban-American history. A third is the Sanctuary of Our Lady of Charity (Nuestra Señora de la Caridad), the patron saint of Cuba. It was built by the Catholic Church on the shores of Biscayne Bay, with its main altar pointing toward Cuba. These sites also serve as locations for mass rallies, protests, and Catholic masses on the occasions when outside events provoke the animus of the community. Although irregular, these occasions are not rare because interest of machine leaders lies in cultivating a mobilized, emotional state among the mass of exiles. It also helps that clashes between this community and its perennial island communist foes are quite common. After the planes of the exile organization, Brothers to the Rescue had flown several times over Havana distributing anti-Castro leaflets, the Cuban government sent a Mig fighter to shoot them down. The incident, in November 1996, triggered instant mass protests in Miami and led directly to passage by the U.S. Congress of the Helms-Burton bill, which aimed at decisively choking the island's economy. Only weeks later, several streets in Miami were rebaptized with the names of the downed exile pilots.

The incident provoked by the Brothers to the Rescue planes is just one of a long chain of events triggering mass mobilizations in South Florida. At the forefront of these rallies are multiple pocket organizations whose very raison d'être lies in stoking the fires of anti-Castro sentiment. While supporting and benefiting from these rituals, the top leadership of the Cuban machine seldom takes part in these street actions. That task is left to the pocket organizations whose leaders vie with each other in their patriotic militancy and fervor. Table 7.1 presents a partial list of these organizations grouped in two umbrella federations—Unidad Cubana (Cuban Unity [UC]), and the Junta Patriotica (Patriotic Junta [JP]). As their names indicate, they are a motley crew, ranging from fictitious military commandos to various occupational and municipal associations.

During the Elián González episode, several of the most exalted grassroots groups vowed to "shut down Miami" in protest for the U.S. government's decision to return the child to Cuba. They blocked traffic and sought to paralyze the harbor and airport of Miami with utter disregard for the opinions and wishes of the non-Cuban inhabitants of the city. When Elián was forcibly removed by federal authorities, the protests turned violent with torched cars and repeated confrontation with police forces throughout the city.[25] Plans were subsequently announced by the CANF to turn the house where Elián lived into a shrine and museum, still another sacred site for the celebration of future public rituals.

Table 7.1   Confederations of Cuban Political Groups of Miami

Junta Patriotica	Unidad Cubana
Founded in April 1980	Founded in June 1991
First led by Tony Varona, former Cuban Prime Minister	First led by Armando Pérez Roura, a radio commentator
Organizations	
Puente de Jóvenes Profesionales Cubanos	Movimiento Demócrata Cristiano
Coalición de Profesionales Cubano-Americanos	Grupo Táctico Cubano
Movimiento de Recuperación Revolucionaria	Asociación Nacional de Mujeres Cubanoamericanas
Partido Revolucionario Cubano Auténtico	Alianza Fraternal José Martí
Pro Cuba	Federación de Masones Cubanos Exiliados
Municipios de Cuba en el Exilio	"Cuba Primero" Federación Mundial de Ex-Presos Políticos
Brigada 2506	Alpha 66
Central de Trabajadores de Cuba en el Exilio	Bloque de Organizaciones Anticomunistas
Colegio de Arquitectos de Cuba	Federación de Logias Unidas Orden "Caballeros de la Luz"
	Alianza "17 de Abril"
	Federación de Trabajadores Azucareros
	Claustro de Profesores de la Universidad de la Habana
	Comandos Martianos
	Centro de Derechos Humanos
	Municipio de Remedios
	"Stop Dollars to Castro"
	Coalición Democrática Cubana
	Republican Hispanic Association
	Movimiento Comando F4
	Vigilia Mambisa
	Municipio Santiago de las Vegas
	Asociación Ideológica Combativa
	Partido Revolucionario Cubano Auténtico
	Frente de Liberación Cubano
	Movimiento Insurreccional Martiano
	Asociación de Veterinarios

Source: Ariel Hidalgo, "Las corrientes políticas cubano-americanas del sur de la Florida," Commissioned Report, Center for Migration and Development, Princeton University, March 2001.

The rituals, periodic and circumstantial, help keep the mass of the exile population in a state of heightened emotional tension. There is little chance that the classic assimilation process can play itself out among Cuban émigrés when every few weeks another event jolts their collective conscience, leading to poignant reminders of why they left and who the real enemy is. The subsequent protests and rallies, spearheaded by the pocket organizations, but with the support and connivance of their superiors help explain the paradoxes noted at the start of this chapter: just as it is difficult to assimilate to American society in such an atmosphere, it is impossible to forego an ideology reaffirmed so often by highly charged public rituals.

Speaking over Radio Mambí, one of the exile leaders had this to say about one of the latest episodes triggering collective mobilization in Miami—the expulsion of 21 young Cubans who had sought refuge in the Mexican embassy in Havana in late February, 2002: The great Mexican patriot Benito Juárez declared that "respect for the rights of others is peace." Conversely, "lack of respect for the rights of others is war. The Mexican government has shown a complete lack of respect for the rights of oppressed Cubans. Therefore, we are at war with Mexico. We call on all Cubans to boycott Mexican products and on our elected representatives in Washington to decisively oppose President Fox's request to legalize illegal Mexicans living in America."[26] That such declarations are taken seriously is a testimony to the narrowing outlook brought about by the machine's ideology of intransigence.

Conclusion: Future Prospects

The Cuban government and its organized opposition in Miami share many things, including frequent predictions of their demise. So far these predictions have come to naught. Both political systems have demonstrated remarkable resilience. There are indisputable forces arranged against the Miami machine, most significantly those of demography: the segment of the Cuban-American population most identified with the ideology of intransigence—pre-1980 exiles—is aging and dying fast. Simultaneously, the faster growing segments of this population—second- and third-generation Cuban-Americans and new arrivals from Cuba—are less militant, when not alienated by the reigning exile ideology. Nevertheless, it is not likely that demographic trends by themselves will produce significant political changes in Miami. The machine is so well entrenched that even aspiring second-generation politicians must abide by its dictates. Young Cuban-American politicians continue to utter the same old anti-Castro mantras; the same right-wing representatives to U.S. Congress continue to be elected unopposed; and no sane Miami merchant would dream of sponsoring a radio or TV program that challenges the machine's ideology.

In this context, political change in Miami can only came about through deliberate, concerted action by moderate elements of the Cuban-American community in alliance with other non-Cuban groups in the area. With some exceptions, however, moderate voices are seldom heard in Miami since those who hold these views have generally preferred to pursue their individual careers and avoid open confrontation with the dominant ideology. They may despair in private but fail to enact their beliefs in public. A few first- and second-generation Cubans have become so disgusted with the antics of the machine that they have swung to the other side, reenlisting themselves as supporters of the Cuban government in Miami. Obviously, that is a dead end.

While Cuban exiles may continue to believe that they will bring change to Cuba, the opposite may actually be the case. In the absence of deliberate efforts for change within the Cuban-American community itself, the only remaining option is significant political change in Cuba that alters the overarching political equation of the past four decades. Throughout this lengthy period, exile politics has been the faithful mirror of events in the island, reacting vigorously and always in opposition to every move by Castro and his government. It is impossible that a momentous change in the Cuban regime would not affect Miami as well. That possibility is uncertain, however, since Castro and his closest followers appear strongly committed to the perpetuation of communism. Thus, the most plausible outlook for the foreseeable future is more of the same—a sad and unending saga that would be comic if its results had not been so tragic.

Notes

This chapter was originally prepared for the conference on Cuba sponsored by the Center for International Studies of the *Colegio de México*, which took place on March 15, 2002, and subsequently published as "The Cuban-American Political Machine," *Foro Internacional* (Mexico) XLIII, July–September 2003: 608–626. The author thanks the conference participants for their comments.

1. Luis J. Botifoll, *Introducción al futuro de Miami* (Miami: Laurenty, 1988), pp. 3 and 10.
2. Alejandro Portes and Alex Stepick, *City on the Edge: The Transformation of Miami* (Berkeley, CA: University of California Press, 1993), chapter 2.
3. Ibid., p. 35.
4. "Study: Cuban Exile Lobby is Most Cost-Effective," *Miami Herald*, January 24, 1997, pp. 1a and 15a.
5. Joan Didion, *Miami* (New York: Simon and Schuster, 1987); David Rieff, *Going to Miami* (Boston, MA: Little, Brown, 1987); and Guillermo J. Grenier and Alex Stepick, *Miami, Now!* (Gainesville, FL: University of Florida Press, 1992).
6. Jorge I. Domínguez, "The Secrets of Castro's Staying Power," *Foreign Affairs*, 72 (2), Spring 1993: 97–107; Susan Eva Eckstein, *Back from the Future, Cuba under Castro* (Princeton, NJ: Princeton University Press, 1994); and Miguel Ángel Centeno, "Lessons for the Transition: Cuba after Fidel?" *Cuban Affairs/Asuntos Cubanos*, 3–4, Fall–Winter 1998: 1–14.
7. Portes and Stepick, *City on the Edge*, p. 138.
8. Susan Eva Eckstein and Lorena Barberia, "Cuban-American Cuba Visits: Public Policy, Private Practices," *Report of the Mellon-MIT Inter-University Program on Non-Governmental Organizations and Forced Migration*, Center for International Studies, MIT, Boston, MA, January 2001.
9. A standard finding in the literature on naturalization and citizenship change is that immigrants and refugees whose return to their home country is blocked are significantly more likely to naturalize than those able to return. See Alejandro Portes and Rubén G. Rumbaut, *Immigrant America: A Portrait* (Berkeley, CA: University of California Press, 1996), pp. 115–124.
10. John Logan and Harvey Molotch, *Urban Fortunes: The Political Economy of Place* (Berkeley, CA: University of California Press, 1987).
11. Portes and Stepick, *City on the Edge*, chapter 6; and María Cristina García, *Havana-USA: Cuban Exiles and Cuban Americans in South Florida, 1959–1994* (Berkeley, CA: University of California Press, 1996).

12. Rieff, *Going to Miami*, chapter 12; T. D. Allman, *Miami, City of the Future* (New York: Atlantic Monthly Press, 1987), chapter 16; and Lisandro Pérez, "Cuban Miami," in Guillermo J. Grenier and Alex Stepick III (eds.) *Miami Now! Immigration, Ethnicity, and Social Change*, 83–108 (Gainesville, FL: University Press of Florida).

13. James S. Coleman, "A Rational Choice Perspective on Economic Sociology," in N. J. Smelser and R. Swedberg (eds.), *Handbook of Economic Sociology* (Princeton, NJ: Princeton University Press and Russell Sage Foundation, 1994), pp. 166–180; and Mark S. Granovetter, *Getting a Job: A Study of Contacts and Careers* (Cambridge, MA: Harvard University Press, 1974).

14. Howard Becker, *Outsiders: Studies in the Sociology of Deviance* (New York: Free Press, 1963); Coleman, "A Rational Choice Perspective on Economic Sociology"; and Robert K. Merton, "The Self-Fulfilling Prophecy," in *Social Theory and Structure* (New York: Free Press, 1968), pp. 475–490.

15. Portes and Stepick, *City on the Edge*, chapter 6.

16. Eckstein and Barberia, "Cuban-American Cuba Visits," p. 15.

17. Ibid., p. 19.

18. Ibid., pp. 19–20.

19. Portes and Stepick, *City on the Edge*, pp. 137–144.

20. Pierre Bourdieu, "Le capital social: Notes provisoires," *Actes de la Recherche en Sciences Sociales*, 31, 1980: 2–3; James S. Coleman, "Social Capital in the Creation of Human Capital," *American Journal of Sociology*, 94, 1988: 95–121; Alejandro Portes, "The Two Meanings of Social Capital," *Sociological Form*, 15, 2000: 1–12.

21. Portes, "The Two Meanings of Social Capital"; Alejandro Portes and Julia Sensenbrenner, "Embeddedness and Immigration: Notes on the Social Determinants of Economic Action," *American Journal of Sociology*, 98, May 1993: 1320–1350.

22. Portes and Sensenbrenner, "Embeddedness and Immigration"; Mark S. Granovetter, "The Economic Sociology of Firms and Entrepreneurs," in Alejandro Portes (ed.), *The Economic Sociology of Immigration: Essays on Networks, Ethnicity, and Entrepreneurship* (New York: Russell Sage Foundation, 1995), pp. 128–165.

23. García, *Havana, USA*, chapter 1; Pérez, "Cuban Miami"; and Alejandro Portes, "The Social Origins of the Cuban Enclave Economy of Miami," *Sociological Perspectives*, 30, October 1987: 340–371.

24. Personal interviews by author with three participants in these early meetings, Miami, Spring 1993.

25. "INS: Send Elián Back" and "Cuban Exiles Vow Widespread Protests," *Miami Herald*, January 6, 2000, pp. 1a, 12a, 13a.

26. "La Mesa Revuelta," *Radio Mambí*, March 2, 2002.

Chapter 8

Rethinking Civil Society and Religion in Cuba

Margaret E. Crahan and Ariel C. Armony

Introduction

The interplay of religion, culture, and society in any country, at any given time, is one of the most complex phenomena experts have attempted to understand and explain. This is true in the case of democratic regimes where empirical evidence is accessible and conceptual categories are grounded in long-standing scholarly discourse, and the attempt to study these themes in a system such as Cuba's presents considerable challenges. For example, the study of Cuba forces us to grapple with concepts that, notwithstanding broad and sometimes serious disagreements among scholars, can be employed with more or less consensus in mainstream cases. One such concept is civil society itself, which we broadly define as a complex network of individuals and groups through which people participate in community and polity. As such it includes not only civic associations and institutions, but also informal networks that are linked horizontally and, at times, vertically to political elites and the state, particularly in an effort to secure the public's interests.

If one of the defining attributes of civil society is its clear-cut differentiation from the state, then the corollary is that civil society is extremely narrow and weak in Cuba. But if one recognizes the degree to which associations in Cuba, including those initially organized by the government, have carved out increasingly autonomous spaces in which to operate in recent years, then it is possible to analyze civil society on the island in a more comparative and insightful fashion. Furthermore, networking among fully nongovernmental organizations (NGOs) and those with some governmental connection has stimulated the broadening of civil society activity especially in recent years. One should remember the degree to which such linkages helped determine substantial change in other countries in the past 30 years.

A critical question is how much space the Cuban government is willing to accord nonoppositional civil society that may not be mobilizing for regime change, but is increasingly critical of socioeconomic and political conditions.

Furthermore, it is hard not only for experts, but also for the Cuban leadership, to disentangle oppositional, dissident, and nonoppositional sectors of Cuban civil society. Yet it is imperative to do so given that Cuba is clearly in the midst of a transition whose outcome is unclear.[1] Closer examination of the role of civil society in a transition, as well as the nature of the participation of major actors could help clarify that process. Among those actors are a wide variety of religions that constitute the most broad-based sector with a national reach within Cuban civil society. This is obviously no easy task. Nevertheless, a better understanding of the role of religions, past and present, in the context of the evolution of Cuban civil society can help establish the dynamics of citizen participation, nuances in the relationship between state and society and, to some extent, the future of Cuban civil society.[2]

Cuban Civil Society and Religions: How Strong?

Much of the literature on Cuba has concluded that one of the prime reasons for the triumph of the revolutionary 26th of July Movement in 1959 and the subsequent consolidation of a Marxist-Leninist government was the weakness of civil society, and religion. Such assertions are without a strong basis. Civic and other organizations were common in Cuba as early as the nineteenth century, and they continued to proliferate throughout the twentieth century. By 1959 Cuban civil society had developed into one of the most advanced in Latin America in spite of periodic prerevolutionary government attempts to regulate it both legally and through repression.[3]

The tendency for religions to be regarded as relatively weak in Cuba flows, in part, from a focus on institutional attributes such as formal participation, levels of activism, and direct political influence. It is true that attendance at services and participation in religious groups was historically relatively low in Cuba and political influence was evaluated rather superficially, as compared to other Latin American countries. What has not been sufficiently studied is the very real penetration of Cuban society by indigenous, Judeo-Christian, and spiritist religions that have made the vast majority of Cubans believers, normative religious values prevalent, and popular religiosity widespread. Historically, religious beliefs have permeated Cuban culture and molded societal attitudes. At the same time, the very multiplicity of religions and the weak presence of religious institutions, especially in rural areas, contributed to low levels of practice and a high level of syncretism and permeability in terms of both religious and secular belief systems.[4]

Nominally a Catholic country beginning in the sixteenth century, Cuba's religious evolution has deviated substantially from that of other Latin American countries. Initially a commercial entrepôt and sugar colony and later a republic with relatively loose emigration regulations, the ongoing encounters of indigenes, Europeans, Africans, Chinese, Jews, and North Americans, among others, resulted in an intense process of interchange, adaptation, borrowing, overlapping, and the abandonment of some beliefs and practices in favor of the construction of more syncretic ones. All religions in Cuba have been characterized by a high degree of flexibility and permeability.

With respect to the Catholic Church this is clearly reflected in the image of Cuba's patron saint, the Virgen de la Caridad de Cobre, whose statue was "found" floating in the Bay of Nipe in 1613. The statue stands poised on a half circle, the indigenous sign for the moon, and is associated with life, growth, fertility, solace, and caring for the poor as is the Afro-Cuban spirit Ochún with which she is identified. Soldiers going into battle during the Cuban wars of independence (1868–1878, 1895–1898) carried her image, as did some of those same troops who subsequently participated in the 1912 insurrection to oppose racial discrimination and gain more jobs for Afro-Cubans in the public and private sectors.[5] Throughout the twentieth century she was identified largely with the working class, although few middle- and upper-class homes were without her image. In the 1950s both pro- and anti-Batista forces appealed to La Caridad, while Fidel and Raúl Castro's mother affixed *ex-votos* to the Virgin's altar to protect her sons during the guerrilla struggle that brought them to power in 1959. To commemorate that triumph a mass of thanksgiving was said in La Caridad's sanctuary in Oriente Province.[6] That same year the statue was transported to Havana for the National Catholic Congress attended by an estimated 1 million Cubans, including Fidel, at which shouts of *Cuba sí, comunismo no* rang out.[7] The statue of La Caridad did not return to Havana until shortly before the visit of Pope John Paul II in January 1998 when the government allowed public processions in her honor as part of efforts to demonstrate its openness to religious expression. Devotion to La Caridad not only cuts across ethnic and class divisions in Cuba, but also the fragmentation of Cubans within and outside the island.

In the midst of the debate in Miami over whether to travel to Cuba for the pope's visit, Miami Bishop Agustín Román called for unity because, as he phrased it, Cubans "are not divided, because we all love the virgin."[8] The widespread devotion to the Virgen de la Caridad de Cobre and her role as the prime symbol of national identity illustrate the degree to which popular religiosity and syncretic traditional beliefs are prevalent among Cubans, even if traditional indicators of religious participation are low. Hence, while surveys in both the pre- and postrevolutionary periods indicate that 75–85 percent of the population harbors some religious beliefs, Cubans historically have not scored high on traditional measures of loyalty to religious institutions.[9]

Even before the 1959 revolution, many Cuban believers supported separation of church and state, religious freedom and tolerance, and eclecticism in practice to a greater extent than most other traditional Catholic countries. A history of weak institutional presence, chronic limitations in terms of material and human resources, together with the intermingling of a variety of belief systems has resulted in lower levels of institutional identification and loyalty than in most Latin American countries. Nevertheless, Cuban culture and society was and is permeated with religious beliefs, values, symbolism, icons, and referents. Belief in the divine has long been an integral part of Cubans' self-identification or *cubanidad*.[10] Therefore, Cuba is somewhat contradictory: although it is a nation of believers, institutional religion, especially Catholicism, has been weaker than in most of Latin America's formerly Spanish colonies, thereby giving rise to the notion that religion in general has enjoyed relatively little sway in Cuba.

This is also a result of the fact that during the colonial period the relative isolation of Cuba encouraged a greater degree of autonomy and adaptive response to local conditions on the part of both the Catholic clergy and the laity than in the mainland Spanish possessions. This contributed to considerable religious heterodoxy including in the Catholic Church that had within it a strain of independent thinkers who in the early nineteenth century began championing independence, the abolition of slavery, a republican form of government, and expanded citizens' rights. One result was Spain's cracking down on individuals and groups regarded as subversive. Chief among them was Father Félix Varela y Morales (1787–1853), a professor at the Seminary of San Carlos and San Ambrosio in Havana, who was exiled in 1823 to the United States. Varela was one of the first to champion individual rights and the reform of Cuban political, economic, religious, and social structures according to the needs of the citizenry. His writings provided one of the earliest elaborations of a liberal polity and civil society.[11] Varela's ideas influenced the independence leader José Martí and were adduced as recently as 1997 at a University of Havana colloquium as suggesting how a just society should be organized.[12] Catholic priests varied widely in terms of their religious and political attitudes, as well as their political behavior, as did other religious leaders including those involved in indigenous or Afro-Cuban religions.[13] Most reflected the belief systems of the communities they inhabited where daily concerns mingled with religion to mold values and behavior.

The diversity of attitudes among religious personnel was intensified as a result of the gaining of independence first by the French colony of Haiti in 1804 and then by the Spanish mainland colonies in the 1820s. This resulted in an influx of Catholic clerics who generally reinforced conservative sectors of the Catholic Church to the dismay of Bishop José Díaz y Espada y Landa who served from 1802 to 1832. The latter attempted to curb their influence by promoting liberal republican ideas. This caused conservative church sectors to conspire against him eventually forcing him from office. His actions did succeed, however, in identifying a sector of the Catholic Church with the independence struggle and citizens' rights. Nevertheless, the church as an institution continued to be identified with Spain.[14] Such cleavages contributed further to the institutional weakness of the Cuban Catholic Church in a period when Afro-Cuban and Protestant beliefs were more identified with an independent republic.

Protestant ministers and laypersons, whose numbers increased in the latter part of the nineteenth century, were effective transmitters of liberal political ideas. Some Protestant ministers, like their Catholic counterparts, fell afoul of the colonial administration and were forced into exile generally in the

United States where their ideas concerning citizen participation and rights were further developed. Be it abroad or on the island, many of them contributed to the movement for independence.[15] The level of civil society organization immediately prior to the 1895–1898 war of independence was notable and some religious leaders were active not only in legitimizing the movement, but also as combatants.

The influence of spiritist beliefs imported from Africa by slaves in the definition of Cuban civil society was also substantial. Religious ceremonies helped to define community and transmit concepts of governance, as well as legitimate resistance and ultimately stimulate participation in the struggle for independence, together with the ongoing struggle for full citizen rights. Overall civil society in late nineteenth-century Cuba was highly mobilized in opposition to continued Spanish control and awash in a welter of differing concepts of a reformed society that would allow for expansion of the full spectrum of civil, political, socioeconomic, and religious rights. Catholic, Protestant, and Afro-Cuban religious beliefs were all used in the legitimization of the independence movement, albeit the institutional Catholic Church maintained its identification with continued Spanish control.[16]

The failure of the new republic, under the U.S.-imposed Platt Amendment,[17] to provide for broadly expanded citizen rights contributed to ongoing strife and civil society mobilization. Religious beliefs were employed to challenge the leadership of the new republic, particularly given its failure to redeem promises of greater social equality and participation in politics and the expanding economy for Afro-Cubans. In 1912 the dissatisfaction boiled over into an armed uprising during which both Catholic and spiritist iconography was invoked to mobilize and legitimize. Religious networks were employed to organize the movement and transmit information and resources. In the aftermath of the suppression of that revolt, religions once again served as mechanisms of resistance and subterranean organization particularly by Afro-Cubans.[18]

Sectors of the revolutionary movements of the 1930s and 1950s also used religious beliefs and networks not only to legitimate their objectives, but also to mobilize resources and collaborators. Protestant and Catholic university students were active in both movements, while some church groups and leaders served to generate monies for the efforts. Reformist movements, including Catholic Action (Acción Católica [AC]) and the Catholic Grouping (Agrupación Católica) grew particularly in the 1950s.[19] In short, while formal church attendance in Cuba throughout the twentieth century may have been low, religious beliefs and generalized identification with religious norms were common and, at times, coexisted with interest in socialism. The latter was stimulated by interpretations of the social doctrines of the churches, which increasingly emphasized socioeconomic justice, and, in particular, workers' rights. This helped justify movements in support of regime change or at least less governmental corruption and abuse of power.

Hence, while the percentage of Cubans actually engaging in regular religious practice was not high, religiously informed beliefs were widely held and influenced concepts of polity and society, as well as Cubans' involvement in civil society.[20] Furthermore, the level of belief in the divine has remained remarkably stable in Cuba from the 1950s to the present (approximately 75–85 percent), albeit formal religious practice remains low.[21] This suggests that while institutional religion in Cuba has historically been somewhat weak according to such indicators as frequency of attendance at services, institutional loyalty, and practice, the influence of religious beliefs in civil society has been pervasive.

Since 1959 the revolutionary government has tried, largely through executive orders, to limit the autonomy and development of associative organizations. Laws adopted from 1976–1985 to institutionalize the revolutionary process codified the state's efforts to control civil society.[22] Nevertheless, in recent years there has been a revitalization and expansion of civic and other organizations not dominated by the government together with increased autonomy on the part of government-organized associations (GONGOs) and their leadership. Indeed, there is a sense of mild ferment within Cuban civil society. While networking among sectors is somewhat limited, there is a positive disposition among influential sectors such as intellectuals, artists, labor, and church leaders toward the fortification of civil society. As a result they are increasingly assuming roles as community organizers and leaders, providers of food and medicine to those in need, and molders of public opinion. That is, they are occupying more and more public space.

Does Civil Society Lack Autonomy in Cuba?

As noted, traditional concepts of civil society include autonomy from the state as a definitional attribute. Legally, citizen organizations in Cuba must be under the supervision of state agencies and most comply.[23] However, a closer look at the associational sphere in the country reveals a high degree of complexity along a continuum that ranges from fully autonomous groups with or without government licenses through state-initiated organizations that operate somewhat autonomously and beyond to government mass organizations that contain within them sectors that generate counterdiscourses to those of the state. In terms of political attitudes and behavior the spectrum ranges from sharp opposition to the government and Cuban socialism through criticism of Castro regime, but not necessarily of socialism, to dissidence within not only the state's mass organizations, but also within the government bureaucracy.

Cuban civil society, then, can be said to incorporate opponents of the present government, dissident groups that range along a reformist spectrum, together with critical and heterodox individuals within the state that participate in civil society networks. Given this level of articulation of alternative discourses to the state's, it is not surprising that a growing number of organizations have carved out a certain degree of autonomy from the government, which allows them to function as a source of new ideas, debate, and citizen action. Conceptually speaking, these associations contribute to an expanding public sphere in Cuba, contrary to the expectation that the circulation of discourses is essentially determined from the commanding heights of the state.[24]

This sphere has the potential to create spaces for debate over power, claims to authority and policy making, and norms and practices in society.[25] Of course, the level of civic engagement and debate in Cuba is limited when compared to some other societies, but it is crucial to recognize the existence of an expanding public sphere constituted by an increasing number of minispheres within the country and sustained by higher levels of voluntary associational activity. Some of the discourses that circulate in the public sphere concern models of socialism and economic reform, nonpolitical descriptors that shape the identity of youth (particularly rap music and fashion), and the responsibilities of religious believers in a society, which until the early 1990s was described in its constitution as an materialist atheist one.[26]

The expansion of associational autonomy in Cuba is a result, in large measure, of the interaction between two processes. The first is society's increased capacity, skills, and motivation to organize outside the realm of the state. Second there is the decreased capacity of the state to control and regulate society, as well as provide governmental services and ensure basic needs.[27] The provision of the latter is at the core of the Cuban government's claim to legitimacy and adherence to Marxism-Leninism. Failure to do so is a result, in part, of the vast economic transformations that took place in the 1990s following the collapse of the Soviet Union and the Eastern European communist regimes, as well as the ongoing U.S. embargo. Because of the increased activity on the part of civil society, including those directly challenging the ideological and political hegemony of the government, the 1990s witnessed an increase in government sanctions on those sectors that tended to be most outspoken. This included groups that challenged the legitimacy of the Castro regime, intellectuals who questioned economic policies of the government, and independent journalists. Sanctions ranged from loss of jobs within the public sector to imprisonment. In addition, the government increasingly emphasized in the late 1990s and early 2000s mass public demonstrations and TV roundtables that were aimed at generating broad-based popular support for the government and its policies. U.S. pressure, for example, via the tightening of restrictions on family reunification visits of Cuban-Americans and remittances in May 2004 has been used to resurrect nationalism in the face of perceived threats to the country's sovereignty. The pattern has historically been rather cyclical, that is, to allow for a greater or lesser degree of public space for dissidence, as opposed to outright opposition, until a serious threat is perceived. Alternatively, the government has been eager to take advantage of opportunities as they arise to generate nationalistic sentiment in support of the regime as in the Elián González case, as well as capitalizing on criticisms of the United States based on the war in Iraq, and generalized Latin American discontent particularly with neoliberal economic policies. The emergence of leftist leaders in Brazil, Chile, and Uruguay, and most especially in Venezuela has encouraged Cuba to challenge the United States more strongly in international forums. Attempts to influence U.S. public opinion together with that of Cuban-Americans have proved to have little impact. Rather the internal dynamics of such communities appear to be more relevant.

Overall, the capacity of the Cuban government to stem the expansion of the public sphere in the face of growing criticism of economic conditions in Cuba is tied to the internal dynamics of a regime that has been in power for close to 50 years without major advances in the capacity of the Cuban economy to meet citizens' socioeconomic demands. While the government may crack down, at times, on opponents and dissidents, it does not appear to have the capacity to quell the complaints of ordinary citizens arising out of the rigors of their daily lives. Hence, while organized civil society may not be widespread in Cuba, dissidence is and this is what most characterizes contemporary Cuban civil society.

In addition, there is a tendency to overstate the lack of autonomy of Cuban associations. While the official ones, together with the GONGOs, are circumscribed in their leadership and activities, there is, even among them, varying degrees of autonomous action. For example, since the early 1970s the Cuban Confederation of Workers (Confederación de Trabajadores de Cuba [CTC]) has lobbied, sometimes successfully and, at times, allied with sectors of the armed forces, for changes in government economic policies. Currently there are in Cuba not only some small independent labor groups, but also sectors of the CTC that work discreetly for some of the same goals as the former, including more negotiating space. The proliferation of informal sector enterprises employing anywhere from two or three to twenty to thirty workers has contributed to an expanded labor sector that defines its agendas somewhat differently from those employed by the government.[28]

Another mass organization, the National Association of Small Farmers (Asociación Nacional de Agricultores Pequeños de Cuba [ANAP]) has traditionally exercised some autonomy and leverage with respect to the government precisely because such farmers have been the most productive, generally outstripping the state farms. Their members in the Cuban National Assembly tend to vote as a bloc and lobby for changes in proposed legislation that they deem negatively impacts their interests.[29] With dollarization beginning in the early 1990s,[30] small farmers became more prosperous and in some cases invested in expanding sectors of the informal economy, including the *paladares*, licensed and unlicensed restaurants in homes. As tourism, including from the United States, grew in the 1990s, a good number of *paladares* prospered given the generally better quality of the cuisine and service than in state-run enterprises.[31] The private production of crafts for tourists also flourished. Some artists, particularly those in the plastic arts, developed substantial new outlets for their works among foreigners.

During the 1990s skilled workers and professionals also became more involved in nonstate employment with or without licenses. With increased access to foreign currency not only as a result of tourism, but also as a result of remittances from families and friends abroad, demand grew for the services of skilled workers such as plumbers, carpenters, electricians, and others.

This also stimulated the hiring and training of apprentices. Some professionals, such as medical doctors and dentists, set up private offices where they provided services outside of state-operated hospitals and clinics, with or without state permits. In fact, there was something of an exodus of professionals and skilled workers, such as medical and educational personnel, from state employment into tourism and the informal sector. This drain of medical and educational personnel ultimately prompted the government to place restrictions on such career switches. Overall, these developments resulted in some labor and professional associations increasingly serving as channels for alternative discourses and policy recommendations to those of the state.

International developments and networks also impacted state-linked associations. For example, as international bodies of jurists have expanded their focus on human rights and humanitarian law, so have their counterparts in Cuba. The National Union of Jurists (Unión Nacional de Juristas de Cuba [UNJC]) has spearheaded training in international human rights law by the Inter-American Institute of Human Rights (IAIHR) that has substantially increased Cuban expertise in this realm. In addition, in 2005 the UNJC, together with the University of Havana's Law School and The Cuban Society for Philosophical Research, organized an international conference on constitutions, democracy, and political systems. At this meeting a representative of the IAIHR gave a presentation on "Lessons Learned with Regard to the Strengthening of Political Parties in Latin America."[32] Such courses and conferences have had the effect of inserting Cuban professionals into international networks where values and concerns may raise issues for Cubans. The desire on the part of professionals to update their knowledge and skills through training and international exchanges is strong and cannot avoid affecting political and other discourses within Cuba.

Traditionally artists and intellectuals have been in the vanguard of civil society movements as witnessed by Eastern Europe in recent years.[33] In Cuba members of the Writers and Artists Union (Unión de Escritores y Artistas de Cuba [UNEAC]) and the Cuban Institute of Cinematographic Art and Industry (Instituto Cubano de Arte e Industria Cinematográficos [ICAIC]) have repeatedly generated public debates about the role of artists in a socialist society, as well as the operation of the government and its policies. They are critical contributors to the expansion of space for civil society to debate public policy issues and purveyors of alternative opinions. While they have at times been restrained by the government and engage in some self-censorship, this sector has been frequently outspoken in pointing out through art the limitations of the government. Films such as *Death of a Bureaucrat* have been an important means of generating widespread discussion of public policy issues. In this respect, they have served as an important alternative to state TV, radio, and the press.

Government-organized nongovernmental organizations have also played a leading role in creating spaces for somewhat independent political discourses. Principal among them are research centers, some of which were spun off from the Central Committee of the Communist Party. A number of these have produced serious research analyzing government policies and programs and offered extensive critiques, as well as alternative policy proposals.[34] Sometimes the criticism has resulted in government response as witness the purging of some members of the Center for the Americas (Centro de Estudios sobre América [CEA]) in 1996 after they produced a series of papers questioning some government policies, particularly economic.[35] Remarkably enough some of those purged were absorbed into other state-organized research centers suggesting the extent of their autonomy and heterodoxy. Indeed, these centers generate some of the most substantial counterdiscourses relating to public policy issues within Cuba.

Others among those who have been purged not only from research centers, but also from government ministries and universities, have left the country, while some have found work with international organizations in Cuba, in tourism, or the informal economy. Those who have left the country have often contributed to more heterodox opinions within Cuban communities abroad. Among those who remain in the country, whether within state-linked institutions or without, such individuals continue to contribute largely nonoppositional, but critical discourses, to civil society debates. These individuals often maintain their contacts within their former institutions and belong to interlocking networks that tend to exchange information and ideas about Cuba's present and future. The extent and weight of such networks should not be underestimated. They help create spaces for analysis and debate about the course of the Cuban polity and society and possible solutions to current problems. In particular they help undercut the state's monopoly of information concerning internal decision making and even, in some cases, allow for input prior to the public announcement of new policies. Hence, the traditional channels for informing the citizenry, that is, the mass organizations and mass media have been joined by expanding networks that not only transmit information, but also analyze it, and offer policy recommendations. Some of these find their way into the independent press and almost always are circulated among both governmental and nongovernmental elites.

In addition, a fully autonomous sector of Cuban civil society has been developing. This sector includes organizations such as the Catholic Center for Civic and Religious Formation (Centro de Formación Cívica y Religiosa [CFCR]) in Pinar del Río, the Protestant Christian Center for Reflection and Dialogue (Centro Cristiano de Reflexión y Diálogo [CCRD]) in Cardenas, and a plethora of Afro-Cuban cultural groups that span the entire country.[36] Not infrequently they have undertaken social welfare activities previously provided by the state, thereby undercutting, if not intentionally, the latter's claim to legitimacy via meeting the basic needs of all citizens. For example, the CCRD in Cardenas, an impoverished area, is a major provider of socioeconomic assistance through its meals on wheels program, community gardens, educational and recreational groups for youths and the elderly, as well as environmental work.[37] The Center maintains good relations with government and party officials and receives most of its financial support from church organizations in Europe.[38] It is currently initiating an ecumenical project to promote reconciliation among Cubans both on the island and abroad. In addition, in Pinar del Río the CFCR, through its publication *Vitral*, has been a prime outlet for the expression of the opinions of ordinary citizens about government policies and programs. This Center has also disseminated alternative views on the relationship between state and society.[39] Among autonomous international humanitarian organizations, the Catholic Relief Service (CARITAS) has developed a national distribution network in Cuba in order to help provide for nutritional and health care needs in cooperation with the government.

At the local level government officials, hospitals, and churches frequently work together for the common good of the community. Such efforts have served to increase nongovernmental input into governmental operations, as well as increase the dependence of the state on nonstate actors. International organizations such as the Oxford Committee for Famine Relief (OXFAM) and the American Friends Service Committee (AFSC) have assisted grassroots projects, in conjunction with Cuban organizations, including the ecumenical Martin Luther King, Jr. Memorial Center (Centro Memorial Martin Luther King, Jr.). All have contributed over the past 15 years to increased community organization in a context of needs that the government is unable to meet. In addition, considerable emphasis has been placed on strengthening civil society, although more recently the emphasis has been on inculcating mechanisms for conflict resolution and reconciliation with a view toward the future. Not surprisingly, the organizations and networks involved are increasing the level of citizen dependence on them, as well as their influence. This cannot but help increase public space and perhaps erode somewhat the government's ideological and political hegemony.

Other autonomous organizations and movements, some more political than others, have responded to nonhumanitarian societal needs. These groups derive their autonomy, in part, from their international networks and entrepreneurship in obtaining support from abroad sometimes because of shared political orientations. The independent libraries' movement, for example, is constituted by small operations established in homes offering diverse publications including some not available in public libraries. It has received support from international sources, including the former prime minister of the Czech Republic, Vaclav Havel. The Masons, whose presence in Cuba dates from well before the 1959 revolution, have reassumed, to a degree, their historical role as a center for intellectual debate and social welfare activities assisted by their international counterparts. Afro-Cuban religious groups, such as Regla de Ocha and Palo Monte, which are pervasive throughout Cuba, provide readymade networks of groups and individuals who share similar belief systems and definitions of society. Historically they have served as mechanisms of resistance and survival and today include a broad cross-section of Cubans of all classes.[40] In recent years Afro-Cuban groups have been active in organizing local communities to help solve environmental, food, and safety issues. During the economic difficulties in the 1990s some communities, such as Guanabocoa, that are strongly identified with Afro-Cuban religions, were the sites of street protests against government policies.[41]

As indicated there are varying degrees of independence depending, in part, on the skills of the leadership, the organization's resources, and its international links. For example, those organizations under the jurisdiction of the Ministry of Culture have historically had more independence than those under other ministries, in part, because of their greater capacity for communication with the general public, as well as their insertion in and access to international resources. On the other hand, some of the largest associations linked to the government—the unions, for example—have used the power of their numbers to influence government policies. The GONGOs sometimes express alternative opinions and advance new policies by using traditional channels and the strength of their expertise, as well as their informal networks. Still, and particularly for those groups without large constituencies including those that are clearly oppositional, the margins for operating are limited. The decline in the state's capacity to maintain ideological and political consensus in society has led to the use of coercion against some groups, including both those fully autonomous and those operating under the supervision of the state.

Is Civil Society in Cuba Synonymous with Opposition?

Cuba's historically highly heterogeneous society with diverse identities and interests contributes to a high degree of sectoralism in its associational sphere. This feature distinguishes the Cuban case from Eastern European cases, such as Poland, which are more homogeneous in terms of social composition, religion, and culture. Poland, for example, did not have as much of a tradition of tolerating diversity in a number of areas that made mobilizing via mass organizations (Solidarity—with 11 million members at its height in the 1980s) and institutions (the Catholic Church) easier than in Cuba. Nothing comparable to Solidarity exists in Cuba and the difficulties of mobilizing are apparent in the limited numbers involved in organized civil society, which suggests perhaps the utility of rethinking where the weight of the peculiarly Cuban civil society lies. In addition to the heterogeneity and sectoralism of Cuban society, the Polish communist government allowed much more space for civil society, for example, allowing the religious press a degree of freedom, as well as religious instruction in public schools, reflecting the ongoing strength of the Catholic Church as an institution.

The role that the Polish Catholic Church played in rendering illegitimate the communist regime was made possible by its greater institutional strength and popular support than its counterpart in Cuba where institutional identity and loyalty has historically been more diffuse. During the communist era the Polish government recognized the Catholic Church as a powerful actor to be contended with and, as a consequence, it conceded considerable public space to it. The alliance of the Polish Catholic Church with Solidarity presented the Polish regime with a formidable foe that is unequaled in Cuba. In sum, religions in Cuba face more substantial impediments to constructing a highly integrated and mobilized civil society than the countries it has frequently been compared with.

The high degree of sectoralism in Cuban civil society was clearly reflected in the composition of the May 20, 2005 Assembly to Promote Civil Society (Asamblea para la Promoción de la Sociedad Civil [APSC]). Held at a private home on the outskirts of Havana, the organizers claimed to represent over 300 organizations.[42] However, some of Cuba's best known dissidents and organizations were not represented including Osvaldo Payá founder of the Varela Project aimed at reforming the 1976 constitution to expand political participation. Payá is also active in the Christian Liberation Movement (Movimiento Cristiano de Liberación [MCL]) linked to the Christian Democratic International. In a particularly harsh attack, the MCL accused the organizers of the meeting of coordination with state security and being supported by the most extreme sectors of the Cuban-American community in Miami. Such events, it argued, benefited the government by portraying the opposition as allied with extremists. The MCL further asserted that the most effective strategy for a transition was to pursue a national dialogue representing a broader cross-section of Cubans.[43] Competition among human rights, reformist, dissident, and oppositional groups in Cuba is high and impedes attempts to achieve a common agenda. Efforts such as Consenso Cubano and Principios Arcos to build a consensual agenda appear to have drawn more support abroad than from the island revealing additional cleavages between internal and external civil society groups.[44]

The nature of Cuban civil society does not, as a result, lend itself to the building of a single mobilizing agenda, in large measure, because of its multicentrism. There is in Cuba continued support for socialism, albeit reformed, as well as a deep-seated resistance to outside interference rooted in an extended colonial past and infringed sovereignty that helped give rise to nationalist sentiments that continue to cut across the political spectrum. Hence, some critics of the current government, as well as opponents, agree on the desirability of retaining aspects of the socialism, particularly in view of the poverty of some neighboring countries with free-market capitalist systems. In Cuba, itself, the increase in poverty and the emergence of new social strata (e.g., the new mixed enterprise entrepreneurs, rural-urban migrants, and the impoverished elderly) suggest the utility of examining Cuban civil society as an intense arena of contestation over discourses and policies particularly those related to resource distribution. It is thus important to distinguish between the characterization of civil society coming from the government—either exclusively "socialist" or as a "fifth column" on behalf of the United States—and the complex reality of civic activity within the island. Civil society in Cuba is neither an exclusive space for the maintenance of the existing order nor an exclusive space of political opposition to the regime.

It is also important to realize that the symbolic apparatus of the state still gives it an important source of power to stimulate consensus in society. This is especially true in regards to the defensive project of the state vis-à-vis the continued hostility of the U.S. toward the revolutionary regime, which many Cubans, including dissidents, identify as a threat to Cuban sovereignty. Beyond domestic realities in Cuba, the increased global criticism of neoliberalism has also helped the Castro regime to retain some legitimacy, particularly in Latin America. This means that it is not accurate to pose a clear-cut division between civil society and the dominant state project. Sectors of civil society with the potential to generate spaces of legitimacy for democratization are not necessarily opposed to the socialist model and may support the state's position vis-à-vis the United States. While horizontal links within civil society are still limited, there is a complex set of networks that connect civil society and the state, creating a scenario that cannot be reduced to a model of "civil society against the state" as in other transition processes.

As noted, the state still controls, to an important extent, the symbolic framework that identifies "fatherland" with "socialism." The resulting discourse excludes from the political community those who challenge the socialist project. This state-driven discourse has a sustained level of legitimacy across society, making it difficult for some organizations to attain legitimacy in the eyes of the average citizen, even among those critical of the current government. However, some experiences show that civil society groups have been able to generate new spaces of inclusion in the political community on the basis of identities such as race, religion, and sexual orientation. For instance, the resignification of Che Guevara by the Regla de Ocha-Ifa—which reassigns meaning to the figure of Che in light of the symbolism of *santería*—illustrates these recent trends. *Santería* has reformulated the theme of individuality without rejecting the notion of "pueblo" and the model of participatory democracy of the revolution.[45]

Religion and Civil Society in Cuba Today

How have close to 50 years of Marxist-Leninist revolution affected the role of religions in civil society in Cuba today? Largely marginalized in the 1960s, institutional religions began to recoup in the 1970s and 1980s and experienced a resurgence in the 1990s, including of Pentecostal and charismatic groups.[46] The government has from the outset justified its policies and actions, including organizing civil society into government-created mass organizations, on the grounds that this was necessary to ensure equitable distribution of the benefits of a socialist economy. As mentioned, redemption of the latter promise has been at the core of the government's claim to legitimacy. While religious leaders supported the revolutionary government's objective of greater socioeconomic justice by the 1980s—and particularly with the economic crisis of the 1990s—they were increasingly questioning the costs, including political and psychological, as well as the actual results of governmental policies and programs.

Failure of the government's economic model to fully realize the basic socioeconomic needs of Cubans has been linked by some religious leaders, in part, to a lack of effective citizen participation in determining public policies and securing governmental accountability. In a 1999 visit to Rome the Cardinal of Havana, Monsignor Jaime Ortega y Alamino stated that given that the Cuban Revolution had raised the hopes of so many, as well as mobilized Cubans to create a more just society, the Catholic Church had a duty to help preserve the achievements of the revolution. At the same time, he argued, the Church had an obligation to help the Cuban people transcend the revolution's limitations, particularly through increased popular participation in government decision making. The latter, he posited, could best be achieved through intensifying evangelization so that the laity would be better prepared to act through a mobilized civil society.[47] In order to facilitate this, the Catholic Church adopted Global Pastoral Plans for 1997–2000 and 2000–2005. The stated principal objective was to promote evangelization via prophetic and inculturated communities that would disseminate the gospel message in order to promote human dignity, reconciliation, and the construction of a society characterized by love and justice. This would require the strengthening of faith-based communities in which all individuals would be regarded as children of God and therefore treated justly.[48] And this required substantial resources, both in terms of monies and personnel, which were in short supply.[49]

Some clerical and lay leaders felt that the 1997–2000 Plan was too general and not sufficiently proactive. A group of priests issued a public critique arguing that a basic prerequisite had to be overcoming the profound passivity of citizens inculcated by the political system. In addition, they felt that calls by both the Catholic and other churches for a national dialogue were flawed as they were premised on the government's willingness to dialogue. Some priests proposed that what the Catholic Church should do instead was create a national dialogue that included a broad coalition of civil society sectors including other churches, fraternal organizations, and autonomous groups.[50] None of these proposed national dialogues have been undertaken by the churches as the latter, as well as organized civil society, is not sufficiently strong and cohesive enough to sustain such an initiative. In addition, the government appears not to be disposed to dialogue. More recently, the Christian Democratic-linked MCL has called for a dialogue among all Cubans.[51] To date, however, there has not been the necessary strength and unity of purpose within the religious sphere, nor civil society more generally, to realize such an effort. While some have suggested that the Varela Project, which calls for constitutional and other reforms to make Cuban political life more participatory and pluralistic, could serve as a basis for dialogue and the construction of a consensual agenda, there has not been broad-based mobilization within Cuba to support it. Indeed, as indicated, the leadership of the Varela Project is at odds with substantial portions of organized civil society in Cuba.

There are additional impediments to the religious community mobilizing civil society. Virtually all religions in Cuba suffer from a scarcity of resources and face increasing demands for humanitarian assistance from the Cuban populace. Most of the material resources available come from abroad and are subject to government regulation and control, thereby encouraging caution on the part of churches and other religious organizations. They, as well as foreign religious donors, have been careful not to become identified with some of the dissident or oppositional sectors of civil society. Even so, the increased role of religions in responding to the socioeconomic needs of the population has expanded the credibility and influence of most religions within civil society. Overall, while religions are emerging as critical elements of a slowly revitalizing civil society, there is an understandable desire on their part not to precipitate serious conflicts with the government. While religious leaders, by and large, may have become more publicly critical of the government this has not translated into substantial efforts on their parts to mobilize civil society. The 1998 visit of Pope John Paul II had raised hopes that religion would occupy substantially more political space than it had previously. Such hopes were not realized, in part because religions in Cuba have never exercised power comparable to that of their counterparts in Poland, Chile, or Spain. The visit was, in fact, the pragmatic result of the conjunction of limited agendas on the part of the Vatican and the Cuban government.

The Vatican and the Cuban episcopacy aimed at consolidating the revitalization of the Catholic Church and thereby facilitating the reevangelization of the island. Preaching the gospel and disseminating Catholic social doctrine with its emphasis on socioeconomic justice has been a principal goal not only of the Cuban episcopacy, but also the Vatican, and the Latin American Catholic Church. Transforming societies was to be achieved through the conversion of hearts and minds, not armed struggle, in spite of what some interpretations of liberation theology may have suggested. Indeed, the Cuban Catholic Church appears to be committed to positioning itself to stabilize the transition currently underway and infusing it with normative values rather than assuming a leadership role. That does not mean that the Catholic Church does not want to influence whatever leadership and policy prescriptions that may emerge. The pursuit of this agenda requires more public space than resulted from the pope's visit leaving the Catholic, as well as Protestant leadership, discouraged, but not to the extent of allying themselves with oppositional sectors of civil society in Cuba or without.

In the face of increasing international isolation and economic crisis, the government viewed the papal visit as an important step in the war against the U.S. economic embargo. The position of the pope, as well as Protestant, Jewish, and spiritist leaders, in and outside the country was that the embargo was immoral and illegal under international law. U.S. Catholic bishops echoed this sentiment after the pope's visit. In the end, neither the Vatican nor the Castro government achieved their major objectives as a result of the pope's visit.

Since 1998 church-state relations in Cuba have been characterized by a level of discomfort on both sides. The Catholic bishops have been increasingly publicly critical of the government. The latter has responded by questioning the motives of the episcopacy and alleging that they are giving support to Cuba's enemies. Protestant and Jewish leaders have been less publicly critical of the government focusing more on consolidating gains in membership and securing resources to tend to the needs of their members and the broader community. Spiritist leaders range across the spectrum in terms of their positions, with many focusing on meeting the socioeconomic needs of their communities, including through cultivating government sources. Horizontal links among the various religious communities are not strong due to historical rivalries, residual prejudices, and differing agendas. Sectorialism within the religious sector of civil society continues to be strong.

Conclusion: Assessing Future Trends

There is currently a "ripening" of civil society underway in Cuba. Citizens are occupying new spaces outside government control and gradually reshaping the everyday experience of state-society and citizen-citizen interaction. There has been a concurrent ceding of public space by the government, the assumption of greater autonomy by some official organizations, and a mild revitalization of some historical organizations. The result is obviously increased ferment as such groups tentatively attempt to exert greater influence over politics and society. A principal objective is to secure greater enjoyment of socioeconomic rights and freedom from want in a context of greater political participation on which the government has based its claims to legitimacy. Although widespread societal discontent and hence pressure exist, this has not been transformed into civil society mobilization.

In order for civil society's potential to be realized, there are a number of prerequisites that need to be fulfilled. One such precondition is that there exists sufficient space to allow for generalized pressures for a greater role for civil society to be effectively exerted, together with an increasing capacity on the part of civil society to occupy it. There has been some progress in this arena, but it is limited. The government since the late 1970s, for example, has increasingly allowed some autonomous civic, cultural, and religious actors to move away from the margins of society, to which they had been relegated in the 1960s. This is partially a result of the government's need for assistance in meeting the basic needs of the population, as well as its efforts to compensate for the erosion of support from some other sectors. The government's inclination to accord more public space for religious actors was confirmed in the early 1990s by the elimination of the prohibition on believers becoming members of the Communist Party, which had blocked religious activists from holding influential positions in government or in education. In 1992 a constitutional amendment transformed Cuba from officially an atheistic state to a lay state.

There has been, however, a concurrent ceding of public space by the government, the assumption of greater autonomy by some official organizations, and a mild revitalization of some historical organizations. The result is obviously increased ferment as such groups tentatively attempt to exert greater influence over politics and society. Few are questioning the socialist nature of the government, although a fair number are challenging the government to deliver more enjoyment not only of socioeconomic, but also of civil and political rights. The upshot is that the government's claim to legitimacy rooted in the guaranteeing of greater freedom resulting from increased socioeconomic justice is also being challenged. There are some indications that this is striking a responsive chord among the population in general, but it is in the nature of agreement rather than mobilization.

Such a situation raises a critical question: can the principles and norms that sustain a strong civil society be a basis for the incorporation of self-organized groups into a socialist system, thus making it more pluralistic and participatory? If a pluralistic civil society were deemed compatible with socialism, then a program of reforms would have to focus on expanding structures of participation in such a way that they would not be totally subsumed by centralized political or economic structures.[52] Some analysts posit that Cuba could deepen the autonomy of mass organizations as a way of allowing civil society to help rebuild social and political consensus. Others question the realism of a pluralistic concept of civil society in a context where 47 years of governmental ideological hegemony has resulted in a fairly high degree of suspicion of ideological heterodoxy.

A second issue concerns the fact that the Cuban political class has restricted the debate about civil society and limited the broadening of the public sphere arguing that civil society could become a "fifth column" on behalf of the United States. A third issue results from the effects of globalization on Cuba, particularly the penetration of nonsocialist norms and behaviors, including those transmitted by religious actors.[53] Indeed one of the most notable developments in contemporary Cuba is the intensification of international exchanges between religious organizations at both the macro- and microlevels. This has been stimulated by a variety of humanitarian efforts, as well as the natural impulse to build community with one's counterparts.[54] It has resulted in more discussion of the need for religions to formally undertake a role in promoting reconciliation, including developing a theology of reconciliation, among Cubans on the island and with Cubans abroad. Such a development could help increase the likelihood of a consensual civil society agenda.

Given that religions in Cuba are increasingly playing an intermediary role (both formally and informally) between state and society in meeting the latter's basic needs, can religious actors gradually assume a mediating role in the current transition? Does increasing governmental and societal dependence on religious actors, national and international, provide a real opportunity for religions to influence the direction of society? The indications to date are that the government would resist such a possibility, but there is no guarantee that it will continue to be able to do so. To what degree, then, will religious actors be able to take advantage of the situation? Furthermore, given the broad spectrum of opinions within the religious sector over the nature of the transition and the extent of the restructuring to be undertaken, would there be a consensus that goes much beyond the need for change? Such was the case in the 1950s when the vast majority of Cubans supported an end to the Batista regime, but there was no overall agreement on what precisely would replace it, thereby providing Fidel Castro with a considerable opportunity to introduce his own ideas. And will a civil society with strong strains of secularism be willing to accept a substantial leadership role by religions even if the latter have the most extensive institutional resources and networks? In short, what is the disposition of Cuban citizens to accept the leadership of religions in building the Cuban society of the future?

In recent years, religions have been recognized often providing a stimulus for activism in civil societies, particularly in countries experiencing substantial pressures for change. In Cuba, where the revolutionary government has attempted to subsume organized civil society into the state and marginalize religions, the possibilities for religions to assume a major leadership role via a revitalizing civil society in determining Cuba's future is unclear. Not only are there obstacles resulting from the limits imposed by the state, but there are also signs that religions in Cuba are not decisively disposed to work for such incorporation, though there is, at present, considerable difference of opinion on this point. While there has been an upsurge in church attendance and involvement in religious groups in recent years, it is possible that if there were more secular associational alternatives the current popularity of religious involvement might decline. Furthermore, there are no strong indicators that nascent Cuban civil society is committed to according religions a major role in a resurgent civil society, even if they are one of the strongest elements within it.

At present there is no acknowledged leadership representing a broad cross-section of Cuban civil society; rather there is sectoral representation. The generation of consensual leadership requires increased construction of horizontal links and interaction among proactive citizens and associations. Can religious groups facilitate the development of such leadership? There have been some efforts by various religions to train community leaders, professionals, youths, and others to take a more active role in civil society, but there has not been a coalescing of such individuals around a consensual agenda. While there has been some acquisition of leadership skills, they do not appear as substantial as those developed through government mass organizations.

To date there is also a lack of leadership, either individual or institutional, that might define what forms Cuban society and polity should take in the future. In addition, there is hardly any connection between existing spokespersons of change-oriented associations and the bulk of Cuban citizens. In order for the latter's desires to become clearer, it would be necessary for the right of association to be exercised more broadly. It would also require the political space for civil society leaders to generate broader bases. At present only religious leaders appear to represent substantial national networks. Yet they have not been used extensively to consolidate a transitional agenda, although there have been occasional flurries of debate.

While there has been some discussion of goals and agendas within a revitalizing civil society, the proposals circulated to date tend to be quite schematic. The topic has been explored in various sectors and to a degree in secular and religious publications, conferences, and within informal networks, but again without any strong indication that there is a consensus about what forms Cuba's polity, economy, and society might take in the future. This reflects the degree to which Cuban civil society is somewhat adrift conceptually. For their part, religious actors have not yet offered specific proposals nor succeeded in stimulating a discussion that could result in greater consensus in this realm. In short, although Cuba has a strong history of associational activity, with deep historical roots and a society permeated with religious belief, these historical legacies have not succeeded in mobilizing civil society. The state continues to maintain ideological and political hegemony in the face of a variety of counterdiscourses that have had limited impact over society in general, in large measure given historical cleavages and sectoralism that have been exacerbated by tensions among Cubans within and without the island. As a result, while Cubans have a history of strong associationalism, together with a tradition of religious beliefs informing civil society, neither appears to have sufficient strength to guarantee that a religiously informed civil society could determine the outcome of the transition that is currently underway in Cuba.

Notes

This essay is an elaboration of the authors' ideas initially presented in Margaret E. Crahan (ed.), *Religion, Culture, and Society: The Case of Cuba* (Washington, DC: Woodrow Wilson International Center for Scholars, 2003). The authors wish to acknowledge the support of the Rockefeller Foundation's Bellagio Study and Conference Center and the Center for Philanthropy and Civil Society of the City University of New York in revising this work.

1. Reportedly the Cuban government has created units to analyze and make recommendations concerning a transition.
2. The proliferation of literature on civil society since Robert D. Putnam's landmark study, *Making Democracy Work: Civic Traditions in Modern Italy* (Princeton, NJ: Princeton University Press, 1993), is well known. Following are a few of the works that suggest the complexity and diversity of civil society's actors, as well as the degree to which civil society does not always support the deepening of democracy: Juan J. Linz and Alfred Stepan, *Problems of Democratic Transition and Consolidation: Southern Europe, South America, and Post-Communist Europe* (Baltimore, MD: Johns Hopkins University Press, 1996); Ariel C. Armony, *The Dubious Link: Civic Engagement and Democratization* (Stanford, CA: Stanford University Press, 2004); Patricia Bayer Richard and John A. Booth, "Civil Society and Democratic Transition," in Thomas W. Walker and Ariel C. Armony (eds.), *Repression, Resistance, and Democratic Transition in Central America* (Wilmington, DE: Scholarly Resources, 2000), pp. 233–254; Theda Skocpol and Morris P. Fiorina (eds.), *Civic Engagement in American Democracy* (Washington, DC: Brookings Institution Press, 1999); Mark E. Warren, *Democracy and Association* (Princeton, NJ: Princeton University Press, 2001); and Michael Edwards, *Civil Society* (Cambridge: Polity Press, 2004).
3. Alfonso Quiróz, "The Evolution of Laws Regulating Associations and Civil Society in Cuba," in Crahan (ed.), *Religion, Culture, and Society*, pp. 59–63.

4. A 1957 survey of 4,000 agricultural workers in Cuba revealed that while 96.5 percent believed in God, 41.4 percent claimed no religious affiliation. In addition, although 52.1 percent claimed to be Catholic more than half of them (53.5 percent) stated they had never laid eyes on a priest and only 7.8 percent ever had any contact with one. Oscar A. Echevarría Salvat, *La Agricultura Cubana, 1934–1966: Régimen social, productividad y nivel de vida del sector agrícola* (Miami, FL: Ediciones Universal, 1971), pp. 14–15.

5. Olga Portuondo Zúñiga, *La Virgen de la Caridad del Cobre: Símbolo de cubanía* (Santiago de Cuba: Editorial Oriente, 1995), pp. 58–63.

6. Ibid., pp. 260–271.

7. Claude Julien, "Church and State in Cuba: Development of a Conflict," *Cross Currents*, II, Spring 1961: 188; and Alfred L. Padula Jr., "The Fall of the Bourgeoisie: Cuba 1959–1966," PhD Dissertation, University of New Mexico, 1974, pp. 458–459.

8. Joan Maria Pique, "Thousands Celebrate Virgin of Charity," *Miami Herald*, September 9, 1997, p. 4B.

9. Margaret E. Crahan, "Cuban Diasporas: Their Impact on Religion, Culture, and Society," in Crahan (ed.), *Religion, Culture, and Society*, pp. 35–54.

10. Ibid., pp. 37–54; Christine Ayorinde, *Afro-Cuban Religiosity, Revolution, and National Identity* (Gainesville, FL: University Press of Florida, 2004).

11. Eduardo Torres-Cuevas, *Félix Varela: Los orígenes de la ciencia y con-ciencia cubanas* (Havana: Editorial de las Ciencias Sociales, 1997); Félix Varela, *Escritos políticos* (Havana: Editorial de Ciencias Sociales, 1977); and Sheldon B. Liss, *Roots of Revolution: Radical Thought in Cuba* (Lincoln, NE: University of Nebraska Press, 1987), p. 12.

12. Eduardo Torres-Cuevas et al., *Félix Varela: Ética y anticipación del pensamiento de la emancipación Cubana* (Havana: Imagen Contemporánea, 1999).

13. Ayorinde, *Afro-Cuba Religiosity*, pp. 30–39; Crahan, "Cuban Diasporas"; Manuel Maza, S.J., *El Clero Cubano y la independencia: Las investigaciones de Francisco González del Valle (1881–1942)* (Santo Domingo: Compañía de Jesús en las Antillas, 1993); and Manuel Maza, S.J., *El alma del negocio y el negocio del alma: Testimonios sobre la iglesia y la sociedad en Cuba, 1878–1894* (Santiago: Pontificia Universidad Católica Madre y Maestra, 1990).

14. John Kirk, *Between God and the Party: Religion and Politics in Revolutionary Cuba* (Tampa, FL: University of South Florida Press, 1989), pp. 20–22.

15. Crahan, "Cuban Diasporas"; Crahan, "Protestantism in Cuba," in *PCCLAS Proceedings* IX (San Diego, CA: Campanile Press, 1982), pp. 59–70; Marcos A. Ramos, *Protestantism and Revolution in Cuba* (Miami, FL: University of Miami, 1989), pp. 20–27; Jason M. Yaremko, *U.S. Protestant Missions in Cuba: From Independence to Castro* (Gainesville, FL: University Press of Florida, 2000), pp. 3–5.

16. Margaret E. Crahan, "Salvation through Christ or Marx," in Crahan (ed.), *Religion, Culture, and Society*, p. 241.

17. The Platt Amendment, which was incorporated into the 1901 Cuban constitution, protected U.S. economic and political interests in the country while impinging upon the new republic's sovereignty. Lack of full sovereignty debilitated the new republic's capacity to govern and therefore provide the benefits of citizenship to all Cubans, especially those regarded by U.S. troops and representatives as not meriting them, namely Afro-Cubans. It was abrogated in 1934.

18. The Independent Party of Color (Partido Independiente de Color [PIC]) whose leaders led the uprising used a rearing horse as their symbol, identified with the Yoruban spirit Shangó whose Catholic counterpart is Santa Barbara. Aline Helg, *Our Rightful Share: The Afro-Cuban Struggle for Equality, 1886–1912* (Chapel Hill, NC: University of North Carolina Press, 1995), pp. 150–151.

19. Catholic Action, which originated in Europe in the 1920s championed political and economic reforms that could undercut the appeal of socialism, was identified with Christian Democratic parties and movements. *Agrupación Católica* members tended to be identified with social democracy. In recent years European Christian Democrats, as well as Social Democrats, have encouraged the development of their counterparts in Cuba.

20. A 1958 survey of Las Villas Province revealed that only 3.8 percent of male Catholic respondents had attended Mass the previous month, while 5.1 percent of females had. Close to 90 percent of the females and 92.6 percent of males did not generally attend religious services. This pattern was common throughout Cuba. Universidad Central "Marta Abreu" de Las Villas, *La educación rural en las villas: Bases para la redacción de unos cursos de estudios* (Santa Clara, Cuba: Universidad Central, 1959): 32.

21. In 1960 nominal Catholics constituted approximately 70–75 percent of the total population of 7,500,000, while Protestants amounted to 3–6 percent. The Jewish community numbered approximately 12,000 in the 1950s, while spiritists were estimated at about 65 percent of the total population, overlapping with other religions. In the late 1980s the Centro de Investigaciones Psicológicas y Sociológicas of the Cuban Academy of Sciences estimated that 65–85 percent of Cubans believed in the supernatural, while 13.60 percent did not. In the mid-1990s believers were estimated to constitute approximately 85 percent of the population. Currently regular practitioners are estimated by various religious sources to be around 1–3 percent. For an examination of Cuban religious statistics see Margaret E. Crahan, "Cuba," in Paul E. Sigmund (ed.), *Religious Freedom and Evangelization in Latin America: The Challenge of Religious Pluralism* (Maryknoll, NY: Orbis Books, 1999), pp. 297–298; Crahan, "Salvation through Christ or Marx"; and Margaret E. Crahan, "The Church of the Past and the Church of the Future," in Max Azicri and Elsie Deal (eds.), *Cuban Socialism in a New Century: Adversity, Survival, and Renewal* (Gainesville, FL: University Press of Florida, 2004), pp. 123–146.

22. Quiróz, "The Evolution of Laws Regulating Associations and Civil Society in Cuba," pp. 63–64.

23. Ibid.

24. Broadly speaking, the public sphere is the public space where individuals "engage in negotiations and contestations over political and social life." Margaret R. Somers, "Citizenship and the Place of the Public Sphere: Law, Community, and Political Culture in the Transition to Democracy," *American Sociological Review*, 58 (5), October 1993: 589.

25. See Mary P. Ryan, "Civil Society as Democratic Practice: North American Cities during the Nineteenth Century," in Robert I. Rotberg (ed.), *Patterns of Social Capital: Stability and Change in Historical Perspective* (Cambridge: Cambridge University Press, 2001), p. 242; Warren, *Democracy and Association*, pp. 162–181; and Iris Marion Young, "State, Civil Society, and Social Justice," in Ian Shapiro and Casiano Hacker-Cordón (eds.), *Democracy's Value* (Cambridge: Cambridge University Press, 1999), p. 157.

26. For varieties of discourses see Juan Valdés Paz, "Cuba in the 'Special Period':
From Equality to Equity"; Jorge Luis Acanda González, "Changes in Cuban
Society and their Reflection in Cuban Thought from the Nineties to the
Present"; Rafael Hernández, "Mirror of Patience: Notes on Cuban Studies,
Social Sciences and Contemporary Thought"; on youth see María Isabel
Domínguez, "Cuban Youth: Aspirations, Social Perceptions, and Identity";
on religion see Margaret E. Crahan, "Civil Society and Religion in Cuba: Past,
Present, and Future"; Aurelio Alonso, "Relations between the Catholic
Church as of 2003"; and Raimundo García Franco, "Notes on the Role of
Religious Organizations in Community Work and Service Provision in Cuba
After 1990," in Joseph S. Tulchin et al. (eds.), *Changes in Cuba since the
Nineties* (Washington, DC: Woodrow Wilson International Center for
Scholars, 2005).
27. See Adrian H. Hearn, "The Spirit of Development: Community Welfare,
Grassroots Religion, and Transculturation in Contemporary Cuba," manu-
script, 2005.
28. On recent Cuban economic developments, including the evolution of the infor-
mal sector, see Philip Peters, "Cuba's Small Businesses: Taking a Wild Ride," in
Beyond Transition: The Newsletter about Reforming Economies (Washington,
DC: World Bank Group, 2001); "Cuba's International Strategy Pays Off,"
Cuba Policy Report, February 4, 2005: 1–4; and Theodore A. Henken,
"Condemned to Informality: Cuba's Experiments with Self-Employment
During the Special Period," PhD dissertation, Tulane University, 2002.
29. Peter Roman, "The Lawmaking Process in Cuba: Debating the Bill on
Agricultural Cooperatives," *Socialism and Democracy*, 19 (2), July 2005: 37–56.
30. In 1993 the Cuban government decriminalized possession of foreign currency
by Cubans. This, together with an upsurge of tourism and remittances,
resulted in widespread circulation of dollars, as well as other foreign currencies
in Cuba. On October 25, 2004 the Cuban government announced the institution of a convertible peso as a substitute for the dollar. A 10 percent surcharge was added to the purchase of convertible pesos with foreign currencies.
No new deposits of dollars into bank accounts were allowed, although other
foreign currencies were. This effectively limited the circulation of dollars
and was in partial response to the U.S. imposed restrictions on travel
to Cuba, as well as remittances, adopted in mid-2004. Lexington Institute,
"De-Dollarization," *Cuba Policy Report*, October 29, 2004: 1–4.
31. Henken, "Condemned to Informality."
32. Inter American Institute of Human Rights, "IIHR Takes Part in Third
International Meeting: Constitution, Democracy and Political Systems,"
IIHR in the Americas 62, June 15–30, 2005: 4.
33. Linz and Stepan, *Problems of Democratic Transition and Consolidation*.
34. Some of these can be found in Pedro Monreal (ed.), *Development Prospects in
Cuba: An Agenda in the Making* (London: Institute of Latin American
Studies, School of Advanced Study, University of London, 2002).
35. Maurizio Giuliano, *El caso CEA: Intelectuales e inquisidores en Cuba
¿Perestroika en la isla?* (Miami, FL: Ediciones Universal, 1998).
36. Adrian Hearn's "The Spirit of Development" describes in detail the role of
Afro-Cuban religious groups in a variety of community development projects.
37. For the breadth of the Center's work see its Web site at http://www.ccrd.org.
Accessed November 5, 2005.

38. Religious groups in Cuba have formed ties to their counterparts, particularly in Europe and the United States, at both the micro and macro levels, including congregation to congregation as well as between national religious organizations such as the Cuba's and the U.S. National Councils of Churches. On balance these linkages have tended to encourage greater cooperation and even reconciliation. Katrin Hansing and Sarah J. Mahler, "God Knows No Borders: Transnational Religious Ties Linking Miami and Cuba," in Crahan (ed.), *Religion, Culture, and Society*, pp. 123–129.

39. See www.vitral.org. Accessed November 5, 2005.

40. Hearn, "The Spirit of Development."

41. Ayorinde, *Afro-Cuban Religiosity*, pp. 158–160.

42. Committee to Protect Journalists, "Cuba Detains, Expels Several Foreign Journalists," at http://www.cpj.org/news/2005/Cuba20may05na.html. Accessed November 5, 2005.

43. Movimiento Cristiano Liberación, "Una aclaración necesaria," May 19, 2005, Havana, Cuba, at http://www.mclpaya.org/pag.cgi?page=viewnotandid=not.7641598.30244. Accessed November 5, 2005.

44. Consenso Cubano, at http://www.consensocubano.org/eng/whatiscc.htm; cubafacts.com and "New Dissident Initiatives," at http://www.cubafacts.com/Humanrights/HRPers99/hrpers99p.5.htm. Accessed November 5, 2005.

45. Lázara Menéndez, "In Order to Wake Up Tomorrow, You Have to Sleep Tonight," in Tulchin et al. (eds.), *Changes in Cuban Society since the Nineties*, pp. 267–286.

46. Currently religious practitioners tend to fall into three groups: traditionalists, renovators who are noncharismatic and renovators who are charismatic. Traditionalists, who are a minority, tend to adhere to historical doctrines, liturgy, and practices. The noncharismatic renovators emphasize participation in Cuban society as a community of believers and evangelization. They tend to fault the charismatic renovators for a lack of doctrinal clarity and introspection that reduces their participation in the broader community. The latter generally require a second baptism by the Holy Spirit in order to be saved, therefore setting up a barrier between themselves and the society more generally. Religious leaders most committed to revolutionary goals tend to be critical of charismatics, as well as Pentecostals, for contributing to an erosion of societal solidarity and identification. Elizabeth Carillo, "El protestantismo histórico en Cuba hoy: ¿Carismátismo renovación?" *Temas*, 6, April–June 1997: 20–30. While all religions have experienced resurgence in Cuba, those that have demonstrated the strongest growth are those that emphasize community and solidarity. Mainline Protestant, as well as Catholic churches and Jewish congregations that emphasize the latter have grown as strongly as Pentecostal and charismatic groups.

47. Jaime Ortega y Alamino, "Discurso de Mons. Jaime Ortega y Alamino: Visita Ad Limina de los Obispos de Cuba, 25.VI.94," manuscript, Rome, June 25, 1994.

48. Conferencia de Obispos Católicos de Cuba, *Plan Global Pastoral, 1997–2000* (Havana: Secretariado General de la COCC, 1996), pp. 2–4.

49. Ibid., p. 6.

50. "Cuba, Its People and Its Church," *LADOC*, XXX, July/August 2000: 11–17.

51. Organización Demócrata Cristiana de América, "Cubanos presentan diálogo nacional como guía para realizar una consulta popular," *ODCA On Line*, at www.odca.cl; "Diálogo Nacional: Programa Transitorio," December 15, 2003.
52. Ariel C. Armony, "Civil Society in Cuba: A Conceptual Approach," in Crahan (ed.), *Religion, Culture, and Society*, p. 26.
53. Ibid., pp. 17–36.
54. Hansing and Mahler, "God Knows No Borders," pp. 123–130.

Chapter 9

The Knots of Memory:
Culture, Reconciliation, and
Democracy in Cuba

Rafael Rojas

Introduction: Two Politics of Memory

At the beginning of the twenty-first century, the transition to democracy in Cuba is developing in an historical context marked by commercial, financial, migratory, technological, and cultural globalization, and simultaneously by the normative diffusion, on a planetary scale, of the Western philosophy of human rights.[1] Against this background—which makes the political limitations of the nation-state more ostensible and also incites a revamping of nationalist discourses and practices—a pact of national reconciliation must take effect among Cubans of all political persuasions, without which it is virtually impossible to imagine an actual transition to democracy.

The new "culture of memory in times of globalization," of which Andreas Huyssen talks, began to grow during the 1960s with the retroactive application of justice to Adolf Eichmann and other Nazis in hiding.[2] The maximum expression of the institutionalization of such a retroactive juridical conception was reached in the United Nations International Convention on the Non-Applicability of Statutory Limitations to War Crimes and Crimes against Humanity in 1968. Since then, until the establishment of the bylaws of Rome and the efforts made to establish an International Criminal Court (ICC), in the Hague, the global diplomatic pressure in favor of the juridical prosecution of past crimes has grown in strength, and in some cases has induced such processes so as to affirm the national sovereignty of the affected states.

However, in the last few years, the experience of transition from authoritarian or totalitarian regimes in Latin America and Eastern Europe, in Russia and Portugal, in Spain and South Africa, shows that national reconciliation—understood not only as the concession of political rights to all citizens, but also as the free and public circulation of all *memories*, and in its case, the testimonial recognition or juridical prosecution of past crimes—has a very complex relationship with the processes of regime change and democratic construction. This complexity results from the fact that the actors who must negotiate the transition originate for the most part in four spheres with varying historical *legitimacies*: government, civil society, opposition, and exile.

In almost all of these new Western democracies, a change of political regime has occurred. However, the problem of memory and reconciliation remains alive and, in some cases, unresolved. In spite of this, it is possible to group these experiences in two categories: those countries whose governments created "justice and truth commissions" such as South Africa, Argentina, Chile, Uruguay, Peru, Guatemala, and El Salvador and those, such as Spain, Portugal, Mexico, Russia, and the former socialist countries of Eastern Europe, which preferred not to do this, be it on account of the fact that the actors of the transition valued the advantages of a policy of "general oblivion"—so common in Latin American history—or because they considered that, after a few emblematic prosecutions, the issue could be left in the hands of public opinion, educational and cultural policies, and the intellectuals.[3]

In South Africa, the Truth and Reconciliation Commission (TRC), promoted by Nelson Mandela and spearheaded by Desmond Mpilo Tutu was created as a moral rather than a judicial institution. It was charged with the documented exposition of the crimes of apartheid and the prosecution of those found guilty. In Peru, the Commission of Truth and Reconciliation (Comisión de Verdad y Reconciliación [CVR]), chaired by Salomon Lerner Ferbes, registered in August 2003, 69,280 victims of crimes against humanity attributed to the Shining Path, the Tupac Amaru Revolutionary Movement (Movimiento Revolucionario Tupac Amaru [MRTA]), and to the successive Peruvian governments that ruled the country between 1980 and 2000. The government of Alejandro Toledo, however, insisted that justice would be applied rationally and that the prosecution of those guilty for past crimes would have to be assumed autonomously by the Peruvian judicial power.[4]

As opposed to Central America, in Latin America's Southern Cone the tendency toward granting amnesties in the mid-1980s, typified by the laws of Punto Final (Full Stop) and Due Obedience, has reverted in the last few years with several successes: the revision of such legislation by the supreme courts of Argentina and Chile, the extradition request presented by the Spanish Judge Baltazar Garzón, in the first place against the Chilean Dictator Pinochet, and then against 46 members of the Argentine military junta and, finally, the declaration by representatives and senators of the "irremediable nullity" of these laws of impunity.[5] The announcement, at the end of August 2003, that the Spanish government was rejecting the extradition of the Argentine military requested by Judge Garzón simply asserts—as in the case of Pinochet—the sovereignty of Argentina's judicial power in the prosecution of criminals of the past.[6]

Yet, in transitions where the new democratic regime was more flexible with the old regime's elite, the demands for justice by the victims and their defenders do not disappear with the wounds of the past in a sort of "clean slate." The difference, though, rests on the fact that these demands—the declassification of archives, the release of secret information, and the exculpation by means of cultural and educational policies of the state—are debated and disputed. In Spain, for instance, each summer, families of the members of the International Brigades dig up unmarked cemeteries where republican soldiers are known to rest. Meanwhile the debate about the civil war and Franquismo, in historiography, literature, and journalism is progressively more intense. Carmen Franco, the daughter of the dictator, presides over a private foundation favored by state grants, which holds the documents of the Franco regime and which is devoted to promoting the knowledge of the "human, political, and military" work "of the *Generalisimo*." Each November 20, the day of the death of the caudillo, it organizes a memorial service at the Basilica del Valle de los Caidos.[7]

In Russia, there is a constant contest between pro-Soviets and anti-Soviets, between monarchists and Stalinists, which forces Vladimir Putin's government to satisfy, with gestures of state, both offended memories. In Germany, the movie *Good-Bye Lenin* (2003) by Wolfgang Becker and the important art exhibition *Art in the GDR* (2003) are symptoms of the cultural phenomenon called *ostalgie* (nostalgia for the society of the communist East).[8] In Mexico, the new textbooks on national history, which are edited by the Secretariado de Educación Pública (Secretariat of Public Education [SPE]), include for the first time, a very critical vision of the regime of the Revolutionary Institutional Party (Partido Revolucionario Institucional [PRI]), and in particular the student massacre of 1968 in the Tlatelolco Square. This, despite the fact that the special prosecutor—established by Vicente Fox to investigate state violence in the 1960s and 1970s—has not yet presented the fruit of his labor.[9]

Therefore, in broad strokes we could divide the politics of memory associated with processes of democratic transition into two types. The first takes recourse in institutions of judicial power or generates new mechanisms for the exercise of justice in order to achieve the prosecution of past crimes. The other is concentrated in the public sphere (mass media, intellectual circles, cultural and educational policy) with the aim of fomenting the free circulation of contradictory discourses about the past, which are capable of mutual toleration. The first type of transition is, therefore, a politics of memory defined by the notions of *truth* and *justice*; the second type, on the other hand, is a politics of memory rather defined by the concepts of *reconciliation* and *tolerance*.[10]

The choice between the two approaches is related to the duration and type of the old regime. It would be understandable, thus, that in the Southern Cone and in Central America, given the fact that the authoritarian regimes were very repressive and relatively brief, reconciliation would be associated with the prosecution of crimes against humanity or genocide that might have occurred in the past. In a similar manner, the prolonged totalitarian or authoritarian regimes, such as in the cases of the Soviet Union, Spain, Eastern Europe, and Mexico, where the state played a constitutive role in society, the process of reconciliation was, from the very start, characterized by an amnesty pact among the actors in the democratic transformation. The exception has been South Africa. Once the country left behind not only an authoritarian regime but also an order of racial segregation, it had to rediscover itself as a nation. This had to be done by intermingling two conflicting practices: the elucidation of the past and the reconciliation of political rivals.

Which of these politics of memory is a more suitable model for the Cuban transition? Is it the prosecution of past crimes through judicial institutions or the elucidation of the past by means of a commission of *truth* and *justice*? Is it the general amnesty, legally typified or not, which can provide a point of departure for the elucidation of past crimes? Is it perhaps a combination of both as in the South African case?

It is extremely difficult and perhaps impossible to respond to these questions. In fact probably the only valid response can be given by the historical actors as they negotiate the transition to democracy. I will limit myself to pointing out some knots in the memory, which will have to be untied by three historical subjects: the revolution, the opposition, and the exile community. I will do this by relying on contemporary Cuban literature and historiography. These knots, insofar as they are part of the historical imagery of political actors, might present themselves as obstacles to the process of national reconciliation.

I will try to reconstruct these knots with the exposition of two discourses: on the one hand, the official memory of the opposition, and on the other, the exiled memory of the revolution. It is evident that the confrontation of both discourses, to some extent, resolves the conflict of the legitimacy of the past and, for that reason, the possibility of the emergence of a new symbolic repertoire for national reconciliation. Memory, as Reinhart Koselleck points out, is nothing more than the discourse of identity of a historical subject that wishes to gain strength in the present through its past.[11] Thus, national reconciliation among Cubans, the change of regime, and the democratic transition are for the most part subordinated to the recognition of the historical legitimacy of all political actors.

The first serious attempt to tackle the issue of national reconciliation in Cuba from an intellectual angle, resulted from the work of the Memory, Truth and Justice Working Group (Grupo de Trabajo Memoria, Verdad y Justicia), coordinated by Marifeli Pérez-Stable, Jorge I. Domínguez, and Pedro A. Freyre. This group, in which only Cubans living outside of the country participated, proposed that once the time of transition arrived, and in accordance with the norms of international law, there would be three areas where crimes against humanity in the recent past of Cuba could be investigated and debated. The first is "the violation of human rights by the government of Fidel Castro"; the second is "the abuses, felonies and atrocities committed by the violent opposition"; and the third is "the subversive operations and covert actions of the government of the United States."[12] The thoughts I present hereafter are deliberately situated closer than that, which is to say, in the still lively dispute among the political actors in search of historical legitimacy.

The Official Memory of the Opposition

The creation of a pluralist political system always implies the cohabitation of diverse narratives about the past of a country. In the case of Cuba, one of the main forms of resistance to the creation of a democratic culture is, precisely, the preponderance of an official discourse of national history, which, to a large extent, defines the educational, cultural, and ideological policy of the government of Fidel Castro. The focus of such a discourse is the revolution of 1959 as the inaugural event of a "glorious and definitive" time "in the history of Cuba, in which, finally, the modern project of a sovereign nation is realized." According to the official narrative that the ideological apparatus of the state reproduces, the history prior to the revolution is divided in two fundamental epochs: the colony (1492–1898), and the republic (1902–1959), which represent, in fact, the colonial prehistory of the island.[13]

This discourse, far from weakening, has grown stronger since 1992, when the constitutional reforms of that year shifted the ideological emphasis from Marxist-Leninism to revolutionary nationalism, and all the more so after the campaign for the repatriation of Elián González in 1999 gave the initial thrust to the so-called battle of ideas.[14] The hegemony of this narrative is manifested as an eternal and irrevocable present, which cancels, for that reason, the perception of future and change and which maintains only a relation with those events of the past such as the wars of independence of the nineteenth century and the revolution of 1933, which provide a revolutionary teleology. The mythological and teleological character of this narrative is very similar to the one that supports the "politics of oblivion," those "white pages" of which Adam Michnik spoke, and which are so frequent in the historical ideology of authoritarian and totalitarian regimes.[15]

In the past 10 years, a significant paradox has occurred in Cuban culture: while the official narrative of the ideology accentuates its mythical roots in revolutionary nationalism, professional historiography—and most of all that which is practiced by young researchers on the island—begins to show a strong interest in the white pages of the revolution, that is, the old colonial and republican regime. The period following the Pact of Zanjón (1878–1895) has been explored by a new generation of historians: María Antonia Marqués Dolz, Imilcy Balboa Navarro, and Ana Meilyn de la O Torres.[16] But probably the theme that has most attracted the attention of the new historiography of the island is the intellectual and political history of the republic. This is made evident in the latest research of Marial Iglesias, Jorge Núñez Vega, Reinaldo Funes Monzote, Ricardo Quiza Moreno, and Duanel Díaz.[17]

This displacement of the historiographical interest from the three mythological reserves of revolutionary nationalism—the wars of independence, the revolution of 1933, and the revolution of 1959—toward the old colonial and republican regime occurs, as we pointed out, against the grain of an ideological discourse associating the prerevolutionary past with the negative values of capitalism and democracy. Thus, the political actors, who live in or outside of the country, as dissidents or in exile, who defend peaceful and legal projects of transition to a market economy and to a regime of public liberties, are not identified in the official discourse as legitimate opposition but as enemies of the revolution or counterrevolutionaries, who wish to restore the neocolonial order of the republic. Such rigidity does not only place itself in opposition to the new historical horizon, but it also disputes a politics of culture that attempts to transmit the prerevolutionary and exiled intellectual legacy.[18]

At the core of the absence of an elemental culture of opposition stands the very idea of the Cuban Revolution. The most eloquent account of this process might be that advanced by Jean Paul Sartre in *Sartre visita a Cuba* (Hurricane over Sugar), in which he claims that the revolution is not just a historical period of social change, such as the destruction of a capitalist system and the creation of a socialist one. Neither is it the abandonment of a bourgeois democracy and the installation of a proletarian dictatorship. The Cuban Revolution, according to its most profound mythology, is not just its "social achievements," the revolutionary government, or the figure of Fidel Castro. It is, in fact, the unity of the caudillo and the people, of Fidel and the nation in a permanent war against the external enemy—Yankee imperialism and its potential allies on the island. Sartre put it in the following manner in the spring of 1960: "When *La Coubre* exploded, I discovered the occult face of all revolutions, its shady face: the foreign threat sensed in *anguish*. And I discovered the Cuban anguish because suddenly I shared it."[19]

The idea, which is so deeply rooted in the mentality of the Cuban political class, that the revolution is a permanent state of war against the internal and external enemies makes it virtually impossible for Cuba to elaborate a juridical culture of opposition. Such an idea does not only nullify any representative dimension in Cuban politics by gulping in one historic entity such diverse notions as *nation and state* or *government and people*, but it also locates the regime of the country in a continual past that, as Margalit argues, permits the fragmentation of collective memory by means of well-promoted myths, and dissolves the sense of responsibility of power in a communitarian subjectivity.[20] In establishing this equivalence between *opposition* and *enmity*, the discourse of the revolution creates, therefore, the conditions that make possible the history of the counterrevolution.

La contrarrevolución cubana (The Cuban Counterrevolution), by Jesús Arboleya, is an ideal text in which one can read about the official memory of the opposition process. This account argues that the Cuban counterrevolution is, from 1959 to date, a single movement created by the government of the United States with the object of overthrowing the Cuban socialist system and restoring the neocolonial order. The historical roots of the counterrevolution, according to Arboleya, can be found in the social fabric of the republican bourgeoisie, in the "reformist middle class," and, politically, in all the associations and tendencies of the 1950s–from the *batistianos*, *auténticos*, and *ortodoxos*, up to members of the 26th of July Movement (Movimiento 26 de Julio [M-26]), the Revolutionary Directorate (Directorio Revolucionario), and the Partido Socialista Popular (PSP).[21] From 1960 onward, Arboleya continues, the broad and diverse array of organizations and political personalities that confronted the revolution—the Movement for the Revolutionary Recuperation (Movimiento de Recuperación Revolucionaria [MRR]), the Christian Democratic Movement (Movimiento Demócrata Cristiano [MDC]), the Revolutionary Movement of the People (Movimiento Revolucionario del Pueblo [MRP]), the 30 November Movement (Movimiento 30 de Noviembre), Revolutionary Democratic Action (Acción Democrática Revolucionaria [ADR]), the Montecristi Group (Grupo Montecristi [GM]), Manuel Artime and Manuel Antonio de Varona, Manuel Ray and José Miró Cardona, Rufo López Fresquet and Raúl Chibás, Huber Matos and Eloy Gutiérrez Menoyo—experienced a total subordination to the administrations of Eisenhower and Kennedy through the labors of the Central Intelligence Agency (CIA).[22]

During 20 years at the very least, all counterrevolutionary activity was coordinated from Miami, which translated into two major invasion projects (one undertaken, yet defeated, at the Bay of Pigs in 1961, and the other discarded in 1962 after the Russian Missile Crisis, called Operation Mongoose), the guerrillas in the Escambray Mountains and several other armed groups that undertook thousands of sabotage operations and terrorist attacks on the island, responded, according to this account, to a clear, subversive agenda defined by Washington and geared toward the violent destruction of the government of Fidel Castro.[23] The Cuban opposition was no more than a terrorist militia, financed by the State Department and trained by the CIA. The repressive record of the Cuban government in those decades—hundreds of executions, tens of thousands of incarcerations, public migration of disenfranchised citizenry—not only is recognized in this discourse but is also tactically justified as the political imperative of the *"counter-beat revolution"* brought up by Ernesto Guevara in reference to the permanent threat of a neighboring empire.[24]

Arboleya, Escalante, Báez, and other official historians admit that at the end of the 1970s, with Carter's human rights policies, the dialogue with emigrant groups and the Mariel exodus, a generational and political change in the counterrevolution began to take place.[25] The results of such a transformation can be seen in the 1980s and 1990s within four institutional processes. First is the emergence of new associations of émigrés such as the Cuban-American National Foundation (CANF), which is devoted to exercising geopolitical pressure over Fidel Castro through the support of the U.S. trade embargo and the preservation of the Cuban Adjustment Act. Second, there is the emergence of important coalitions such as the Cuban Democratic Platform (Plataforma Democrática Cubana [PDC]), an alliance of Christian Democrats, Social Democrats, and Liberals, which defends the idea of a transition to democracy, negotiated with the government of the island. Third, there is the creation of organizations such as Cambio Cubano (Cuban Change) and the Cuban Committee for Democracy (Comité Cubano por la Democracia [CCD]), openly opposed to the embargo and its legislative tightening (Toricelli Legislation of 1992 and the Helms-Burton Act of 1996) and supporters of a process of normalization in the relations between the United States and Cuba. Finally, there is the appearance of a new political actor, internal Cuban dissidence, which is a movement that managed to consolidate itself in the mid-1990s with projects for a peaceful and gradual transition to democracy, departing from the regime's own legislative and institutional legitimacy, through groups such as Concilio Cubano (Cuban Council) (1995), La Patria es de Todos (The Fatherland Belongs to Everybody, 1997), and the Varela Project (2002).

However, the official discourse considers this transformation of the opposition movement as a mere change of tactics within the same counterrevolutionary strategy. Abandoning violence and supporting a normalization of the relations between the United States and Cuba are, according to this logic, attitudes perfectly compatible with the foreign policy of the United States. Even the more moderate currents of that internal opposition are subtle forms of the same counterrevolutionary genealogy that, because of its lack of a social base, "cannot define itself based on what they want for Cuba, but must be defined by what they do not want for the island," such as the economic embargo, a migratory crisis, or social collapse.[26] That is to say that the only value that the Cuban government recognizes in this political actor is that it is a circumstantial and external ally in the promotion of the advancement of Cuban-American relations. Arboleya summarizes, in this manner, the official perception of the new peaceful and moderate opposition:

> This counter-revolutionary variant responds to an organizational body less structured, which functions on diffuse ideological premises and, as a consequence, is more deceitful. Therefore, on many occasions it is confused with efforts which are truly geared towards the normalization of the relations between Cuba and the United States, and with a legitimate internal debate geared towards surmounting the imperfections of the system. This complicates the Cuban response and induces errors at the time when the enemy must be identified, which constitutes, indeed, one of the purposes. This sector distinguishes itself from other trends within the contemporary ideological debate and bestows upon it a specific counterrevolutionary character, whose territory of operation is not limited to the ideological sphere but is structured in such a way as to affect all Cuban reality with evident political objectives destined to organize the internal opposition from positions that are more acceptable for certain European and Latin American sectors and better adjusted to the new international situation.[27]

This official memory of the Cuban opposition is also manifested in the recent laws approved by the National Assembly of Popular Power (Asamblea Nacional del Poder Popular de la República de Cuba [ANPP]) and conceived as the antidote to the Helms-Burton Law. Law 80 of 1996 on the Reaffirmation of Cuban Dignity and Sovereignty passed by the ANPP, establishes that the United States must pay reparation to the Cuban people for the harms caused by the embargo and by the counterrevolution since Washington "during four decades devoted itself to promoting, organizing, financing and directing counter-revolutionary and *annexationist* elements within and without the territory of the Republic of Cuba and has invested vast material and financial resources in the realization of numerous covert actions aimed at destroying the independence and the economy of Cuba, using for such ends, among other things, individuals recruited within the national territory." In Article 11 of this law, the Cuban legislators announced their intention to add to the amount of the reparations for the "effects of the economic, commercial and financial embargo and the aggression against the country"—which should be prorated each year, the "demands for harm and damage caused by the thieves, counterfeiters, corrupt politicians and mobsters" of the republic, and the "torturers and murderers of Batista's tyranny by whose actions the government of the United States has made itself responsible in the promulgation of the Helms-Burton legislation."

This same connection between the old prerevolutionary regime and the Cuban opposition in the past 44 years appears in the "for how much" of Law 88 of 1999, titled Protection of National Independence and the Economy of Cuba. Here any exercise of internal opposition within the country is typified as a criminal infraction due to the fact that such exercise will irremediably respond, in some fashion or other, to the interests of the U.S. government. In chapter four of the law, the first and second sections of this law, penalties of between eight and twenty years of prison are contemplated for those who "supply, directly or through third persons, to the government of the United States, its offices, its dependencies, its representatives, or its functionaries, information with the object of facilitating the goals of the Helms-Burton legislation, the embargo and the economic war against our people aimed at the disintegration of internal order, the destabilization of the country, the liquidation of the socialist state and of the independence of Cuba." This felony of opinion, of which only duly accredited foreign journalists are exempted, is also a felony of association since it contemplates the aggravating factor that it is "committed with the participation of two people or more."

As a result the historical memory of the Cuban opposition that is preponderant in the government of Fidel Castro is guided by a revolutionary conception of the political present according to which the United States, as it promotes democracy in Cuba, is attempting to destroy the Cuban nation and restore the neocolonial order. The opposition groups, inside and outside of the island, that work peacefully for change or for a reform of the political system from the institutional legitimacy of the regime and the existing, socialist constitutional legislation are not only taken as enemies of the country who must be punished but also as direct descendents of the political class of the pre-1959 republic and of the counterrevolutionary groups of the 1960s and 1970s. That is the official memory of the revolution as it is reflected in the legitimating discourse of the regime, which the ideological apparatus of the state promotes and, over all, as it is manifested in the island's penal legislation.[28]

The Exiled Memory of the Revolution

One of the great difficulties that the construction of an opposition movement has faced in Cuba, besides the absence of public freedoms to sustain its development, is the prevalence of an illegitimate vision of the government of

Fidel Castro. During several decades, the Cuban opposition within and without the island assumed that the regime was illegitimate because it had emerged from the popular revolution and its leadership was never validated with the electoral norms of a representative democracy. This discourse of the illegitimacy of the Cuban regime was always supported by the fact that the leadership of exile was headed by nationalist and liberal politicians such as José Miró Cardona, Manuel Antonio de Varona, Manuel Ray Rivero, and Manuel Artime Buesa, some of them former members of the first revolutionary government who broke with Fidel Castro between 1960 and 1961 in protest of the radicalization of the socialist process.

In the first historiography of exile, which was written in many cases by intellectuals who sympathize with the revolutionary movement (people such as Jorge Mañach, Carlos Márquez Sterling, Herminio Portell Vilá, Mario Llerena, or Leví Marrero) the main topic was the "betrayed revolution." These authors reiterated the idea of the revolutionary project that had assured the fall of Fulgencio Batista in 1959, and that had been based on the social-democratic ideological consensus, which was abandoned by Fidel Castro and the more intractable wing of the 26th of July Movement in alliance with the communists.[29] The topic of the betrayed revolution converged in the anticommunist political culture of the Cuban opposition and facilitated the alliance of the Cuban exiles with the U.S. government during the Cold War. The nationalism and violence of this first exile were mingled in political and military activity, conceived with the aim of overthrowing the illegitimate regime, which was subordinating the island to "Soviet imperialism." The alliance of the Cuban exile with the United States was always justified by a perfectly nationalist mentality and rhetoric, which was very similar to that which, from the perspective of the Castro government, sustained the necessity of a defensive pact with the Soviet Union.[30]

Along with this a peculiar nationalism, which simultaneously defended the identity of the Cuban Revolution and of the Exile, a very similar discourse of national victimization surfaced on both sides. According to the government of Fidel Castro, the island was a victim of the United States and of the Cuban bourgeoisie, first in Havana, now in Miami, which had to be transformed and defended. According to the discourse of the Cuban exile, Cuba was, in truth, a victim of Fidel Castro, the Soviet Union, and international communism that had to be rescued and protected. While the government was quantifying the damages caused by counterrevolutionary terrorism, the Cuban exile measured the repression: executions, incarcerations, tortures, forced labor, marginalization, and exodus. A good dose of the symbolic patrimony of the exile has been constructed upon the certainty that the regime of Fidel Castro is highly repressive. Such certainty has been relatively well documented by a voluminous corpus of testimonies and memories, which demands a place in official archives and deserves public or juridical attention.[31]

Another reflection of the idea of the illegitimacy of the regime in the memory of the exile was the perception of the revolutionary moment as a calamity or an accident in the history of Cuba, which had to be negated or overcome in order to resume the correct path of the republican tradition. The instinct to turn ones back on the island's present granted to the political language of emigration a tone of restoration. To a large extent, the identification of change with restoration, so efficiently used by the Castro government in its constant degradation of opposition politics, had its origins in those first years.[32] The idealization of the republican past and the deprecation of the revolutionary present in the memory of the Cuban exile was the reverse of the exaltation of the socialist *today* and the vituperation of the republican *yesterday*. The war of memory between the two shores has been grounded for many decades on the symbolic skirmish around the two temporalities of Cuban history (the republic and the revolution), and the two spaces of national life (the island and the exile). The symbolic battle between the two communities, which aspire to a mutual dissolution, takes recourse in those "abuses of memory" of which Tzvetan Todorov speaks.[33]

Propelled by this nationalist discourse of the tragedy and the victim, the theme of *guilt* also emerges in the memory of the exile. The treatment of the issue oscillates between universal formulas of distribution of responsibility, as the one advanced by Guillermo de Zéndegui, an important cultural functionary in the days of Batista, in his book *We Are All Guilty* (1993), and the complete personalization of guilt in the figure of Fidel Castro, with which the book of Reinaldo Arenas *Antes que anochezca* (Before Night Falls) ends. In any case, it is important to point out that each emigrated generation reaches exile with its own file of complaints and its particular localization of guilt. In this way, for instance, the memory of intellectuals who emigrated in the two first decades, after having taken part in the revolution, such as Carlos Franqui, Guillermo Cabrera Infante, Nivaria Tejera, or César Leante, manifests a frustration with the political regime and with Fidel Castro himself, which is not based on the idea of the betrayed revolution because of the turn to Marxist-Leninism as was the case in the first generation of exile, since they themselves had been socialists. The principal motive for the rupture in these memories is the *Stalinization* of socialism, which until then had been *autochthonous*, certified by the chain of positions that went from the "Revolutionary Offensive" in 1967, the support of the Soviet invasion of Czechoslovakia in 1968, the incarceration and "self-criticism" of the poet Heberto Padilla in 1971, and the National Congress of Education and Culture that same year.[34]

The generation of the Mariel exodus, on the other hand, introduces to the memory of exile one of the most bitter and painful accounts of Cuban cultural history. As it is registered in testimonies such as *Before Night Falls* (1992) by Reinaldo Arenas or in *A la sombra del mar. Jornadas cubanas con Reinaldo Arenas* (In the Shade of the Sea. Cuban Days with Reinaldo Arenas) by Juan Abreu and the poetic narratives and fiction of other authors of that generation such as Carlos Victoria, Guillermo Rosales, or Néstor Díaz de Villegas, the wounds of the Mariel exodus have to do with the rejection of all forms of moral authoritarianism rather than a political disappointment with the Cuban regime. Due to the fact that this generation was not only the victim of social and political repression but also of the disdain and the discrimination of the traditional exile, its memory is strongly branded by a type of pain that shows itself resistant to any pact of reconciliation. At the end of *Before Night Falls,* Arenas remembers each time in New York that he felt nostalgia for Cuba or for Old Havana, his "furious memory, more powerful than any nostalgia" would be interposed.[35] The testimonial rage of Mariel is, in the words of Juan Abreu, the "beautiful insurrection" of a "generation decimated, humiliated and outraged by the Cuban dictatorship."[36]

As opposed to the bitterness that characterizes the memory of the Mariel generation, the Cuban diaspora of the 1990s arrived in exile with a vision much more reconciled to the revolutionary past. Many intellectuals of that migratory wave, such as Manuel Díaz Martínez, Jesús Díaz, Zoé Valdés, Daína Chaviano, and Eliseo Alberto, have written personal testimonies of their own rupture with the regime in which one can sense a less traumatic experience, more contemplation of the revolution, and even a recognition of its important cultural legacy.[37] In the most emblematic book of the memories of the diaspora, *Informe contra mí mismo* (Report against Myself) by Eliseo Alberto, one can observe a constant appeal to rescue the revolutionary culture of the 1960s and 1970s, and an obsessive attempt at reconciliation between that heritage and its opposite, the exile culture.[38] A sentence of the text clearly depicts the integrative will of those two memories: "The sterile bipolarity of the judgment has cost too much oblivion, which is like neglecting a lot of fertile memory, because the memories are nothing other than moments that we have forgotten to forget for pure oblivion."[39]

The *disencounter* between the memories of Mariel and the Cuban diaspora of the 1990s is, in fact, part of the critique Juan Abreu makes in the opening pages of *In the Shade of the Sea* of Eliseo Alberto's *Informe contra mí mismo.* Abreu says that "the book of Eliseo Alberto seems to me to be useful and necessary, but the author's obstinate attempts to legitimize certain aspects of the dictatorship of Fidel Castro is a way to justify himself and his class. The author does not succeed in understanding or does not want to understand that we are all victims, us and them—but not all were guilty. He does not succeed in understanding that the best way to examine the past is to be that which we were not permitted to be: free, totally and painfully free. And that freedom does not admit camouflage, self-pity, or *tabula rasa* for that sinister time in the life of our country."[40] Similar reproaches to writers and artists of the island fill the pages of the book of memory *Mi vida saxual* (My Saxual Life*)* by Paquito Rivera and Enrico Mario Santí's essay "*Contra la doble memoria*" (Against the Double Memory), a study of the autobiography of Lisandro Otero, *Llover sobre mojado* (When it Pours it Rains).[41]

In these texts, the "easy pardon," as Paul Ricoeur would say, of victims of memory is inscribed in a debate about the responsibility of the intellectual under the authoritarian or totalitarian regime, which in the past few years has begun to be articulated on the island and in the diaspora. In the more recent Cuban narrative, there are two important novels that, through the history of separation and reconciliation, tackle the theme of the responsibility of intellectuals under totalitarianism. One is *Las palabras perdidas* (The Lost Words) by Jesús Díaz and the other is *La novela de mi vida* (The Novel of my Life) by Leonardo Padura.[42] Two treatments of the same topic from essayist perspectives appear in the book *La memoria frente al poder* (Memory Facing Power) by Jacobo Machover and the essay *"Cuba y los intelectuales"* (Cuba and the Intellectuals) by Enrico Mario Santí. These two authors insist that any political reconciliation in Cuban intellectual circles must begin with recognition of the moral responsibility of a totalitarian order, which restricted the freedom of expression.[43] The difficulty of asking for forgiveness and forgiving in societies that have suffered the harshness of dictatorial regimes or civil wars, as Ricoeur points out, has to do with the thick moralization of political culpability.[44]

Along with the memory of Mariel and the diaspora of the 1990s, in the past two decades an autobiographical corpus by Cuban-American authors (most of them sons of the first exiles) has surfaced, which introduces yet another vision of the past. Texts such as *Exiled Memories: A Cuban Childhood* by Pablo Medina, *Next Year in Cuba: A Cubano's Coming-of-Age in America* by Gustavo Pérez Firmat, and *Cuba on my Mind: Journeys to a Severed Nation* by Román de la Campa establish a symbolic relation with the revolutionary event and with the exodus to the United States, which differs from those of the first exile, Mariel, and the diaspora of the 1990s.[45] Here the evocation of the republic, associated with childhood, lacks all the idealization that had been assigned to it by the first exiles. And at the same time, the judgment of the revolution is hard, revealing a period of violence and want. It is interesting to see that in this generation, as opposed to the historic exile as in the case of Mariel and of the later diaspora, the theme of the return occupies a decisive place, either to be rejected (Pérez Firmat), or to be experienced critically (Medina), or to be undertaken (Román de la Campa).

We also owe another achievement to the Cuban-American generation regarding the thaw in the memories of the Cuban exile: academic historiography. The studies about the revolution and Cuban socialism that Cuban-American academia has produced since the 1970s contribute to abandoning the theme of the illegitimacy of the revolution. In books such as *Cuba: Order and Revolution* by Jorge I. Domínguez, *The Cuban Revolution: Origins, Course and Legacy* by Marifeli Pérez-Stable, *On Becoming Cuban: Identity, Nationality, and Culture* by Louis A. Pérez Jr., and *Cuba and the Politics of Passion* by Damián J. Fernández, the "Cuban revolution" appears as a social process from Cuba's past and not as a current government, making its legitimacy not political but historical.[46] The historiographic corpus, although it circulates above all in North American academic circles, helps to ease the memory of exile and to stimulate national reconciliation within the intellectual horizon.

Nonetheless, the notion of the illegitimacy of the Cuban regime has subsisted in the memory of the organized exile in spite of abandoning violence and terrorism as political methods. The change experienced in the political sociability of the emigration since the mid-1980s and which today registers itself as the virtual absence of armed opposition groups has not completely taken root in the imagery of the exile. The idea that the Cuban political system must be transformed from within by its own actors and institutions has gained ground among dissidents and the diaspora, especially after 1992. But the Cuban-American political class continues to hold a subversive strategy that combines punitive diplomatic and commercial pressure on the part of the U.S. government with the destabilization of the regime by means of civil disobedience and social detonation. In fact, it is becoming progressively easier to detect a dissonance between the loyal opposition that is constitutional, peaceful, and *gradualist* in the internal dissidence, and the project of quick transition, which is defended by the Cuban-American congressional members, many exile associations, and the U.S. government.

The Narrative of Reconciliation

In a novel greatly acclaimed by the Spanish public by Javier Cercas called Soldados de Salamina (Soldiers of Salamina), Cercas told the story of the novelist Rafael Sánchez Mazas, ideologist and founder of the *Falange*, and of the soldier Antonio Miralles, veteran of the fourth regiment, who had fought under the command of Lister, afterward joined the French Foreign Legion, and finally joined De Gaulle in the Second World War. In light of an investigation to determine the possibility that Miralles had been that young republican soldier who forgave and spared the life of his enemy, the writer Sánchez Mazas, on the hills of Catalonia at the beginning of 1939, Cercas set himself a task more becoming to a historian than to a novelist: to narrate the civil war without vanquisher or vanquished, without heroes or traitors, with only decent, responsible people involved in political conflicts whose moral implications far exceeded their capacities.

In one passage of the novel, Cercas remembered a statement by Andrés Trapiello, who argued that the Spanish republicans lost the war in arms but won the war in letters.[47] Both themes—the one about the biography of the rivals, the hero, and the traitor as interchangeable figures in a civil war, and the old topic of the letters and the arms, incarnated in the intellectual Sánchez Mazas and the warrior Miralles—shed light on the Cuban Revolution and, beyond that, on all other modern epics in the history of Latin America, such as the Mexican and the Nicaraguan revolutions. Sergio Ramírez, author of *Sombras nada más* (No More than Shadows), for instance, also tries to construct a tale about the civil war, the Nicaraguan Revolution of 1979, in which the character of Alitio Matinica is a former private secretary of Anastacio Somoza whom the Sandinista National Liberation Front (Frente Sandinista de Liberación Nacional [FSLN]) puts on trial, and Sandinistas and Somocistas are treated without rigid moral asymmetries or uplifting political arguments.[48]

The first difficulty that the Cuban case offers to this new type of historical narrative is that the revolution of Fidel Castro is not yet perceived as a civil war, in which rivals with the same legitimacy or with the same lack of legitimacy confronted each other. In fact, since the first two years of the war (1957–1959), the legitimacy was defined in negative terms; the government of Batista was a dictatorship imposed through a coup d'état, while the revolution was a popular and armed movement. After the triumph of January 1, 1959, the government of Fidel Castro began to be perceived as illegitimate in the democratic ranks of the revolutionary camp on account of its refusal to hold the promised elections. After 1961, because of its alliance with the Soviet Union and the sharp turn toward communism, something never contemplated in the original program of the revolution. Between 1959 and 1967, the armed opposition to the revolutionary government in the Escambray Mountains and in the main cities of the island was composed primarily of ex-combatants of the revolution, who continued to be loyal to the project of Moncada.

This opposition, nationally articulated by organizations such as the MRR and the MRP, had the stage set for its major confrontation in the spring of 1961 with the landing of the Brigade 2506 in Playa Girón. In the historical and literary narrative of the Cuban Revolution this event occupies the place of the enemy and of the traitor. A place that those "counterrevolutionaries," "bandits," or "mercenaries" (Manuel Artime, Tony Varona, José Miró Cardona, Eloy Gutiérrez Menoyo, Huber Matos, among others) share with the adversaries of the old regime, the Batistians, the bourgeois, and today's rivals: exile and distance. Despite the fact that it has been years since the political opposition inside and outside the country recognized the legitimacy of the regime, it calls for a peaceful change and does not propose the destruction, but rather the reform of the system; the government of Fidel Castro continues to assume itself as a revolution in perpetual war against the counterrevolution that must be annihilated.

The presence of this polarization in the Cuban government's apparatus of symbolic legitimization has defined the literary treatment of the civil war in the past 40 years. The authors, who wrote novels and short stories about the years of the insurrection against Batista (Guillermo Cabrera Infante, Lisandro Otero, Jaime Sarusky, Edmundo Desnoes, Noel Navarro, José Soler Puig, Humberto Arenal, César Leante, Hilda Perera, and others), as collaborators or sympathizers of the insurrection movement, described with great detail the virtue of the revolutionaries and with just as much detail the vices of the sympathizers of Batista. Their disciples, the young narrators who have tackled the topic of the war against the armed opposition in the 1960s and 1970s, promoted under the label of "the struggle against the bandits" (among them, David Buzzi, Norberto Fuentes, Jesús Díaz, Eduardo Heras León, Osvaldo Navarro, Hugo Chinea, and Raúl González Cascorro), scolded, in most cases, the rebels of Escambray as abominable beings, half way between cattle thieves and the chief of a savage tribe, wanting in political ideas and totally relegated to the interests of the United States.[49]

The moments of closest approximation to the humanity of the enemy, in *Los años duros* (The Hard Years) by Jesús Díaz, *El condenado del condado* (The Condemned of the Condado) by Norberto Fuentes, or *El caballo de*

Mayaguara (The Horse of Mayaguara) by Osvaldo Navarro, for instance, are inscribed within the atmosphere of political tension in which the discovery of a certain dignity in the adversary accentuates the greatness of the battle. Due to the fact that the best Cuban storytellers supported the revolution precisely during the years of the civil war (1957–1967), it is difficult to find a solid narrative of exile that will defend the vanquished. Perhaps the exceptions are *Enterrado vivo* (Buried Alive) by Andrés Rivero Collado or *Now the World Grows Dim* by Salvador Díaz Versón.[50] The great Cuban narrative of exile is precisely the one that is often associated with authors who were well established by the time of the triumph of the revolution, such as Lino Novás Calvo or Carlos Montenegro, or with writers who broke with the regime in the decades after the revolution as are the cases of Guillermo Cabrera Infante, Severo Sarduy, or Reinaldo Arenas. In this sense, in Cuba as opposed to Spain, it is possible to say that the literary and the political wars were won by the revolutionaries.

In the past few years, however, several books written by Cuban authors living outside of the island have been published. These books seem to suggest a new historical narrative in which two sides of the civil war begin to be taken up in their reason and in their madness, in their violence and their legitimacy. This is the case, for example, of *Cómo llegó la noche* (Because the Night Arrived), the memoirs of a commander of the revolution, Huber Matos, who was incarcerated by the government of Fidel Castro due to his resignation in protest at the turn toward communism that the regime took by the end of 1959. Matos, a victim of the revolution who spent 20 years in prison and then another 20 years in exile, wrote an autobiography without rancor in which two-thirds of the text are devoted to the reconstitution of the anti-Batista epic between 1957 and 1959, and the first year of the triumphant revolution; only a third is devoted to the account of the calamities of reclusion. In spite of the pain that invades the pages, this victim is able to defend the justice of the revolution: "Our national independence was not the work of politicians. They only prepared the path, but it was the revolutionaries who moved history forth, changing the structures of society. In reality, the revolutionary is a politician seriously committed to freedom, justice, and the popular interests in the manner of Simón Bolívar, Benito Juárez and José Martí."[51]

Other memories, of a revolutionary intellectual woman, *Espero la noche para soñarte, Revolución* (I Await the Night to Dream You, Revolution!) by Nivaria Tejera, besides sharing the same nocturnal metaphor of the failure of utopia, contrast such a tone of reconciliation with an idealist past that, as a mirror, reflects the lost political illusions. But Tejera, as opposed to Matos, rather than recuperating the nobility of the original revolutionary commitment, is interested in evoking the moment of disenchantment, the very instant in which the spiritual metamorphosis occurred. It is only that the search for this evocation is not dictated by the mere desire to break with the revolutionary past but rather by the will to understand and perhaps to recuperate the moral fabric of the change. In an admirable passage Nivaria Tejera shows her fervent desire to capture, as transparently as possible, that moment of mutation that will permit her to be reconciled with the two halves of her biography—the revolutionary and the exiled: "Terrible anguish of abandoning a revolution, its well rounded dogmas and climb with no hesitation the extramural of its line of conduct, of its incessantly renewed tasks in visits to who knows what concealed end. Always quivering, well-calculated end: today against ones, tomorrow against others. Sharpened line of fire that ends, which *a priori* and as *in fraganti*, made of all of us, its irremediable targets. Sooner or later its condemned ones. Behind that train, whose run took me closer to an inextricable exile that would place a quote to the desperate purpose of running away, which had obsessed me from day to day, was being left behind in its flamboyant despotism, seaweed-like, sponge-like, floating as a landscape of dry leaves, an ideal revolution."[52]

Another feminine voice, that of Uva de Aragón, in a fictional exercise although quite close to what Javier Cercas calls a "real tale," reconstructs the memories of two identical twin sisters, Menchu and Lauri, separated for 40 years by revolution and exile. The novel, impeccably entitled *Memoria del silencio* (Memory of the Silence), tells the story of the parallel lives of these sisters through the daily resource of journal accounts. That is to say through the autobiographical accounts in which different historical perspectives are juxtaposed upon the same events: the dictatorship of Batista, the triumph of the revolution, the Bay of Pigs, the Soviet missile crisis, the wars in Vietnam and Angola, the exodus of Mariel, the collapse of communism, and the depression of the 1990s. These two sisters who maintained a dialogue in the silence of their memories assume that their lives could have been exchangeable. Lauri, the one in Miami, puts it this way: "Menchu is the mirror of what I was not and could have been."[53] However, when the reencounter takes place, first in Havana and then in Miami, the personalities are affirmed and at the same time relinquish mutual space in a perfect ritual of reconciliation. In this way, the sister left in Havana proclaims the dignity of her choice to stay in Cuba: "Well, what do you want me to say? That I should have not fallen in love with Lázaro because he was a Marxist, that all the hours I spent *alfabetizando* (teaching to read and write), that all the cane I cut, that all the schools I designed, that the only place where I have traveled, the Soviet Union, that all the misery that I have undergone and all the sacrifices that we have endured are worth nothing . . . that my life is worth nothing, that the lives of twelve million on the island are worth nothing, that we should bow before the exile?" And the sister in Miami responds, "We have lived for forty years sighing for Cuba, filling our houses with photographs, with flamboyant paintings of Cuba, writing poetry about Cuba, writing songs about Cuba, talking to our sons about Cuba, denying this country the possibility to swallow us, thinking of Cuba day and night, waiting for news of Cuba, founding a Cuba House wherever there is a Cuban colony, feeling as foreigners in all places . . . and now you are going to tell me that not even in Cuba we are going to be entitled to our opinions!?"[54]

This clash of two worthy actors involved in a conflict of great moral costs is also rendered in the novel *No siempre gana la muerte* (Death Does Not Always Win) by the American writer David Landau. This book tells the story of Mariano José Núñez Hidalgo, also known as Rodrigo, a young Cuban who, after participating in the clandestine movement against the dictatorship of Fulgencio Batista, joins the opposition to the revolutionary government in 1960. The young man is employed by the CIA to perpetrate an assassination attempt on Fidel Castro. The attempt failed, and he is imprisoned in La Cabaña for more than 20 years. The interesting thing about the account is that upon evoking his mission, the character insists on underscoring his reservations concerning the role of the United States in the history of Cuba, as if he were trying to put the ambivalence that was implied in the aspirations of a nationalist political end by imperial means on trial.[55] As in the memoirs of Huber Matos, in this novel the discourse of the victim comes close to the serenity, to the suspension of rancor: "I have even reached the point," says the main character, "of being in agreement with Goethe that the way to clean the world is that each sweeps the yard of his own house . . . in jail, in war, in all that I have done, I have had the privilege of seeing what the human condition has to offer."[56]

A similar approach to that "vision of the vanquished" can be found in the novel of Osvaldo Navarro, *Hijos de saturno* (Sons of Saturn). The biography of the imaginary commander of the revolution, Eustaquio de la Peña, who was displaced from power after the triumph of 1959, permits Navarro to introduce a complex and tempered perspective of the Cuban civil war. At the end of the novel, Navarro describes how the fundamental core of the seditious soldiers, who fought in the Escambray Mountains against the government of Fidel Castro, had originated in the very revolutionary army that fought against the dictatorship of Batista in the central part of the island, and which now was opposing the edification of a Marxist-Leninist regime. The accusations of "cow-eaters" and "bandits" against these disaffected military men, according to Navarro, seeks to disqualify the armed opposition that was doing nothing other than continuing the revolutionary sociability generated by the anti-Batista movement.[57] The deranged rivals appear here as actors who share the discourse and the practice of the same political culture.

This new historical narrative, which we have briefly reviewed here, establishes a noticeable tension with the official narration of contemporary Cuban history, which is based on the certainty that the revolution lives in a "continual past." As Avishai Margalit points out in his 2002 book *The Ethics of Memory* the symbolic actualization of past conflicts allows authoritarian powers to legitimize the state of perpetual war against a transhistorical enemy.[58] The prevalence of this narration among intellectual circles moves a certain will of recollection of moral testimonies belonging to those subjects involved in civil wars toward literary poetics, who attempt to draw a background upon which to undertake a process of reconciliation. This politics of memory, however, establishes a kind of dialectic between forgiveness and oblivion in which, in general, the actors must cede emotional quotas of their identity for the benefit of being completely recognized as legitimate subjects of history.

Notes

1. Michael Ignatieff, *Los derechos humanos como política e idolatría* (Barcelona: Paidós, 2003), pp. 29–73; and Martha C. Nussbaum, *Los límites del patriotismo* (Barcelona: Paidós, 1999), pp. 13–42.

2. Andreas Huyssen, *En busca del futuro perdido. Cultura y memoria en tiempos de globalización* (Mexico: FCE/Goethe Institut, 2002), pp. 13–40; Hannah Arendt, *Eichmann en Jerusalén. Informe sobre la banalidad del mal* (Barcelona: Lumen, 1997), pp. 200–210; and Rony Brauman and Eyal Sivan, *Elogio de la desobediencia* (Mexico: FCE, 2000), pp. 11–27.

3. Tomás Moulián, *Chile actual. Anatomía de un mito* (Santiago de Chile: Arcis Universidad/Ediciones Lom, 1998), pp. 354–382; Nelly Richard, *Residuos y metáforas. Ensayos de crítica cultural sobre el Chile de la transición* (Santiago de Chile: Editorial Cuarto Propio, 1998), pp. 32–54; Rita Arditti, *Searching for Life: The Grandmothers of the Plaza de Mayo and the Disappeared Children of Argentina* (Berkeley, CA: University of California Press, 1999), pp. 70–85; Ben Fowkes, *The Post-Communist Era: Change and Continuity in Eastern Europe* (London: Palgrave Macmillan, 1999), pp. 9–22; "Amnesia y amnistía. La participación del historiador," *Istor: Revista de Historia Internacional* (CIDE-Mexico), 2 (5), 2001: 7–24; Grupo de Trabajo Memoria, Verdad y Justicia, *Cuba. La reconciliación nacional* (Miami, FL: Centro para América Latina y el Caribe, Florida International University, 2003), pp. 39–57; Javier Tussel, *La transición española* (Madrid: Club Internacional del Libro, 1995), pp. 73–92; and Áurea Matilde Fernández, *España. Franquismo y transición* (Havana: Editorial de Ciencias Sociales, 2002), pp. 156–163.

4. *El Independiente* (Mexico), August 29, 2003, p. 20.

5. *El País* (Madrid), July 26, 2003, pp. 3–4; *La Jornada* (Mexico), July 26, 2003, pp. 26–29; *La Jornada* (Mexico), August 13, 2003, p. 26; and *Reforma* (Mexico), August 22, 2003, p. 24.

6. *El Independiente* (Mexico), August 30, 2003, p. 21.

7. *El País* (Madrid), July 14, 2003, pp. 12–13; and *El Independiente* (Mexico), August, 29, 2003, p. 21.

8. *El Independiente* (Mexico), August, 23, 2003, p. 21.

9. José Antonio Aguilar, "Las batallas por la historia en México y Estados Unidos," *Istor. Revista de Historia Internacional* (CIDE-Mexico), 1 (1) 2000: 52–84. See also by the José Antonio Aguilar, *La sombra de Ulises. Ensayos sobre intelectuales mexicanos y norteamericanos* (Mexico: CIDE/Porrúa, 1998), pp. 57–103.

10. For a flexible interpretation of the relationship between truth and justice, see Michel Foucault, *La verdad y las formas jurídicas* (Barcelona: Gedisa, 1991), pp. 13–33.

11. Reinhart Koselleck, *Futuro pasado. Para una semántica de los tiempos históricos* (Barcelona: Paidós, 1993), pp. 173–201.

12. Grupo de Trabajo Memoria, Verdad y Justicia, *Cuba*, pp. 59–69.

13. Rafael Rojas, *Isla sin fin. Contribución a la crítica del nacionalismo cubano* (Miami, FL: Ediciones Universal, 1998), pp. 20–60.

14. Ann Louise Bardach, *Cuba Confidential. Love and Vengeance in Miami and Havana* (New York: Random House, 2002), pp. 254–282.

15. Adam Michnik, *La segunda revolución* (Mexico: Siglo XXI, 1993), pp. 151–169; Avishai Margalit, *The Ethics of Memory* (Cambridge, MA: Harvard University

Press, 2002), pp. 55–74; Marc Augé, *Las formas del olvido* (Barcelona: Gedisa, 1998), pp. 20–34; Paul Ricoeur, *La memoria, la historia y el olvido* (Madrid: Editorial Trotta, 2003), pp. 539–591; and Harald Weinrich, *Leteo. Arte y crítica del olvido* (Madrid: Editorial Siruela, 1999), pp. 301–322.

16. María Antonia Marqués Dolz, *Las industrias menores. Empresas y empresarios en Cuba (1880–1920)* (Havana: Editora Política, 2002); Imilcy Balboa Navarro, *Los brazos necesarios. Inmigración, colonización y trabajo libre, 1878–1898* (Valencia: Centro Francisco Tomás y Valiente, UNED/Fundación Instituto de Historia Social, 2000); and Ana Meilyn de la O Torres, "La construcción del espacio público moderno en la Habana del siglo XIX," Masters Thesis in Social Science, FLACSO, Mexico, 2001.

17. Marial Iglesias, "Pedestales vacíos," *Encuentro de la cultura cubana*, 24, Spring 2002: 17–34; Jorge Núñez Vega, "La fuga de Ariel," *Encuentro de la cultura cubana*, 24, Spring 2002: 53–67; Reinaldo Funes Monzote, "Cuba: República y democracia (1901–1940)," in Rafael Acosta de Arriba et al., *Debates historiográficos* (Havana: Editorial de Ciencias Sociales, 1999), pp. 177–221; and Ricardo Quiza Moreno, "Fernando Ortiz, los intelectuales y el dilema del nacionalismo en la República (1902–1930)," *Temas. Cultura, ideología, sociedad*, 22–23, July–December 2000: 46–54. See also José Antonio Piqueras (ed.), *Diez nuevas miradas a la historia de Cuba* (Castellón de la Plana: Publicaciones de la Universidad Jaume, 1998).

18. Ambrosio Fornet, *Memorias recobradas. Introducción al discurso literario de la diáspora* (Santa Clara, Cuba: Ediciones Capiro, 2000), pp. 9–15. Volumes 22–23 (July–December, 2000) and 24–25 (January–June, 2001) of the journal *Temas* are dedicated to the Republic.

19. Jean Paul Sartre, *Sartre visita a Cuba* (Havana: Ediciones R, 1960), p. 243.

20. Margalit, *The Ethics of Memory*, pp. 48–65.Concerning the relation between memory and totalitarian regimes see Agnes Heller and Ferenc Fehér, *El péndulo de la modernidad. Una lectura de la era moderna después de la caída del comunismo* (Barcelona: Ediciones Península, 1994), pp. 47–59.

21. Jesús Arboleya, *La contrarrevolución cubana* (Havana: Editorial de Ciencias Sociales, 1997), pp. 25–42.

22. Ibid., pp. 65–104.

23. Fabián Escalante Font, *Cuba: La guerra secreta de la CIA* (Havana: Editorial Capitán San Luis, 1993), pp. 30–52; and Luis Báez, *El mérito es vivir* (Barcelona: Editorial La Buganville, 2002), pp. 21–70

24. Arboleya, *La contrarrevolución cubana*, p. 3.

25. Ibid., pp. 168–182.

26. Ibid., p. 285.

27. Ibid., p. 279.

28. See Rosa Miriam Elizalde and Luis Báez, *"Los disidentes." Agentes de la Seguridad Cubana revelan la historia real* (Havana: Editora Política, 2003); and Arleen Rodríguez and Lázaro Barredo, *El Camaján* (Havana: Editora Política, 2003).

29. Jorge Mañach, *Teoría de la frontera* (San Juan, Puerto Rico: Editorial Universitaria, 1970), pp. 140–160; Carlos Márquez Sterling, *Historia de Cuba* (New York: Las Americas Publishing Company, 1969), pp. 655–676; Herminio Portell Vilá, *Nueva historia de la República de Cuba* (Miami, FL: La Moderna Poesía, 1986), pp. 727–770; Mario Llerena, *La revolución insospechada. Origen y desarrollo del castrismo* (Buenos Aires: Editorial

Universitaria de Buenos Aires, 1981), pp. 11–21; and Leví Marrero, *Escrito ayer* (Puerto Rico: Ediciones Capiro, 1992), pp. 155–160.

30. James G. Blight and Peter Kornbluh, *Politics of Illusion: The Bay of Pigs Invasion Reexamined* (Boulder, CO: Lynne Rienner, 1998), pp. 10–20.

31. Efrén Córdova, "Represión e intolerancia," in *40 años de Revolución. El legado de Castro* (Miami, FL: Ediciones Universal, 1999), pp. 253–279. Also see the dossier "El presidio político en Cuba," *Encuentro de la Cultura Cubana*, 20, Spring 2001: 154–238.

32. Alejandro Portes and Alex Stepick, *City on the Edge: The Transformation of Miami* (Berkeley, CA: University of California Press, 1993), pp. 89–107; María Cristina García, *Havana-USA: Cuban Exiles and Cuban Americans in South Florida, 1959–1994* (Berkeley, CA: University of California Press), pp. 13–45; and María de los Ángeles Torres, *In the Land of Mirrors. Cuban Exile Politics in the United States* (Ann Arbor, MI: University of Michigan Press, 1999), pp. 42–61.

33. Tzvetan Todorov, *Los abusos de la memoria* (Barcelona: Paidós Asterisco, 2000), pp. 11–18, 49–59.

34. Carlos Franqui, "Libertad y socialismo," *Libre* (Paris), 2, December–Feburary 1972: 9–10; Guillermo Cabrera Infante, *Mea Cuba* (Mexico: Editorial Vuelta, 1993), pp. 38–40; Nivaria Tejera, *Espero la noche para soñarte, Revolución* (Miami, FL: Ediciones Universal, 2002), pp. 30–35; and César Leante, *Volviendo la mirada* (Miami, FL: Ediciones Universal, 2002), pp. 17–37.

35. Reinaldo Arenas, *Antes que anochezca* (Barcelona: Tusquets, 1992), p. 314.

36. Juan Abreu, "Bella insumisión," *Mariel. Revista de Literatura y Arte* (special anniversary edition), Miami, Spring 2003: 23.

37. Manuel Díaz Martínez, *Sólo un leve rasguño en la solapa* (Logroño: AMG Editor, 2002), pp. 120–150; and René Vázquez Díaz, *Voces para cerrar un siglo* (Stockholm: Olof Palme Center, 2000), p. 2.

38. Eliseo Alberto, *Informe contra mí mismo* (Madrid: Alfaguara, 2002), pp. 134–154.

39. Ibid., p. 315.

40. Juan Abreu, *A la sombra del mar. Jornadas cubanas con Reinaldo Arenas* (Barcelona: Editorial Casiopea, 1998), p. 34.

41. Paquito D'Rivera, *Mi vida saxual* (San Juan, Puerto Rico: Plaza Mayor, 1999), pp. 174–189; and Enrico Mario Santí, *Bienes del siglo* (Mexico: Fondo de Cultura Económica, 2002), pp. 363–384.

42. Jesús Díaz, *Las palabras perdidas* (Barcelona: Ediciones Destino, 1992); and Leonardo Padura, *La novela de mi vida* (Barcelona: Tusquets, 2002).

43. Jacobo Machover, *La memoria frente al poder* (Valencia: Valencia University, 2001), pp.11–19; and Santí, *Bienes del siglo*, pp. 359–362.

44. Ricoeur, *La memoria, la historia y el olvido*, pp. 616–620.

45. Pablo Medina, *Exiled Memories: A Cuban Childhood* (New York: Persea Books, 2002), pp. 108–114; Gustavo Pérez Firmat, *Next Year in Cuba: A Cubano's Coming-of-Age in America* (New York: Anchor Books/Doubleday, 1995), pp. 17–45; and Román de la Campa, *Cuba on my Mind: Journeys to a Severed Nation* (London: Verso, 2000), pp. 1–21.

46. Jorge I. Domínguez, *Cuba: Order and Revolution* (Cambridge, MA: Harvard University Press, 1978); Marifeli Pérez-Stable, *The Cuban Revolution: Origins, Course, and Legacy* (New York: Oxford University Press, 1993); Louis A. Pérez Jr., *On Becoming Cuban: Identity, Nationality, and Culture*

(Chapel Hill, NC: University of North Carolina Press, 1999); and Damián J. Fernández, *Cuba and the Politics of Passion* (Austin, TX: University of Texas Press, 2000).

47. Javier Cercas, *Soldados de Salamina* (Barcelona: Tusquets, 2001), p. 22.

48. Sergio Ramírez, *Sombras nada más* (Madrid: Alfaguara, 2002), pp. 13–45.

49. Seymour Menton, *Caminata por la narrativa latinoamericana* (Mexico: Fondo de Cultura Económica, 2002), pp. 349–386.

50. Carlos Espinosa Domínguez, *El peregrino en comarca ajena. Panorama crítico de la literatura cubana del exilio* (Boulder, CO: University of Colorado, Society of Spanish and Spanish American Studies, 2001), pp. 13–16.

51. Huber Matos, *Cómo llegó la noche* (Barcelona: Tusquets, 2002), p. 47.

52. Tejera, *Espero la noche para soñarte, Revolución*, pp. 14–15.

53. Uva de Aragón, *Memoria del silencio* (Miami, FL: Ediciones Universal, 2002), p. 240.

54. Ibid., pp. 226–227.

55. David Landau, *No siempre gana la muerte* (Los Angeles, CA: Pureplay Press, 2002), p. 130.

56. Ibid., pp. 262–264.

57. Osvaldo Navarro, *Hijos de saturno* (Mexico: Editorial Debate, 2002), pp. 264–267.

58. Margalit, *The Ethics of Memory*, pp. 48–83.

Conclusions: Cuban Exceptionalism Revisited

Bert Hoffmann and Laurence Whitehead

Introduction

What are the social laws or "rules" to which twentieth-century Cuba appears such a flagrant exception? Those who believed that the fall of the Berlin Wall had inaugurated "the end of history" will need to concede that at least in this corner of the Caribbean history seems to be taking another generation to extinguish itself. It is still just about possible to counter that triumphalist claim with Castro's equally resonant slogan "history will absolve me." Those who believe that state intervention to control the entire economy and marginalize the price system had been proven unviable and doomed to collapse will have to cope with the evidence that, compared to other post-Soviet economies, after the initial slump between 1989 and 1993 Cuba's economic performance has been at least average, or perhaps even slightly better than most. Those who have argued that there is now only one hegemonic "superpower," and that U.S. military, economic, political, and cultural supremacy is now such that outright resistance to it has become futile, must face the fact that the Castro regime, as tiny as the Cuban economy may be in a global perspective, still continues to flaunt its resistance, and even to attract occasional new allies to its cause. Those who would argue that no single autocrat can remain sane and politically effective after exercising virtually unlimited power over his home territory for up to half a century, have still not come to terms with the secrets of Fidel Castro's psychology and his personal authority. Those who believe that the unquestionable yearnings of ordinary Cuban citizens for personal freedom, economic opportunity, the right to travel and access information must be sufficient to overwhelm all the artificial props used to sustain a "closed" system of Communist Party control, have not yet grasped either the offsetting power of the regime's "David versus Goliath" imagery or the density of its formal and informal social controls beyond the security apparatus. In all these, as in other related respects, contemporary Cuba is an outlier, a challenge to conventional assumptions, a demonstration that there are "more things in heaven and earth" than are dreamt of in what passes for philosophy inside the Washington beltway.[1] This book is therefore an open-minded, collaborative and uncommitted collective attempt to revisit Cuban "exceptionalism" more than a decade and a half after the dismantling of the Berlin Wall.

Many announced the end of Cuban exceptionalism after 1989.[2] Cuban state socialism was seen as an offshoot of the bipolar Cold War era, bound to disappear with the dissolution of its potent overseas allies. According to widespread expectations, the Caribbean "domino" had to fall sooner rather than later. The forces of globalization would not allow an island just 90 miles off the U.S. coastline to maintain a state-socialist economic order and one-party rule, and defy its powerful Northern neighbor. Cuba would become part of the "third wave" of democratization that swept away socialist regimes from Berlin to Vladivostok. Whatever the scenario and outcome of a Cuban transition, in the 1990s many saw it as only a matter of time before Cuban exceptionalism gave way, and the island joined the ranks of other "really existing democracies" in Latin America. But what has happened instead is that Cuban state socialism not only survived the end of the Cold War and the demise of the Soviet Union, but it has actually managed to consolidate its position in new and unexpected ways.

The contributions in this volume explore how it has done so from various different angles and address the question of what the persistence of Cuban exceptionalism tells us about the particularities of the Cuban case and, what is more important, about the general assumptions underlying post-1989 expectations of regime change in Cuba. Transition studies have been criticized for focusing on success stories. The study of Cuba partially redresses this criticism and sheds light on the conditions for "nontransition." Hence, the hope is that by focusing on the "deviant case" of Cuban exceptionalism, this volume will contribute to the study of comparative politics and democratization theory.

Cuban Exceptionalism

Cuban exceptionalism does not preclude the considerations of comparative analyses relevant to the Cuban case. As can be seen from Andrew Arato's chapter (chapter 2), exercises in comparison are as much about specifying and explaining contrasts as identifying similarities.[3] From a comparative social scientific perspective, it is necessary to pay attention to "exceptions" and "deviant cases" as well as to average and exemplary examples. Such nonstandard or deviant experiences help us to specify the scope and limits of the normal outcomes that can be explained by a generally applicable theory. Thus, for example, studying Cuba as a case of nontransition can sharpen our theories of democratic transition and counter the bias toward "successful outcomes" that can easily distort our retrospective theory building.

But it is not just with regard to theories of democratic transition that the Cuban case has proved so challenging and intractable. Twentieth-century Cuba has appeared thus far to falsify the predictions of a long list of cherished social science theories. According to "modernization" theory the Cuba of the 1950s was the most unlikely setting for a socialist revolution. Its high levels of urbanization, literacy, income per capita, and exposure to the U.S. market and culture should have favored irreversible democratization, not the installation of a highly personalist one-party regime. Traditional Marxism was equally confounded. The "stage theory" embraced by (among others) the pre-Castro Cuba Communist Party (then called the PSP) was that further development of capitalism was necessary before socialism could become a reality. But the Cuban Revolution both defied modernization theory and skipped stages. Similarly, the realist school of thought in international relations would have predicted that of all the subordinate allies of the United States, Cuba was virtually the one that was most securely "locked into" the so-called Free World. But the Cuban Revolution achieved the unthinkable: it defied Washington, survived, and successfully reversed alliances. Once that shocking result had been absorbed, standard realism would then predict that an isolated and vulnerable Castro regime, only able to survive thanks to Soviet support, would become a pliable "proxy" for Moscow foreign policy objectives. Instead, Havana provided the "small motor" that drove the Soviet bloc as a whole to adopt policies (especially in Africa) that were much more active and radical than those envisaged by the sclerotic bureaucrats in the Kremlin. So realism has been twice falsified. Cuba has also defined Fukuyama's "End of History" thesis, an overarching frame of interpretation it seemed to work for the rest of Latin America—and indeed much of the world—at least in the 1990s. Again, Cuba proved to be the exception throughout that decade, and the Castro regime has now lasted long enough to witness a "return of history" both globally and in its own region. This list of standard theories that have all spectacularly failed to work in the Cuban context is illustrative rather than exhaustive. But it is long enough to raise a fundamental question of method. What more would have to happen in Cuba that falsifies macrohistorical social science predictions, before the island's historical trajectory can be acknowledged as distinctively "exceptional"? Or is "exceptionalism" a taboo category, which should never be used whatever the evidence, for fear of subverting the commitment of modern social science to universalism?

A focus on the Cuban case also draws attention to the multidimensionality of key concepts in the theoretical literature. Thus, for example, if democracy is understood to refer to the ideal of popular sovereignty, this has, at least, two components—self-determination and rule by the people. Facing massive and sustained external pressure the Cuban revolutionary regime has made resistance to foreign domination its central claim to democratic legitimacy. But the internal dimension (the sovereign struggle of the citizenry to choose and control its government) is an equally indispensable component of popular sovereignty that has been severely relegated in revolutionary Cuba.

Contemporary Cuban exceptionalism is both political and economic. Not only did Cuba not undergo the standard post-Soviet transition to a market economy via collapse and privatization, but it also resisted the more gradualist—or a "social democratic"—variant of a managed transition as envisaged by many European advisers. Indeed, despite the continuing and even tightened U.S. embargo and in spite of the failure of *acercamientos* (rapprochements) with Canada, Mexico, and the European Union (EU), the Cuban economy, although weak and distorted, is displaying unexpected signs of resilience and even of partial recovery, as the chapter by Emily Morris (chapter 3) shows. In addition, as Javier Corrales illustrates in chapter 4, in its management of the economic crisis the government has shown an uncanny ability to blend politics and economics in such a way as to ensure economic survival and purchase a new generation of political loyalties.

It is said that Castro is better at politics than at economics. The statement is hard to refute when one considers the fact that he has remained in power for more than 47 years, and when one notes the material shortcomings suffered by his subject population over this nearly half century. But this statement overlooks something that is a key to understanding the survival of the Cuban regime: that the political trumps the economic logic in Cuba or in official parlance: "Our political system, which enshrines the people's power, is the foremost accomplishment that we must safeguard, because all others depend on it."[4] If potential economic benefits mean compromising on political essentials, Fidel Castro will renounce those benefits, even when this entails such extraordinarily high economic costs that it leaves foreign observers baffled. This is what European leaders had to deal with in 2003 when Castro fell out with the EU, shunning development cooperation and disrupting commercial relations over the European attempt to impose "political conditionality." This is even clearer in the case of U.S. Cuba policy: all sanctions and embargo measures imposed by Washington since 1959 have manifestly failed to elicit political compliance. This is so not only because the Cuban leadership found an ally in Moscow, but also, as the post-1989 years show, because Havana was willing to bear enormously high costs and adopt "virtually a war economy"[5] to cope with the quasi-collapse of the island's trade, production, and monetary systems.

However, this is only one part of the story. As Emily Morris (chapter 3) argues, there has not only been austerity but also more liberalization than either Cuban policy makers or their detractors like to admit. The survival of a socialist state at the heart of the Americas rests as much on the Cuban propensity to respond to change as on its insistence on pursuing a separate path. As Corrales (chapter 4) also shows, the dual economy that emerged in the 1990s, with a stagnant domestic economy and a dynamic externally linked sector, has created severe economic disparities as well as generated social and political tensions.

Recent changes in economic management, such as the replacement of U.S. dollar circulation by a convertible peso, have been widely interpreted as a reversal of prior reforms and as likely to compound existing difficulties. Increases in salaries, consumer spending, and public investment have been made possible by changing external conditions. The always-politicized external economic relations of the Cuban Revolution have been profoundly altered again by the arrival of two new saviors: a political partner and economic benefactor in the form of Venezuela's Hugo Chávez; and communist China, a new source of commercial credit given that country's increased outreach activities in Latin America in general and in Cuba in particular. Both changes appear to be reinforcing a statist, centrally directed model of economic management. And yet, as with earlier reforms, appearances can be deceptive: above all, the

Cuban model of "defiance" is one of creative adaptation to circumstances. There is no reason to expect this to change.

In the 1990s the impact of the economic crisis led to the erosion of the state's economic capacity and to the emergence of new inequalities which Centeno has taken as an indication of Cuba's "return to Latin America": "The great Cuban exceptionalism in health and education may be wearing thin."[6] While the quality of health and educational services on the island have suffered severely compared to the 1980s, the universality and gratuity of these services has remained untouched. And illustrating the argument of cumulative causation Laurence Whitehead spells out in his chapter, what started out as exceptional social coverage for the domestic population has now translated into an at least as exceptional transformation of such "revolutionary accomplishments" into nontraditional exports that generate hard currency income as well as important political benefits as key elements of Cuba's current foreign policy. Similarly, the inequalities that emerged in the 1990s have not led to ever-growing social polarization but, quite to the contrary, have come under attack from the state's drive to recentralize and reideologize the economy, which has been striking out emphatically against the "nouveaux riches" and (legal or illegal) market actors. Informality, although always present in socialist Cuba (as in other socialist states), peaked in the mid-1990s but has since experienced a gradual decline. And while the "Chávez bonanza" may arguably be based on shaky economic grounds, it is difficult to see the island as being currently "just as much involved in the infamous 'race to the bottom' as its neighbors."[7]

If Cuba's economic policy can be subordinated to the logic of survival of the political system, a reverse feedback is equally possible: an economic policy such as Cuba's is viable only in a vertical political system that is able to administer a dramatic decline in living standards without being "disturbed" by public protest or subjected to the negotiating capacity of independent social actors. In chapter 1, Laurence Whitehead traces the path dependency of Cuba's current political exceptionalism, linking it to its historic origins, to the special role that the country played in the Spanish Empire, to its belated independence and to its subordinate position to the United States during the first half of the twentieth century. This historical perspective contrasts with the understanding of Cuban exceptionalism as being limited to the "revolutionary epoch" after 1959. This is Centeno's perspective, for instance,[8] and leads him to argue that the current "return to Latin America" he diagnoses translates into the "end of Cuban exceptionalism." Such a long-term perspective highlights the role of geopolitics, and the discursive power of revolutionary nationalism, and suggests that theories of cumulative causation can explain much of the political course taken since 1959. This is a product both of structure and of choice. At the structural level, the concentration of economic and political power at the apex of the revolutionary system made possible the authoritarian implantation of a project of social transformation, which has now lasted for almost half a century, and has systematically deepened the gulf separating the Cuban people from most of the major tendencies at work in the rest of the Western Hemisphere. This objective parting the ways has also created a subjective and discursive divide, which makes continuing "exceptionalist" choices not only possible but also probable. Strategic options that would be almost unthinkable in most Latin American countries become logical first preferences in Cuban conditions.

"History will absolve me," reads the title of Fidel Castro's famous defense in the trials after the attack on the Moncada barracks in 1953. When state socialism in the Soviet Union and Eastern Europe collapsed after 1989, history seemed to have turned against the Cuban leader who had tied Cuba's political and economic destiny closely to those powerful overseas allies. In the official rhetoric of the early 1990s history no longer signaled a bright future on the horizon but became the legitimizing framework for a stubborn defense of the duty to *resistir!* (resist), in the name of the century-old struggles for Cuban independence, first against Spanish colonial rule and then U.S. neocolonial tutelage. This has changed. Cuban state socialism managed to survive the painful decade of the 1990s, and in the first decade of the new millennium Cuba's leadership no longer sees itself as the last bulwark of the just cause holding out against all odds but, once again, as the vanguard of the epic struggles of the Latin American continent.

In the second half of the 1990s, a gradual economic recovery began, led by tourism earnings and the high level of remittances from Cuban emigrants. Living conditions still are precarious in many ways, but they are a far cry from the "this-ship-is-sinking" atmosphere of 1993–1994 when the crisis hit bottom. While the world of the regular Cuban peso certainly illustrates all too well what Kornai had called "the economics of shortage," it is routine, not despair that marks daily life in Cuba today.[9]

In terms of political economy, this recovery has led to a virtual halt of reform measures. Introduced under the pressure of crisis, such reforms are increasingly seen as concessions or as erroneous, and as no longer necessary, and so ought to be corrected. While in the mid-1990s foreign observers discussed the "when" and "how," rather than the "if" of Cuban reform toward more market-driven mechanisms, a full-scale rollback in the form of a *perfeccionamiento del socialismo* (the perfecting of socialism) is now under way. If the legalization of the U.S. dollar in 1993 was a highly symbolic step, so is the ban of U.S. dollar circulation and its substitution with the convertible Cuban peso in 2004. In fact, the government has declared the end of the *período especial* (special period), understood as the phase when Cuban socialism was forced to resort to what Fidel Castro referred to as "measures we do not like" in his 1993 speech legalizing the U.S. currency.[10] In May 2005, Fidel Castro announced an overnight hike of minimum wages by 225 percent and a 300 percent rise in minimum pensions. As the government was quick to point out, this spectacular increase involves dedicating an additional 2.25 billion Cuban pesos to the annual budget—roughly $100 million at the rate of the official Cuban exchange houses. With this act of largesse, that to many observers is reminiscent of the voluntarism of the early years of the Revolution, Havana signals what it claims to be the light at the end of the tunnel of daily hardship.

The measure has led some economists to warn against the potentially negative inflationary consequences, and, indeed, the material base for such a spending increase cannot possibly be found in Cuban domestic production. In the very short run the ban of the U.S. dollar has filled the state coffers with a considerable amount of cash as Cubans rushed to exchange their greenbacks for convertible pesos before the announced 10 percent surcharge came into force. But the new economic confidence displayed by the Cuban authorities is based on a more long-term reason: the ever-closer alliance with the Venezuelan government and the apparent consolidation and radicalization of Chávez's "Bolivarian Revolution." This is just the most recent in the long line of external patrons or sponsors that has characterized Cuban politics since the nineteenth century (as described in chapter 1 by Laurence Whitehead). And it signals that Cuba is not only "returning to Latin America" as argued by Centeno, but also that important emerging actors in Latin America are "returning to Cuba" with rather unexpected enthusiasm, with Chávez and Bolivia's Evo Morales being the most prominent cases.

A New International Patron

At the rhetorical level Hugo Chávez emphatically embraces the revolutionary legacy of Fidel Castro and has willingly played on the father-son imagery, presenting himself as the only successor who is ready to carry the historic relay baton of the continent's epic anti-imperialist struggle. Although the Bolivarian Revolution has shied away from clear ideological definition, Chávez now seems to have embraced the rhetoric of "Socialism of the twenty-first century" (this could still mean many disparate things, but it does have the virtue, from a Cuban point of view, of opting for the term socialist and of clearly rhyming with *Cuba Socialista*). This political affinity is accompanied by no less important economic support. In the streets in Havana the news that the country has *nuevos rusos* (New Russians) is already making the rounds. This is obviously an exaggeration, but Venezuelan oil revenues mean that this is an ally with great economic potential, all the more so at current world market oil prices. In 2004, the Venezuelan state-owned oil company PdVSA officially handed over a record $11.9 billion to the Caracas government, 60 percent more than the government had budgeted; and the oil bonanza continues unabated in 2006. While most of this is absorbed by domestic priorities, Caracas has diverted major sums to further its international priorities.

Cuba has been tapping these resources successfully through a series of cooperation agreements, the most prominent of which is a barter arrangement allowing Cuba to pay for Venezuelan oil shipments by sending thousands of medical doctors and sports trainers to work in Chávez's social programs. The precise terms of the agreements and the dimension of de facto Venezuelan subsidies to Cuba are open to speculation, and one can only guess what credit lines Venezuela is or will be willing to grant Cuba. So while current oil prices allow for much generosity, the question remains how sustainable this lifeline will be. Oil prices and political conditions in Venezuela may change, and Venezuelan support for Cuba may not prove to be such a blank check as some currently assume. For the time being, however, relations between both countries are more intense than ever. In October 2005, Cuban politburo member Carlos Lage declared in Caracas that the destinies of both countries are now so closely bound that "Cuba now has two presidents, Fidel and Chávez."[11] Since then, the launch of the ALBA integration scheme, however unclear its substance, the use of health and educational service exports as foreign policy vehicles, and the prominently displayed new bonds of friendship with the government of Evo Morales in Bolivia have underscored Havana's renewed internationalist appeal and ambitions.

Thus, if in the mid-1990s the achievement of the Cuban leadership was to steer a process of limited economic opening while maintaining its political control—well described as the "gatekeeper state" in the chapter by Javier Corrales—what we have witnessed since about 2000, is not just the persistence of a centrally planned economy long abandoned elsewhere, but even the reimposition of a degree of state direction and management that faltered during the most acute phase of the crisis. This has been possible not just because of tourism and remittances, important though they have been in cushioning the dollar shortage but also because of the continued ability of the Cuban regime to engage with external benefactors seeking a counterweight to U.S. hegemony. This recurring logic is now being played out with Chávez's Venezuela and China, a new source of commercial credit. For Chávez, the main incentive to subsidize Cuba is the symbolic importance of Fidel Castro and of Cuban socialism as a bulwark against the dominance of the U.S. and neoliberal economics; and for China there is some geopolitical advantage in moderately supporting a regime so strategically located at the center of the Caribbean and so persistently in confrontation with the United States. And so once again, as argued by the thesis of cumulative causation, it is the survival of exceptionalism in itself that creates the conditions allowing for the perpetuation of that exceptionalism.

The recent announcements that "good times are coming" may also reflect a serious concern of the Cuban leadership: that the patience of its people is not an infinite resource. The relative economic stabilization the regime has achieved does not automatically translate into a parallel recovery of political prestige. The government has launched a massive "ideological offensive," kicked off by the infamous 1996 "Report of the Politburo" that frontally attacked the intellectual reform debate then underway. This campaign reached a first climax with the mass mobilizations over the Elián case in 2000 and is by now firmly entrenched in the emphatic rhetoric of the "battle of ideas." But the *mesas redondas* (roundtables) and *tribunas abiertas* (public tribunes) that flood the official media play to a largely passive audience. The calls for heroic causes and self-disinterested commitment contrast sharply with the realities of everyday life, deeply marked by what the Cubans call the need to *resolver* their daily needs by resorting to a wide array of formal and informal means, from networks of relatives or friends, to black or gray market activities, to contacts with foreigners or with *socios* (buddies) somewhere in the bureaucratic structure. The ritualized mass mobilizations of today are a far cry from the enthusiasm of the early 1960s that they pretend to emulate. The younger generation that has known nothing but the hardships and retreats of the special period is particularly alienated.

The gap between private and public attitudes has become so wide that it hardly seems sustainable over time. While open political defiance remains limited to a small minority of the population, there is a very blurred line between what Haroldo Dilla calls "passive consensus" (chapter 5), and resigned acceptance or quiet obedience. There are no reliable ways to measure just how severe this popular dissatisfaction has become. Nevertheless, the income and pensions hike and similar measures can be read as a signal that the Cuban leadership is well aware of the need to regain some of its eroding social base, that heroic rhetoric alone will not do, and that quite ordinary material underpinnings are necessary. At the same time, however, the path of "perfecting socialism" does not necessarily mean a full return to the orthodox economic model of the defunct bureaucratic socialism with central planning and Moscow-style five-year plans. The gatekeeper state—which incorporates quasi-capitalist structures under state control—seems to be here to stay. When Fidel Castro personally goes on television to explain the benefits of a new Chinese rice cooker that is to be massively distributed to the population, these kinds of distributive measures may have less to do with orthodox socialism than with older populist traditions that are so resilient in much of Latin America.

There is a similar process at work at the political level. Hidden beneath the overwhelming continuity of the political system as embodied by the sustained leadership of Fidel Castro, are the significant changes undergone by the regime. Perhaps the most stunning of these is the ongoing process of deinstitutionalization. Although the official structures of party and state apparatus have remained very much untouched, it is notable that the next party congress is long overdue (it is ostensibly held every five years and is formally the highest body of authority of what is the backbone institution of classic Communist rule). And nobody is bothering (or daring) to ask when it may take place. The office of the battle of ideas has evolved into a parallel superministry with a wide array of programs covering the most diverse fields, and has effectively sidelined the competencies of the respective ministries or other established government authorities. And, while the country's leader is visibly aging, the personalist nature of the regime has been accentuated in multiple domains, from the recruitment of cadres for top positions to the ideological discourse of the battle of ideas.

The Exceptionalism of Cuban Regime Change

Various arguments and theories have been developed in the study of democratization processes that, when applied to Cuba, seem to lose their explanatory power, or at least to become sufficiently subverted that they end up reemphasizing the thesis of Cuban exceptionalism. Let us now look at some of the challenges that the Cuban case presents to the comparative study of transition or democratization.

A first example of how Cuba subverts expectations that seem reasonable elsewhere is apparent when looking at the role of the Internet in political change.[12] A key argument in the thesis of globalization as a force of democratization is that new digital communication technologies, particularly the Internet, cannot be controlled by states because of their intrinsic border-crossing and decentralized nature, and that free access to information will eventually make it very difficult if not impossible to contain freedom. In the words of former U.S. President Bill Clinton in March 2000, "[I]n the new century liberty will spread by cell phones and cable modem!"[13]

The Cuban government was initially highly cautious. The so-called Torricelli law enacted by the U.S. Congress in 1992 promoted intensified communication with Cuba as a strategy to undermine the political system. Cuba only decided to establish an IP connection to the Internet in 1996— the last country in the hemisphere to do so—when it felt sufficiently assured that political risks could be minimized. It did so after the Report of the Politburo, which attacked the reform debate in the harshest terms, decried the concept of civil society (used by Cuban scholars as means to introduce a more pluralist approach within the socialist framework) as a "Trojan Horse of Imperialism" (in the words of Raúl Castro in 1996).[14] It also did so only after keenly observing how the Peking government made Internet use compatible with one-party rule. Cuba not only imports most of the technological hardware of its networks but also know-how in security and administration matters from China. So although Cuba is now online, the government keeps a close watch on access to international networks by ensuring that computer and network density remains low, and that most connected computers only have access to closed domestic networks (what the government calls Cubanet) rather than the World Wide Web. Access to computers that are connected to the latter is generally only possible from within institutions or in public spaces (both subject to social control mechanisms that are reinforced by the technical controls, which the quasi-state monopoly on provider services make possible). Domestic residential access is forbidden, and in 2002 the government launched an effective campaign against unauthorized Internet access, squeezing the limited black market for passwords and Internet access even further.

Thus, articles by dissident journalists, which are transmitted by phone to supporters outside the island and put online abroad, or the homepage of the U.S. Department of State, nor indeed any other web-based media, reach a broad audience on the island on a regular basis. Cuba has not experienced the transnationalization of its domestic public sphere, as proponents of the thesis that the Internet is a force for democratization have argued. The backdrop to these restrictions on Internet access is that they not only minimize the political impact of the new communication technologies but that they also severely limit their potential developmental benefits. So here too the economic logic remains subordinated to the political logic. The government is ready to assume the high economic costs implicit in manifold restrictions on Internet access if in this way the Internet will not pose any immediate threat to the state monopoly over mass media or to regime stability.

A second example of Cuba's exceptionalism is related to the expected role of civil society in processes of political change. Studies of democratization have often highlighted the key role played by civil society in such processes. As Margaret Crahan and Ariel Armony argue (chapter 8), there has been a revitalization of civic and other organizations not dominated by the government in recent years. This has contributed to an expanding public sphere through the development of various "minispheres" of discourse throughout Cuba, contradicting the expectation that the circulation of discourse is essentially determined from the commanding heights of the state. The reaction of the Cuban political class has been to restrict the debate about civil society and to limit the broadening of the public sphere by denouncing "civil society" as "fifth column" operating on behalf of U.S. interests. As a consequence, although there is widespread societal discontent, although Cuba has a strong history of associational activity and a society permeated with religious belief, and although the everyday experience of state-society and citizen-citizen interactions has been reshaped, this has not translated into civil society mobilization. At some local levels and in various discrete social domains (as in cinema, music, and some areas of science) there have been significant manifestations of pluralism and outreach to the external world, but the state continues to maintain ideological and political hegemony on the core issues of revolutionary continuity and defiance of Washington. There is a notable variety of counterdiscourses that have no more than a limited social impact, in part because collective action outside the state is too costly, but also because dissent from within must always guard against identification with subversion from the outside.

A third example of the difficulties of extrapolation lies in the logic of Latin American transition studies. Ever since the onset of crisis in Cuba in the late 1980s observers have been keen to identify individual political figures as "hard-liners" or "soft-liners." But there has been a lot more speculation than evidence. People identified by foreign observers as potential leaders of a "reformist" or "perestroika-minded" wing within the party have been ousted at too early a stage for one to know whether such claims were well founded (this was the case with General Arnaldo Ochoa, the highest-ranking military man after Raúl Castro, who was executed following a show trial on drug and conspiracy charges in 1989; or of Carlos Aldana, who at the peak of his career in 1992 was the highest-ranking member of the Politburo after the Castro brothers and who was dismissed after being publicly charged with corruption, obliged to undertake a "self-criticism," and then stripped of all influence). The most sustained "reformer thesis" was based on generational change, and embodied by three Politburo members who are a generation younger than Fidel and Raúl Castro: Carlos Lage who was born in 1951 and is usually credited as the architect of the economic reforms of the mid-1990s, former foreign minister Roberto Robaina, who was born in 1956, and Abel Prieto, the long-haired President of the writers' and artists' association (UNEAC) born in 1950. The fate of these "potential reformists" has been more complex and varied. Robaina was dismissed in 1999 under corruption charges much like Aldana, but Prieto remains Minister of Culture and member of the Politburo despite some moments of isolation, and Carlos Lage is still vice president of the Council of State and a member of the politburo. This may look a lot like continuity, but their status and the popular perception of their influence has changed. Lage embodied hopes for economic reform but was then a loyal servant when the reversal came; Prieto embodied the hope for greater cultural and intellectual heterodoxy and autonomy, but he also closed ranks with the party line when the tide turned back to the crude ideological campaigns, narrowing the room for intellectual debate. In the process, both lost popular credibility as potential exponents of a reform option from above.

Time has taken its toll on their standing within the party as well. They were once regarded as the people who would replace the "old guard," but the leadership of this generation is being eclipsed by that of a younger generation of party cadres who are not identified with any reformist attitudes of any kind. First among these is Felipe Pérez Roque, who replaced Robaina as foreign minister and who was presented in the National Assembly session of December 2005 in a way that fell just short of declaring him as Fidel Castro's designated successor; Otto Rivero, who heads the "office for the battle of ideas," is another prime example.[15] Neither the reformers nor the intransigents possess sufficient security of tenure to open up a sustained competition over the scope and limits of liberalization. The Castro regime remains so verticalist that only the very highest levels of leadership can exercise that degree of strategic choice. The *comandante* (commander) has observed how democratization emerged in other postrevolutionary and postcommunist regimes, and he retains the discretion to block or manipulate any such developments on his island.

A fourth—perhaps one of the most familiar—example of Cuban exceptionalism is the unique role played by its emigrant population since 1959. Certainly, having roughly a tenth of one's population abroad is hardly exceptional for the region, but the characteristics of that emigration as its implications for the sending country are indeed exceptional. The economic success story of Cuban *émigrés*, embodied by the transformation of Miami from a secondary tourist resort into a dynamic business metropolis, is singular.[16] No other Latin American migrant group in the United States has a parallel history or political impact. Providing almost five decades of staunch political opposition to the Castro regime has been crucial for the social cohesion and identity of a community that ceased to be one of "exiles" and took on the "hyphen identity" of today's Cuban-Americans. As Alejandro Portes points out in chapter 7, politically defined cohesion has been a core element of the social capital of the Cuban community. And it was precisely the blocked option of return to the island that led exiled Cubans to acquire U.S. citizenship, and this in turn laid the foundation for their extraordinarily successful involvement in U.S. politics. They succeeded in establishing a political-economic exchange network that not only served the intransigently anti-Castro line of U.S. Cuba policy but was also crucial in fostering the growth of Cuban-American businesses, which initially serviced a purely ethnic market and then became major players as purveyors of goods and services to the mainstream population and the state.

As Portes argues and the case of the Cuban exile community vividly illustrates, the downside of social capital based on political homogenization is that while it creates opportunities for members of the group it simultaneously imposes social controls over them; strong feelings of solidarity within the group and the rewards for toeing the line have their counterpart in intolerance and the imposition of severe negative sanctions against those who deviate from that line. So dissident life is under siege not only on the island but also because of the Cuban-American political machine, and an individual who deviates from dominant political attitudes in Miami must have more personal courage than is usually necessary in a democratic environment.

The attitude of the Cuban *diaspora* to their homeland differs significantly from attitudes of other migrant groups. The Chinese *diaspora* (including conservative businessmen) may be politically opposed to the Beijing government, but a resurgent China does appeal to their nationalist sentiments and opens up highly attractive business and professional opportunities for the community abroad—albeit under the watchful eye of the Communist Party. Mexican-Americans, Irish-Americans and Jewish-Americans all wish to see their home countries doing better, if only to enhance their prestige and influence within the United States. By contrast, the social, political, and economic success of the Cuban-American community in the United States has been closely linked to its ability to capitalize by opposition on the "symbolic capital" of the Cuban Revolution embodied by Fidel Castro. This particular cold war has outlived the Cold War even a decade and a half after the demise of the Soviet Union and with it the oversized symbolic importance of Fidel Castro that is so essential a facet of the high-profile political standing of the exile in the U.S. Cuban community. This is bound to change in any pos-Castro transition scenario. Cuban-American identity and the Cuban-American insertion in U.S. politics will face a serious challenge if Cuba is "resized" to its "true" dimensions (a rather small and poor Caribbean island again dependent on the goodwill of the United States).

The specificities of Cuban emigration have contributed to the longevity of the Castro regime. Unlike the Eastern Europe state-socialist regimes, Cuba's tended to keep the emigration door open. This not only served as an important safety-valve function along the lines described by Hirschman in his "exit and voice" scheme,[17] but has also helped stabilize the regime in other ways, as Bert Hoffmann argues in chapter 6. The explicit political alliance between the dominant exile groups and Washington's foreign policy-making elite has always nourished a key element of regime survival: the melding of the Cuban "political question" and its "national question." And emigration is far from being such a dichotomous "exit" category as per the Hirschman model.

Despite sharp political polarization, Cuban emigrants have maintained strong transnational ties with those living on the island. These surfaced in a particularly spectacular form during the crisis years of the 1990s, when the massive inflow of U.S. dollar remittances not only helped many Cuban families to make ends meet. Again, the increasing importance of family remittances from emigrants is a feature of many Latin American countries and hardly exceptional; however, it is certainly exceptional that those who emigrate provide a crucial financial lifeline for the regime even though the majority define themselves explicitly in opposition to the government in their home country. So the exceptional story of Cuban emigration and the ambiguities of Cuba's "exiles" are part and parcel of explaining the country's political exceptionalism.

A fifth aspect of Cuban exceptionalism is the way that it will have to deal with its past and generate mutually tolerant and divergent "memories" of that past. Any Cuban democratization process will entail a painful reconciliation between Cubans on both sides of the Florida straits, a historical and ideological revision for Cuban-Americans and islanders alike. The Task Force on Memory, Truth, and Justice initiated by Mariféli Pérez-Stable at Florida International University tries to anticipate what Cuba can learn from other experiences with "transitional justice" and truth commissions. While this exercise is antiexceptionalist in structure, Cuban exceptionalism comes across in various places in the Task Force report.[18] Rafael Rojas (chapter 9) addresses the issue of memory but from a broader perspective. He points to the "culture of memory in times of globalization" and explores Cuban "memory knots" in the light of the experiences of Eastern European and other democratizing countries. He differentiates between two kinds of "dealing with the past," one that is primarily judicial and is based on prosecution of past crimes (centered on notions of truth and justice), and another that operates in the public sphere and is about the free circulation and coexistence of contradictory interpretations of the past (and centered on reconciliation and tolerance). Rojas argues that without a pact of national reconciliation among Cubans of all political persuasions it will be virtually impossible to imagine a transition to democracy. Here, reconciliation is understood not only as the concession of political rights to all citizens, but also as the free and public circulation of all memories. If a pluralist political system implies the cohabitation of diverse narratives about a nation's past, in Cuba it implies the recognition of the historical legitimacy of all political actors, whether revolutionary, oppositionist, or of the exile community.

A final and perhaps the most striking feature of most contemporary analyses of Cuban politics is the way it so closely identifies any political change with the death of Fidel Castro. Of course there can be no doubt that the "Castro regime" will enter into a profound period of change when that inevitable event finally occurs. But we may need to differentiate between the physical death of the *comandante* and the "demise of authoritarian rule" to use the catchphrase of the transitology literature. The Yugoslav regime survived for a considerable period after the death of Tito, as did Salazarism after the death of Salazar. Spain, where the death of Franco cleared the path to a rapid democratic transition, represents an extreme rather than a dominant pattern. Arguably conditions in Spain were "overripe" and it was only the survival of the dictator that disguised underlying changes. This was not the case in Vietnam after Ho Chi Minh or in China after Mao either. The aim here is not to engage in futurology but to explore the impact of future *expectations* on the present. The excessive focus on the mortality of Fidel Castro distorts current analysis and Cuban politics dynamics. The oft-heard phrase "once Castro dies . . ." may often be intended to raise expectations, but what it also does is imply that as long as he remains alive nothing of interest will or can change in Havana.

It is misguided to imagine that ruling groups in Havana are simply waiting passively for an endgame that they can neither foretell nor control. On the contrary, rival factions (and different generational cohorts) compete with one another for control of strategic positions that are likely to prove decisive in the struggle for power that they foresee when the unifying leader is gone. And that old ruler himself is equally active in promoting and demoting these succession competitors so as to prolong his ascendancy as long as possible and also as a way to steer the course of his regime in the direction he judges most conducive to its long-term survival. A generation of young "reformists" came to the fore in the 1990s, who believed they would be in the pole position to capitalize on any "normalization" of relations with the rest of the world. But now there is an even younger generation of hard-line militants being promoted, who are persuaded by the idea that it will be the *pure et dure* (hardcore purists) who may prove to be the true heirs of Castroism. It is unclear whether either of these two groups will be the final beneficiaries of Fidel's patronage when the balance of his rule is eventually made. Indeed, the personal power of Fidel is served at home and abroad by analyses that focus on his eventual death.

Broader questions about the real inheritance of the regime and the best options for preserving its achievements and correcting its deficiencies should be debated in the interim. During the 1990s the prevailing conventional wisdom about Cuba among Western social scientists was broadly a liberal internationalist one. The assumption has been that democratization and convergence on a standard template of liberal politics and open market economies was inevitable and that the only question was how quickly and painlessly individual nations undertook these linked transitions. According to this "end of history" and "third wave" framework of analysis the future of post-Castro Cuba was predetermined, leaving room only for debate about whether the "ever-faithful isle" would take that step very much later than the rest of the Western Hemisphere, or how much international pressure and guidance might be required, or how far behind Cuban economy and society would have to fall before it could be turned around. Since the (questionable) election of George W. Bush to the U.S. presidency in 2000 this kind of liberal triumphalism has suffered a series of setbacks, but as far as Cuba is concerned the dominant interpretation has remained largely intact. As Fidel Castro grows older and visibly frailer and as Havana passes up successive opportunities to soften its course, the predetermined denouement is assumed to be drawing ever-nearer. It was in that spirit that U.S. Secretary of State Condoleezza Rice appointed a "Cuba transition coordinator" in July 2005, and that the U.S. National Intelligence Council reportedly added Cuba to its secret watch-list of countries in which instability might require U.S. intervention.[19] But the reconsiderations of Cuban exceptionalism in this volume cast doubt on the reliability of such an interpretative framework. So much time has elapsed since the dismantling of the Berlin Wall, and so many developments have occurred that make sense of events within an "exceptionalism" framework that are anomalous according to the orthodox view, that intellectual honesty demands some reanalysis.

The image of a Cuba that is politically paralyzed and waiting for an act of God is both erroneous and politically convenient for those who are not interested in seriously preparing for the future. It is a particularly perverse manifestation of Cuban political exceptionalism, one that this volume has sought to challenge and indeed contest. A more positive variant of the exceptionalism thesis would point to a different conclusion. To think constructively about the scope for regime change and the dynamics of a potential transition requires breaking with the stalemate over Castro's personalism and focusing instead on the distinctive collective structures and memories that drive island politics (and make them differ from standard templates). If it falls to the Cuban people to decide their own future they will have an unusually rich array of precedents to draw upon, and an exceptionally large number of foundational issues to resolve. For example, they could in principle base an eventual post-Castro political settlement on the 1976 Socialist Constitution (with Varela-type modifications). Or they could revert to the 1940 precedent. Indeed, if Washington's will were to prevail, the Helms-Burton Act would take them back to the semisovereign electoral system of 1902–1933. In addition to this unusual variety of constitutional starting points, they would have to define who could be included in a democratic settlement (one in which émigrés could take part) and on what terms (with wholesale property restitution, or on the basis of the current socialized distribution of assets). Deeply entangled with these basic choices about the "rules of the game" would be the question of how to renegotiate their relations with the rest of the world, not only with Washington and Miami but also with Madrid, Caracas, Beijing, and others.

After all, the United States is most unlikely to envisage annexation of the island, so any post-Castro settlement will have to be on the basis of an international reaffirmation of its formal sovereignty. All this means that Cuba's exceptional political trajectory leaves their eventual future extraordinarily underdetermined and potentially open to choice and institutional innovation.

However, to capitalize on this potential the Cuban people would need an extended space for collective reflection and deliberation, something that may not be easy to attain in the most likely transition scenarios If they could secure that opportunity for autonomous political construction they might freely conclude that the costs of continuing to deviate so far from standard models of economic and political liberalization are too high. They might therefore choose to terminate their record of exceptionalism. But they could also conclude that after all the sacrifices they have made and all the costs they have borne, they were not willing to relinquish all aspects of their past half century's political legacy, however contrary to prevailing international prescriptions that choice might seem. This more positive variant of the exceptionalism thesis would invoke the liberating potential of continuing to be different, of understanding why, and choosing a suitable course, regardless of external requirements and expectations.

One of the impediments to fresh thinking about the course of Cuban development is the pressure to pass quickly from analysis to prescription. This volume is not concerned with the standard prescriptive questions of what Washington policy should be, or how Europe should react, or how the transition might be shaped. The focus has been rather on a prior, and easily underestimated, task: that of understanding and explaining where Cuba has been heading. The "third wave" metaphor—open to some severe criticism on more general grounds—has been particularly unhelpful here.[20] Whatever the trajectory of the Cuban revolution, it is radically out of sync with such loosely postulated tendencies. It follows a dynamic of its own, one much more driven by the island's distinctive sociopolitical experience and geopolitical predicament than by any imagined oceanic rhythms. Equally, it would be superficial to attribute the unforeseen survival of the Castro regime to purely accidental factors, such as the temporary ascendancy of a generous ally in Caracas. Our longer-term historical perspective highlights the recurrent features of the island's relationship with external benefactors, both predating and providing the key to explaining the otherwise improbable circumstances of today's Chávez-Castro partnership. (More generally, the combined influences of the Bush administration and the Chávez regime are shifting the axis of political alignment in a large number of Latin American countries, potentially redirecting their energies away from the course foreseen by liberal international teleology. But if this turns out to be the case it will reflect unresolved tensions and neglected tendencies within the various countries concerned, rather than simply being the product of external pressures and interventions).

Viewed from this perspective a mistaken and inflexible external orthodoxy about what must (and therefore will) transpire in Cuba when Castro dies becomes a critical feature of the situation to be explained, rather than an article of faith beyond empirical verification. Any future demise of the Castro regime may precipitate yet a further round of unsuspected outcomes and deviant responses, not just because of the momentum derived from a past history of exceptionalism, but also because opportunities to support conventional liberalization will be missed, owing to the preconceptions and analytical failings of various actors in contention. The risk is high that ill-informed and unreflective policymakers in Miami and Washington (or indeed in Brussels, London, Madrid, or Berlin) will be caught by surprise and react suboptimally when developments in Cuba fail to correspond to their expectations and requirements. Advance planning based on a sober and realistic appreciation of the distinctive features of the Cuban issue could perhaps reduce the chance of a dangerously unexpected outcome, but on present evidence it would be more plausible to forecast that a refusal to analyze the implications of Cuban exceptionalism will increase the chances of its perpetuation.

The exceptionalism experienced by Cubans means that their future is open to choice and innovation, but at the same time, if they are to capitalize on that possibility they need space for unconstrained reflection, something that both Havana and Washington have always denied them. As noted above, if they could reflect on their exceptional past, Cubans might either decide that the costs of continuing to deviate so much from prevailing international patterns are too high, *or* they may conclude that after all the sacrifices they have made and the costs they have borne, they deserve the fruits of their efforts, or they might devise some intermediate path. On this basis, we can distinguish between a negative kind of exceptionalism, which we aim to criticize and try to change—the exceptionalism that keeps Cubans in a state of polarization and unable to initiate a comprehensive evaluation of their predicament—from an exceptionalism with positive connotations, which is the liberating potential of being different, understanding why, and choosing one's own course accordingly, regardless of external impositions. In social science terms our use of exceptionalism runs counter to the dominant tendency to break up complex realities into more short time periods or into partial fragments, to separate economics from politics or social structure, or to seek out universal covering laws or generalizations to explain patterns in each separate sphere. Our perspective is long-term, holistic, combining features from across different disciplines, relying on broad-gauge historical comparisons and contrasts to shed light on how different features combine together in a particular context. Collective memories serve to bind together these complexities into distinctive patterns. That is why non-Cubans have difficulty making sense of what the Cubans are really talking about. It is why simple moral messages are inappropriately extracted from their embedded contexts. It is why Cubans may find it helpful to see their problems from a more detached and comparative perspective in order to get a handle on the real choices available to them.

Notes

1. Hamlet: "There are more things in heaven and earth, Horatio, than are dreamt of in your philosophy" (*Hamlet*, Act I, Scene V).
2. The most recent example is Miguel Ángel Centeno, "The Return of Cuba to Latin America. The End of Cuban Exceptionalism?" Plenary Lecture at the Society for Latin American Studies 2004, published in the *Bulletin of Latin American Research*, 23 (4), October 2004.
3. In this sense, this volume is a "sisterly" endeavor rather than an anti-thesis to projects that analyze Cuba in comparative perspective.
4. Partido Comunista de Cuba, "El Partido de la unidad, la democracia y los derechos humanos que defendemos: Proyecto para el V Congreso del PCC, Octubre de 1997," *Granma Internacional*, June 1, 1997.

5. Fidel Castro, *Presente y futuro de Cuba. Entrevista concedida a la revista "Siempre!"* (Havana: Oficina de Publicaciones del Consejo de Estado, 1991), p. 57.

6. Centeno, "The Return of Cuba to Latin America," p. 404.

7. Ibid., p. 408.

8. "Prior to 1959, Cuba exemplified many of these issues, but for the past four decades, it has represented the great exception to the Latin American trend." Ibid., p. 404.

9. Janos Kornai, *The Economics of Shortage* (Amsterdam: North-Holland, 1980).

10. Fidel Castro, "Discurso en la clausura del 40 aniversario del asalto al Cuartel Moncada," *Granma*, July 28, 1993, pp. 3–7.

11. "Lage en el acto de clausura de la VI reunión de la Comisión Mixta Cuba–Venezuela," *AFP, October 7*, 2005.

12. Bert Hoffmann, *The Politics of the Internet in Third World Development: Challenges in Contrasting Regimes with Case Studies of Costa Rica and Cuba* (New York: Routledge, 2004).

13. Bill Clinton, "America Has a Profound Stake in What Happens in China," Transcript of President Clinton speech on U.S.-Chinese Trade Relations, Washington, DC: White House/Office of the Press Secretary, March 8, 2000, at http://usinfo.state.gov/regional/ea/uschina/clint308.htm.

14. Raúl Castro, "Informe del Buró Político en el V. Pleno del Comité Central del Partido, 23.3.1996," *Granma Internacional*, April 10, 1996, pp. 4–8.

15. In May 2005 Wilfredo López Rodríguez who had been head of the *Grupo de Apoyo y Coordinación del Comandante en Jefe* since 1995, was dismissed and as far as we can tell has not yet been replaced. His ouster was not reported publicly until August 2005, and so gave rise to much speculation.

16. Alejandro Portes and Alex Stepick, *City on the Edge: The Transformation of Miami* (Berkeley, CA: University of California Press, 1993).

17. Albert O. Hirschman, *Exit, Voice, and Loyalty: Responses to Decline in Firms, Organizations, and States* (Cambridge, MA: Harvard University Press, 1970).

18. Task Force on Memory, Truth, and Justice, *Cuban National Reconciliation* (Miami, FL: Florida International University, 2003), at http://memoria.fiu.edu.

19. As reported by *The Financial Times*, November 1, 2005.

20. See Laurence Whitehead "Freezing the Flow: Theory about Democratization in a World in Flux," *Taiwan Journal of Democracy*, 1 (1), July 2005: 1–20.

Notes on Contributors

Andrew Arato was born in Budapest (1944) and has lived in the United States since 1957. He has a PhD from the University of Chicago, and is currently the Dorothy Hirshon Professor in Political and Social Theory, New School for Social. Among his publications are the books *The Young Lukacs and the Origin of Western Marxism* (1979), *Civil Society and Political Theory* (1992), *From Western Marxism to Democratic Theory* (1993), *Civil Society, Constitution and Legitimacy* (2000). He is editor of the journal *Constellations*. His current research focuses on the theory of constitution making, the history of dictatorship, and the politics of transition in Iraq.

Ariel C. Armony was born and raised in Buenos Aires, Argentina. He is Associate Professor of Government and CoDirector of the Goldfarb Center. He is the author of *The Dubious Link: Civic Engagement and Democratization*, Stanford, which made the University Press Bestsellers List in 2004, and *Argentina, the United States, and the Anti-Communist Crusade in Central America, 1977–1984* (1997). He is coeditor of *Repression, Resistance, and Democratic Transition in Central America* and *Repensando la Argentina*. His essays on state-sponsored terror, transnational military cooperation, civil society, citizenship, and comparative democratization have appeared in several edited volumes and journals, including recent contributions in the *Journal of Democracy, Latin American Politics and Society*, and *Textos*. He has received funding from the Aspen Institute, the National Science Foundation, and the Mellon, Kellogg and Inter-American Foundations, and has been a residential fellow at the Woodrow Wilson International Center in Washington, DC, and at the Rockefeller Foundation's Bellagio Study Center in Italy.

Javier Corrales is associate professor of political science at Amherst College in Amherst, Massachusetts. In 2005, he was a Fulbright Scholar in Caracas, Venezuela. He obtained his PhD in Political Science in 1996 from Harvard University. His areas of interest include the politics of economic and social policy reform in developing countries. He is the author of *Presidents without Parties: The Politics of Economic Reform in Argentina and Venezuela in the 1990s* (2002). His research has been published as chapters in several books and in academic journals such as *Comparative Politics, World Development, Political Science Quarterly, International Studies Quarterly, World Policy*

Journal, Latin American Politics and Society, Latin American Research Review, Studies in Comparative International Studies, The European Review of Latin American and Caribbean Studies, and *Current History*. In 2000, he became one of the youngest scholars to be selected as a Fellow at the Woodrow Wilson International Center for Scholars in Washington, DC. He has also been a consultant for the World Bank, the United Nations, and the American Academy of Arts and Sciences.

Margaret E. Crahan is the Dorothy Epstein Professor of Latin American History at Hunter College and the Graduate Center of the City University of New York. She received her doctorate from Columbia University where she is a Senior Research Associate at the Institute of Latin American Studies. From 1982 to 1994 she was the Henry R. Luce Professor of Religion, Power and Political Process at Occidental College, and from 1993 to 1994, the Marous Professor at the University of Pittsburgh. She has served on the Executive Councils of the Latin American Studies Association and the Pacific Coast Council of Latin American Studies, as well as on the Kellogg Institute of the University of Notre Dame, and the Council for International Exchange of Scholars (Fulbright Program). She is currently a member of the Board of Trustees of St. Edward's University, the Inter-American Institute of Human Rights, and For CHILDREN, Inc. She has authored, coauthored, edited, and coedited over 100 articles and books including *Africa and the Caribbean: Legacies of a Link* (1979); *Human Rights and Basic Needs in the Americas* (1982); *The City and the World: New York's Global Future* (1997); *Religion, Culture and Society: The Case of Cuba* (2003); and *The Wars on Terrorism and Iraq: Human Rights, Unilateralism, and US Foreign Policy* (2004). She has received various grants and fellowships, including from the Social Science Research Council, the American Philosophical Society, and the National Endowment for the Humanities, and the Ford and Rockefeller foundations.

Haroldo Alfonso Dilla is a Cuban historian and sociologist. He was a researcher at the Centro de Estudios sobre América for about two decades, and the Director of its Department of Latin American Studies. In 2002, he immigrated to the Dominican Republic, where he still resides. Between 2000 and 2005 he was the general coordinator for research at FLACSO. Currently, he is an independent consultant and the coordinator of the CIECA Grupo de Estudios Fronterizos. He has published more than a dozen books, among them *Participación y desarrollo en los municipios cubanos* (1993); *La democracia en Cuba y el diferendo con los Estados Unidos* (1995); *Alternativas de izquierda al neoliberalismo* (1997); *Community Power and Grassroots Democracy* (1997); *Mercados globales, gobernabilidad local* (2001); *Los recursos de la gobernabilidad en la Cuenca del Caribe* (2002); and *Globalización e intermediación urbana en América Latina* (2004). He has also published dozens of articles in specialist journals from various continents. He has been a professor and researcher at various universities in Latin America, Europe, Canada, and the United States. He is a specialist consultant for various international development agencies. He is currently working on a book about frontiers and globalization, and finishing a doctorate with the Federal Polytechnic Institute, in Lausanne, Switzerland.

Bert Hoffmann is a Senior Researcher at the Institute of Latin American Studies of the German Institute of Global and Area Studies (GIGA—formerly German Overseas Institute), Hamburg, and academic coordinator of the GIGA publications department. He teaches at the University of Hamburg. He holds a doctoral degree in political science from the Free University of Berlin, where he has been teaching from 1998 to 2003. He has published numerous articles and books on Cuba, among them *The Politics of the Internet in Third World Development: Challenges in Contrasting Regimes with Case Studies of Costa Rica and Cuba* (2004); *Kuba* (2000); *The Cuban Transformation as a Conflict Issue in the Americas: The Challenges for Brazil's Foreign Policy* (1999); and *Cuba. Apertura y reforma económica: Perfil de un debate* (1995). He is Deputy Director of the German scholarly journal on Latin America *Lateinamerika Analysen;* from 1993 to 2005, he served as coeditor of the German language yearbook *Lateinamerika—Analysen und Berichte.*

Emily Morris was a Lecturer in Development Economics at London University's School of Oriental and African Studies from 1993 to 1995. Since 1995, she has been working at the Economist Intelligence Unit Country Analysis division, and is currently Senior Editor/Economist for Latin America and the Caribbean, responsible for EIU coverage of Cuba. This includes quarterly Country Reports, monthly updated two-year forecasts, Risk Service Reports, and annual Country Profiles. She has also been working on a doctoral thesis on Cuban economic policy and performance since 1990.

Claus Offe, born in 1940, is Professor of Political Science at Humboldt University, Berlin, where he holds a chair of Political Sociology and Social Policy. His previous positions include professorships at the universities of Bielefeld and Bremen, where he has served as the director of the Center of Social Policy Research. His fields of research are Democratic Theory, Transition Studies, EU Integration, and Welfare State and Labor Market Studies. He has published numerous articles and book chapters in these fields, a selection of which was reprinted as *Herausforderungen der Demokratie. Zur Integrations- und Leistungsfähigkeit politischer Institutionen* (2003). Recent books in English include *Varieties of Transition* (1996); *Modernity and the State: East and West* (1996); *Institutional Design in Post-Communist Societies* (1998, with J. Elster and U. K. Preuss); and the English translation of *Selbstbetrachtung aus der Ferne: Tocqueville, Weber, und Adorno in Amerika* (2004).

Alejandro Portes is Howard Harrison and Gabrielle Snyder Beck Professor of Sociology and Director of the Center for Migration and Development at Princeton University. He has formerly taught at Johns Hopkins University, where he held the John Dewey Chair in Arts and Sciences, Duke University, and the University of Texas in Austin. In 1997, he was elected President of the American Sociological Association and served in that capacity in 1998–1999. Born in Havana, Cuba, he came to the United States in 1960. He was educated at the University of Havana, the Catholic University of Argentina, and Creighton University. He received his MA and PhD from the University of Wisconsin in Madison. Portes is the author of about 220 articles and chapters on national development, international migration, Latin American and Caribbean urbanization, and economic sociology. His books include *City on the Edge: The Transformation of Miami* (1993), coauthored with Alex Stepick and winner of the Robert Park Award for best book in Urban Sociology and the Anthony Leeds Award for best book in Urban Anthropology in 1995; and *Immigrant America: A Portrait* (1996), designated as a Centennial Publication by the University of California Press. His current research is on the adaptation process of the immigrant second generation and the rise of transnational immigrant communities in the United States. His most recent books, coauthored with Rubén G. Rumbaut, are *Legacies: The Story of the Immigrant Second Generation* (2001) and *Ethnicities: Children of Immigrants in America* (2001). *Legacies*, which was the winner of the 2002 Distinguished Scholarship Award from the American Sociological Association (ASA) and of the 2002 W. I. Thomas and Florian Znaniecki Award for best book from the International Migration Section of ASA. His most recent articles on immigrant transnationalism have been published in the *American Sociological Review* (2002); *American Journal of Sociology* (2003); and the *International Migration Review* (2003). Portes is a former Fellow of the Center for Advanced Studies in the Behavioral Sciences, in Stanford, California, and of the Russell Sage Foundation. He has received honorary doctorates from the New School for Social Research and the University of Wisconsin and the Distinguished Career Award from the Section on International Migration of the American Sociological Association. He is a Fellow of the American Academy of Arts and Sciences and a member of the National Academy of Sciences.

Rafael Rojas is a Cuban historian and writer residing in Mexico since 1991. He has been a professor and researcher at the CIDE (Mexico) since 1997. He holds a BS in Philosophy from Havana University and a PhD in History from the Colegio de México. He is the author of several books on cultural history and Cuban politics, among them *El arte de la espera: notas al margen de la política cubana* (1998); *Isla sin fin. Contribución a la crítica del nacionalismo cubano* (1999); *Un banquete canónico* (2000) *José Martí. La invención de Cuba* (2000); *Cuba mexicana. Historia de una anexión imposible* (2001)—for which he was awarded the Matías Romero de Historia Diplomática prize in 1999—and *La escritura de la independencia. El surgimiento de la opinión pública en México* (2003). He was the recipient of a Rockefeller Foundation scholarship in 1996, and he is codirector of *Encuentro de la cultura cubana* (Madrid) and *Istor: Revista de Historia Internacional* (Mexico). He contributes to *Letras Libres, Nexos,* and *Historia Mexicana* (in Mexico), *Apuntes Postmodernos* and *Cuban Studies* (in Miami), and *Encuentro de la cultura cubana* and *Claves de la razón práctica* (published in Madrid).

Laurence Whitehead is an Official Fellow in Politics at Nuffield College, Oxford University, and Senior Fellow of the College. During 2005–2006, he served as Acting Warden of the College. He currently chairs Research Committee 13 of the International Political Science Association (Comparative Democratization), and the section on Europe and Latin America of the Latin American Studies Association. He belongs to the Steering Committee of the Red Eurolatinoamericana de Gobernabilidad para el Desarrollo, and serves as a Region Head for Latin America at Oxford Analytica. In 2002, he became the first Director of the Centre for Mexican Studies at Oxford University. His most recent books are *Latin America: A New Interpretation* (2005); *Democratization: Theory and Experience* (2002); and *Emerging Market Democracies: East Asia/Latin America* (2002)—a *Journal of Democracy* book generated by a conference he coorganized in Santiago at the end of 1999, and coedited with Lourdes Sola, *State-Crafting Monetary Authority: Brazil in Comparative Perspective* (2006). He is editor of an Oxford University Press Studies in Democratization series, the first book of which, *International Dimensions of Democratization: Europe and the Americas* (1996) he edited. Over a dozen books have been published in this series so far.

Bibliography

Abreu, Juan, *A la sombra del mar. Jornadas cubanas con Reinaldo Arenas* (Barcelona: Editorial Casiopea, 1998).

———, "Bella insumisión," *Mariel. Revista de Literatura y Arte* (special anniversary edition) (Miami), Spring 2003.

Acanda González, Jorge Luis, "Changes in Cuban Society and Their Reflection in Cuban Thought from the Nineties to the Present," in Tulchin, Bobea, Prieto, and Hernández (eds.), *Changes in Cuba since the Nineties*, pp. 125–138.

Ackerman, Holly, "The *Balsero* Phenomenon, 1991–1994," *Cuban Studies* 26, 1996: 169–200.

Acosta de Arriba, Rafael et al., *Debates historiográficos* (Havana: Editorial de Ciencias Sociales, 1999).

Afanasiev, Victor, "Fuerzas armadas y política revolucionaria: El caso de Cuba de 1959 a los años 90," in Bobea (ed.), *Soldados y ciudadanos en el Caribe*, pp. 207–254.

Aguilar, José Antonio, "Las batallas por la historia en México y Estados Unidos," *Istor. Revista de Historia Internacional* (CIDE-Mexico) 1 (1), 2000: 52–84.

———, *La sombra de Ulises. Ensayos sobre intelectuales mexicanos y norteamericanos* (Mexico: CIDE/Porrúa, 1998).

Aguilar, Luis E., "Cuba, c. 1860–c. 1930," in Bethell (ed.), *Cuba: A Short History*, pp. 21–56.

Aguirre, Benigno, "Social Control in Cuba," *Latin American Politics and Society* 44 (2), Summer 2002: 67–98.

———, "The Stability of Cuba's Political System," in Linger and Coleman (eds.), *Cuban Transitions at the Millennium*, pp. 273–278.

Alberto, Eliseo, *Informe contra mí mismo* (Madrid: Alfaguara, 2002).

Allman, T. D., *Miami, City of the Future* (New York: Atlantic Monthly Press, 1987).

Alonso, Aurelio, "Relations between the Catholic Church as of 2003," in Tulchin, Bobea, Prieto, and Hernández (eds.), *Changes in Cuba since the Nineties*, pp. 243–256.

"Amnesia y amnistía. La participación del historiador," *Istor: Revista de Historia Internacional* (CIDE-Mexico) 2 (5), 2001: 7–24.

Amuchastegui, Domingo, "Las FAR: Del poder absoluto al control de las reformas," *Encuentro de la Cultura Cubana* 26–27, 2002–2003: 133–147.

Añé, Lia, "La reforma económica y la economía familiar en Cuba," in de la Miranda (ed.), *Reforma económica y cambio social en América Latina y el Caribe*, pp. 126–145.

Arato, Andrew, "Interim Imposition," *Ethics and International Affairs* 18 (3), Winter 2004: 25–51.

Arato, Andrew, "Interpreting 1989," in *Civil Society, Constitution and Legitimacy* (Lanham, MD: Rowman and Littlefield, 2000), pp. 1–42.

———, "The Occupation of Iraq and the Difficult Transition from Dictatorship," *Constellations* 10 (3), September 2003: 408–424.

———, "The Round Tables, Democratic Institutions and the Problem of Justice," in Bozoki (ed.), *The Round Table of 1989*, pp. 223–236.

Arboleya, Jesús, *La contrarrevolución cubana* (Havana: Editorial de Ciencias Sociales, 1997).

Arditti, Rita, *Searching for Life: The Grandmothers of the Plaza de Mayo and the Disappeared Children of Argentina* (Berkeley, CA: University of California Press, 1999).

Arenas, Reinaldo, *Antes que anochezca* (Barcelona: Tusquets, 1992).

Arendt, Hannah, *Eichmann en Jesrusalén. Informe sobre la banalidad del mal* (Barcelona: Lumen, 1997).

Armony, Ariel C., "Civil Society in Cuba: A Conceptual Approach," in Crahan (ed.), *Religion, Culture, and Society*, p. 26.

———, *The Dubious Link: Civic Engagement and Democratization* (Stanford, CA: Stanford University Press, 2004).

Asian Development Bank, *Asian Development Outlook* (Oxford: Oxford University Press, 2003).

———, *Country Economic Review: People's Republic of China*, Asian Development Bank, mimeo, August 2002. Manila, Philippines.

Augé, Marc, *Las formas del olvido* (Barcelona: Gedisa, 1998).

Ayorinde, Christine, *Afro-Cuban Religiosity, Revolution, and National Identity* (Gainesville, FL: University Press of Florida, 2004).

Azcuy, Hugo, "Cuba: ¿Reforma Constitucional o Nueva Constitución?" Cuadernos de Nuestra América 19 (Havana: Centro de Estudios sobre América, 1994).

———, "Estado y sociedad civil en Cuba," *Temas* (Havana), October 4–December 1995: 105–110.

Azicri, Max, and Deal, Elsie (eds.), *Cuban Socialism in a New Century: Adversity, Survival, and Renewal* (Gainesville, FL: University Press of Florida, 2004).

Báez, Luis, *El mérito es vivir* (Barcelona: Editorial La Buganville, 2002).

Balboa Navarro, Imilcy, *Los brazos necesarios. Inmigración, colonización y trabajo libre, 1878–1898* (Valencia: Centro Francisco Tomás y Valiente, UNED/Fundación Instituto de Historia Social, 2000).

Banco Nacional de Cuba (ed.), *Economic Report 1994*, Banco Nacional de Cuba, August 1995, Havana.

Barberia, Lorena, "Remittances to Cuba: An Evaluation of Cuban and U.S. Government Policy Measures," Working Paper 15, September 2002, at http://web.mit.edu/cis/www/migration/pubs/rrwp/15_remittances.doc. Accessed September 2003 and January 2007.

Bardach, Ann Louise, *Cuba Confidential. Love and Vengeance in Miami and Havana* (New York: Random House, 2002).

Bayer, Patricia, and Booth, John A., "Civil Society and Democratic Transition," in Walker and Armony (eds.), *Repression, Resistance, and Democratic Transition in Central America*, pp. 233–254.

Becker, Howard, *Outsiders: Studies in the Sociology of Deviance* (New York: Free Press, 1963).

Bengelsdorf, Carollee, *The Problem of Democracy in Cuba: Between Vision and Reality* (Oxford: Oxford University Press, 1994).

Bethell, Leslie A. (ed.), *Cuba: A Short History* (Cambridge: Cambridge University Press, 1993).

Blanco, Juan Antonio, "Sin patria pero ¿con amo?" *Encuentro en la Red*, May 17, 2004.

Blight, James G., and Kornbluh, Peter, *Politics of Illusion: The Bay of Pigs Invasion Reexamined* (Boulder, CO: Lynne Rienner, 1998).

Boas, Taylor C., "The Dictator's Dilemma: The Internet and U.S. Policy toward Cuba," *Washington Quarterly* 23 (3), 2000: 62–63.

Bobea, Lilian (ed.), *Soldados y ciudadanos en el Caribe* (Santo Domingo: FLACSO, 2002).

Bodemer, Klaus, Grabendorff, Wolf, Jung, Weinfried, and Thesing, Josef et al. (eds.), *El Triángulo Atlántico. América Latina, Europa y los Estados Unidos en el sistema internacional cambiante* (Sankt Augustin: Konrad-Adenauer-Stiftung/ Arbeitsgemeinschaft Deutsche Lateinamerika-Forschung, 2002).

Botifoll, Luis J., *Introducción al futuro de Miami* (Miami, FL: Laurenty, 1988).

Bourdieu, Pierre, "Le capital social: Notes provisoires," *Actes de la Recherche en Sciences Sociales* 31, 1980: 2–3.

Bozoki, András (ed.), *The Round Table of 1989. The Genesis of Hungarian Democracy: Analysis and Documents* (Budapest: Central European University Press, 2002).

Brauman, Rony, and Sivan, Eyal, *Elogio de la desobediencia* (Mexico: Fondo de Cultura Económica, 2000).

Brundenius, Claes, and Weeks, John (eds.), *Globalization and Third World Socialism: Cuba and Vietnam* (New York: Palgrave Macmillan, 2001).

Bueno de Mequita, Bruce, Morrow, James D., Siverson, Randolph M., and Smith, Alastair, "Political Institutions, Political Survival, and Policy Success," in de Mesquita and Root (eds.), *Governing for Prosperity*, pp. 59–84.

Bunce, Valerie, "Comparing East and South," *Journal of Democracy* 6 (3), July 1995: 133–145.

Burawoy, Michael, and Lucás, János, *The Radiant Past: Ideology and Reality in Hungary's Road to Capitalism* (Chicago, IL: University of Chicago Press, 1992).

Cabrera Infante, Guillermo, *Mea Cuba* (Mexico: Editorial Vuelta, 1993).

Capella, Juan R., *Fruta prohibida* (Madrid: Editorial Trotta, 1997).

Carillo, Elizabeth, "El protestantismo histórico en Cuba hoy: ¿carismátismo o renovación?" *Temas* 6, April June 1997: 20–30.

Carlsnaes, Walter, Risse, Thomas, and Simmons, Beth A. (eds.), *A Handbook of International Relations* (New York: Sage, 2001).

Carranza Valdéz, Julio, Gutiérrez Urdantea, Luis, and Monreal González, Pedro, *Cuba: Restructuring the Economy: A Continuing Debate* (London: Institute of Latin American Studies of the University of London, 1996).

Castro, Fidel, "Discurso en la clausura del 40 aniversario del asalto al Cuartel Moncada," *Granma*, July 28, 1993, pp. 3–7.

———, *Presente y futuro de Cuba. Entrevista concedida a la revista "Siempre!"* (Havana: Oficina de Publicaciones del Consejo de Estado, 1992).

Castro, Raúl, "Informe del Buró Político en el V. Pleno del Comité Central del Partido, March, 23, 1996," *Granma Internacional*, April 10, 1996, pp. 4–8.

Centeno, Miguel Ángel, "Lessons for the Transition: Cuba after Fidel?" *Cuban Affairs/Asuntos Cubanos* 3–4, Fall–Winter 1998: 1–14.

Centeno, Miguel Ángel, and Font, Mauricio (eds.), *Toward a New Cuba?: Legacies of a Revolution* (Boulder, CO: Lynne Rienner, 1997).

Centeno, Miguel Ángel, and Silva, Patricio (eds.), *The Politics of Expertise in Latin America* (New York: St. Martin's, 1998).

Cercas, Javier, *Soldados de Salamina* (Barcelona: Tusquets, 2001).

Chen, An, "Capitalist Development, Entrepreneurial Class and Democratization in China," *Political Science Quarterly* 117 (3), Fall 2002: 401–422.

Coleman, James S., "A Rational Choice Perspective on Economic Sociology," in Smelser and Swedberg (eds.), *Handbook of Economic Sociology*, pp. 166–180.

———, "Social Capital in the Creation of Human Capital," *American Journal of Sociology* 94, 1988: 95–121.

Colomer, Josep M., "Exit, Voice, and Hostility in Cuba," *International Migration Review* 34 (2), 2000: 423–442.

———, "Los militares 'duros' y la transición en Cuba," *Encuentro de la Cultura Cubana* 26–27, Fall–Winter 2002–2003: 148–167.

Comisión Económica para América Latina y el Caribe (CEPAL), *La economía cubana: Reformas estructurales y desempeño en los noventa* (Santiago de Chile: CEPAL, 2001).

Conferencia de Obispos Católicos de Cuba, *Plan Global Pastoral, 1997–2000* (Havana: Secretariado General de la COCC, 1996).

Constant, Benjamim, *Écrits politíques* (Paris: Gallimard, 1997).

Córdova, Efrén, "Represión e intolerancia," in *40 años de Revolución. El legado de Castro* (Miami, FL: Ediciones Universal, 1999), pp. 253–279.

Corrales, Javier, "Lessons from Latin America," in Simon, Corrales, and Wolfenson (eds.), *Democracy and the Internet*, pp. 30–66.

———, *Presidents without Parties: The Politics of Economic Reform in Argentina and Venezuela in the 1990s* (University Park, PA: Pennsylvania State University Press, 2002).

Crahan, Margaret E., "The Church of the Past and the Church of the Future," in Azicri and Deal (eds.), *Cuban Socialism in a New Century*, pp. 123–146.

———, "Civil Society and Religion in Cuba: Past, Present, and Future," in Tulchin, Bobea, Prieto, and Hernández (eds.), *Changes in Cuba since the Nineties*, pp. 231–242.

———, "Cuba," in Sigmund (ed.), *Religious Freedom and Evangelization in Latin America*, pp. 297–298.

———, "Cuban Diasporas: Their Impact on Religion, Culture, and Society," in Crahan (ed.), *Religion, Culture, and Society*.

———, "Protestantism in Cuba," in *PCCLAS Proceedings*, IX (San Diego, CA: Campanile Press, 1982).

———, (ed.), *Religion, Culture, and Society: The Case of Cuba* (Washington, DC: Woodrow Wilson International Center for Scholars, 2003).

Cruz, Consuelo, and Seleny, Anna, "Reform and Counter-Reform: The Path to Market in Hungary and Cuba," *Comparative Politics* 34 (2), January 2002: 211–231.

"Cuba's International Strategy Pays Off," *Cuba Policy Report* (February 4, 2005): 1–4. http://lexingtoninstitute.org/910.shtml, accessed January 11, 2007.

De Aragón, Uva, *Memoria del silencio* (Miami, FL: Ediciones Universal, 2002).

De la Campa, Román, *Cuba on My Mind: Journeys to a Severed Nation* (London: Verso, 2000).

De la Miranda, Mauricio (ed.), *Reforma económica y cambio social en América Latina y el Caribe* (Cali, Colombia: TM Editores, 2000).

Del Águila, Juan M., "The Party, the Fourth Congress, and the Process of Counter Reform," in Pérez-López (ed.), *Cuba at a Crossroads*, pp. 19–40.

De la O Torres, Ana Meilyn, "La construcción del espacio público moderno en la Habana del siglo XIX." Masters Thesis in Social Science, FLACSO, Mexico, 2001.

De Mesquita, Bruce Bueno, and Root, Hilton L. (eds.), *Governing for Prosperity* (New Haven, CT: Yale University Press, 2000).

Díaz, Jesús, *Las palabras perdidas* (Barcelona: Ediciones Destino, 1992).

Díaz Martínez, Manuel, *Sólo un leve rasguño en la solapa* (Logroño: AMG Editor, 2002).

Didion, Joan, *Miami* (New York: Simon and Schuster, 1987).

Dilla, Haroldo Alfonso, "Cuba: Los escenarios cambiantes de la gobernabilidad," in Dilla (ed.), *Los recursos de la gobernabilidad en la Cuenca del Caribe*, pp. 1–38.

———, "Cuba: La reforma económica, la reestructuración social y la política," *Estudios Latinoamericanos: Nueva Época* 4 (7), January–June 1997: 165–178.

———, *La democracia en Cuba y el diferndo con los Etados Unidos* (Havana: Ediciones Centro de Estudios sobre América [CEA], 1995).

———, *La participacíon en Cuba y los retos del futuro* (Havana: Ediciones Centro de Estudios sobre América [CEA], 1996).

———, (ed.), *Los recursos de la gobernabilidad en la Cuenca del Caribe* (Caracas: Nueva Sociedad, 2002).

Dilla, Haroldo Alfonso, and Oxhorn, Philip, "The Virtues and Misfortunes of Civil Society in Cuba," *Latin American Perspectives* 124 (4), July 2002: 11–30.

Dilla, Haroldo Alfonso, Gerardo Gonzalez, and Ana, Vincentelli, T. (eds.), *Participación y desarrollo en los municipios cubanos* (Havana: Centro de Estudios sobre América, 1993).

Directorio Democrático Cubano, *Informe parcial de violaciones a los derechos humanos en Cuba, Febrero 2001–Febrero 2002*, at http://www.procubalibre.org.ar. Accessed September 2003 and January 2007.

Dirmoser, Diezmar, and Estay, Jaime, *Economía y reforma económica en Cuba* (Caracas: Nueva Sociedad, 1997).

Domínguez, Jorge I., "Comienza una transición hacia el autoritarismo en Cuba?" *Encuentro de la Cultura Cubana* 6/7, *Cuba a la luz de otras transiciones* (Madrid), 1997: 7–23.

———, "Cuba in a New World," in Lowenthal and Treverton (eds.), *Latin America in a New World*, pp. 203–216.

———, "Cuba since 1959," in Bethell (ed.), *Cuba: A Short History*, pp. 95–148.

———, *Cuba: Order and Revolution* (Cambridge, MA: Harvard University Press, 1978).

———, "The Political Impact on Cuba of the Reform and Collapse of Communist Regimes," in Mesa-Lago (ed.), *Cuba after the Cold War*, pp. 99–132.

———, "The Secrets of Castro's Staying Power," *Foreign Affairs* 72 (2), Spring 1993: 97–107.

———, *To Make a World Safe for Revolution: Cuba's Foreign Policy* (Cambridge, MA: Harvard University Press, 1989).

Domínguez, Jorge I., Everleny Pérez Villanueva, Omar, and Barberia, Lorena (eds.), *The Cuban Economy at the Start of the Twenty-First Century* (Cambridge, MA: Harvard University Press, 2004).

Domínguez, Jorge L. (ed.), *Technopols: Freeing Politics and Markets in Latin America in the 1990s* (University Park, PA: Pennsylvania State University Press, 1997).

Domínguez, María Isabel, "Cuban Youth: Aspirations, Social Perceptions, and Identity," in Tulchin, Bobea, Prieto, and Hernández (eds.), *Changes in Cuba since the Nineties*, pp. 155–170.

———, "Generaciones y mentalidades: Existe una conciencia generacional entre los jóvenes cubanos," in Monereo, Riera, and Valdés (eds.), *Cuba: Construyendo futuro*, pp. 55–75.

Dowding, Keith, John, Peter, Mergoupis, Thanos, and Van Vugt, Mark, "Exit, Voice and Loyalty: Analytic and Empirical Developments," *European Journal of Political Research* 37 (4), 2000: 469–495.

D'Rivera, Paquito, *Mi vida saxual* (San Juan, Puerto Rico: Plaza Mayor, 1999).

Durán, Alfredo, "Testimony to the U.S. Senate of June 14, 1995," *Cuban Affairs/Asuntos Cubanos* 2 (1–2), Spring–Summer 1995: 2–3.

Echevarría Salvat, Oscar A., *La Agricultura Cubana, 1934–1966: Régimen social, productividad y nivel de vida del sector agrícola* (Miami, FL: Ediciones Universal, 1971).

Eckstein, Susan Eva, *Back from the Future: Cuba under Castro* (Princeton, NJ: Princeton University Press, 1994).

———, "Transnational Networks and Norms, Remittances, and the Transformation of Cuba," in Domínguez, Everleny Pérez Villanueva, and Barberia (eds.), *The Cuban Economy at the Start of the Twenty-First Century*, pp. 319–351.

Eckstein, Susan Eva, and Barberia, Lorena, "Cuban-American Cuba Visits: Public Policy, Private Practices," *Report of the Mellon-MIT Inter-University Program on Non-Governmental Organizations and Forced Migration*, MIT, Center for International Studies, January 2001, Boston, MA.

Elizalde, Rosa Miriam, and Báez, Luis, *"Los disidentes": Agentes de la Seguridad Cubana revelan la historia real* (Havana: Editora Política, 2003).

Enzensberger, Hans Magnus, "Bildnis einer Partei: Vorgeschichte, Struktur und Ideologie der PCC," *Kursbuch* 18, October 1969: 192–216.

Escalante Font, Fábian, *Cuba: La guerra secreta de la CIA* (Havana: Editorial Capitán San Luis, 1993).

Espina, Mayra, "Transición y dinámica de los procesos socio-estructurales," in Monereo, Riera, and Valdés (eds.), *Cuba: Construyendo futuro*, pp. 9–54.

Espinosa, Juan Carlos, "Vanguard of the State: The Cuban Armed Forces in Transition," *Problems of Post-Communism* 48 (6), November/December 2001: 19–30.

Espinoza Domínguez, Carlos, *El peregrino en comarca ajena. Panorama crítico de la literatura cubana del exilio* (Boulder, CO: University of Colorado, Society of Spanish and Spanish American Studies, 2001).

European Bank for Reconstruction and Development (EBRD), *Transition Reports* (London: EBRD, 1988).

Europa World Year Book (London: Europa Publications Limited, 1979–2003).

Evans, Peter B., *Dependent Development: The Alliance of Multinational, State and Local Capital in Brazil* (Princeton, NJ. Princeton University Press, 1979).

Evans, Peter B., Rueschemeyer, Dietrich, and Skocpol, Theda (eds.), *Bringing the State Back In* (New York: Cambridge University Press, 1985).

Everhart, Stephen S., and Sumlinski, Mariusz A., "Trends in Private Investment in Developing Countries, 1970–2000." International Finance Corporation Discussion Paper no. 44, International Finance Corporation, Washington, DC, September 2001.

Everleny, Omar, "Ciudad de la Habana: desempeño económico y situación social," *La Economía Cubana en el 2000*, CEEC, April 2001, Havana, pp. 36–45.

Fabienke, Rikke, "Labor Markets and Income Distribution during Crisis and Reform," in Brundenius and Weeks (eds.), *Globalization and Third World Socialism*, pp. 102–128.

Feng, Yi, Huckeba, Margaret, Nguyen T, Son, and Williams, Aaron, "Political Institutions, Economic Growth, and Democratic Evolution: The Pacific Asian Scenario," in de Mesquita and Root (eds.), *Governing for Prosperity*, pp. 172–208.

Fernández, Áurea Matilde, *España. Franquismo y transición* (Havana: Editorial de Ciencias Sociales, 2002).

Fernández, Damián J., *Cuba and the Politics of Passion* (Austin, TX: University of Texas Press, 2000).

Figueras, Miguel Alejandro, "Cuba's Tourism Sector." Seminar at Smith College, September 10, 2001, Northhampton, MA.

Font, Mauricio, "Crisis and Reform in Cuba," in Centeno and Font (eds.), *Toward a New Cuba?* pp. 109–133.

Fontana, Biancamaría (ed.), *Constant: Political Writings* (Cambridge: Cambridge University Press, 1988).

Fornet, Ambrosio, *Memorias recobradas. Introducción al discurso literario de la diáspora* (Santa Clara, Cuba: Ediciones Capiro, 2000).

Foucault, Michel, *La verdad y las formas jurídicas* (Barcelona: Gedisa, 1991).

Fowkes, Ben, *The Post-Communist Era: Change and Continuity in Eastern Europe* (London: Palgrave Macmillan, 1999).

Franqui, Carlos, "Libertad y socialismo," *Libre* (Paris) 2, December–Feburary 1972: 9–10.

Friedman, Milton (with Rose D. Friedman), *Capitalism and Freedom* (Chicago, IL: University of Chicago Press, 1962).

Fukuyama, Francis, "The End of History," *National Interest* 16, Summer 1989: 3–18.

Funes Monzote, Reinaldo, "Cuba: República y democracia (1901–1940)," in Acosta de Arriba et al., *Debates historiográficos*, pp. 177–221.

Gallagher, Mary E., "Reform and Openness: Why China's Economic Reforms Have Delayed Democracy," *World Politics* 54 (3), April 2002: 338–372.

García, María Cristina, *Havana-USA: Cuban Exiles and Cuban Americans in South Florida, 1959–1994* (Berkeley, CA: University of California Press, 1996).

García Franco, Raimundo, "Notes on the Role of Religious Organizations in Community Work and Service Provision in Cuba After 1990," in Tulchin, Bobea, Prieto, and Hernández (eds.), *Changes in Cuba since the Nineties*, pp. 257–266.

Geddes, Barbara, *Politician's Dilemma: Building State Capacity in Latin America* (Berkeley, CA: University of California Press, 1994).

———, "What Do We Know about Democratization after Twenty Years?" *Annual Review of Political Science* 2, 1999: 115–144.

Gibson, Edward, "The Populist Road to Market Reform: Policy and Electoral Coalition in Mexico and Argentina," *World Politics* 49 (3), April 1997: 339–370.

Giuliano, Maurizio, *El caso CEA: Intelectuales e inquisidores en Cuba ¿Perestroika en la isla?* (Miami, FL: Ediciones Universal, 1998).

González Planas, Ignacio, "La conectividad es clave (entrevista)," *Giga: Revista Cubana de Computación* 3, 2000: 4–7.

Granovetter, Mark S., "The Economic Sociology of Firms and Entrepreneurs," in Portes (ed.), *The Economic Sociology of Immigration*, pp. 128–165.

———, *Getting a Job: A Study of Contacts and Careers* (Cambridge, MA: Harvard University Press, 1974).

Grenier, Guillermo J., and Stepick, Alex, *Miami, Now!* (Gainesville, FL: University of Florida Press, 1992).

Grupo de Trabajo Memoria, Verdad y Justicia, *Cuba. La reconciliación nacional* (Miami, FL: Centro para América Latina y el Caribe, Florida International University, 2003).

Haggard, Stephen, and Kaufmann, Robert, *The Political Economy of Democratic Transitions* (Princeton, NJ: Princeton University Press, 1995).

Hansing, Katrin, and Mahler, Sarah J., "God Knows No Borders: Transnational Religious Ties Linking Miami and Cuba," in Crahan (ed.), *Religion, Culture, and Society*, pp. 123–130.

Hawkins, Darren, "Democratization Theory and Non-Transitions: Insights from Cuba," *Comparative Politics* 33 (4), July 2001: 441–461.

Hearn, Adrian H., *The Spirit of Development: Community Welfare, Grassroots Religion, and Transculturation in Contemporary Cuba*, manuscript, 2005, under review by Durham NC: Duke University Press.

Helg, Aline, *Our Rightful Share: The Afro-Cuban Struggle for Equality, 1886–1912* (Chapel Hill, NC: University of North Carolina Press, 1995).

Heller, Agnes, and Fehér, Ferenc, *El péndulo de la modernidad. Una lectura de la era moderna después de la caída del comunismo* (Barcelona: Ediciones Península, 1994).

Hellman, Joel, "Winners Take All," *World Politics* 50 (2), January 1998: 203–234.

Henken, Theodore A., "*Balseros, Boteros,* and *El Bombo*: Cuban Immigration to the United States since the 1994 Rafter Crisis And the Persistence of Special Treatment." Paper prepared for the Symposium the Balseros Ten Years Later: No Longer *Adrift?*" Cuban Research Institute, Florida International University, Miami, FL, July 16–17, 2004.

———, "Condemned to Informality: Cuba's Experiments with Self-Employment During the Special Period." PhD dissertation, Tulane University, New Orleans, 2002.

———, "Condemned to Informality: Cuba's Experiments with Self-Employment during the Special Period (The Case of the Bed and Breakfasts)," in Lisandro Pérez, *Cuban Studies* 33 (Pittsburgh, PA: University of Pittsburgh Press, 2002), pp. 1–29.

———, " '*Vale Todo*' (Anything Goes): Cuba's Paladares." Paper presented at the XII Annual Meeting of the Association for the Study of the Cuban Economy, Coral Gables, FL, August 1–3, 2002.

Hernández, Rafael, "Mirror of Patience: Notes on Cuban Studies, Social Sciences and Contemporary Thought," in Tulchin, Bobea, Prieto, and Hernández (eds.), *Changes in Cuba since the Nineties*, pp. 139–154.

———, "Sin urna de cristal: Reordenamiento y transición socialista en Cuba," in Lozano (ed.), *Cambio político en el Caribe*, pp. 23–36.

———, "La sociedad civil y sus alrededores," *La Gaceta de Cuba* (Unión Nacional de Escritores y Artistas de Cuba) 1, 1994.

Hidalgo, Ariel, *Las corrientes políticas cubano americanas del sur de la Florida*, commissioned report, Princeton University, Center for Migration and Development, Princeton, NJ, March 2001.

Hirschman, Albert O., "Abwanderung, Widerspruch und das Schicksal der Deutschen Demokratischen Republik," *Leviathan* 20 (3), 1992: 330–358.

———, (ed.), *Essays in Trespassing. Economics to Politics and Beyond* (Cambridge: Cambridge University Press, 1981).

———, "Exit and Voice: An Expanding Sphere of Influence," in Hirschman (ed.), *Rival Views of Market Society*, pp. 77–101.

———, "Exit, Voice, and the Fate of the German Democratic Republic: An Essay in Conceptual History," *World Politics* 45 (2), 1993: 173–202.

———, "Exit, Voice, and Loyalty: Further Reflections and a Survey of Recent Contributions," in Hirschman (ed.), *Essays in Trespassing*, pp. 227–228.

———, *Exit, Voice, and Loyalty: Responses to Decline in Firms, Organizations, and States* (Cambridge, MA: Harvard University Press, 1970).

————, (ed.), *Rival Views of Market Society* (New York: Viking, 1986).

Hoffmann, Bert, "El cambio imposible: Cuba como 'asunto interméstico' en la política de EE. UU: Consecuencias y perspectivas," in Bodemer et al. (eds.), *El Triángulo Atlántico*, pp. 352–362.

————, "Cuba: La reforma desde adentro que no fue," *Encuentro de la Cultura Cubana* (Madrid) 10, 1998: 71–84.

————, "¿Helms-Burton a perpetuidad? Repercusiones y perspectivas para Cuba, EEUU y Europa," *Nueva Sociedad* (Caracas) 151, 1997: 57–72.

————, *The Politics of the Internet in Third World Development. Challenges in Contrasting Regimes with Case Studies of Costa Rica and Cuba* (New York: Routledge, 2004).

Huang, Yasheng, *Selling China: Foreign Direct Investment during the Reform Era* (New York: Cambridge University Press, 2003).

Huyssen, Andreas, *En busca del futuro perdido. Cultura y memoria en tiempos de globalización* (Mexico: FCE/Goethe Institut, 2002).

Iglesias, Marial, "Pedestales vacíos," *Encuentro de la cultura cubana* 24, Spring 2002: 17–34.

Ignatieff, Michael, *Los derechos humanos como política e idolatría* (Barcelona: Paidós, 2003).

Instituto de Relaciones Europeo-Latinoamericanas (IRELA), *Documentación del seminario El refuerzo del embargo de EEUU contra Cuba: Implicaciones para el comercio y las inversiones*, Sitges, Spain, IRELA, Madrid, July 8–10, 1996.

Inter American Institute of Human Rights, "IIHR Takes Part in Third International Meeting: Constitution, Democracy and Political Systems," *IIHR in the Americas* 62, June 15–30, 2005: 4.

Jatar-Hausmann, Ana Julia, *The Cuban Way* (West Hartford, CT: Kumarian Press, 1999).

Jorge, Antonio, "A Preliminary Approach to a Social Market Economy for Post-Castro Cuba," in Association for the Study of the Cuban Economy (ASCE) (ed.), *Cuba in Transition* 14, 2004: 410–419.

Julien, Claude, "Church and State in Cuba: Development of a Conflict," *Cross Currents* 11(2), Spring 1961.

Karl, Terry Lynn, and Schmitter, Philippe C., "Dilemas de la democratización en América Latina," *Foro Internacional* 3, January–March 1991: 27–43.

————, "Modes of Transition in Latin America, Southern and Eastern Europe," *International Social Science Journal* 43, May 1991: 269–284.

Kirk, John, *Between God and the Party: Religion and Politics in Revolutionary Cuba* (Tampa, FL: University of South Florida Press, 1989).

Kornai, Janos (ed.), *Contradictions and Dilemmas: Studies on the Socialist Economy and Society* (Harvard, MA: MIT Press, 1986).

————, *The Economics of Shortage* (Amsterdam: North-Holland, 1980).

————, "The Reproduction of Shortage," in Kornai (ed.), *Contradictions and Dilemmas*, pp. 6–32.

Koselleck, Reinhardt, *Futuro pasado. Para una semántica de los tiempos históricos* (Barcelona: Paidós, 1993).

Landau, David, *No siempre gana la muerte* (Los Angeles, CA: Pureplay Press, 2002).

Leante, César, *Volviendo la mirada* (Miami, FL: Ediciones Universal, 2002).

LeoGrande, William M., "The Cuban Communist Party and Electoral Politics: Adaptation, Succession, and Transition," *Cuban Transition Project, Institute for Cuban and Cuban-American Studies Mimeo* (Coral Gables, FL: University of Miami, 2002).

Lexington Institute, "De-Dollarization," *Cuba Policy Report*, October 29, 2004, pp. 1–4.

Linger, Eloise, and Coleman, John (eds.), *Cuban Transitions at the Millennium* (Largo, MD: International Development Options, 2000).

Linz, Juan J., and Alfred Stepan, *Problems of Democratic Transition and Consolidation: Southern Europe, South America, and Post-Communist Europe* (Baltimore, MD: Johns Hopkins University Press, 1996).

Liss, Sheldon B., Roots of Revolution: Radical Thought in Cuba (Lincoln, NE: University of Nebraska Press, 1987).

Llerena, Mario, *La revolución insospechada. Origen y desarrollo del castrismo* (Buenos Aires: Editorial Universitaria de Buenos Aires, 1981).

Logan, John, and Molotch, Harvey, *Urban Fortunes: The Political Economy of Place* (Berkeley, CA: University of California Press, 1987).

Lora, Eduardo, *Index of Economic Reforms in Latin America* (Washington, DC: Inter-American Development Bank, mimeo, 2001).

Lowenthal, Abraham F., and Treverton, Gregory F. (eds.), *Latin America in a New World* (Boulder, CO: Westview Press, 1994).

Lozano, W. (ed.), *Cambio político en el Caribe* (Caracas: Nueva Sociedad, 1998).

Machover, Jacobo, *La memoria frente al poder* (Valencia: Universitat de Valencia, 2001).

Mañach, Jorge, *Teoría de la frontera* (San Juan, Puerto Rico: Editorial Universitaria, 1970).

Margalit, Avishai, *The Ethics of Memory* (Cambridge, MA: Harvard University Press, 2002).

Marquéz Dolz, María Antonia, *Las industrias menores. Empresas y empresarios en Cuba (1880–1920)* (Havana: Editora Política, 2002).

Márquez Sterling, Carlos, *Historia de Cuba* (New York: Las Americas Publishing Company, 1969).

Marrero, Leví, *Escrito ayer* (Puerto Rico: Ediciones Capiro, 1992).

Maseda, Héctor, "El presidio político en Cuba," *Encuentro de la Cultura Cubana* 20, Spring 2001: 154–238.

Massey, Douglas S., Arango, Joaquín, Graeme, Hugo, Kouaouci, Ali, Pellegrino, Adela, and Taylor, Edward J., *Worlds in Motion: Understanding International Migration at the End of the Millennium* (New York: Greenwood Press, 1998).

Masud-Piloto, Félix, *From Welcomed Exiles to Illegal Immigrants: Cuban Migrants to the U.S., 1959–1995* (Lanham, MD: Rowman and Littlefield, 1996).

Matos, Huber, *Cómo llegó la noche* (Barcelona: Tusquets, 2002).

Maza, Manuel, S. J., *El alma del negocio y el negocio del alma: Testimonios sobre la iglesia y la sociedad en Cuba, 1878–1894* (Santiago de los Caballeros, Dominican Republic: Pontificia Universidad Católica Madre y Maestra, 1990).

———, *El Clero Cubano y la Independencia: Las Investigaciones de Francisco González del Valle (1881–1942)* (Santo Domingo: Compañía de Jesús en las Antillas, 1993).

Medina, Pablo, *Exiled Memories: A Cuban Childhood* (New York: Persea Books, 2002).

Menéndez, Lázaro, "In Order to Wake Up Tomorrow, You Have to Sleep Tonight," in Tulchin, Bobea, Prieto, and Hernández (eds.), *Changes in Cuban Society since the Nineties*, pp. 267–286.

Menton, Seymour, *Caminata por la narrativa latinoamericana* (Mexico: Fondo de Cultura Económica, 2002).

Merton, Robert K., "The Self-Fulfilling Prophecy," chapter 13 in *Social Theory and Social Structure* (New York: Free Press, 1968), pp. 475–490.

Mesa-Lago, Carmelo (ed.), *Cuba after the Cold War* (Pittsburgh, PA: University of Pittsburgh, 1993).

———, "Cuba's Raft Exodus of 1994: Causes, Settlement, Effects, and Future," North–South Center Agenda Paper 12, Miami, FL, 1995.

———, "Testing the Assumptions Concerning the Effects of German Pension Reform Based on Latin American and Eastern European Outcomes," *European Journal of Social Security* 4, 2002: 285–330.

———, "Un ajiaco cubano-alemán sobre la tercera reforma agraria de Cuba," *Encuentro* (Madrid) 18, Fall 2000: 254–258.

Mesa-Lago, Carmelo, Arenas de Mesa, Alberto, Brenes, Ivan, Montecinos, Verónica, and Samara, Mark, *Market, Socialist, and Mixed Economies: Comparative Policy and Performance, Chile, Cuba and Costa Rica* (Baltimore: Johns Hopkins University Press, 2000).

Michnik, Adam, *La segunda revolución* (Mexico: Siglo XXI, 1993).

Milán, Guillermo, *Los procesos anómicos en la sociedad cubana* (Havana: Instituto de Filosofía, 1998).

Monreal González, Pedro (ed.), *Development Prospects in Cuba: An Agenda in the Making* (London: Institute of Latin American Studies, School of Advanced Study, University of London, 2002).

———, "Las remesas familiares en la economía cubana," *Encuentro de la Cultura Cubana* 14 (Madrid), Fall 1999: 148–167.

Monereo, Manuel, Riera, Migual, and Valdés, Juan (eds.), *Cuba: Construyendo futuro* (Madrid: Editorial El Viejo Topo, 2000).

Mora, Frank O., "From Fidelismo to Raulismo: Civilian Control of the Military in Cuba," *Problems of Post-Communism* 46 (2), March–April 1999: 25–38.

Moulián, Tomás, *Chile actual. Anatomía de un mito* (Santiago de Chile: Arcis Universidad/Ediciones Lom, 1998).

Mujal-León, Eusebio, and Busby, Joshua W., "Much Ado about Something? Regime Change in Cuba," *Problems of Post-Communism* 48 (6), November–December 2001: 6–18.

Multilateral Investment Fund (MIF), *Sending Money Home: An International Comparison of Remittance Markets* (Washington, DC: Inter-American Development Bank, 1993).

Muse, Robert, "Legal and Practical Implications of Title III of the Helms-Burton Law," in IRELA, *Documentación del seminario El refuerzo del embargo de EEUU contra Cuba.*

Navarro, Osvaldo, *Hijos de saturno* (Mexico: Editorial Debate, 2002).

Nova, Armando, "La nueva relación de producción en la agricultura," *Revista Cuba: Investigaciones Económicas*, January–March 1998: 65–82.

Núñez Vega, Jorge, "La fuga de Ariel," *Encuentro de la cultura cubana* 24, Spring 2002: 53–67.

Nussbaum, Martha C., *Los límites del patriotismo* (Barcelona: Paidós, 1999).

O'Donnell, Guillermo, "Delegative Democracy," *Journal of Democracy* 5 (1), January 1994: 55–69.

———, "Introduction to the Latin American Cases," in O' Donnell, Schmitter, and Whitehead (eds.), *Transitions from Authoritarian Rule*, pp. 3–18.

———, "The State, Democratization and Some Conceptual Problems: A Latin American View with Glances at Some Post-Communist-Countries," in Smith, Acuña, and Gamarra (eds.), *Latin American Political Economy in the Age of Neo Liberal Reform*, pp. 117–125.

O'Donnell, Guillermo, and Schmitter, Philippe C., *Transitions from Authoritarian Rule: Tentative Conclusions about Uncertain Democracies* (Baltimore: Johns Hopkins University Press, 1986).

O' Donnell, Guillermo, Schmitter, Philippe C., and Whitehead, Laurence (eds.), *Transitions from Authoritarian Rule: Latin America* II (Baltimore, MD: Johns Hopkins University Press, 1986).

Offe, Claus, "Capitalism by Democratic Design? Democratic Theory Facing the Triple Transition in East Central Europe," *Social Research* 58 (4), 1991: 865–892.

Olson, Mancur, *Power and Prosperity: Outgrowing Communist and Capitalist Dictatorships* (New York: Basic Books, 2000).

Oppenheimer, Andrés, *Castro's Final Hour. The Secret Story Behind the Coming Downfall of Communist Cuba* (New York: Simon and Schuster, 1992).

Organisation for Economic Cooperation and Development, *China in the World Economy: The Domestic Policy Challenges* (Paris: OECD Synthesis Report, 2002).

Orozco, Manuel, "Globalization and Migration: The Impact of Family Remittances in Latin America," *Latin American Politics and Society* 44 (2), Summer 2002: 41–65.

Ortega y Alamino, Jaime, "Discurso de Mons. Jaime Ortega Y Alamino: Visita Ad Limina de los Obispos de Cuba, June 25, 1994" (Rome), June 25, 1994, at http://www.nacub.org/nacub/vozigcub/94.htm, accessed January 11, 2007.

Oxhorn, Philip, and Ducatenzeiler, Graciela, "The Problematic Relationship between Economic and Political Liberalization: Some Theoretical Considerations," in Oxhorn and Starr (eds.), *Markets and Democracy in Latin America*, pp. 13–41.

Oxhorn, Philip, and Starr, Pamela K. (eds.), *Markets and Democracy in Latin America: Conflict or Convergence?* (Boulder, CO: Lynne Rienner, 1999).

Padula Jr., Alfred L., "The Fall of the Bourgeoisie: Cuba 1959–1966." PhD Dissertation, University of New Mexico, 1974.

Padura, Leonardo, *La novela de mi vida* (Barcelona: Tusquets, 2002).

Pastor Jr., Manuel, "After the Deluge? Cuba's Potential as a Market Economy," in Purcell and Rothkopf (eds.), *Cuba*, pp. 31–55.

Pastor Jr., Manuel, and Wise, Carol, "The Politics of Second Generation Reforms," *Journal of Democracy* 10 (3), July 1999: 34–48.

Pedraza, Silvia, "Democratization and Migration: Cuba's Exodus and the Development of Civil Society—Hindrance or Help?" in Association for the Study of the Cuban Economy (ASCE) (ed.), *Cuba in Transition* 12, 2002: 247–261.

Pérez, Lisandro, "Cuban Miami," in Grenier and Stepick, *Miami, Now!*, pp. 83–108.

———, "De Nueva York a Miami: El desarrollo demográfico de las comunidades cubanas en Estados Unidos," *Encuentro de la Cultura Cubana* (15), 1999: 13–23.

Pérez Firmat, Gustavo, *Next Year in Cuba: A Cubano's Coming-of-Age in America* (New York: Anchor Books/Doubleday, 1995).

Pérez-López, Jorge F., *Cuba's Second Economy* (New Brunswick, NJ: Transaction Books, 1995).

———, (ed.), *Cuba at a Crossroads: Politics and Economics after the Fourth Party Congress* (Gainesville, FL: University Press of Florida, 1994).

———, "Waiting for Godot: Cuba's Stalled Reforms and the Continuing Economic Crisis," *Problems of Post-Communism* 48(6), November/December 2001: 43–55.

Pérez-López, Jorge F., and Travieso-Díaz, Matías F. (eds.), *Perspectives on Cuban Economic Reforms* (Phoenix, AZ: Arizona State University Center for Latin American Studies, 1998).

Pérez Jr., Louis A., "Cuba, c. 1930–c. 1959," in Bethell (ed.), *Cuba: A Short History*, pp. 57–94.

———, "Fear and Loathing of Fidel Castro: Sources of US Policy toward Cuba," *Journal of Latin American Studies* 34 (2), May 2002: 227–254.

————, *On Becoming Cuban: Identity, Nationality, and Culture* (Chapel Hill, NC: University of North Carolina Press, 1999).

Pérez-Stable, Marifeli, "Caught in a Contradiction: Cuban Socialism Between Mobilization and Normalization," *Comparative Politics* 32 (1), October 1999: 63–82.

————, *The Cuban Revolution: Origins, Course and Legacy* (New York: Oxford University Press, 1993).

Peters, Philip, "Cuba's Small Businesses: Taking a Wild Ride," in *Beyond Transition: The Newsletter about Reforming Economies* (Washington, DC: World Bank Group, 2001). www.worldbank.org/transitionnewsletter/.

Piqué, Joan Maria, "Thousands Celebrate Virgin of Charity," *Miami Herald*, September 9, 1997.

Piqueras, José Antonio (ed.), *Diez nuevas miradas a la historia de Cuba* (Castellón de la Plana: Publicaciones de la Universidad Jaume, 1998).

Poirine, Bernard, "A Theory of Remittances as an Implicit Family Loan Arrangement," *World Development* 25 (4), 1997: 589–611.

Portell Vilá, Herminio, *Nueva historia de la República de Cuba* (Miami, FL: La Moderna Poesía, 1986).

Portes, Alejandro, "The Cuban-American Political Machine," *Foro Internacional* (Mexico) XLIII, July–September 2003: 608–626.

————, (ed.), *The Economic Sociology of Immigration: Essays on Networks, Ethnicity, and Entrepreneurship* (New York: Russell Sage Foundation, 1995).

————, "The Social Origins of the Cuban Enclave Economy of Miami," *Sociological Perspectives* 30, October 1987: 340–371.

————, "The Two Meanings of Social Capital," *Sociological Form* 15, 2000: 1–12.

Portes, Alejandro, Guarnizo, Luis Eduardo, Landolt, and Patricia Landolt, "Transnational Communities," (special issue) *Ethnic and Racial Studies* 22 (2), 1999: 316–339.

Portes, Alejandro, and Rumbaut, Rubén G., *Immigrant America: A Portrait* (Berkeley, CA: University of California Press, 1996), pp. 115–124.

Portes, Alejandro, and Sensenbrenner, Julia, "Embeddedness and Immigration: Notes on the Social Determinants of Economic Action," *American Journal of Sociology* 98, May 1993: 1320–1350.

Portes, Alejandro, and Stepick, Alex, *City on the Edge: The Transformation of Miami* (Berkeley, CA: University of California Press, 1993).

Portuondo Zúñiga, Olga, *La Virgen de la Caridad del Cobre: Símbolo de cubanía* (Santiago de Cuba: Editorial Oriente, 1995).

Pries, Ludger, *Migration and Transnational Social Spaces* (Aldershot: Ashgate, 1999).

Przeworski, Adam, *Democracy and the Market: Political and Economic Reforms in Eastern Europe and Latin America* (Cambridge: Cambridge University Press, 1991).

Przeworski, Adam, Álvarez, Michael E., Cheibub, José Antonio, and Limongi, Fernando, *Democracy and Development: Political Institutions and Well-Being in the World, 1950–1990* (New York: Cambridge University Press, 2000).

Purcell, Susan Kaufman, and Rothkopf, David (eds.), *Cuba: The Contours of Change* (Boulder, CO: Lynne Rienner, 2000).

Putnam, Robert D., *Making Democracy Work: Civic Traditions in Modern Italy* (Princeton, NJ: Princeton University Press, 1993).

Quiróz, Alfonso, "The Evolution of Laws Regulating Associations and Civil Society in Cuba," in Crahan (ed.), *Religion, Culture, and Society*, pp. 55–68.

Quiza Moreno, Ricardo, "Fernando Ortiz, los intelectuales y el dilema del nacionalismo en la República (1902–1930)," *Temas. Cultura, Ideología, Sociedad* 22–23, July–December 2000: 46–54.

Ramírez, Sergio, *Sombras nada más* (Madrid: Alfaguara, 2002).

Ramos, Marcos A., *Protestantism and Revolution in Cuba* (Miami, FL: University of Miami, 1989).

Remmer, Karen L., "Elections and Economics in Contemporary Latin America," in Wise and Roett (eds.), *Post-Stabilization Politics in Latin America*, pp. 31–55.

Richard, Nelly, *Residuos y metáforas. Ensayos de crítica cultural sobre el Chile de la transición* (Santiago de Chile: Editorial Cuarto Propio, 1998).

Ricoeur, Paul, *La memoria, la historia y el olvido* (Madrid: Editorial Trotta, 2003).

Rieff, David, *Going to Miami* (Boston, MA: Little, Brown, 1987).

Ritter, Archibald R. M. (ed.), "Cuba's Economic Strategy and Alternative Futures," in Pérez-López (ed.), *Cuba at a Crossroads*, pp. 67–93.

———, *The Cuban Economy* (Pittsburgh, PA: University of Pittsburgh Press; Pitt Latin American Series, 2004).

Ritter, Archibald R. M., and Rowe, Nicholas, "Cuba: From 'Dollarization' to 'Euroization' or Peso Reconsolidation?" *Latin American Politics and Society* 44 (2), Summer 2002: 99–124.

Rodríguez, Arleen, and Barredo, Lázaro, *El Camaján* (Havana: Editora Política, 2003).

Rodríguez Chávez, Ernesto, *Emigración cubana actual* (Havana: Editorial de Ciencias Sociales, 1993).

Rojas, Rafael, *Isla sin fin. Contribución a la crítica del nacionalismo cubano* (Miami, FL: Ediciones Universal 1998).

———, "Políticas invisibles," *Cuba a la luz de otras transiciones: Encuentro de la Cultura Cubana* (Madrid) 6/7, 1997: 24–35.

Roman, Peter, "The Lawmaking Process in Cuba: Debating the Bill on Agricultural Cooperatives," *Socialism and Democracy* 19 (2), July 2005: 37–56.

Roque Cabello, Marta Beatriz, and Sánchez Herrero, Manuel, "Background: Cuba's Economic Reforms: An Overview," in Pérez-López and Travieso-Díaz (eds.), *Perspectives on Cuban Economic Reforms*, pp. 9–17.

Rotberg, Robert I. (ed.), *Patterns of Social Capital: Stability and Change in Historical Perspective* (Cambridge: Cambridge University Press, 2001).

Ryan, Mary P., "Civil Society as Democratic Practice: North American Cities during the Nineteenth Century," in Rotberg (ed.), *Patterns of Social Capital*, pp. 221–246.

Santí, Enrico Mario, *Bienes del siglo* (Mexico: Fondo de Cultura Económica, 2002).

Sartre, Jean Paul, *Sartre visita a Cuba* (Havana: Ediciones R, 1960).

Schamis, Hector, "Distributional Coalitions and the Politics of Economic Reform in Latin America," *World Politics* 51 (2), January 1999: 236–268.

Schoultz, Lars, "Blessings of Liberty: The United States and the Promotion of Democracy in Cuba," *Journal of Latin American Studies* 34 (2), May 2002: 397–425.

Schmitter, Philippe C., and Karl, Terry Lynn, "The Conceptual Travels of Transitologists and Consolidationists: How Far to the East Should They Attempt to Go?" *Slavic Review* 53, Spring 1994: 173–185.

Shapiro, Ian, and Hacker-Cordón, Casiano (eds.), *Democracy's Value* (Cambridge: Cambridge University Press, 1999).

Shiffman, Gary M., "Castro's Choices: The Economics of Economic Sanctions." Paper presented at the XII Annual Meeting of the Association for the Study of the Cuban Economy, Coral Gables, FL, August 1–3, 2002.

Sigmund, Paul E. (ed.), *Religious Freedom and Evangelization in Latin America: The Challenge of Religious Pluralism* (Maryknoll, NY: Orbis Books, 1999).

Simon, Leslie, Corrales, Javier, and Wolfenson, Don (eds.), *Democracy and the Internet* (Washington, DC: Woodrow Wilson Center Press, 2002).

Skocpol, Theda, and Fiorina, Morris P. (eds.), *Civic Engagement in American Democracy* (Washington, DC: Brookings Institution Press, 1999).

Smelser, N. J., and Swedberg, R. (eds.), *Handbook of Economic Sociology* (Princeton, NJ: Princeton University Press and Russell Sage Foundation, 1994)

Smith, Wayne S., "Cuba's Long Reform," *Foreign Affairs* 75 (2), March–April 1996: 99–112.

Smith, William C., Acuña, Carlos H., and Gamarra, Eduardo A. (eds.), *Latin American Political Economy in the Age of Neo Liberal Reform: Theoretical and Comparative Perspectives for the 1990s* (New Brunswick, NJ: Transaction Books, 1994).

Solinger, Dorothy J., "Ending One-Party Dominance: Korea, Taiwan, Mexico," *Journal of Democracy* 12 (1), January 2001: 30–42.

Somers, Margaret R., "Citizenship and the Place of the Public Sphere: Law, Community, and Political Culture in the Transition to Democracy," *American Sociological Review* 58 (5), October 1993.

Spadoni, Paolo, "The Impact of the Helms-Burton Legislation on Foreign Investment in Cuba." Paper presented at the XI Annual Conference of the Association for the Study of the Cuban Economy, Miami, FL, August 2–4, 2001.

Stepan, Alfred (ed.), *Democratizing Brazil: Problems of Transition and Consolidation* (Oxford: Oxford University Press, 1989).

Suárez, Luis, *El siglo XXI: posibilidades y desafíos para la Revolución Cubana* (Havana: Editorial de Ciencias Sociales, 2000).

Suchlicki, Jaime, "Castro's Cuba: Continuity Instead of Change," in Purcell and Rothkopf (eds.), *Cuba*, pp. 57–79.

Tejera, Nivaria, *Espero la noche para soñarte, Revolución* (Miami, FL: Ediciones Universal, 2002).

Tilly, Charles, "War-Making and State-Making as Organized Crime," in Evans, Rueschemeyer, and Skocpol (eds.), *Bringing the State Back In*, pp. 169–191.

Todorov, Tzvetan, *Los abusos de la memoria* (Barcelona: Paidós Asterisco, 2000).

Torres, María de los Ángeles, *In the Land of Mirrors. Cuban Exile Politics in the United States* (Ann Arbor, MI: University of Michigan Press, 1999).

Torres-Cuevas, Eduardo et al., *Félix Varela: Etica y anticipación del pensamiento de la emancipación cubana* (Havana: Imagen Contemporánea, 1999).

———, *Félix Varela: Los orígenes de la ciencia y con-ciencia cubanas* (Havana: Editorial de las Ciencias Sociales, 1997).

Travieso-Díaz, Matías F., and Trumbull, Charles P., "Foreign Investment in Cuba: Prospects and Perils," mimeo, 2002.

Tulchin, Joseph S., Bobea, Lilian, Prieto, Mayra P. Espina, and Hernández, Rafael (eds.), *Changes in Cuba since the Nineties* (Washington, DC: Woodrow Wilson International Center for Scholars, 2005).

Tussel, Javier, *La transición española* (Madrid: Club Internacional del Libro, 1995).

Universidad Central "Marta Abreu" de Las Villas, *La educación rural en las villas: bases para la redacción de unos cursos de estudios* (Santa Clara, Cuba: Universidad Central, 1959).

U.S. Department of Homeland Security, *Yearbook of Immigration Statistics 2003* (Washington, DC: Government Printing Office, 2004).

Valdés Paz, Juan, "Cuba in the 'Special Period': From Equality to Equity," in Tulchin, Bobea, Prieto, and Hernández (eds.), *Changes in Cuba since the Nineties*, pp. 103–124.

Varela, Félix, *Escritos políticos* (Havana: Editorial de Ciencias Sociales, 1977).

Vázquez Díaz, René, *Voces para cerrar un siglo* (Stockholm: Olof Palme Center, 2000).

Vera, Esther, and Colomer, Josep M., "El Nacional-Catolicismo de Fidel Castro," *Claves de Razón Práctica* 81, 1998: 14–19.

Walker, Thomas W., and Armony, Ariel C. (eds.), *Repression, Resistance, and Democratic Transition in Central America* (Wilmington, DE: Scholarly Resources, 2000).

Weinrich, Harald, *Leteo. Arte y crítica del olvido* (Madrid: Editorial Siruela, 1999).

Werlau, Maria C., "Foreign Investment in Cuba: The Limits of Commercial Engagement," *World Affairs* 160 (2), Fall 1997: 51–69.

Weyland, Kurt, *The Politics of Market Reform in Fragile Democracies: Argentina, Brazil, Peru, and Venezuela* (Princeton, NJ: Princeton University Press, 2002).

Whitehead, Laurence, *Democratization: Theory and Experience* (Oxford: Oxford University Press, 2002).

———, "Freezing the Flow," *Taiwan Journal of Democracy* 1 (1), 2005: 1–20.

Williamson, John, "What Should the World Bank Think About the Washington Consensus," *World Bank Research Observer* 15 (2), August 2000: 251–270.

Wise, Carol, and Roett, Riordan (eds.), *Post-Stabilization Politics in Latin America* (Washington, DC: Brookings Institution Press, 2003).

World Bank, *Transition: The First Ten Years. Analysis and Lessons for Eastern Europe and the Former Soviet Union* (Washington, DC: World Bank, 2002).

Yaremko, Jason M., *U.S. Protestant Missions in Cuba: From Independence to Castro* (Gainesville, FL: University Press of Florida, 2000).

Young, Iris Marion, "State, Civil Society, and Social Justice," in Shapiro and Cordón (eds.), *Democracy's Value*.

Zimbalist, Andrew, "Reforming Cuba's Economic System from Within," in Pérez-López (ed.), *Cuba at a Crossroads*, pp. 220–237.

———, "Whither the Cuban Economy?" in Purcell and Rothkopf (eds.), *Cuba*, pp. 13–29.

Index

Marginalization, 108, 174
Marginalized
  Groups, 80
  Institutionalized religions, 152
Mariel, 32, 107, 108, 119, 123, 171,
    175, 176, 177, 181
Market
  Agricultural, 40, 43, 44
  Black or gray, 43, 44, 48, 195
  Farm, 61
  Economy, 3, 38, 41, 78, 79, 80,
    115
  International, 39
  Labor, 57, 71, 113
  Price(s), 37, 41, 44, 48
  Reforms, 62, 63, 64, 71, 73, 78, 80
  U.S., 57
Marqués Dolz, María Antonia, 169
Márquez Sterling, Carlos, 174
Marrero, Leví, 174
Marshall Islands, 4
Martí, José, 142, 180
Martin Luther King, Jr. Memorial
    Center, 149
Martínez, Raúl, 127
Marxist-Leninist
  Regime, 140, 182
  Revolution, 152
  Vanguard, 117
Más Canosa, Jorge, 124, 127, 130, 133
Mass
  Mobilization/protests/rallies, 111,
    133, 145, 194, 195
  Organizations, 144, 148, 150, 152,
    156, 157
Matos, Huber, 171, 179, 180, 182
Media, 4, 29, 33, 37, 92, 109, 114,
    148, 167, 194, 196, 197
Medina, Pablo, 177
Meilyn de la O Torres, Ana, 169
Memories
  Knots of, 168, 200
  Official, 168, 169, 172, 173
Mexican-Americans, 199
Mexico, 2, 3, 27, 30, 31, 34, 63, 64,
    74, 76, 103, 135, 166, 167, 168,
    190
Miami Herald, 123
Michnik, Adam, 169
MIG fighter, 133

Military
  Commandos, 133
  Cuban, 3, 4, 63, 72–74, 77, 96, 104
  In Angola, 84
  Intervention, 28, 30, 33
  Officers, 67, 68, 72, 74
  Purge, 65
  Regime, 3, 31, 77
Minister of Culture, 198
Ministry of Computing and
    Communications, 70
Ministry of Foreign Trade, 70
Miró Cardona, José, 171, 174, 179
Missile Crisis, 21, 171, 181
Mixed enterprises, 73
Monarchists, 167
Moncada Barracks, 3, 6, 10, 11, 192
Monopoly, (of state)
  Banks, 74
  Capitalist rewards, 78
  Distribution economic resources, 91
  Dollar trade, 69, 108
  Elected office, 128
  Information, 148, 197
  Ownership, 46
  Single Party, 22
Montecristi Group, 171
Montenegro, Carlos, 180
Moscow, 4, 13, 105, 189, 190, 195
Movimiento 26 de Julio (M-26), 171
Movimiento Comando F4, 134
Movimiento Cristiano de Liberación
    (MCL), 151
Movimiento de Recuperación
    Revolucionaria (MRR), 134, 171
Movimiento Demócrata Cristiano
    (MDC), 171
Movimiento Insurreccional Martiano,
    134
Multilateral organizations, 28
Multinationals, 73
Multiparty system, 117
Municipios de Cuba en el Exilio, 134

Napoleon, 2, 17, 18, 19, 20, 21
Napoleonic Empire, 20
National Association of Small Farmers
    of Cuba (ANAP), 146
National Endowment for Democracy
    (NED), 35